PRAISE FOR *THE GLOI*

"With capitalism battering the Third World and forcing the First World to lower its expectations of opportunity, human rights and a future, getting an unflinching, intelligent look at so-called recessions, superprofits and resistance is needed more than ever. Who better to illuminate politics, social movements and finance than this constellation of authors? None better can present matters of such urgency as accessibly or sharply."
—**Ernesto Aguilar**, program director, KPFT, Pacifica Radio

"*The Global Industrial Complex* makes an immense contribution to the literature by engaging the key thoughts and ideas of some of the most important, influential and outspoken public intellectuals of our time. In doing so the book provides not only a searing and devastating critique of contemporary 'capitalist' society, but also engages in a full frontal assault on the poverty of imagination evident in those who refuse to believe that there are real alternatives, and that active resistance is necessary to achieve them. It deserves to be read widely."
—**Richard White**, editor of the *Journal for Critical Animal Studies*

"Human society is organized in a way that privileges a tiny minority at the expense of the vast majority of humanity and to the detriment of the entirety of the non-human world. With this collection, Best, Kahn, Nocella, and McLaren intervene in that and ask the question: 'Might things be done another way?' The answer, of course, is a resounding 'Yes!' Read this book and join us in creating a world free of the constraints placed on us by domination in all of its myriad forms!"
—**Deric Shannon**, co-author of *Political Sociology: Oppression, Resistance, and the State*

"This penetrating, insightful book written by a collection of the world's most prominent public intellectuals, is a skilled combination of lucid explanation and cogently argued critique of what the contributors term the 'global industrial complex.' The authors combine scholarship with insight, erudition with moral passion as they critique the fundamental direction in which our world is moving financially, politically and economically. The conclusions are radical and profound. No activist, academic or student can afford to ignore their arguments."
—**Susan L. Thomas**, director of gender and women's studies, Hollins University

"In this book, leading American radical scholars provide important insights into interlocking networks of power under global capitalism. This fine collection of essays is a useful tool for those seeking to understand and alter the corporate structures that dominate our world."

—**John Sorenson**, chair of the department of sociology, Brock University

— if workers were Richer the
eco would be More Stable
but the who would also
be More politically demand.

The Global Industrial Complex

Complex

Frank Catano

The Global Industrial Complex
Systems of Domination

Steven Best, Richard Kahn, Anthony J. Nocella II, and Peter McLaren

LEXINGTON BOOKS
Lanham • Boulder • New York • Toronto • Plymouth, UK

Published by Lexington Books
A wholly owned subsidiary of The Rowman & Littlefield Publishing Group, Inc.
4501 Forbes Boulevard, Suite 200, Lanham, Maryland 20706
www.lexingtonbooks.com

Estover Road, Plymouth PL6 7PY, United Kingdom

British Library Cataloguing in Publication Information Available

Library of Congress Cataloging-in-Publication Data

The global industrial complex : systems of domination / Steven Best . . . [et al.].
    p. cm.
  Includes bibliographical references and index.
  ISBN 978-0-7391-3697-3 (cloth) — ISBN 978-0-7391-3698-0 (pbk. : alk. paper) —
ISBN 978-0-7391-3699-7 (electronic : alk. paper)
  1. Capitalism—Social aspects. 2. Capitalism—Political aspects. 3. Big business.
4. Power (Social sciences) 5. Social institutions. I. Best, Steven.
  HB501.G5495 2011
  306.3'42—dc23   2011030966

♾ ™ The paper used in this publication meets the minimum requirements of American National Standard for Information Sciences—Permanence of Paper for Printed Library Materials, ANSI/NISO Z39.48-1992.

Printed in the United States of America

Contents

Acknowledgments

We, the editors, would like to thank all of the contributors for taking time out of their schedules to contribute to this book. We would also like to thank Erin Currier, the artist of the powerful front cover. Additionally, we would like to thank everyone at Lexington Books, especially Michael Sisskin and Eric Wrona, for their assistance and support of this project. Finally, we would like to thank our human and nonhuman friends and family throughout our lives that have supported us.

Introduction

Pathologies of Power and the Rise of the Global Industrial Complex

Steven Best

Investigations of various topics and levels of abstraction that are collected here are united in the intention of developing a theory of the present society.

—Max Horkheimer

Since trade ignores national boundaries and the manufacturer insists on having the world as a market, the flag of his nation must follow him, and the doors of the nations which are closed against him must be battered down. Concessions obtained by financiers must be safeguarded by ministers of state, even if the sovereignty of unwilling nations be outraged in the process. Colonies must be obtained or planted, in order that no useful corner of the world may be overlooked or left unused.

—Woodrow Wilson, 1919

Globalization has considerably accelerated in recent years following the dizzying expansion of communications and transport and the equally stupefying transnational mergers of capital. We must not confuse globalization with "internationalism" though. We know that the human condition is universal, that we share similar passions, fears, needs and dreams, but this has nothing to do with the "rubbing out" of national borders as a result of unrestricted capital movements. One thing is the free movement of peoples, the other of money.

—Eduardo Galeano

MATRICES OF CONTROL: MODERNITY, INDUSTRIALISM, AND CAPITALISM

In the transition to what is called "modernity"—a revolutionary European and American social order driven by markets, science, and technology—reason awakens to its potential power and embarks on the project to theoretically comprehend and to practically "master" the world. For modern science to develop, heretics had to disenchant the world and eradicate all views of nature as infused with living or spiritual forces. This required a frontal attack on the notion that the mind participates in the world, and the sublation of all manner of the animistic and religious ideologies—from the Pre-Socratics to Renaissance alchemists to indigenous cosmological systems—which believed that nature was magical, divine, or suffused with spirit and intelligence.[1]

This became possible only with the dethronement of God as the locus of knowledge and value, in favor of a secular outlook that exploited mathematics, physics, technology, and the experimental method to unlock the mysteries of the universe. Modern science began with the Copernican shift from a geocentric to a heliocentric universe in the sixteenth century, advanced in the seventeenth century with Galileo's challenge to the hegemony of the Church and pioneering use of mechanics and measurement, while bolstered by Bacon's and Descartes's call to command and commandeer nature; and reached a high point with Newton's discoveries of the laws of gravity, further inspiring a mechanistic worldview developed by Enlightenment thinkers during the eighteenth century.

For the major architects of the modern worldview—Galileo Galilei, Francis Bacon, Rene Descartes, and Isaac Newton—the cosmos is a vast machine governed by immutable laws which function in a stable and orderly way that can be discerned by the rational mind and manipulated for human benefit. Beginning in the sixteenth century, scientific explanations of the world replace theological explanations; knowledge is used no longer to serve God and shore up faith, but rather to serve the needs of human beings and to expand their power over nature. Where philosophers in the premodern world believed that the purpose of knowledge was to know God and to contemplate eternal truths, modernists exalted applied knowledge and demystified the purpose of knowledge as nothing more than to extend the "power and greatness of man" to command natural forces for "the relief of man's estate."[2]

Through advancing mathematical and physical explanations of the universe, modernists replaced a qualitative, sacred definition of reality with a strictly quantitative hermeneutics that "disenchanted" (Berman)[3] the world and ultimately presided over the "death of nature" (Merchant).[4] This involved transforming the understanding of the universe as a living cosmos into a dead machine, thus removing any qualms scientists and technicians might have in the misguided project of "mastering" nature for human purposes.

The machine metaphor was apt, not only because of the spread of machines and factories throughout emerging capitalist society, but also because—representing something orderly, precise, determined, knowable, and controllable—it was the totem for European modernity. Newton's discoveries of the laws of gravity vindicated the mechanistic worldview and scores of eighteenth and nineteenth century thinkers (such as Holbach and La Mettrie) set out to apply this materialist and determinist paradigm to the earth as well as to the heavens, on the assumption that similar laws, harmonies, and regularities governed society and human nature. Once the laws of history, social change, and human nature were grasped, the new "social scientists" speculated, human behavior and social dynamics could be similarly managed through application of the order, harmony, prediction, and control that allowed for the scientific governance of natural bodies.

The rationalization, quantification, and abstraction process generated by science, where the natural world was emptied of meaning and reduced to quantitative value, is paralleled in dynamics unleashed by capitalism, in which all things and beings are reduced to exchange value and the pursuit of profit. In both science and capitalism, an aggressive *nihilism* obliterates intrinsic value and reduces natural, biological, and social reality to instrumental value, viewing the entire world from the interest of dissection, manipulation, and exploitation. Science sharply separates "fact" from "value," thereby pursuing a "neutral" or "objective" study of natural systems apart from politics, ethics, and metaphysics, as capitalism bifurcates the public and private sectors, disburdening private enterprise of any public or moral obligations. The kind of rationality that drives the modern scientific, economic, and technological revolutions—instrumental or administrative reason (*herrschaftwissen*)—is only one kind of knowledge, knowledge for the sake of power, profit, and control.[5] Unlike the type of rationality that is critical, ethical, communicative, and dialogical in nature, the goal of instrumental reason is to order, categorize, control, exploit, appropriate, and commandeer the physical and living worlds as means toward designated ends. Accordingly, this general type of reason—a vivid example of what Nietzsche diagnoses as the Western "will to power"—dominates the outlook and schemes of scientists, technicians, capitalists, bureaucrats, war strategists, and social scientists. Instrumental knowledge is based on prediction and control, and it attains this goal by linking science to technology, by employing sophisticated mathematical methods of measurement, by frequently serving capitalist interests, and by abstracting itself from all other concerns, often disparaged as "nonscientific," "subjective," or inefficient.

The dark, ugly, bellicose, repressive, violent, and predatory underbelly of the "disinterested" pursuit of knowledge, of "reason," and of "democracy," "freedom," and "rights" as well, has been described through a litany of ungainly sociological terms, including, but not limited to: secularization, rationalization, commodification, reification ("thingification"), industrialization, standardization, homogenization, bureaucratization, and globalization. Each term describes a different aspect of modernity—reduction of the universe to mathematical symbols and equations, the mass production of identical objects, the standardization of individuals into the molds of conformity, the evolution of capitalist power from its competitive to monopolist to transnational stages, or the political and legal state apparatus of "representative" or "parliamentary" democracies. Each dynamic is part of a comprehensive, aggressive, protean, and multidimensional system of power and domination, co-constituted by the three main engines incessantly propelling modern change: science, capitalism, and technology.[6] In industrial capitalist societies, elites deploy mathematics, science, technology, bureaucracies, states, militaries, and instrumental reason to render the world as something abstract, functional, calculable, and controllable, while transforming any and all things and beings into commodities manufactured and sold for profit.

From Exploitation to Administration

Critical theorists and postmodernists resisted Marxist economic reductionism to work out the implications of Weber's "iron cage of rationality" that tightly enveloped the modern world by the nineteenth century. A critical counter-enlightenment trajectory leads from Nietzsche to Weber to Georg Lukács through Frankfurt School theorists like Theodor Adorno, Max Horkheimer, Herbert Marcuse, and Jurgen Habermas, to postmodernists such as Michel Foucault and Jean Baudrillard. Although many relied on key Marxist categories, they sought a more complex concept of power and resistance than allowed by the economistic emphasis on capital, alienated labor, and class struggle. Where Marx equates power with exploitation, the capital-labor relation, the factory system, and centralized corporate-state power, modern and postmodern theorists of administrative rationality brought to light the autonomous role that knowledge, reason, politics, and technique serve in producing systems of domination and control.

Thus, on this line of reasoning, in the early twentieth century German philosopher Martin Heidegger theorized modernity as a huge system of

reason is a Value b/c we Value it

"enframing" that reduced things to mere objects and functions available for human use.[7] Adorno and Horkheimer revealed the "total administration" of society through instrumental reason that sought control over objects, the environment, and human individuals and populations by eliminating difference and treating everything as resources suited to manipulation and control.[8] They witnessed how culture and the arts had been colonized by capitalist values and industrial methods, such that creative works once judged on aesthetic criteria such as originality, sublimity, and edification were assessed instead on economic grounds as commodities with potential mass appeal capable of generating enormous profits. Culture, in short, had become a culture industry, where artworks became commodities for mass production, distribution, and consumption, designed according to rationalized formulae, and administered through a bureaucratic chain of command.

Similarly, Marcuse documented the loss of critical reason, autonomy, and individual transformation in a "one dimensional" society ruled by capital, state bureaucracy, and technoscience. This system precludes, represses, or absorbs dissent and opposition amid a monotone culture of corporatism and conformity devoid of opposition and dissent.[9] Rather than a centralized control system dominated by corporations and the state, Foucault analyzed modernity as a plurality of mcro-institutions such as hospitals, schools, and prisons. Foucault argues that capital exploitation of labor is only one aspect of power, which is far more general in its nature, strategies, and range of effects. Power should be understood not as exploitation, but as *rationalization,* or rather, as a series of discursive-institutional employments of rationality that seek to "normalize" and "discipline" individuals and populations through the liquidation of alterity and the production of docile minds and bodies.[10] In works such as *For a Critique of the Political Economy of the Sign* (1981) and *The Mirror of Production* (1975), Jean Baudrillard interprets political economy as a gigantic system of bureaucratic administration of all social life, such that capitalism is less a structure in itself than an institutional instantiation of a larger rationalization process. In a notable more recent updating of a Weber-Marx synthesis, analyzing the logic and consequences of industrialization and capitalism, sociologist George Ritzer described the "McDonaldization of society." For Ritzer, this process describes a global phenomenon in which society and culture come under the logic of mass production, standardization, mass consumption, and capital markets. As McDonaldization spreads insidiously, it dulls consciousness, destroys diversity and difference, and integrates people into the global factory system in spheres of production and consumption, work and everyday life, while spreading markets and commodification imperatives in all directions, always with the intent to amass capital and power for the minority elite.[11]

Clearly, instrumental reason targets not only objects and things for control, but also subjects and society; and just as mechanistic science moved seamlessly from objectifying heavenly bodies to policing social bodies, so administrative rationality moved from controlling nature to manipulating society. The disciplining of bodies in eighteenth century schools, the ubiquitous gaze of guards over prisoners in nineteenth century penitentiaries, the Taylorization process in twentieth century factories that studied workers' movements to minimize wasted energy and maximize surplus value; the eugenics discourse and mass sterilization policies in the United States during the 1920s; the networks of mass culture, electronic media, and advertising that constitute a vast "society of the spectacle" (Guy Debord) that transforms citizens from active agents to passive consumers; the colonization of minds of children, youth, and adults through a cornucopia of chemical toxins that dull, deaden, and neutralize minds through pharmaceutical warfare—these are only some of the seemingly infinite methods and techniques used to regiment populations, pacify resistance, neutralize activity, and eliminate opposition.

A Light Snuffed Out

Despite the optimistic predictions of sundry eighteenth century Enlightenment thinkers in Germany, France, the United States, and elsewhere, the rise of science, technology, global markets, rationality, and critical thinking did not lead to universal peace, happiness, and prosperity for the world's peoples. In the alchemy of capitalist modernity, things morph into their opposites, and thus dreams spawned nightmares, visions of light brought darkness, knowledge bred ignorance, productive forces evolved into destructive forces; competition led to monopoly; wealth produced misery; automation extended the regime of labor, and freedom multiplied domination. The unfettered development of reason, science, technology, and markets did not eliminate wars, abolish poverty, or annul want. Like "democracy" and "rights," the discourse of "Progress"—the Gospel of Modernity—disguises private interests (the small minority who comprise the financial, political, and cultural elite) under the mask of universal discourse (e.g., "the rights of man"). "Progress" thus works to obscure unjust social relations and to legitimate science, technology, and capitalism, and thus is a mantra created by and for elites.

The underbelly of the Enlightenment and "Age of Reason" was riddled with racism, patriarchy, genocide, slavery, and colonialism, and the leaders and ambassadors of modernity had the audacity to uphold capitalism, science, and industry as a "civilization" *par excellence,* generating a society that allegedly transcends the legacy of "savage" and "barbaric" cultures.

This "pinnacle" of human evolution, this "mature" realization of promise in relation to which non-Western and pre-modern societies were but "infants," proved its superiority through two world wars, fascism, totalitarianism, genocide, and atomic warfare, followed by a nuclear arms race and ecological destruction on a planetary scale. In the tragic "dialectic of enlightenment," Adorno and Horkheimer noted, reason morphed into its opposite as "catastrophe radiated over the earth."

Whereas modern theorists of the eighteenth and nineteenth centuries championed the spread of reason, science, and technology as emancipatory, "postmodern" critics of the late twentieth century attacked these forces as coercive and oppressive. They rejected the naïve coupling of reason and freedom to argue that reason aided by science, technology, and capitalism produces monsters and catastrophes. Accordingly, Lyotard finds the main characteristic of the "postmodern condition" and *fin-de-siècle* malaise to be "incredulity toward metanarratives" (i.e., modern progressivist visions of history as a linear and purposive movement of events toward the confluence of reason and freedom.)[12]

Habermas, however, rejects postmodern critiques themselves as totalizing, as one-sided polemics that conflate different forms of rationality into one oppressive force that allegedly has colonized all of society.[13] For Habermas, the problem with modernity is not too much rationality, but too little. That is, whereas modernity is characterized by the hegemony of instrumental rationality which seeks a technical mastery of nature and society, the Enlightenment culture generated a *communicative rationality* that is concerned not with power and control but rather the logic of raising different validity claims which require redemption under conditions of argumentation while seeking consensus over important issues of government and social regulation. Whereas Habermas agrees with critical modernists and postmodernists that instrumental reason has bolstered the domination of human over nature and human over human, he insists that communicative rationality can decouple reason and domination. Thus, he believes, there are positive aspects of the Enlightenment and modern liberalism that can be redeemed and developed toward emancipatory ends. The Enlightenment, therefore, is not dead or unqualifiedly disastrous; rather, Habermas declares it and modernity as a whole to be an "unfinished project."[14]

Systems of Command

After World War II, and the huge gains made by U.S. corporate and military interests, the idea of a manifold and structured power system—an *industrial*

complex—was first articulated and became common vernacular. In his seminal work, *The Power Elite* (1956), sociologist C. Wright Mills theorized the
structural outcomes arising from the mutual class interests uniting military,
governmental, and business leaders within an anti-democratic oligarchy.[15]
During his January 1961 Farewell Address to the Nation, President Dwight
D. Eisenhower warned of a menacing new "military-industrial complex,"
a post-war power bloc composed of the armed forces, private defense
contractors, weapons suppliers, the Pentagon, Congress, and the Executive
Branch of government. Invoking this unholy alliance among industrialism,
capitalism, and state militarism, Eisenhower cautioned that weapons and
warfare had become new industries and capital markets that may boost the
economy but undermine the Constitution and upset the "balance of powers"
among the executive, legislative, and judicial branches of government.

But it was not only the military that had exploited science and technology,
appropriated industrial models of production and organization, used bureaucratic organization techniques, and produced commodities—deadly weapons
of war—for capital markets and profit motivations. As Eisenhower delivered
his somber address, the foundations of the military-industrial complex were
already set and began multiplying and manifesting in different institutions,
disciplines, fields of research, and social institutions. The military-industrial
complex was but part of a larger revolution bent on remaking American
society, Western Europe, and ultimately the entire globe in its own image
of power, subjugation, and profit. At the same time, its autonomy congealed
within basic paradigms or structures rooted in imperatives of control, domination, efficiency, and profit within various hierarchical systems of rule. In this
sense, as Noam Chomsky has described it, the military-industrial complex is
"a misnomer . . . There is no military-industrial complex: it's just the industrial system operating under one or another pretext."[16]

In the decades since Eisenhower's speech, one sees in capitalist societies the fluid and dynamic merging of science, technology, mass production,
capitalism, bureaucracy, and hierarchical power systems. It was not only the
military that had merged with market models, industrial paradigms, systems
of mass production, growth and efficiency imperatives, and bureaucratic
administration, but also every other institution of society. By the mid-
twentieth century, in sectors ranging from medicine, agriculture, media, and
entertainment, to security, education, criminal justice, and transportation,
virtually all institutions were reconceived and reconstructed according to
capitalist, industrial, and bureaucratic models suited to the aim of realizing
profit, growth, efficiency, mass production, and standardization imperatives.

These systems, moreover, interrelate and reinforce one another. We can see
this, for instance, in how the constellation in which the academic industrial

complex does research for the medical industrial complex and Big Pharma, exploiting the nonhuman animal slaves of the animal industrial complex in university, military, and private vivisection laboratories and producing fraudulent research financed by and for pharmaceutical capital. The dubiously researched drugs are patented, typically fast-tracked into market sales by the obliging Food and Drug Administration, and then advertised through the media industrial complex. Up to 115 million animals die worldwide annually to perpetuate this fraud, and the human victims of research-for-profit succumb to the medical industrial complex for costly "disease management" (not "health care") treatment that treats only symptoms to focus on the ultimate objective of profit. The dissent of animal rights activists is criminalized by the security industrial complex, and many are sent off to languish, along with one out of every one hundred adults in the U.S. population incarcerated in the prison industrial complex.

Similarly, in the fast-growing academic industrial complex, universities are no longer noble institutions of "higher education" but rather profit-seeking corporations that treat students as commodities; replace costly tenured professors with the cheap labor of part-time, contract, and adjunct instructors; and emphasize the highly lucrative fields of science, engineering, and athletics, while marginalizing "non-performing" disciplines such as philosophy, sociology, and anthropology. Universities also opens their doors to the military and security industrial complexes to staff the U.S. global war machine and repressive state apparatus with well-trained functionaries.[17] Meanwhile, our food system has become thoroughly industrialized and corporatized as small, family farms have been bankrupted and assimilated into the giant conglomerate holdings of agribusiness. Thus, factory farms have become the international business standard, as agribusiness giants such as Cargill and Monsanto absorb remaining traditional farms into their global networks by coercive attempts to impose seeds, pesticides and herbicides, and service technologies they patent and own, and taking advantage of "genetic pollution" on neighboring farms to sue, destroy, and control their land as well. But to announce the role of these multinational companies in determining the shape and nature of our lives is to recognize that the capitalist-industrial complex has become global, diversified, interconnected and networked.

The Dialectic of Globalization

In a classic work, Karl Polyani (1957) described the "great transformation" from preindustrial to industrial society.[18] With Douglas Kellner, I attempted previously to theorize the transformation of twenty-first century global industrial society—the postmodern adventure (which designated dramatic changes in the economy and society, but also in science, technology, politics, culture, nature, and human identity itself).[19] The contributors to *The Global Industrial Complex: Systems of Domination* contribute their trenchant sociological and political analysis toward further exploring the argument that a momentous change of the social order is taking place today with the emergence of the global industrial complex.

The termination of the Bretton Woods financial system and the collapse of the Soviet Union followed in the wake of centuries of capital-driven globalization. Neoliberal capitalism has become the new paradigm of permanent growth. The implications of the neoliberal stage of capitalist marketization are enormous, as capitalism universalizes its rule, throws off "superfluous" and "injurious" constraints on "free trade," and increasingly realizes the goal of purity of function and purpose through the autonomization of the economy from society, so that the social *is* the economic. Over the last few decades, Takis Fotopoulos notes, "A neoliberal consensus has swept over the advanced capitalist world and has replaced the social-democratic consensus of the early post-war period."[20] Not only have "existing socialist societies" been negated in the global triumph of capitalism, so too have social democracies and the bulk of institutional networks designed to protect individuals from the ravages of privatization and the relinquishment of responsibilities to people in need to case them into barbaric barrenness of the "survival-of-the-fittest."

Over the last several decades, the capitalist production process itself has become increasingly transnationalized and thereby relatively autonomous (but not in total negation) of the archipelago of nation-states in favor of global institutions and power blocs of unprecedented influence and might. We have moved from a world economy to a new epoch known as the global economy. Whereas formerly the world economy was composed of the development of national economies and state-based circuits of accumulation interlinked through commodity trade and capital flows in differentiated world markets, today corporations and national production systems are reorganized and functionally integrated into porous global circuits, creating a single and increasingly homogenous field for massive and mobile capitalism.

Fuelled by new forms of science and technology, military expansion, and aggressive colonization of southern nations and the developing world, capitalism evolved into a truly global system. Global capital is inspired by neoliberal visions of nations as resource pools and open markets operating without restrictions. The process euphemistically termed "globalization" is driven by multinational corporations such as ExxonMobil and DuPont; financed by financial goliaths such as the World Bank and the International Monetary Fund (IMF), and legally protected by the World Trade Organization (WTO). It homogenizes nations into a single economic organism and trading bloc through arrangements such as the North American Free Trade Agreement (NAFTA), the Free Trade Area of the Americas (FTAA), and the European Union (EU). Multinationals seduce, bribe, and coerce nations to open their markets and help drive down labor costs to a bare minimum, and rely heavily on corrupt dictators, loans and debt, and "hit men" and armies to enforce the rule of their "structural transformations" of societies into conduits for the flow of resources and capital. Globalization has produced trade laws that protect transnational corporations at the expense of human life, biodiversity, and the environment. It is accompanied by computerization of all facets of production and expanding automation, generating heightened exploitation of labor, corporate downsizing, and greater levels of unemployment, inequality, insecurity, and violence.

Debates rage over issues such as when globalization dynamics began and if current ones are continuous developments of centuries of global markets and exchange or something qualitatively new; whether corporate globalization is mainly a positive or negative dynamic; the degree to which globalization is largely under the command of U.S. capital and military interests or more diverse and plural powers; whether the United States is a declining empire and a power shift is underway from American-European capital to the rapidly modernizing and growing economies of the East (China and India) and the South (Latin America); the extent to which the nation state is still a significant force amidst the growing power of international corporate and financial networks; whether or not industrial logics such as standardization have been displaced by postindustrial developments (such as are organized more around communications, science, knowledge, and service industries than traditional manufacturing operations) and post-Fordist "flexible" production schemes, and so on. While a vast literature explains recent epochal shifts in terms like postindustrialism, post-Fordism, or postmodernity, we grasp numerous novelties but nevertheless insist that significant changes and reorganization in technology, organization, culture, and capital are best understood not as something qualitatively different, but rather as new stages in capitalism still dominated by profit and growth imperatives. And as theorists such as Claus Offe, John Keene, Scott Lash, and John Urry describe the restructuring process as "disorganized capitalism," we see this as a complex form of the reorganization of capitalism, constituting a new mode of economic and social organization with momentous consequences.[21]

There has been less realization, however, that structures of power are multiple, plural, and decentralized, and that we live amidst a tangled matrix of systems anchored in logics of control, standardization, exploitation, and profit. Taken together, this "power complex" continues to expand throughout the globe and to grow new tentacles, each system or network overlapping with and reinforcing others, and the totality integrating nature, animals, and human beings ever deeper into a veritable global industrial complex. The expansive, colonizing, interconnected network is comprised of numerous industry-capital specific systems such as the criminal industrial complex, the agricultural industrial complex, the medical industrial complex, the animal industrial complex, the academic industrial complex, the military industrial complex, the prison industrial complex, the entertainment industrial complex, and the communication industrial complex, to name some of the more salient configurations.

Thus, a major thesis of this volume is that the powerful logics of industrialization and capitalism, symbiotically interlocked at least since the nineteenth century, have expanded, diversified, and colonized ever more institutions and organizing systems, and expanded into a world system. In any one institutional node of this protean and rhizomatic network, one can find logics, functions, and procedures that include commodification, profit-seeking, corporatization, and privatization; hierarchical command and bureaucratic administration; exploitation of technoscience and expertise; electronic information networks and profit-making goals; and structures of state and military repression, coercive violence, and prison to enforce institutional power.

By no means is globalization to be understood as an inherently negative dynamic or consequence of human history, as if the desideratum is fragmentation, isolation, provincialism, and nationalism. Ever since *Homo sapiens* migrated out of Africa and dispersed itself globally across the continents, human existence has been a global dynamic and knowledge, culture, and technologies have spread in all directions, such as with the influence of Islam on the West. Certainly, from the standpoint of the natural environment and the countless animal species driven into extinction, the rapid global growth of human populations, technologies, and economies has not been a positive development. But dissemination of knowledge, culture, and people is a positive and enriching process; indeed, it is now urgent that the paradigm shift from economics and growth to ecology and sustainability take root on a global scale. A salient distinction to be made here is between globalization from above (as dictated by multinational capital) and globalization from below (as realized in self-organizing and democratic ways by people in cultural exchange and open movement).[22] And just as we reject the false option of seeing power as either macrological or micrological, recognizing both that power, resources, and wealth are concentrated like never before and yet distributed throughout societies in a wide range of institutions, none of which are reducible to ruling elites or a dominant class, so we reject framing the issue as Marx *or* Weber, in favor of Marx *and* Weber, while affirming the need for

Power is amorphous - adhering to whoever is using it but able to move quickly away.

a host of other fruitful perspectives, such as the standpoints of gender, race, and species.

Moreover, it would be a serious mistake to think that the octopus of inter-locked power networks covering the globe does not generate appropriate responses and relevant modes of resistance and struggle. Through even per-functory perusal of sites such as *Indymedia, Infoshop, 325nostate.net, Guerilla News,* and *Bite Back,* one can see that resistance is intense, global, and total, against every system of hierarchy ever devised, giving rise to diverse and vital struggles for human, animal, and earth liberation. As dramatically evident in battles such as raged in Madrid in 1994, in Seattle in 1999, and in Genoa in 2001, "anti-" or, more accurately, "alter-globalization" groups throughout the world recognized their common interests and fates, and formed unprecedented kinds of alliances to fight against the globalization of capital.[23] Global capitalism has emerged as the common enemy recognized by world groups and peoples, and resistance movements have come together in alliances that bridge national boundaries, North-South divisions, and different political causes.

Yet struggles have not kept pace with the scope and speed of planetary plunder; resistance movements are winning some battles, but losing the larger war against greed, violence, expanding corporate power, militariza-tion, and against metastasizing systems of economic growth, technological development, overproduction, overconsumption, and overpopulation. The deterioration of society and nature demands a profound, systematic, and radi-cal political response, yet in recent decades Left opposition movements have tended to become more reformist and co-opted on the whole, growing weaker in proportion to their strategic importance and the power of global capital. As the world spirals ever deeper into disaster, with all things becoming ever more tightly knit into the tentacles of global capitalism, there is an urgent need for new conceptual and political maps and compasses to help steer humanity into a viable mode of existence.

Pluralizing Power, Multiplying Resistance

We hope that this volume advances understanding of some of the most ominous and important developments of recent decades, such as those involving "the global industrial complex." While many have written on the different aspects of neoliberal globalization, and some have written histories or critical analyses of one type of "industrial complex" or another (e.g., military, academic, media, medical, agricultural, and so on), no one has yet brought together these disparate critical perspectives into a comprehensive

we are not a Cancer but suffer from one: Capitalism - as practised.

and coherent framework, such as *The Global Industrial Complex*, which analyzes the global industrial complex dominated by capitalist growth and profit imperatives, bureaucratic efficiency requirements, technological mass production standardization, and hierarchical administration, and is backed by punishment, jail, and military force.

We believe that a major issue thus far preventing a more successful resistance to global systemic domination has been the inability of alter-globalization writers and activists to theorize the nature of the opposition. Some have successfully named and analyzed strands in the global industrial complex. Others have exhaustively clarified the relentless marketization campaign of neoliberal capitalism, such as which undermine the last forms of social democracy and relegating socialists and communists to corrupt variants of capitalism. Still others have sought to pinpoint the manner in which global imperialism has instituted a new bureaucratic ordering of life for the world's citizens. But few, if any, have managed to reveal the *co-constructive, interdependent, and imbricative* nature of multiple systems of domination and oppression dispersed throughout the globe.

Far from a slogan or catchphrase, we use the "global industrial complex" category to highlight the growing influence and dominance of corporations, bureaucracies, and technological control models, while showing how independent power complexes evolved into interdependent networks of control. More bluntly, theorizing the present era via the lens of a global industrial complex helps to expose the real dangers and potential today for a new paradigm of worldwide fascism or some mode of authoritarian control reinforced by threats of "terrorism" and ecological breakdown.

Consequently, it is crucial to understand how diverse institutions that spread throughout the globe are being pieced together as part of an interlocking system of imperialist domination that extends the classical capitalist factory operation (however much it has changed since the nineteenth century) into all domains of social life, by exporting the ideals, techniques, and models used for mass production, standardization, commodification, bureaucratic administration, and hierarchical control. *The Global Industrial Complex: Systems of Domination* hopes to inspire new thinking among critical theorists, public intellectuals, and radical activists and to educate a broader public about the transformations underway, the threats they pose, and the need to resist these changes and dismantle multiple systems of hierarchy, domination, and control.

Maude Barlow has written, "We are committed with our lives to building a different model and a different future for humanity, the Earth, and other species. We have envisaged a moral alternative to economic globalization and we will not rest until we see it realized." This book is itself intended to be a modest artifact of resistance along these lines, an attempt to be proactive and engaged rather than reactive and passive, or to merely study social changes academically and "objectively" with the sublime detachment available only to the emotionally dead and morally impaired. *The Global Industrial Complex* is not a blueprint or handbook, obviously, but rather it offers critical insights and provisional perspectives on the evolution, structure, operation, function, and consequences of the intensification, globalization, and interpenetration of capitalism, technoscience, bureaucratic domination, and industrialization paradigms and processes, such as play out globally in various institutional spheres. As the global industrial complex is emergent and still novel and inchoate, this volume's essays gesture to some of its complexity but do not pretend to offer definitive statements, and many retain a focus on U.S. dynamics of American imperialism as a key catalyst in this emergent process. Indeed, more than any other nation still, the U.S. is the fabled "belly of the beast" and much can be gained from this focus, which can be judiciously applied to developments in other areas of the world, especially as these are also extensions of, or significantly influenced by, the U.S. context. Understanding the role of the "Washington consensus," of America as a core nation-state within the world system of capitalism, imperialism, and the domination of nature generally, while not adequate to delineate all the complexity of any aspect of the global industrial complex, remains a necessary (or at least useful) foundation stone for further analysis in globalization studies and anticapitalist political movement struggle.

It bears repeating that the forces of death, destruction, and domination today are not only capitalism, transnational corporations, and the banking and finance institutions, but are also states, militaries, bureaucracies, and sundry systems of control that aim to colonize and control nature, animals, and human populations. Additionally, the underlying mentalities of hierarchy and instrumentalism that have driven Western culture and beyond for over two millennia remain instantiated in the global consciousness. As such, they shape not only the materially systemic forms that domination now takes, but also present limiting factors for the planetary realization of liberation struggles.

If every moment is pregnant with revolution, this is an especially pivotal time in history, a crossroads for the future of life. As the social and ecological crisis deepens, with capitalism surging, inequalities growing, control systems tightening, forests disappearing, species vanishing, oceans dying, resources diminishing, and the catastrophic effects of global climate change now immanent and irreversible, windows of reasonable political opportunity for the production of an alternative social order are rapidly closing. The actions that humanity now collectively takes or fails to take will determine whether the future is more hopeful or altogether bleak.

As the corporate machines continue to slash and burn the planet, inequalities widen and power grows, logics of profit and control spread through social institutions, human numbers and the insatiable appetites of the global consumer society swell as the biodiversity of flora and fauna steeply declines, it is easy to become not only cautious or pessimistic about the prospects for planetary peace and freedom, but fatalistic and nihilistic. In the schools and social movement discourse, we are beginning to hear from some who appear resigned to the catastrophe playing out on this planet. Others, however, remain oblivious to this incredible moment in time and the epic tragedy of resigning humanity's fate to be a failed primate species because of its inability to harness the evolutionary advantages of a large forebrain or overcome its predilection to tribalism, xenophobia, hubris, hierarchy, violence, alienation from nature and other life forms, and uncontrolled growth.

Surrender, however, is not an option. Our debt to the past and present is great, and we have no choice but to live in the tension that pits hopes and ideals against grim realities and unprecedented challenges. As Italian theorist Antonio Gramsci wrote, "The challenge of modernity is to live without illusions and without becoming disillusioned." But every crisis harbors opportunities for profound change, and the "grow or die" imperative that ought to shape our priorities is not capitalist in nature, but rather evokes the need for moral, psychological, and social evolution, to be realized in radically new forms of consciousness, species identities, ethics, values, social arrangements, and lifeways. There is no swift economic or technological fix for the myriad complex crises we confront. The only solution lies in organizing informed radical change across all levels of the integrated systems of domination—commencing with an emancipatory education into and critical understanding of the precise nature and dynamics of the systematic barriers blocking our journey into sustainable planetary community. Let us hope that this long march through the institutions does not further transform into a trail of tears.

NOTES

1. See Morris Berman, *The Re-Enchantment of the World* (Ithaca, NY: Cornell University Press, 1981).

2. Francis Bacon, *The New Organon and Other Writings* (New York, NY: Library of Liberal Arts, 1960).

3. Berman, *The Re-Enchantment of the World.*

4. Carolyn Merchant, *The Death of Nature: Women, Ecology, and The Scientific Revolution* (New York, NY: HarperOne, 1990).

5. Rene Descartes, *Discourse on Method* (New York, NY: McMillan, 1960).

6. See Steven Best and Douglas Kellner, *The Postmodern Adventure: Science, Technology, and Cultural Studies at the Third Millennium* (New York, NY: Guilford Press, 2001).

7. Martin Heidegger, *Being and Time* (New York, NY: Harper and Row, 1962).

8. Max Horkheimer and Theodor W. Adorno, *Dialectic of Enlightenment* (New York, NY: Continuum, 1972).

9. Herbert Marcuse, *One Dimensional Man* (Boston, MA: Beacon Press, 1964).

10. Michel Foucault, *Discipline and Punish* (New York, NY: Vintage, 1979); *Power/ Knowledge* (New York: Pantheon Books, 1980).

11. George Ritzer, *The McDonaldization of Society* (revised edition) (Thousand Oaks, CA: Pine Forge Press, 2004).

12. Jean-François Lyotard, *The Postmodern Condition* (Minneapolis, MN: University of Minnesota Press, 1984).

13. Jurgen Habermas, *Theory of Communicative Action, Vol. 1* (Boston, MA: Beacon Press, 1984).

14. Jurgen Habermas, *The Philosophical Discourse of Modernity.* Cambridge, MA: MIT Press, 1987).

15. C. Wright Mills, *The Power Elite* (Oxford, UK: Oxford University Press, 2000).

16. Noam Chomsky, *On Power, Dissent and Racism* (DVD) (Baraka Productions, 2003).

17. See Anthony J. Nocella II, Steven Best, and Peter McLaren (eds.), *Academic Repression: Reflections from the Academic-Industrial Complex* (Oakland, CA: AK Press, 2010).

18. Karl Polyani, *The Great Transformation: The Political and Economic Origins of Our Time* (Boston, MA: Beacon Press, 2001).

19. Best and Kellner, *The Postmodern Adventure.*

20. Takis Fotopoulos, *Toward an Inclusive Democracy: The Crisis of the Growth Economy and the Need for a New Liberatory Project* (London, UK: Cassell Press, 1997), 39.

21. Claus Offe and John Keene, *Disorganized Capitalism: Contemporary Transformation of Work and Politics* (Cambridge, MA: MIT Press, 1985); Scott Lash and John Urry, *The End of Organized Capitalism* (Madison, WI: University of Wisconsin, 1987).

22. Jeremy Brecher, Tim Costello, and Brendan Smith. *Globalization From Below: The Power of Solidarity* (Cambridge, MA: South End Press, 2000).

23. On resistance movements against global capitalism, see Richard Kahn and Douglas Kellner, "Resisting Globalization," in *The Blackwell Companion to Globalization,* ed. George Ritzer (Malden, MA: Blackwell Publishers, 2006).

Chapter One

Crisis and Hope

Theirs and Ours[1]

Noam Chomsky

Perhaps I may begin with a few words about the title. There is too much nuance and variety to make such sharp distinctions as *theirs-and-ours, them-and-us*. And neither I nor anyone can presume to speak for "us." But I will pretend it is possible.

There is also a problem with the term "crisis." Which one? There are numerous very severe crises, interwoven in ways that preclude any clear separation. But again I will pretend otherwise, for simplicity.

One way to enter this morass is offered by the June 11 issue of the *New York Review of Books*. The front-cover headline reads "How to Deal With the Crisis"; the issue features a symposium of specialists on how to do so. It is very much worth reading, but with attention to the definite article. For the West the phrase "*the* crisis" has a clear enough meaning: the financial crisis that hit the rich countries with great impact, and is therefore of supreme importance. But even for the rich and privileged that is by no means the only crisis, nor even the most severe. And others see the world quite differently. For example, in the October 26, 2008 edition of the Bangladeshi newspaper *The New Nation*, we read:

> It's very telling that trillions have already been spent to patch up leading world financial institutions, while out of the comparatively small sum of $12.3 billion pledged in Rome earlier this year, to offset the food crisis, only $1 billion has been delivered. The hope that at least extreme poverty can be eradicated by the end of 2015, as stipulated in the UN's Millennium Development Goals, seems as unrealistic as ever, not due to lack of resources but a lack of true concern for the world's poor.[2]

The article goes on to predict that World Food Day in October 2009 "will bring . . . devastating news about the plight of the world's poor . . . which

1

is likely to remain that: mere 'news' that requires little action, if any at all."[3] Western leaders seem determined to fulfill these grim predictions. On June 11 the *Financial Times* reported, "the United Nations' World Food Programme is cutting food aid rations and shutting down some operations as donor countries that face a fiscal crunch at home slash contributions to its funding."[4] Victims include Ethiopia, Rwanda, Uganda, and others. The sharp budget cut comes as the toll of hunger passes a billion—with over one hundred million added in the past six months—while food prices rise, and remittances decline as a result of the economic crisis in the West.

As *The New Nation* anticipated, the "devastating news" released by the World Food Programme barely even reached the level of "mere 'news.'" In the *New York Times,* the WFP report of the reduction in the meager Western efforts to deal with this growing "human catastrophe" merited 150 words on page ten under "World Briefing."[5] That is not in the least unusual. The United Nations also released an estimate that desertification is endangering the lives of up to a billion people, while announcing World Desertification Day. Its goal, according to the Nigerian newspaper *THISDAY,* is "to combat desertification and drought worldwide by promoting public awareness and the implementation of conventions dealing with desertification in member countries."[6] The effort to raise public awareness passed without mention in the national U.S. press. Such neglect is all too common.

It may be instructive to recall that when they landed in what today is Bangladesh, the British invaders were stunned by its wealth and splendor. It was soon on its way to becoming the very symbol of misery, and not by an act of God.

As the fate of Bangladesh illustrates, the terrible food crisis is not just a result of "lack of true concern" in the centers of wealth and power. In large part it results from very definite concerns of global managers: for their own welfare. It is always well to keep in mind Adam Smith's astute observation about policy formation in England. He recognized that the "principal architects" of policy—in his day the "merchants and manufacturers"—made sure that their own interests had "been most peculiarly attended to" however "grievous" the effect on others, including the people of England and, far more so, those who were subjected to "the savage injustice of the Europeans," particularly in conquered India, Smith's own prime concern in the domains of European conquest.[7]

Smith was referring specifically to the mercantilist system, but his observation generalizes, and as such, stands as one of the few solid and enduring principles of both international relations and domestic affairs. It should not, however, be overgeneralized. There are interesting cases where state interests, including long-term strategic and economic interests, overwhelm the parochial concerns of the concentrations of economic power that largely shape state policy. Iran and Cuba are instructive cases, but I will have to put these topics aside here.

The food crisis erupted first and most dramatically in Haiti in early 2008. Like Bangladesh, Haiti today is a symbol of misery and despair. And, like Bangladesh, when European explorers arrived, the island was remarkably rich in resources, with a large and flourishing population. It later became the source of much of France's wealth. I will not run through the sordid history, but the current food crisis can be traced directly to 1915, Woodrow Wilson's invasion: murderous, brutal, and destructive. Among Wilson's many crimes was dissolving the Haitian Parliament at gunpoint because it refused to pass "progressive legislation" that would have allowed U.S. businesses to take over Haitian lands. Wilson's Marines then ran a free election, in which the legislation was passed by 99.9 percent of the 5 percent of the public permitted to vote. All of this comes down through history as "Wilsonian idealism."

Later, the United States Agency for International Development (USAID) instituted programs to turn Haiti into the "Taiwan of the Caribbean," by adhering to the sacred principle of comparative advantage: Haiti must import food and other commodities from the United States, while working people, mostly women, toil under miserable conditions in U.S.-owned assembly plants. Haiti's first free election, in 1990, threatened these economically rational programs. The poor majority entered the political arena for the first time and elected their own candidate, a populist priest, Jean-Bertrand Aristide. Washington adopted the standard operating procedures for such a case, moving at once to undermine the regime. A few months later came the anticipated military coup, and the resulting junta instituted a reign of terror, which was backed by Bush senior and even more fully by Clinton, despite pretenses. By 1994 Clinton decided that the population was sufficiently intimidated and sent U.S. forces to restore the elected president, but on the strict condition that he accept a harsh neoliberal regime. In particular, there must be no protection for the economy. Haitian rice farmers are efficient, but cannot compete with U.S. agribusiness that relies on huge government subsidies, thanks largely to Reagan, anointed High Priest of free trade with little regard to his record of extreme protectionism and state intervention in the economy.

There is nothing surprising about what followed: a 1995 USAID report observed that the "export-driven trade and investment policy"—that Washington mandated—will "relentlessly squeeze the domestic rice farmer."[8] Neoliberal policies dismantled what was left of economic sovereignty and drove the country into chaos, accelerated by Bush junior's blocking of international aid on cynical grounds. In February 2004 the two traditional torturers of Haiti, France and the United States, backed a military coup and spirited President Aristide off to Africa. Haiti had, by then, lost the capacity to feed itself, leaving it highly vulnerable to food price fluctuation, the immediate cause of the 2008 food crisis.

The story is fairly similar in much of the world. In a narrow sense, it may be true enough that the food crisis results from Western lack of concern: a pittance could overcome its worst immediate effects. But more fundamentally it results from dedication to the basic principles of business-run state policy, the Adam Smith generalization. These are all matters that we too easily evade— along with the fact that bailing out banks is not uppermost in the minds of the billion people now facing starvation, not forgetting the tens of millions enduring hunger in the richest country in the world.

Also sidelined is a possible way to make a significant dent in the financial and food crises. It is suggested by the recent publication of the authoritative annual report on military spending by SIPRI, the Swedish peace research institute. The scale of military spending is phenomenal, regularly increasing. The United States is responsible for almost as much as the rest of the world combined, seven times as much as its nearest rival, China. There is no need to waste time commenting.

• • •

The distribution of concerns illustrates another crisis, a cultural crisis: the tendency to focus on short-term parochial gains, a core element of our socioeconomic institutions and their ideological support system. One illustration is the array of perverse incentives devised for corporate managers to enrich themselves, however grievous the impact on others—for example, the "too big to fail" insurance policies provided by the unwitting public.

There are also deeper problems inherent in market inefficiencies. One of these, now belatedly recognized to be among the roots of the financial crisis, is the underpricing of systemic risk: if you and I make a transaction, we factor in the cost to us, but not to others. The financial industry, that means Goldman Sachs, if managed properly, will calculate the potential cost to itself if a loan goes bad, but not the impact on the financial system, which can be severe. This inherent deficiency of markets is well known. Ten years ago, at the height of the euphoria about efficient markets, two prominent economists, John Eatwell and Lance Taylor, wrote *Global Finance at Risk,* an important book in which they spelled out the consequences of these market inefficiencies and outlined means to deal with them. Their proposals conflicted sharply with the deregulatory rage that was then consuming the Clinton administration, under the leadership of those whom Obama has now called upon to put Band-Aids on the disaster they helped to create.[9]

In substantial measure, the food crisis plaguing much of the South and the financial crisis of the North have a common source: the shift toward neoliberalism since the 1970s, which brought to an end the Bretton Woods system instituted by the United States and United Kingdom after World War II. The architects of Bretton Woods, John Maynard Keynes and Harry Dexter White, anticipated that its core principles—including capital controls and regulated currencies—would lead to rapid and relatively balanced economic growth and would also free governments to institute the social democratic programs that had very strong public support. Mostly, they were vindicated on both counts. Many economists call the years that followed, until the 1970s, the "golden age of capitalism."

The "golden age" saw not only unprecedented and relatively egalitarian growth, but also the introduction of welfare-state measures. As Keynes and White were aware, free capital movement and speculation inhibit those options. To quote from the professional literature, free flow of capital creates a "virtual senate" of lenders and investors who carry out a "moment-by-moment referendum" on government policies, and if they find them irrational—that is, designed to help people, not profits—they vote against them by capital flight, attacks on currency, and other means. Democratic governments therefore have a "dual constituency": the population, and the virtual senate, who typically prevail.

In his standard history of the financial system, Barry Eichengreen writes that, in earlier years, the costs imposed by market inefficiencies and failures could be imposed on the public, but that became difficult when governments were "politicized" by "universal male suffrage and the rise of trade unionism and parliamentary labor parties" and later by the radicalization of the general public during the Great Depression and the anti-fascist war. Accordingly, in the Bretton Woods system, "limits on capital mobility substituted for limits on democracy as a source of insulation from market pressures."[10] There is a corollary: dismantling of the Bretton Woods restrictions on capital during the neoliberal period restores a powerful weapon against democracy.

The neoliberal rollback of democracy—often called "democracy promotion"—has enabled other means of control and marginalization of the public. One illustration is the management of electoral extravaganzas in the United States by the public relations industry, peaking with Obama, who won the industry's award for "marketer of the year for 2008."[11] Industry executives exulted in the business press that Obama was the highest achievement yet of those who "helped pioneer the packaging of candidates as consumer brands

30 years ago,"[12] when they designed the Reagan campaign. The *Financial Times* paraphrased one marketing executive suggesting that the Obama triumph should "have more influence on boardrooms than any president since Ronald Reagan, [who] redefined what it was to be a CEO."[13] Reagan taught, "you had to give [your organization] a vision," leading to the "reign of the imperial CEO" in the 1980s and 1990s. The synergy of running corporations and controlling politics, including the marketing of candidates as commodities, offers great prospects for the future management of democracy.

For working people, small farmers, and the poor, at home and abroad, all of this spells regular disaster. One of the reasons for the radical difference in development between Latin America and East Asia in the last half-century is that Latin America did not control capital flight, which often approached the level of its crushing debt and has regularly been wielded as a weapon against the threat of democracy and social reform. In contrast, during South Korea's remarkable growth period, capital flight was not only banned, but could bring the death penalty.

Where neoliberal rules have been observed since the '70s, economic performance has generally deteriorated and social democratic programs have substantially weakened. In the United States, which partially accepted these rules, real wages for the majority have largely stagnated for 30 years, instead of tracking productivity growth as before, while work hours have increased, now well beyond those of Europe. Benefits, which always lagged, have declined further. Social indicators—general measures of the health of the society—also tracked growth until the mid-'70s, when they began to decline, falling to the 1960 level by the end of the millennium. Economic growth found its way into few pockets, increasingly in the financial industries. Finance constituted a few percentage points of GDP in 1970, and has since risen to well over one-third, while productive industry has declined, and with it, living standards for much of the workforce. The economy has been punctuated by bubbles, financial crises, and public bailouts, currently reaching new highs. A few outstanding international economists explained and predicted these results from the start. But mythology about "efficient markets" and "rational choice" prevailed. This is no surprise: it was highly beneficial to the narrow sectors of privilege and power that provide the "principal architects of policy."

• • •

The phrase "golden age of capitalism" might itself be challenged. The period can more accurately be called "state capitalism." The state sector was, and remains, a primary factor in development and innovation through a variety of measures, among them research and development, procurement, subsidy, and bailouts. In the U.S. version, these policies operated mainly under a Pentagon cover as long as the cutting edge of the advanced economy was electronics-based. In recent years there has been a shift toward health-oriented state institutions as the cutting edge becomes more biology-based. The outcomes include computers, the Internet, satellites, and most of the rest of the IT revolution, but also much else: civilian aircraft, advanced machine tools, pharmaceuticals, biotechnology, and a lot more. The crucial state role in economic development should be kept in mind when we hear dire warnings about government intervention in the financial system after private management has once again driven it to crisis, this time, an unusually severe crisis, and one that harms the rich, not just the poor, so it merits special concern. It is a little odd, to say the least, to read economic historian Niall Ferguson in the *New York Review of Books* symposium on "The Crisis" saying that "the lesson of economic history is very clear. Economic growth . . . comes from techno-logical innovation and gains in productivity, and these things come from the private sector, not from the state"—remarks that were probably written on a computer and sent via the Internet, which were substantially in the state sector for decades before they became available for private profit. His is hardly the clear lesson of economic history.

Large-scale state intervention in the economy is not just a phenomenon of the post–World War II era, either. On the contrary, the state has always been a central factor in economic development. Once they gained their independence, the American colonies were free to abandon the orthodox economic policies that dictated adherence to their comparative advantage in export of primary commodities while importing superior British manufacturing goods. Instead, the Hamiltonian economy imposed very high tariffs so that an industrial economy could develop: textiles, steel, and much else. The eminent economic historian Paul Bairoch describes the United States as "the mother country and bastion of modern protectionism,"[14] with the highest tariffs in the world during its great growth period. And protectionism is only one of the many forms of state intervention. Protectionist policies continued until the mid-twentieth century, when the United States was so far in the lead that the playing field was tilted in the proper direction—that is, to the advantage of U.S. corporations. And when necessary, it has been tilted further, notably by Reagan, who virtually doubled protectionist barriers among other measures to rescue incompetent U.S. corporate management unable to compete with Japan.

From the outset the United States was following Britain's lead. The other developed countries did likewise, while orthodox policies were rammed down the throats of the colonies, with predictable effects. It is noteworthy that the one country of the (metaphorical) South to develop, Japan, also successfully resisted colonization. Others that developed, like the United States, did so after they escaped colonial domination. Selective application of economic principles—orthodox economics forced on the colonies while violated at will by those free to do so—is a basic factor in the creation of the sharp North-South divide. Like many other economic historians, Bairoch concludes from a broad survey that "it is difficult to find another case where the facts so contradict a dominant theory"[15] as the doctrine that free markets were the engine of growth, a harsh lesson that the developing world has learned again in recent decades. Even the poster child of neoliberalism, Chile, depends heavily on the world's largest copper producer, Codelco, nationalized by Allende.

In earlier years the cotton-based economy of the industrial revolution relied on massive ethnic cleansing and slavery, rather severe forms of state intervention in the economy. Though theoretically slavery was ended with the Civil War, it emerged again after Reconstruction in a form that was in many ways more virulent, with what amounted to criminalization of African-American life and widespread use of convict labor, which continued until World War II. The industrial revolution, from the late nineteenth century, relied heavily on this new form of slavery, a hideous story that has only recently been exposed in its shocking detail in a very important study by *Wall Street Journal* bureau chief Douglas Blackmon.[16] During the post-World War II "golden age," African Americans were able for the first time to enjoy some level of social and economic advancement, but the disgraceful post-Reconstruction history has been partially reconstituted during the neoliberal years with the rapid growth of what some criminologists call "the prison-industrial complex," a uniquely American crime committed continuously since the 1980s and exacerbated by the dismantling of productive industry.

The American system of mass production that astonished the world in the nineteenth century was largely created in military arsenals. Solving the major nineteenth-century management problem—railroads—was beyond the capacity of private capital, so the challenge was handed over to the army. A century ago the toughest problems of electrical and mechanical engineering involved placing a huge gun on a moving platform to hit a moving target—naval gunnery. The leaders were Germany and England, and the outcomes quickly spilled over into the civilian economy. Some economic historians compare that episode to state-run space programs today. Reagan's "Star Wars" was sold to industry as a traditional gift from government, and was understood that way elsewhere too: that is why Europe and Japan wanted to buy in. There was a dramatic increase in the state role after World War II, particularly in

the United States, where a good part of the advanced economy developed in this framework.

• • •

State-guided modes of economic development require considerable deceit in a society where the public cannot be controlled by force. People cannot be told that the advanced economy relies heavily on their risk-taking, while eventual profit is privatized, and "eventual" can be a long time, sometimes decades. After World War II Americans were told that their taxes were going to defense against monsters about to overcome us—as in the '80s, when Reagan pulled on his cowboy boots and declared a National Emergency because Nicaraguan hordes were only two days from Harlingen, Texas. Or twenty years earlier when LBJ warned that there are only 150 million of us and 3 billion of them, and if might makes right, they will sweep over us and take what we have, so we have to stop them in Vietnam.

For those concerned with the realities of the Cold War, and how it was used to control the public, one obvious moment to inspect carefully is the fall of the Berlin Wall twenty years ago and its aftermath. Celebration of the anniversary in November 2009 has already begun, with ample coverage, which will surely increase as the date approaches. The revealing implications of the policies that were instituted after the fall have, however, been ignored, as in the past, and probably will continue to be come November.

Reacting immediately to the Wall's fall, the Bush senior administration issued a new National Security Strategy and budget proposal to set the course after the collapse of Kennedy's "monolithic and ruthless conspiracy" to conquer the world and Reagan's "evil empire"—a collapse that took with it the whole framework of domestic population control. Washington's response was straightforward: everything will stay much the same, but with new pretexts. We still need a huge military system, but for a new reason: the "technological sophistication" of Third World powers. We have to maintain the "defense industrial base," a euphemism for state-supported high-tech industry. We must also maintain intervention forces directed at the Middle East's energy-rich regions, where the threats to our interests that required military intervention "could not be laid at the Kremlin's door," contrary to decades of pretense. The charade had sometimes been acknowledged, as when Robert Komer—the architect of President Carter's Rapid Deployment Force (later Central Command), aimed primarily at the Middle East—testified before Congress in 1980 that the Force's most likely use was not resisting Soviet attack, but dealing with indigenous and regional unrest, in particular the "radical nationalism" that has always been a primary concern throughout the world.[17]

With the Soviet Union gone, the clouds lifted, and actual policy concerns were more visible for those who chose to see. The Cold War propaganda framework made two fundamental contributions: sustaining the dynamic state sector of the economy (of which military industry is only a small part) and protecting the interests of the "principal architects of policy" abroad.

The fate of NATO exposes the same concerns, and it is highly pertinent today. Prior to Gorbachev NATO's announced purpose was to deter a Russian invasion of Europe. The legitimacy of that agenda was debatable right from the end of World War II. In May 1945 Churchill ordered war plans to be drawn up for Operation Unthinkable, aimed at "the elimination of Russia." The plans—declassified ten years ago—are discussed extensively in the major scholarly study of British intelligence records, Richard Aldrich's *The Hidden Hand.* According to Aldrich, they called for a surprise attack by hundreds of thousands of British and American troops, joined by one hundred thousand rearmed German soldiers, while the RAF would attack Soviet cities from bases in Northern Europe. Nuclear weapons were soon added to the mix. The official stand also was not easy to take too seriously a decade later, when Khrushchev took over in Russia, and soon proposed a sharp mutual reduction in offensive weaponry. He understood very well that the much weaker Soviet economy could not sustain an arms race and still develop. When the United States dismissed the offer, he carried out the reduction unilaterally. Kennedy reacted with a substantial increase in military spending, which the Soviet military tried to match after the Cuban missile crisis dramatically revealed its relative weakness. The Soviet economy tanked, as Khrushchev had anticipated. That was a crucial factor in the later Soviet collapse.

• • •

But the defensive pretext for NATO at least had some credibility. After the Soviet disintegration, the pretext evaporated. In the final days of the USSR, Gorbachev made an astonishing concession: he permitted a unified Germany to join a hostile military alliance run by the global superpower, though Germany alone had almost destroyed Russia twice in the century. There was a quid pro quo, recently clarified. In the first careful study of the original documents, Mark Kramer, apparently seeking to refute charges of U.S. duplicity, in fact shows that it went far beyond what had been assumed. It turns out, Kramer wrote this year in *The Washington Quarterly,* that Bush senior and Secretary of State James Baker promised Gorbachev that "no NATO forces would ever be deployed on the territory of the former GDR . . . NATO's jurisdiction or forces would not move eastward." They also assured Gorbachev "that NATO would be transforming itself into a more political organization."[18]

There is no need to comment on that promise. What followed tells us a lot more about the Cold War itself, and the world that emerged from its ending.

As soon as Clinton came into office, he began the expansion of NATO to the east. The process accelerated with Bush junior's aggressive militarism. These moves posed a serious security threat to Russia, which naturally reacted by developing more advanced offensive military capacities. Obama's National Security Advisor, James Jones, has a still-more expansive vision: he calls for extending NATO further east and south, becoming in effect a U.S.-run global intervention force, as it is today in Afghanistan—"Afpak" as the region is now called—where Obama is sharply escalating Bush's war, which had already intensified in 2004. NATO Secretary-General Jaap de Hoop Scheffer informed a NATO meeting that "NATO troops have to guard pipelines that transport oil and gas that is directed for the West," and more generally have to protect sea routes used by tankers and other "crucial infrastructure" of the energy system.[19] These plans open a new phase of Western imperial domination—more politely called "bringing stability" and "peace."

As recently as November 2007, the White House announced plans for a long-term military presence in Iraq and a policy of "encouraging the flow of foreign investments to Iraq, especially American investments."[20] The plans were withdrawn under Iraqi pressure, the continuation of a process that began when the United States was compelled by mass demonstrations to permit elections. In Afpak Obama is building enormous new embassies and other facilities, on the model of the city-within-a-city in Baghdad. These new installations in Iraq and Afpak are like no embassies in the world, just as the United States is alone in its vast military-basing system and control of the air, sea, and space for military purposes.

While Obama is signaling his intention to establish a firm and large-scale presence in the region, he is also following General Petraeus's strategy to drive the Taliban into Pakistan, with potentially quite serious consequences for this dangerous and unstable state facing insurrections throughout its territory. These are most extreme in the tribal areas crossing the British-imposed Durand line separating Afghanistan from Pakistan, which the Pashtun tribes on both sides of the artificial border have never recognized, nor did the Afghan government when it was independent. In an April publication of the Center for International Policy, one of the leading U.S. specialists on the region, Selig Harrison, writes that the outcome of Washington's current policies might well be "what Pakistani ambassador to Washington Husain Haqqani has called an 'Islamic Pashtunistan.'"[21] Haqqani's predecessor had warned that if the Taliban and Pashtun nationalists merge, "we've had it, and we're on the verge of that."[22]

Prospects become still more ominous as drone attacks that embitter the population are escalated with their huge civilian toll. Also troubling is the unprecedented authority just granted General Stanley McChrystal—a special forces assassin—to head the operations. Petraeus's own counter-insurgency adviser in Iraq, David Kilcullen, describes the Obama-Petraeus-McChrystal policies as a fundamental "strategic error," which may lead to "the collapse of the Pakistani state," a calamity that would "dwarf" other current crises.[23]

It is also not encouraging that Pakistan and India are now rapidly expanding their nuclear arsenals. Pakistan's were developed with Reagan's crucial aid, and India's nuclear weapons programs got a major shot in the arm from the recent U.S.-India nuclear agreement, which was also a sharp blow to the Non-Proliferation Treaty. India and Pakistan have twice come close to nuclear war over Kashmir, and have also been engaged in a proxy war in Afghanistan. These developments pose a very serious threat to world peace.

Returning home, it is worth noting that the more sophisticated are aware of the deceit that is employed as a device to control the public, and regard it as praiseworthy. The distinguished liberal statesman Dean Acheson advised that leaders must speak in a way that is "clearer than truth."[24] Harvard Professor of the Science of Government Samuel Huntington, who quite frankly explained the need to delude the public about the Soviet threat 30 years ago, urged more generally that power must remain invisible: "The architects of power in the United States must create a force that can be felt but not seen. Power remains strong when it remains in the dark; exposed to the sunlight it begins to evaporate."[25] This is an important lesson for those who want power to devolve to the public, a critical battle that is fought daily.

• • •

Whether the deceit about the monstrous enemy was sincere or not, if Americans a half century ago had been given the choice of directing their tax money to Pentagon programs to enable their grandchildren to have computers, iPods, the Internet, and so on, or putting it into developing a livable and sustainable socioeconomic order, they might have made the latter choice. But they had no choice. That is standard. There is a striking gap between public opinion and public policy on a host of major issues, domestic and foreign, and public opinion is often more sane, at least in my judgment. It also tends to be fairly consistent over time, despite the fact that public concerns and aspirations are marginalized or ridiculed—one very significant feature of the yawning "democratic deficit," the failure of formal democratic institutions to function properly. That is no trivial matter. In a forthcoming book, the writer and activist Arundhati Roy asks whether the evolution of formal democracy in India and the United States—and not only there—"might turn out to be the endgame of the human race."[26] It is not an idle question.

It should be recalled that the American republic was founded on the principle that there *should* be a democratic deficit. James Madison, the main framer of the Constitutional order, held that power should be in the hands of "the wealth of the nation," the "more capable set of men," who have sympathy for property owners and their rights. Possibly with Shay's Rebellion in mind, he was concerned that "the equal laws of suffrage" might shift power into the hands of those who might seek agrarian reform, an intolerable attack on property rights. He feared that "symptoms of a levelling spirit" had appeared sufficiently "in certain quarters to give warning of the future danger." Madison sought to construct a system of government that would "protect the minority of the opulent against the majority."[27] That is why his constitutional framework did not have coequal branches: the legislature prevailed, and within the legislature, power was to be vested in the Senate, where the wealth of the nation would be dominant and protected from the general population, which was to be fragmented and marginalized in various ways. As historian Gordon Wood summarizes the thoughts of the founders: "The Constitution was intrinsically an aristocratic document designed to check the democratic tendencies of the period," delivering power to a "better sort" of people and excluding "those who were not rich, well born, or prominent from exercising political power."[28]

In Madison's defense, his picture of the world was pre-capitalist: he thought that power would be held by the "enlightened Statesman" and "benevolent philosopher," men who are "pure and noble," a "chosen body of citizens, whose wisdom may best discern the true interests of their country and whose patriotism and love of justice would be least likely to sacrifice it to temporary or partial considerations," guarding the public interest against the "mischiefs" of democratic majorities.[29] Adam Smith had a clearer vision.

There has been constant struggle over this constrained version of democracy, which we call "guided democracy" in the case of enemies: Iran right now, for example. Popular struggles have won a great many rights, but concentrated power and privilege clings to the Madisonian conception in ways that vary as society changes. By World War I, business leaders and elite intellectuals recognized that the population had won so many rights that they could not be controlled by force, so it would be necessary to turn to control of attitudes and opinions. Those are the years when the huge public relations industry emerged—in the freest countries of the world, Britain and the United States, where the problem was most acute. The industry was devoted to what Walter Lippmann approvingly called "a new art" in the practice of democracy,

Concentrated P/W/Riv Rees itself
as Rulers by Right.

the "manufacture of consent"[30]—the "engineering of consent"[31] in the phrase of his contemporary Edward Bernays, one of the founders of the public relations industry. Both Lippmann and Bernays took part in Wilson's state propaganda organization, the Committee on Public Information, created to drive a pacifist population to jingoist fanaticism and hatred of all things German. It succeeded brilliantly. The same techniques, it was hoped, would ensure that the "intelligent minorities" would rule, undisturbed by "the trampling and the roar of a bewildered herd," the general public, "ignorant and meddlesome outsiders" whose "function" is to be "spectators," not "participants."[32] This was a central theme of the highly regarded "progressive essays on democracy" by the leading public intellectual of the twentieth century (Lippmann), whose thinking captures well the perceptions of progressive intellectual opinion: President Wilson, for example, held that an elite of gentlemen with "elevated ideals" must be empowered to preserve "stability and righteousness," essentially the Madisonian perspective. In more recent years, the gentlemen are transmuted into the "technocratic elite" and "action intellectuals" of Camelot, "Straussian" neocons, or other configurations. But throughout, one or another variant of the doctrine prevails, with its Leninist overtones.

And on a more hopeful note, popular struggle continues to clip its wings, quite impressively so in the wake of 1960s activism, which had a substantial impact on civilizing the country and raised its prospects to a considerably higher plane.

• • •

Returning to what the West sees as "*the* crisis"—the financial crisis—it will presumably be patched up somehow, while leaving the institutions that created it pretty much in place. Recently the Treasury Department permitted early TARP repayments, which reduce bank capacity to lend, as was immediately pointed out, but allow the banks to pour money into the pockets of the few who matter. The mood on Wall Street was captured by two Bank of New York Mellon employees, who, as reported in *The New York Times*, "predicted their lives—and pay—would improve, even if the broader economy did not."[33]

The chair of the prominent law firm Sullivan & Cromwell offered the equally apt prediction that "Wall Street, after getting billions of taxpayer dollars, will emerge from the financial crisis looking much the same as before markets collapsed."[34] The reasons were pointed out, by, among others, Simon Johnson, former chief economist of the IMF: "Throughout the crisis, the government has taken extreme care not to upset the interests of the financial institutions, or to question the basic outlines of the system that got us here," and the elite business interests [that] played a central role in creating the crisis, making ever-larger gambles, with the implicit backing of the government, until the inevitable collapse . . . are now using their influence to prevent precisely the sorts of reforms that are needed, and fast, to pull the economy out of its nosedive.[35]

Meanwhile "the government seems helpless, or unwilling, to act against them."[36] Again no surprise, at least to those who remember their Adam Smith.

But there is a far more serious crisis, even for the rich and powerful. It is discussed by Bill McKibben, who has been warning for years about the impact of global warming, in the same issue of the *New York Review of Books* that I mentioned earlier. His recent article relies on the British Stern report, which is very highly regarded by leading scientists and a raft of Nobel laureates in economics. On this basis McKibben concludes, not unrealistically, "2009 may well turn out to be the decisive year in the human relationship with our home planet."[37] In December a conference in Copenhagen is "to sign a new global accord on global warming," which will tell us "whether or not our political systems are up to the unprecedented challenge that climate change represents."[38] He thinks the signals are mixed. That may be optimistic, unless there is a really massive public campaign to overcome the insistence of the managers of the state-corporate sector on privileging short-term gain for the few over the hope that their grandchildren will have a decent future.

At least some of the barriers are beginning to crumble—in part because the business world perceives new opportunities for profit. Even *The Wall Street Journal,* one of the most stalwart deniers, recently published a supplement with dire warnings about "climate disaster," urging that none of the options being considered may be sufficient, and it may be necessary to undertake more radical measures of geoengineering, "cooling the planet" in some manner.[39]

As always, those who suffer most will be the poor. Bangladesh will soon have a lot more to worry about than even the terrible food crisis. As the sea level rises, much of the country, including its most productive regions, might be under water. Current crises are almost sure to be exacerbated as the Himalayan glaciers continue to disappear, and with them the great river systems that keep South Asia alive. Right now, as glaciers melt in the mountain heights where Pakistani and Indian troops suffer and die, they expose the relics of their crazed conflict over Kashmir, "a pristine monument to human folly,"[40] Roy comments with despair.

The picture might be much more grim than even the Stern report predicts. A group of MIT scientists have just released the results of what they describe as, "the most comprehensive modeling yet carried out on the likelihood of how much hotter the Earth's climate will get in this century, [showing] that without rapid and massive action, the problem will be about twice as severe as previously estimated six years ago—and could be even worse than that." Worse because the model, "does not fully incorporate other positive feedbacks that can occur, for example, if increased temperatures caused a large-scale melting of permafrost in arctic regions and subsequent release of large quantities of methane."[41]

The leader of the project says, "There's no way the world can or should take these risks," and that "the least-cost option to lower the risk is to start now and steadily transform the global energy system over the coming decades to low or zero greenhouse gas-emitting technologies."[42] There is far too little sign of that.

While new technologies are essential, the problems go well beyond. We have to face up to the need to reverse the huge state-corporate social engineering projects of the post-World War II period, which quite purposefully promoted an energy-wasting and environmentally destructive fossil fuel-based economy. The state-corporate programs, which included massive projects of suburbanization along with destruction and then gentrification of inner cities, began with a conspiracy by General Motors, Firestone, and Standard Oil of California to buy up and destroy efficient electric public transportation systems in Los Angeles and dozens of other cities; they were convicted of criminal conspiracy and given a slap on the wrist. The federal government then took over, relocating infrastructure and capital stock to suburban areas and creating the massive interstate highway system, under the usual pretext of "defense." Railroads were displaced by government-financed motor and air transport.

The programs were understood as a means to prevent a depression after the Korean War. One of their Congressional architects described them as "a nice solid floor across the whole economy in times of recession."[43] The public played almost no role, apart from choice within the narrowly structured framework of options designed by state-corporate managers. One result is atomization of society and entrapment of isolated individuals with self-destructive ambitions and crushing debt. These efforts to "fabricate consumers" (to borrow Veblen's term) and to direct people "to the superficial things of life, like fashionable consumption"[44] (in the words of the business press), emerged from the recognition a century ago of the need to curtail democratic achievements and to ensure that the "opulent minority" are protected from the "ignorant and meddlesome outsiders."

While state-corporate power was vigorously promoting privatization of life and maximal waste of energy, it was also undermining the efficient choices that the market does not provide—another destructive built-in market inefficiency. To put it simply, if I want to get home from work, the market offers me a choice between a Ford and a Toyota, but not between a car and a subway. That is a social decision, and in a democratic society, would be the decision of an organized public. But that is just what the dedicated elite attack on democracy seeks to undermine.

The consequences are right before our eyes in ways that are sometimes surreal. In May *The Wall Street Journal* reported:

> U.S. transportation chief [Ray LaHood] is in Spain meeting with high-speed rail suppliers. . . . Europe's engineering and rail companies are lining up for some potentially lucrative U.S. contracts for high-speed rail projects. At stake is $13 billion in stimulus funds that the Obama administration is allocating to upgrade existing rail lines and build new ones that could one day rival Europe's fastest . . . . [LaHood is also] expected to visit Spanish construction, civil engineering and train-building companies.[45]

Spain and other European countries are hoping to get U.S. taxpayer funding for the high-speed rail and related infrastructure that is badly needed in the United States. At the same time, Washington is busy dismantling leading sectors of U.S. industry, ruining the lives of the workforce and communities. It is difficult to conjure up a more damning indictment of the economic system that has been constructed by state-corporate managers. Surely the auto industry could be reconstructed to produce what the country needs, using its highly skilled workforce—and what the world needs, and soon, if we are to have some hope of averting major catastrophe. It has been done before, after all. During World War II the semi-command economy not only ended the Depression but initiated the most spectacular period of growth in economic history, virtually quadrupling industrial production in four years as the economy was retooled for war, and also laying the basis for the "golden age" that followed.

• • •

Warnings about the purposeful destruction of U.S. productive capacity have been familiar for decades and perhaps sounded most prominently by the late Seymour Melman.[46] Melman also pointed to a sensible way to reverse the process. The state-corporate leadership has other commitments, but there is no reason for passivity on the part of the "stakeholders"—workers and communities. With enough popular support, they could take over the plants and carry out the task of reconstruction themselves. That is not a particularly radical proposal. One standard text on corporations, *The Myth of the Global*

Corporation, points out, "nowhere is it written in stone that the short-term interests of corporate shareholders in the United States deserve a higher priority than all other corporate 'stakeholders.'"[47]

It is also important to remind ourselves that the notion of workers' control is as American as apple pie. In the early days of the industrial revolution in New England, working people took it for granted that those who work in the mills should own them. They also regarded wage labor as different from slavery only in that it was temporary; Abraham Lincoln held the same view.

And the leading twentieth-century social philosopher, John Dewey, basically agreed. Much like nineteenth-century working people, he called for elimination of "business for private profit through private control of banking, land, industry, reinforced by command of the press, press agents and other means of publicity and propaganda."[48] Industry must be changed "from a feudalistic to a democratic social order"[49] based on workers' control, free association, and federal organization, in the general style of a range of thought that includes, along with many anarchists, G. D. H. Cole's guild socialism and such left Marxists as Anton Pannekoek, Rosa Luxemburg, Paul Mattick, and others. Unless those goals are attained, Dewey held, politics will remain "the shadow cast on society by big business, [and] the attenuation of the shadow will not change the substance."[50] He argued that without industrial democracy, political democratic forms will lack real content, and people will work "not freely and intelligently," but for pay, a condition that is "illiberal and immoral"—ideals that go back to the Enlightenment and classical liberalism before they were wrecked on the shoals of capitalism, as the anarchosyndicalist thinker Rudolf Rocker put it 70 years ago.[51]

There have been immense efforts to drive these thoughts out of people's heads—to win what the business world called "the everlasting battle for the minds of men."[52] On the surface, corporate interests may appear to have succeeded, but one need not dig too deeply to find latent resistance that can be revived. There have been some important efforts. One was undertaken 30 years ago in Youngstown Ohio, where U.S. Steel was about to shut down a major facility at the heart of this steel town. First came substantial protests by the workforce and community, then an effort led by Staughton Lynd to convince the courts that stakeholders should have the highest priority. The effort failed that time, but with enough popular support it could succeed.

It is a propitious time to revive such efforts, though it would be necessary to overcome the effects of the concerted campaign to drive our own history and culture out of our minds. A dramatic illustration of the challenge arose in early February 2009, when President Obama decided to show his solidarity with working people by giving a talk at a factory in Illinois. He chose a

Caterpillar plant, over objections of church, peace, and human rights groups that were protesting Caterpillar's role in providing Israel with the means to devastate the territories it occupies and to destroy the lives of the population. A Caterpillar bulldozer had also been used to kill American volunteer Rachel Corrie, who tried to block the destruction of a home. Apparently forgotten, however, was something else. In the 1980s, following Reagan's lead with the dismantling of the air traffic controllers' union, Caterpillar managers decided to rescind their labor contract with the United Auto Workers and seriously harm the union by bringing in scabs to break a strike for the first time in generations. The practice was illegal in other industrial countries apart from South Africa at the time; now the United States is in splendid isolation, as far as I know.

Whether Obama purposely chose a corporation that led the way to undermine labor rights I don't know. More likely, he and his handlers were unaware of the facts.

But at the time of Caterpillar's innovation in labor relations, Obama was a civil rights lawyer in Chicago. He certainly read the *Chicago Tribune,* which published a careful study of these events. The *Tribune* reported that the union was "stunned" to find that unemployed workers crossed the picket line with no remorse, while Caterpillar workers found little "moral support" in their community, one of the many where the union had "lifted the standard of living."[53] Wiping out those memories is another victory for the highly class-conscious American business sector in its relentless campaign to destroy workers' rights and democracy. The union leadership had refused to understand. It was only in 1978 that UAW President Doug Fraser recognized what was happening and criticized the "leaders of the business community" for having "chosen to wage a one-sided class war in this country—a war against working people, the unemployed, the poor, the minorities, the very young and the very old, and even many in the middle class of our society," and for having "broken and discarded the fragile, unwritten compact previously existing during a period of growth and progress."[54] Placing one's faith in a compact with owners and managers is suicidal. The UAW is discovering that again today, as the state-corporate leadership proceeds to eliminate the hard-fought gains of working people while dismantling the productive core of the American economy.

Investors are now wailing that the unions are being granted "workers' control" in the restructuring of the auto industry, but they surely know better. The government task force ensured that the workforce will have no shareholder voting rights and will lose benefits and wages, eliminating what was the gold standard for blue-collar workers.

This is only a fragment of what is underway. It highlights the importance of short- and long-term strategies to build—in part resurrect—the foundations of a functioning democratic society. An immediate goal is to pressure Congress to permit organizing rights, the Employee Free Choice Act that was promised but seems to be languishing. One short-term goal is to support the revival of a strong and independent labor movement, which in its heyday was a critical base for advancing democracy and human and civil rights, a primary reason why it has been subject to such unremitting attack in policy and propaganda. A longer-term goal is to win the educational and cultural battle that has been waged with such bitterness in the "one-sided class war" that the UAW president perceived far too late. That means tearing down an enormous edifice of delusions about markets, free trade, and democracy that has been assiduously constructed over many years and to overcome the marginalization and atomization of the public so that they can become "participants," not mere "spectators of action," as progressive democratic theoreticians have prescribed.

Of all of the crises that afflict us, the growing democratic deficit may be the most severe. Unless it is reversed, Roy's forecast may prove accurate. The conversion of democracy to a performance with the public as mere spectators—hardly a distant possibility—might have truly dire consequences.

NOTES

1. Previously published as Noam Chomsky, "Crisis and Hope: Theirs and Ours," *Boston Review,* September/October 2009, bostonreview.net/BR34.5/chomsky.php (accessed July 2, 2010); based on a talk delivered June 12, 2009, at an event sponsored by the Brecht Forum. Endnotes for this chapter additionally assembled and provided by the book's editors.

2. Quote attributable to Ramzy Baroud, "Bailing-out Rich, Starving Poor to Death," *IslamOnline.net,* www.islamonline.net/servlet/Satellite?c=Article_C&pagename=Zone-English-Muslim_Affairs%2FMAELayout&cid=1224517713838 (accessed July 2, 2010).

3. Baroud, *IslamOnline.net.*

4. Javier Blas, "Funds Crunch Threatens World's Food Aid," *Financial Times,* June 11, 2009, www.ft.com/cms/s/0/524d50da-56ae-11de-9a1c-00144feabdc0.html (accessed July 2, 2010).

5. Reuters, "More Than 1 Million Go Hungry, the World Food Program Says," *New York Times,* June 13, 2009, 10.

6. This Day, "Nigeria; '43 Million under Threat of Desertification,'" *Africa News,* June 20, 2009.

7. Adam Smith, *An Inquiry into the Nature and Causes of the Wealth of Nations,* R. H. Campbell and A. S. Skinner, eds. (Oxford, UK: Oxford University Press, 1976): 481; 721.

8. USAID, "Haiti Agribusiness Assessment," prepared for USAID by Abt Associates, April 1995 draft.

9. John Eatwell and Lance Taylor, *Global Finance at Risk: The Case for International Regulation* (New York, NY: New Press, 2001).

10. Barry Eichengreen, *Globalizing Capital: A History of the International Monetary System* (Princeton, NJ: Princeton University Press, 2008), 3.

11. See Matthew Creamer, "Obama Wins! . . . Ad Age's Marketer of the Year," *Advertising Age,* October 17, 2008, adage.com/moy2008/article?article_id=131810 (accessed July 2, 2010).

12. See Andrew Edgecliffe-Johnson, "Bush Set to be Knocked Off His CEO Pedestal," Financial Times, November 25, 2008, www.ft.com/cms/s/0/3bdbc77e-bb3f-11dd-bc6c-0000779fd18c.html (accessed July 2, 2010).

13. Edgecliffe-Johnson, *Financial Times.*

14. Paul Bairoch, *Economics & World History: Myths and Paradoxes* (Chicago, IL: University of Chicago Press, 2005), 30.

15. Bairoch, *Economics,* 54.

16. Douglas A. Blackmon, *Slavery by Another Name: The Re-Enslavement of Black Americans from the Civil War to World War II* (Norwell, MA: Anchor Press, 2009).

17. Testimony of Robert Komer to the Senate Armed Services Committee, cited by Melvyn Leffler, "From the Truman Doctrine to the Carter Doctrine," *Diplomatic History,* vol. 7, 1983, 245f.

18. Mark Kramer, "The Myth of a No-NATO-Enlargement Pledge to Russia," *Washington Quarterly* 32, no. 2 (April 2009): 39–61.

19. See Paul Ames, "NATO to Talk Energy Security," *Washington Post,* June 28, 2007, www.washingtonpost.com/wp-dyn/content/article/2007/06/28/AR2007062802 700_pf.html (accessed July 2, 2010).

20. See the "Declaration of Principles" between Iraq and the United States issued by the White House on November 26, 2007, www.npr.org/templates/story/story .php?storyId=18357565 (accessed July 2, 2010).

21. Selig S. Harrison, "The Fault Line Between Pashtuns and Punjabis in Pakistan," *Washington Post,* May 11, 2009, www.washingtonpost.com/wp-dyn/content/ article/2009/05/10/AR2009051001959.html (accessed July 2, 2010).

22. Harrison, *Washington Post.*

23. Carlos Lozada, "A Conversation with David Kilcullen," *Washington Post,* March 22, 2009, www.washingtonpost.com/wp-dyn/content/article/2009/03/19/ AR2009031903038.html (accessed July 2, 2010).

24. Dean Acheson, *Present at the Creation: My Years in the State Department* (New York, NY: W. W. Norton & Company, 1987).

25. Samuel P. Huntington, *American Politics: The Promise of Disharmony* (Cambridge, MA: Harvard University Press, 1981), 75.

26. Arundhati Roy, *Field Notes on Democracy: Listening to Grasshoppers* (Chicago, IL: Haymarket Books, 2009), 2.

27. James Madison, *Journal of the Federal Convention Kept by James Madison,* E. H. Scott, ed. (Clark, NJ: Lawbook Exchange, 2003).

28. Gordon S. Wood, *The Creation of the American Republic, 1776–1787* (Chapel Hill, NC: University of North Carolina Press, 1998), 513.

29. Alexander Hamilton, James Madison and John Jay, *The Federalist Papers,* Ian Shapiro, ed. (New Haven, CT: Yale University Press, 2009), 50–51.

30. Walter Lippmann, *Public Opinion* (New York: Free Press, 1997).

31. Edward Bernays, "The Engineering of Consent," *The Annals of the American Academy of Political and Social Science* 250 (1947): 113–20.

32. See Walter Lippmann, *The Essential Lippmann: A Political Philosophy for Liberal Democracy,* Clinton Rossiter and James Lare, eds. (Cambridge, MA: Harvard University Press).

33. Eric Dash, "10 Large Banks Allowed to Exit U.S. Aid Program," *New York Times,* June 9, 2009, www.nytimes.com/2009/06/10/business/economy/10tarp.html (accessed July 4, 2010).

34. Michael J. Moore and Jamie McGee, "Wall Street Firms Will Revert to Pre-Crisis Model, Cohen Says," *Bloomberg,* May 5, 2009, www.bloomberg.com/apps/news?pid=newsarchive&sid=aye5Fzy0L_ss (accessed July 4, 2010).

35. Simon Johnson, "The Quiet Coup," *The Atlantic* (May 2009), www.theatlantic.com/magazine/archive/2009/05/the-quiet-coup/7364/ (accessed July 4, 2010).

36. Johnson, *The Atlantic.*

37. Bill McKibben, "Can Obama Change the Climate?" *New York Review of Books,* June 11, 2009, www.nybooks.com/articles/archives/2009/jun/11/can-obama-change-the-climate/ (accessed July 4, 2010).

38. McKibben, *New York Review of Books.*

39. Jamais Cascio, "It's Time to Cool the Planet," *Wall Street Journal* (June 15, 2009), online.wsj.com/article/SB10001424052970204771304574181522575503150.html (accessed July 4, 2010).

40. Arundhati Roy, "What Have We Done to Democracy?" *TomDispatch.com* (September 27, 2009), www.tomdispatch.com/post/175125/ (accessed July 4, 2010).

41. See David Chandler, "Climate Change Odds Much Worse Than Thought," *MIT News* (May 19, 2009), web.mit.edu/newsoffice/2009/roulette-0519.html (accessed July 4, 2010).

42. Chandler, *MIT News.*

43. Richard B. DuBoff, *Accumulation and Power: An Economic History of the United States* (Armonk, NY: M. E. Sharpe, 1989).

44. Paul Nystrom, *Economics of Fashion* (New York, NY: The Ronald Press Company, 1928), 68.

45. Thomas Catan and David Gauthier-Villars, "Europe Listens for U.S. Train Whistle," *Wall Street Journal* (May 29, 2009), online.wsj.com/article/SB124354749274164117.html (accessed July 4, 2010).

46. Author of *The Permanent War Economy and Pentagon Capitalism,* Melman was a professor of industrial engineering and operations research at Columbia University, who wrote extensively on "economic conversion."

47. Paul Doremus, William M. Keller, Louis W. Pauly, and Simon Reich, *The Myth of the Global Corporation* (Princeton, NJ: Princeton University Press, 1999).

48. John Dewey, "Imperative Need: A New Radical Party," *Common Sense* 2 (September 1933): 6–7.

49. In Robert Westbrook, ed., *John Dewey and American Democracy* (Ithaca, NY: Cornell University Press, 1991): 177.

50. Westbrook, *John Dewey,* 440.

51. Westbrook, *John Dewey,* 177.

52. In Elizabeth A. Fones-Wolf, *Selling Free Enterprise: The Business Assault on Labor and Liberalism* (Champaign-Urbana, IL: University of Illinois Press, 1995): 52.

53. Stephen Franklin, Peter Kendall and Colin McMahon, "Caterpillar Strikers Face the Bitter Truth," Pt. 3 of Series, *Chicago Tribune,* Sept. 6, 7, 9, 1992.

54. In Kim Moody, *An Injury to All: The Decline of American Unionism* (New York, NY: Verso Press, 1997): 147.

is there such
a Thing as Military
Capitalism

C, is oligarchical/monopolistic
Not democratic

Chapter Two

The Corporate War Economy

Carl Boggs

The postwar age of militarized state capitalism in the United States has meant the steady expansion of corporate, government, and Pentagon power reinforced by Empire and globalization—surely the most concentrated and far-reaching system of rule in history. Although many previous theorists—Karl Marx, Max Weber, Joseph Schumpeter, and Franz Neumann among them—foresaw oligopolistic, bureaucratic, and rationalizing tendencies at work in modern capitalism, certainly none could have foreseen the enormous scope of domination that American ruling elites would accrue even before the twentieth century drew to a close. If none of these theorists would have been seduced by pretenses of democratic governance by those same elites, none could have anticipated the rise of a behemoth imposing its presence through every corner of the globe, armed with an ideology of special national entitlement and the largest war machine the world has ever seen. While thinkers of the Frankfurt School like Max Horkheimer, Theodor Adorno, and Herbert Marcuse indeed expected in the advanced capitalist societies something akin to a "totally-administered" system, even their pessimism was not sufficient to capture the awesome sweep of a rogue superpower like the United States. This chapter explores the contemporary structure and ideology of the American power elite first systematically charted by C. Wright Mills nearly a half-century earlier, with focus on the growth of corporate power, the war economy, security state, and authoritarian trends within the political system.

A pressing question immediately arises: insofar as American society is ruled by an increasingly narrow and oligopolistic stratum of privileged elites, could anything resembling classical democratic ideals associated with the Greeks, Locke, Rousseau, Jefferson, and other nineteenth-century liberals have relevance—much less thrive—at the start of the twenty-first century?

25

Could the legitimating, indeed sacred, cornerstone of American politics turn out to be nothing more than a curious fantasy, a grand illusion celebrated only in civics textbooks and ritual political speeches? Whatever the seemingly undeniable reality, the old myths and illusions always die hard—even, or perhaps especially, among the most educated strata. The great democratic myths remain probably the most difficult for Americans to seriously question on the basis of hard evidence. One case in point is the liberal Andrew Bacevich's statement, in *The Limits of Power*, that "Today, no less than in 1776, a passion for life, liberty, and the pursuit of happiness remains at the center of America's civic theology. The Jeffersonian trinity summarizes our common inheritance, defines our aspirations, and provides a touchstone for our influence abroad."[1] Another example is furnished by Jean Bethke Elshtain, who calls for renewal of a "good" American imperialism that can, through its exercise of global power, help restore democracy, human rights, and rule of law in a Hobbesian world filled with terrorists, thugs, and ethnic cleansers. In *Just War Against Terror*, Elshtain unblushingly refers to the United States as a noble, selfless, law-abiding superpower that must, by default, take on the burden of ensuring order in a lawless world.[2] Under conditions of global chaos, with no visible and impartial world body, the leading moral force must fill the void given its time-honored values of "human dignity" and "equal regard."[3] Thus: "At this point in time the possibility of international peace and stability premised on equal regard for all rests largely . . . on American power."[4]

In a universe where the American power structure, reinforced by Empire and globalization, has grown perpetually more concentrated and authoritarian, the claims of such academics as Bacevich and Elshtain make sense only as ideological platitudes, as self-serving legitimating myths. Ritual assertions that Washington has always been dedicated to the spread of democracy, human rights, and rule of law around the globe cannot stand the test of even minimal empirical scrutiny. They are the product of a recycled national exceptionalism fueled nowadays, as before, by imperial arrogance mixed with a vengeful nationalism—the essence not of democracy, however defined, but of authoritarianism both at home and abroad. In his book *Nemesis*, Chalmers Johnson argues that Empire inevitably gives rise to some form of domestic tyranny, on a foundation of war economy and security state.[5] If authoritarian politics is one domestic outcome of imperial power, then its global equivalence is chaos, war, and lawlessness—all components of a Hobbesian state of nature projected, as we have seen, by American leaders. In this setting Americans today are confronted by hierarchical power across the entire landscape— government, workplaces, schools and universities, media, technology daily life—even as the opinion-makers celebrate democratic values. Far removed

Religion as the 3rd objective "force" outside

from convenient academic fictions, Chris Hedges has arrived at a far more realistic view of the current American predicament: "At no period in American history has our democracy been in such peril or has the possibility of totalitarianism been as real. Our way of life is over. Our profligate consumption is finished. Our children will never have the standard of living we had. And poverty and despair will sweep across the landscape like a plague. This is a bleak future."[6] That "future" cannot be grasped without critical understanding of the existing power structure that strips away the familiar illusions and myths.

THE PERMANENT WAR SYSTEM

Crucial to perpetuation of the American ruling stratum has been the growth of U.S. imperial power and the underlying war system, entrenched within a complex economic, cultural, and political network so pervasive as to be nearly invisible for the vast majority of citizens. A nation geared to international supremacy—to full-spectrum dominance—has inevitably given rise to a behemoth reliant on a wide assortment of authoritarian controls, economic coercion, and military violence, at home and abroad. While strongly denied by government and Pentagon leaders, in fact militarism has grown into a powerful hegemonic belief system supported by politicians, the media, the corporate sector, and academia; its premises are unchallengeable within the dominant public sphere. The turning point came with what Sheldon Wolin defines as a new "power imaginary" spawned by the take-off of military Keynesianism during and after World War II.[7] As James Cypher puts it: "In the U.S. militarism is and has been since the late 1940s a hegemonic societal perception—the prism through which global political events and U.S. foreign policy are interpreted."[8] This ideology is hardly the brainchild of a few neocon crazies or the result of a Bush-Cheney coup to push the United States along the path of a more adventurous foreign policy; it is less a rupture with than an extension of longstanding American traditions of national exceptionalism, conquest, and expansion. In any event, a vital function of militarism is to legitimate not only U.S. global agendas but domestic elite power.

In the postwar era the U.S. military has achieved a global reach without historical parallel. While this system is commonly referred to as a "permanent war economy," following Seymour Melman's seminal work, its vast web of political, bureaucratic, cultural, and international as well as economic institutions suggests a broader label is more appropriate.[9] The economic dimension naturally calls attention to the myriad functions performed by the war-making machine within American production and consumption: budgetary allocations and taxes, stimulus to corporate power, impact on R&D, larger consequences for domestic production and work, and trends associated with a militarized society. All these phenomena gain strength within the broad matrix of Pentagon activity extending to land, seas, air, outer space, and even cyberspace. Full-scale mobilization of resources behind the armed forces, begun during World War II, has never slackened, reaching peak levels in the wake of 9/11. The wartime threat of Nazis and fascists was quickly transferred to a new Cold War menace—international Communism—justifying continued massive Pentagon outlays that President Eisenhower would label the "military-industrial complex" in 1961. Meanwhile, the United States became the world's leading superpower, widening its lead over rival USSR as the Pentagon budget exceeded the entire gross domestic product of all but a few industrialized nations. Thus, in the mid-1950s Mills could write: "It is not only within the higher political, economic, scientific, and educational circles that the military ascendancy is apparent. The warlords, along with fellow travelers and spokesmen, are attempting to plant their metaphysics firmly among the population at large."[10] Anticipating future trends, he added: "American militarism in fully developed form would mean the triumph in all areas of life of the military metaphysic, and hence the subordination to it of all other ways of life."[11]

Writing only a few years after Mills, Fred Cook, in his seminal *The Warfare State*, analyzed this military trajectory with equal clarity, identifying a radical shift toward Pentagon power that would forever reshape American politics, economic life, and culture—not to mention foreign policy. Observed Cook: "The crutch of the Warfare State is propaganda. We must be taught to fear and to hate or we will not agree to regiment our lives, to bear the enormous burdens of ever heavier taxation to pay for ever more costly military hardware—and to do this at the expense of domestic programs like medical care and education and healthy urban development."[12] According to Cook, the 1946 elections marked the first real triumph of the military-corporate-government alliance that came to be shared equally by Democrats and Republicans across the decades. It signaled a turning away from FDR's liberal emphasis (before the war) on social Keynesianism toward a military Keynesianism that would become henceforth institutionalized. As Pentagon agendas morphed into the "American way of life," Cold War bipartisan consensus meant that dissent from such agendas would be viewed within mainstream politics as un-American, even treasonous. As the arms race with the USSR intensified, Cook wrote: "The picture that emerges is the picture of a nation whose entire economic welfare is tied to warfare"[13]—a theme later emphasized in the work of Seymour Melman. Expecting fearsome trends that would take decades to

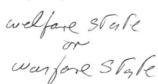

welfare state
or
warfare state

thoroughly unfold, Cook reflected: "The time has come when we can see clearly and unmistakably before us our chosen destiny. The Pied Pipers of the military and big business, who have been drumming into our ears the siren song of 'peace through strength,' can no longer quite conceal the brink toward which they lead us."[14] Like Mills, Cook believed such developments ran counter to the basic requirements of democracy.

Postwar U.S. military expansion grounded in a deepening state capitalism involved an integrative process, both structural and ideological, in which corporate, government, and military interests converged to drive an authoritarian system. In this fashion military Keynesianism served U.S. imperial designs as well as elite power, ensuring massive profits domestically as well as the freest possible terrain for global investments and market control. The enormous staying power of the war economy depended on other factors: corporate lobbying, bureaucratic power, scientific and technological agendas, armed services jockeying for position, the entwined priorities of the two major parties. Every postwar American president, from Truman to Obama, has given full, enthusiastic blessings to a Pentagon behemoth that achieved a life of its own. Some of the most vigorous military interventions—Korea, Vietnam, Central America, and the Balkans, for example—were launched by Democrats. An institutionalized power structure allowed for little elite maneuverability at the summit of governance.

The permanent war system today constitutes a global network of more than a thousand military facilities spread across 40 states and more than 70 nations, from Latin America to Africa, Europe, the Middle East, Asia, and scattered islands in the Pacific and Atlantic oceans. Its sophisticated arms, intelligence, and surveillance webs of power extend to every corner of the earth and space, dependent on a production and distribution apparatus involving several thousand industrial companies and subsidiaries. It is intimately connected to such powerful, and often secretive, institutions as the Central Intelligence Agency, National Security Agency, Federal Bureau of Investigation, Bureau of Alcohol, Tobacco, Firearms and Explosives, National Aeronautics and Space Administration, and the United States Information Agency. It exerts pervasive ideological influence on the mass media, think tanks, universities, popular culture, and the Internet. The Pentagon labyrinth itself, located in Washington D.C., lies at the hub of all this activity, the symbol of American global power since 1947, with 28,000 employees, 30 acres of offices and meeting rooms, and 17.5 miles of hallways. The Pentagon is a major center of communications, transportation, social life, and political engagement, the site of the National Military Command Center, which collects vast amounts of data from around the globe. It is the center of a sprawling network employing

1.6 million armed services personnel, 800,000 reserves, and some two million workers in the industrial sector. In providing far-flung support for troops, logistical operations, and employees, the Pentagon manages a multitude of information sites, entertainment centers, hospitals, schools, family dwellings, officers' and enlisted clubs, churches, restaurants, sports facilities, and transportation systems.

By fiscal year 2010, Pentagon spending had reached nearly one trillion dollars (including veterans' funding), nearly three times what all potential U.S. adversaries were allocating combined (with Russia and China together at less than $200 billion). The United States and its allies were spending roughly 75 percent of total global military allocations in 2009, with Washington alone counting for about half the total. This amount does not include money for intelligence agencies (nearly $100 billion in known resources for 2009), for homeland security (another $50 billion), or for the occupation of Iraq (untold tens of billions more)—numbers likely to increase further with other military ventures in the future. These resource deployments, without parallel in history, have become the sign of something akin to a garrison state, a system routinely oiled by lobbies, politicians of both parties, think tanks, the media, universities, and of course huge military contractors. Arms producers yearly donate several million dollars in campaign funding: Lockheed Martin, Raytheon, TRW, and Boeing gave more than six million to both Democrats and Republicans during the 2000 elections. Such corporations, in turn, hugely benefit from new weapons contracts as well as lucrative overseas arms sales, which totaled $156 billion between 2001 and 2008 (41 percent of world sales). As the ideological apparatus holds up the threat of new enemies, profit-driven corporations seek aggressive military policies to fight rogue states, terrorists, and drug traffickers. Leading military contractors were anxious to see NATO's vaunted push eastward, spurred by the 1990s Balkans interventions—for both geostrategic and market-oriented reasons. Lockheed Martin, among others, secured billions in arms sales to Poland, the Czech Republic, Romania, and Croatia starting in 1999.

The war economy depends on a merging of factors: a deeply-embedded military culture, bureaucratic leverage, political conservatism, fetishism of technology, popular equation of corporate power with "freedom" and "democracy"—all of this underwritten by strong elements of national exceptionalism and imperial hubris. Helen Caldicott has observed that "one could readily diagnose the attitudes of the Pentagon as clinically sick and suggest that all people who subscribe to those theories [e.g., about world domination] need urgent counseling and therapy."[15] Of course the seductive power, material, and status rewards derived from an immense labyrinth of contracts, jobs, and deployments could help reduce the need for psychological help. A more accurate reading of the Pentagon system is that it affirms business-as-usual at the apex of a militarized state capitalism, where elites are pursuing seemingly rational objectives. Indeed the warfare apparatus thrives on an entrenched corporate oligopoly in which myths of free enterprise are scarcely operative insofar as profitability from sales to government alone is typically ensured. By 2000, the top military corporations had been reduced in number to just five: Lockheed Martin, Boeing, Raytheon, General Dynamics, and Northrop Grumman. In 2003 the largest of these remained Lockheed Martin, the result of 1990s mergers involving Lockheed and Martin Marietta, Loral Defense, General Dynamics, and scores of smaller companies to create a $36 billion empire that lobbies tirelessly for aggressive militarism (as in Iraq). After 9/11 these corporations adapted their marketing strategies to accommodate new demands for space militarization, homeland security, and the war on terrorism—signaling a shift toward high-tech production to fit the Bush-Cheney-Rumsfeld emphasis on techno-war. In 2006, it cost more than a million dollars to dispatch a Tomahawk missile, about $2,500 an hour to operate a single M-12A tank, more than $3,000 an hour to fly an F-16 fighter plane, and roughly $40,000 an hour to keep a navy destroyer active. With everything taken into account, moreover, it cost more than a million dollars to deploy and equip a single first-line soldier to Iraq or Afghanistan for a year.

Military Keynesianism has long relied on technology: since World War II upwards of 70 percent of all resources devoted to research and development has come under the auspices of the Pentagon. With its emphasis on remote aerial warfare, robotics, and sophisticated communications systems, techno-war has been a durable feature of U.S. military life at least since the Vietnam War. By the 1990s, however, Pentagon technology, enhanced by computerized systems, made even greater leaps forward, a paradigm shift eventually labeled a "revolution in military affairs" (RMA). Increasing resources were poured into high-tech weapons systems, surveillance, space operations, information networks, and lighter, more mobile combat units for all branches of the armed services. A high-tech military would presumably enable the United States to achieve full-spectrum dominance more efficiently, wedding flexibility, mobility, and computerized responses to an already terrifying arsenal of weapons. A champion of RMA, Secretary of Defense Donald Rumsfeld, saw this as a catalyst for a new phase in the military development once Bush took office. In reality RMA had already been set in motion during Desert Storm, when the Pentagon started relying more fully on high-tech communications and weapons systems as part of an integrated electronic battlefield. While techno-war permits quicker, more flexible, and often more deadly armed responses, it is also extremely costly and limited in the context of asymmetric warfare like that encountered in Iraq and Afghanistan. RMA innovations include pilotless aircraft like the Global Hawk and Predator, used in Afghanistan and Pakistan to pursue dispersed and hard-to-reach military targets such as Al Qaeda base camps. In December 2009, the United States moved to escalate its drone strikes in both Afghanistan and Pakistan, designed to attack not only Al Qaeda but the Taliban, as the Obama administration indicated its readiness to mount high-tech assaults (risking no American lives) against targets in such densely-populated urban areas as Quetta, Pakistan. Such risky and costly operations—run mostly by the CIA—coincided with a new U.S. "surge" strategy in Afghanistan.

As the war economy thrives and expands, the marriage of government, business, and military grows ever more intimate. Under these conditions, "privatization" of military functions simply comes with the terrain, as many corporations shift to greater battlefield engagement. Since the early 1980s, U.S. armed forces operational needs have been increasingly performed by private firms, usually staffed by retired military personnel hoping to mix adventure and fortunes. Enterprises like Military Professional Resources, Inc. (MPRI), Blackwater, Halliburton, and Bechtel have been hired by the Pentagon or State Department to furnish training and assistance to military and law enforcement agencies in countries friendly to the United States. In fact these contractors engage in many tasks—planning, engineering, security, infrastructure rebuilding, etcetera—almost completely beyond the purview of public or legislative oversight. Until Blackwater operatives went on a Baghdad shooting rampage in late 2007, accused of killing at least 17 Iraqi civilians, the PMCs carried out their work largely beneath the political and media radar. Yet their role in the Middle East, with a reported presence exceeding 100,000 "contractors" in Iraq alone (as of 2009), could hardly be discounted. Ken Silverstein, in *Private Warriors*, wrote: "These private warriors have a financial and career interest in war and conflict, as well as the power and connections to promote continued hard-line policies. Their collective influence is one reason the United States seems incapable of making the transition to a post-Cold War world."[16] MPRI, founded in 1987 by retired Army General Vernon Lewis, has been deeply involved in keeping the harsh Saudi Arabian regime in power, working secretly to assist its coercive military and police organs—crucial to protecting U.S. oil interests in the region. The company received more than $500 million in the 1990s to train similar forces in Bosnia and Croatia under repressive governments. Corporations like MPRI and Vinnell have received billions to provide aid and training to dictatorial regimes in Central America, Indonesia, South Korea, Kuwait, and Saudi Arabia. Joint Pentagon-corporate programs have funded and trained thousands of operatives yearly at military schools and training camps in the United States and elsewhere, and these operatives carry out U.S. objectives across the globe. PMCs in collaboration with arms contractors have reaped hundreds of billions of dollars, all subsidized by taxpayers. Such "privatization" of war and related functions allows the Pentagon, working with the CIA and NSA, to escape public scrutiny.

The permanent war system both legitimates and reinforces state power on a grand scale—vital to perpetuation of elite rule. Few politicians have the audacity to oppose or even seriously question this out-of-control behemoth. For most citizens a sprawling Pentagon edifice represents American status and power in a threatening world. In a nation that consumes more than 30 percent of the world's energy supplies and depends on a steady flow of cheap labor, markets, and resources from abroad, imperial wars will continue to drive the mechanisms of statist economic and political organization even as elites loudly proclaim values of small government and free markets. Yet, while the Pentagon functions as stimulus to economic growth, such growth (technology-intensive, top-heavy, wasteful, destructive) has been increasingly detrimental to the social infrastructure not to mention jobs and services. The American developmental model favors the military sector, global priorities, and warfare over a wide range of civilian programs such as public transportation. Fred Cook's description of a "nation whose entire economic welfare is tied to warfare" takes on added meaning decades later, when the cumulative Pentagon budget has reached a staggering $25 trillion. It is hard to resist the conclusion that such unbelievable material, human, and technological resources have produced little beyond overwhelming devastation and waste— the former amounting to millions of human lives since World War II. Put differently, the military sector never contributes to ordinary modes of production and consumption or to the general welfare, except peripherally as in the case of technological spin-offs. More than that: the war economy by its very logic reproduces material decay, social inequality, cultural stresses, and political authoritarianism at the very moment it helps sustain an advanced industrial order. The end of the Cold War signaled a modest and brief decline in military spending as many spoke of armed services reductions, troop demobilizations, and base closings in step with a much-celebrated "peace dividend." A limited shift in this direction did occur, but the focus was on modernization: fewer domestic bases and personnel along with a phasing out of older weapons systems in favor of a higher-tech military. The newer arsenals, of course, had much greater firepower and efficiency than what they replaced. After

9/11, quite predictably, the Pentagon budget soared, fueled by interventions in Afghanistan and Iraq and the war on terrorism.

THE CULTURE OF MILITARISM

As the American people are asked to endure burdensome costs and sacrifices of war and preparation for war, mechanisms of legitimation take on new meaning. Empire, a bloated war economy, recurrent armed interventions, hardships on the home front—all these must be made to appear "natural," routine, even welcome if not noble. The historical myth of national exceptionalism, combined with hubris associated with economic, technological, and military supremacy, contributes to this ideological function. To translate such an ideological syndrome into popular language and daily life, to fully incorporate it into the political culture, is the task not so much of a classical state-run propaganda system as a developed hegemonic ideology reliant more on education and the media. In the United States, media culture has evolved into an outgrowth of megacorporate power that sustains the most far-reaching ideological and cultural network in history. Hollywood films alone have for many decades served as a crucial vehicle for legitimation of Empire.[17] The repetitive fantasies, illusions, myths, images, and storylines of Hollywood movies (not to mention TV and other outlets) can be expected to influence mass audiences in rather predictable ways, much along lines of advertising and public relations. One popular response to the flood of violent combat, action-adventure, sci-fi, and horror films (with their companion video games) is stronger readiness to support U.S. military operations that, in an intensely patriotic, violent milieu will require little overt justification except where American casualties are deemed excessive. Such ideological legitimation is needed in a context where even the ensemble of corporate, military, and government power cannot suffice.

Despite its command of institutional power, tools of violence, and material resources, therefore, the system requires something along lines of a culture of militarism. In the United States, militarism has indeed evolved into an ideology forged by media culture, political messages, academic discourses, and patriotic indoctrination. If the linkage between militarism and daily life goes back in history, it has taken on new dimensions with the dramatic growth of the media and popular culture over the past few decades. If the culture of militarism endows warfare with a popular sense of meaning and purpose, it also constitutes the hegemonic façade behind which the power structure can more or less freely operate, domestically and worldwide. The decay of

American economic, political, and social life cannot be understood apart from this destructive cycle—likely to worsen as the elites strive to maintain the advantages of Empire against new challenges. By the early twenty-first century it was obvious that war, and orientation to war, had become a way of life in the United States, a society in which both leaders and general population could be said to have grown addicted to war. If the United States fails to qualify as a full-fledged "warrior society" at the level of ancient Sparta, Nazi Germany, interwar Japan, or even Israel today, the military influence is perhaps even more pervasive—though not always recognizable as such—owing to the global presence of American power.

Who could expect otherwise, as the Pentagon dominates the globe with its military, technological, and communications presence, with its hundreds of bases and sites, and its status as the world's biggest landlord (overseeing 300,000 housing units globally)? The U.S. military runs its own vast propaganda network with scores of newspapers and magazines, invests in hundreds of movies and TV programs, develops state-of-the-art video games, and is by far the largest sponsor of research and development, allowing it to influence such fields as nuclear physics, chemistry, astronomy, and electrical engineering. What might be called the militarization of the academy is reflected in the capacity of the Pentagon to shape research goals at such respectable universities as UC Berkeley, MIT, Stanford, Johns Hopkins, Penn State, and Carnegie Mellon—a few of the more than 350 institutions that routinely get military contracts. Under the familiar guise of national security, American society has seen a convergence of military, corporate, and academic centers of power.[18] Tens of billions are targeted annually for higher-tech warfare agendas: urban-assault counterinsurgency methods, satellite technology, nuclear modernization, robotics and other forms of remote combat, laser-guided weapons, war-gaming, and database collections among others.[19]

In a militarized society the armed forces experience is bound to touch the lives of tens of millions of people, often in the most intimate ways—and often outside the ranks of the military itself. In her study of the "homefront," Catherine Lutz comments: "In an important sense . . . we all inhabit an army camp, mobilized to lend support to the permanent state of war readiness that has been with us since World War II. No matter where we live, we have raised war taxes at work, and future soldiers at home lived with the cultural atmosphere of racism and belligerence that war mobilization often uses or creates, and nourished the public opinion that helps send soldiers off to war. . . . All experience the problems bred by war's glorification of violent masculinity and the inequalities created by its redistribution of wealth to the already privileged." Lutz adds that "we all have lived with the consequences of the reinvigorated idea that we prove and regenerate ourselves through violence."[20] This reality turns out to be even more all-consuming for military personnel and residents of Fayetteville, North Carolina—home of the sprawling Fort Bragg army base—that Lutz chose as the focus of her research. Here all the contradictions of U.S. militarism came home to roost—a "dumping ground for the problems of the American century of war and empire." Here we have exaggerated problems of poverty, crime, child abuse, alcoholism, prostitution, homelessness, and a wide array of physical and mental injuries.[21] These are the fruits of a permanent war system that transfigures daily life for those within and close to the "homefront" of Empire.

This is a world geared to warfare, preparation for warfare, killing, and refinement of the instruments for killing. In her classic work *Military Brats*, Mary Edwards Wertsch brilliantly weaves together narratives of life in the military, focusing on two lingering motifs—the warrior ethos, and the authoritarian character of social relations. She writes: "Growing up inside the fortress [as she did] is like being drafted into a gigantic theater company. The role of the warrior society, even in peacetime, is to exist in a state of perpetual 'readiness': one continuous dress rehearsal for war. The principal actors are immaculately costumed, carefully scripted, and supplied with a vast array of props. They practice elaborate large-scale stage movements—land, air, sea exercises simulating attacks and defenses."[22] All this is part of a deep socialization process that Wertsch expertly unravels. Well before 9/11 and the subsequent wars, she could remark that "this is a society prepared to wage war with the same relentless attention to detail it brings to every moment of every day."[23] In such a culture authoritarian values inevitably prevail: "The Fortress, in short, is an authoritarian society. The masks worn there are authoritarian masks, each exactly like the others of its rank, each subservient to those of high rungs. The notions of conformity, order, and obedience reign supreme."[24] She adds: "The great paradox of the military is that its members, the self-appointed front-line guardians of our cherished American democratic values, do not live in a democracy themselves. Not only is individuality not valued in the military, it is discouraged. There is no freedom of speech, save on the most innocuous level. There is no freedom of assembly for anything that is not authorized. There is not even a concept of privacy . . ."[25] God, community, family, nation—everything is glorified through the mediations of warfare, violence, hierarchy, and aggression.

The permanent war system undermines democracy at every turn: imperial projects lead to authoritarian controls domestically and globally. Militarization gives rise not only to a warrior ethos but to hierarchy, discipline, secrecy, surveillance, lopsided allocations, and narrowed debate in government operations. Richard Falk writes of a shift toward fascism in the global order that, he argues, permeates American domestic politics as power and wealth come to dominate the field of decision-making.[26] An imperial arrogance that champions U.S. exceptionalism and subverts universal norms of legality on the world scene, that strives toward full-spectrum dominance, sooner or later generates a regime of lawlessness and violence at home. A Hobbesian universe, after all, is predictably rife with fear and hate. Falk observes that an authoritarian scenario will be momentarily disguised as necessary security adjustment to the threats of global terrorism."[27] While this "scenario" has surely gained new credence since 9/11, the pattern was set during World War II with solidification of the war economy and security state. Further, as discussed in the first two chapters, the United States has throughout its history worked tirelessly to defeat democratic possibilities outside its own borders. The neocons, as we have seen, embrace an uncompromising global authoritarianism (while preaching "democracy promotion") driven by U.S. entitlement to world supremacy. Falk argues: " . . . I consider it reasonable to think of something one might call global fascism as the mentality of those seeking to regulate the world, from either above or below, according to their extremist beliefs."[28] In both cases—home and abroad—the rules and laws of political behavior are to be set by the most powerful and wealthy.

When it comes to the actual making of U.S. foreign policy, therefore, even pretenses of democratic participation fall by the wayside. More than elsewhere, American global initiatives—no matter how costly or bloody—have been framed, justified, and carried out from the summits of power. Only a tiny minority of Americans expresses serious interest in foreign-policy issues, while the vast majority have been bombarded by patriotic, even jingoistic messages and warnings to leave such grave issues to the (mostly white-male) "experts." Most people have simply and uncritically followed the dictates of U.S. imperial ambitions as set by the ruling elites. The Constitution, which formally endows Congress with war-making powers, has rarely entered the picture when it comes to matters of war and peace: virtually every U.S. military intervention, from Mexico to Iraq to Afghanistan, was decided by executive power. Support has been readily mobilized through bipartisan embrace of "national security," powerful military lobbies, think tanks, and media manipulation. A long history of national expansion, conquest, and war has followed this decidedly undemocratic pattern.[29] The imperial presidency has only grown in power across the postwar era. Far-reaching exchanges over U.S. global behavior have been a rare occurrence—whether on TV or talk radio shows, congressional deliberations, news broadcasts, "expert" testimony, or presidential debates; consensus is the norm. It follows that the ruling elites enjoy considerable autonomy when it comes to the major issues: military, the budget, arms sales abroad, decisions to intervene, support for Israel, covert

operations, surveillance, space militarization. References to "national security" will typically ensure popular compliance with elite decisions. One real
departure from this pattern came during the final years of the Vietnam War,
when some elite sectors (joined by much of the media) grew disillusioned
with what had become a costly military disaster leading to civic unrest. Even
here, however, the disagreements with official policy revolved mainly around
failure of that policy; the ends were accepted as just and honorable.

Postwar examples of elite-driven interventions abound, from Korea to Vietnam, Laos, Cambodia, Central America, the Balkans, Iraq, and Afghanistan.
All were launched by the White House with minimal, if any, congressional
participation, and all were justified by a litany of distortions, myths, and
outright deceptions. Enough has already been written about an illegal Iraq
War, here and elsewhere, to reveal the utterly manipulative process even as
the Bush administration (belatedly) claimed the purest of democratic motives.
We know that Bush and the neocons were determined to launch their war
long before 9/11—a project that would be shared by politicians of both parties with equal fervor. In December 2001 the House voted 393 to 12 to brand
any Iraqi rejection of new arms inspections (when the Hussein regime had
already disarmed) an "increasing threat" to U.S. security—although no one
questioned how a small, distant nation weakened by years of harsh sanctions,
covert actions, and bombings could present a threat to the world's leading
superpower. By late 2002, the idea of regime change (itself a violation of
international law) had grown into something of an obsession among elites and
media pundits. The 1998 PNAC statement made it clear that no evidence of
terrorist links or WMD possession was needed to justify military action; only
later, for public edification, did the propaganda machine set forth such flimsy
pretexts. By mid-2002 the war drums picked up momentum: in November
Congress voted overwhelmingly to support military force against Iraq—the
Senate by 77 to 23, the House by 296 to 133, as "debates" were limited
to matters of timing, logistics, and strategy. By the end of 2002, therefore,
despite growing antiwar sentiment across the country, Democrats had totally
capitulated to an outrageous Republican foreign-policy scheme destined to
profoundly influence global and domestic politics for years if not decades
into the future.

THE IMPERIAL STATE

At a critical turning point in U.S. history, Democrats could never forge
alternative responses or initiatives, no doubt fearful they would be branded
unpatriotic or soft on terrorism—a familiar postwar bipartisan pattern. The

bankruptcy of Bush's rationale for war went scarcely contested within the political arena, as fear and confusion ruled the day. House majority leader Dennis Hastert (R-Illinois) loudly proclaimed: "We must not let evil triumph!" and Democrats quickly took up the rhetoric. Representative Tom Lantos (D-CA) spoke for the majority of Democrats when he said: "Just as leaders and diplomats who appeased Hitler at Munich in 1938 stand humiliated before history, so will we if we appease Saddam Hussein today."[30] The preposterous equation of Hitler's war machine with Hussein's weak, beaten, surrounded, impoverished nation of 23 million was never made an issue in Congress or the media. Senator Robert Byrd (D-WV) would say: "I'm in my 50th year in Congress and I never thought I would find a Senate which lacks the backbone to stand up against the stampede, this rush to war."[31] That the United States would launch a bloody war against Iraq, without U.N. Security Council approval and in full violation of international law, speaks volumes about the stifling narrowness of American politics.

James Bamford thoroughly documented the shameful trail of propaganda that paved the way toward a war Bush and the neocons had decided to carry out months and even years before the March 2003 invasion, indeed well before 9/11. The Pentagon, CIA, and White House utilized the sprawling public-relations network of the John Rendon Group to wage "perception management" of epic proportions, helping establish the ideological conditions for warfare in the absence of any credible Iraqi threat. The campaign depended on large-scale saturation of the media with false reports, misleading intelligence "data," distorted alarms (visions of "mushroom clouds"), and a variety of contrived pro-war narratives with the collaboration of writers like Judith Miller of the New York Times. Bamford writes that "never before in history had such an extensive secret network been established to shape the entire world's perception of a war."[32] That is not all: with the U.S. military occupation in full force, it was revealed that Pentagon contractors regularly paid Iraqi newspapers to publish glowing stories about the war and the role of U.S. troops as benevolent "liberators"—a propaganda enterprise that, while costly, was completely hidden from the American public. The Washington, D.C.-based Lincoln Group was given tens of millions of dollars to infiltrate Iraqi media over a period of nearly two years.[33] The war, from the outset highly-unpopular around the world, was conducted within a cynical framework of sustained domestic and international media manipulation. Its initial ideological success, at least on the home front, cannot be discounted in the face of enormous material and human costs.

As a protracted buildup to regime change in 2003, Washington had carried out a wide range of programs and schemes—most of them secret and illegal—to complement devastating economic sanctions that cost upwards of 500,000 Iraqi civilian lives. Dilip Hiro, in his book *Iraq* (2002), presents accounts of covert actions, sabotage, arming of opposition groups, and even a coup attempt, often under cover of the U.N. inspections regimen, undertaken by the CIA and other clandestine agencies.[34] American operatives, posing as weapons inspectors, collected valuable intelligence data that would be used for later military operations. Hiro reports on aborted CIA coup efforts in June 1996 after the "White House [Clinton] decided to accelerate its plan to overthrow Saddam and replace him with a small group of generals"—a plan that collapsed when Hussein learned about the conspirators.[35] All these activities took place fully outside any public scrutiny in the United States.

Other cases of undemocratic U.S. foreign-policy initiatives are much too numerous to be catalogued here. Lawrence Davidson, in his *Foreign Policy, Inc.*, chronicles in some detail several examples, including the postwar role of the powerful Cuba and Israel lobbies that, for the most part, strongly influence American global behavior beneath the public radar.[36] For decades anti-Castro lobbyists, based mainly in Florida, have waged successful campaigns to isolate Cuba—through diplomatic maneuvers, propaganda, embargo, cultural boycotts, etc.—even as the island regime posed no recognizable threat to the United States or anyone else, and the ostensible goal of democracy promotion never had much resonance. Congress continued to pass harsh anti-Cuban resolutions even as public opinion was entirely indifferent.[37] The impact of the much-larger Israel Lobby, comprised of several powerful organizations, has been far more egregious, as the lobby has worked tirelessly to discredit even tepid opposition to Israeli behavior, much of it in violation of universal human-rights and legal norms, as "anti-Semitic" and pro-terrorist. As Walt and Mearsheimer also show in *The Israel Lobby*, overwhelming elite consensus behind Israeli military aggression against Palestinians most often actually conflicts with U.S. strategic interests in the Middle East.[38] Open discussion of these policies has long been taboo in both the political and media systems. Any elected member of the U.S. Congress opposing Israeli policies will be quickly rebuked and driven from office—witness the example of Rep. Cynthia McKinney (D-Georgia). Powerful and wealthy lobbies with perhaps tens of thousands of members have thus managed to engineer U.S. foreign policy beyond the reach of any political mechanism. Such lobbies, moreover, typically linked to the corporate establishment, have deeply influenced the work of think tanks, foundations, and universities as well as the mass media. And the impact of these interest groups on the course of international relations should not be minimized.

Yet another case of imperial priorities subverting democracy is what has been called "the secret U.S. war in Pakistan," where the CIA, Special Forces units, and private military contractors (notably Blackwater) combined forces to carry out far-reaching operations inside and outside of Pakistan. These operations include intelligence-gathering, covert actions, and a drone bombing campaign directed against Al Qaeda and Taliban targets in Afghanistan, Pakistan, and elsewhere. The drone strikes were actually increased after Obama entered the White House, often with dreadful civilian casualties in a nation that is not at war with the United States. These initiatives, with potentially disastrous outcomes for the region, have clearly received no official congressional imprimatur. As Jeremy Scahill, writing in *The Nation*, observes: "The use of private companies like Blackwater for sensitive operations such as drone strikes or other covert work undoubtedly comes with the benefit of plausible deniability that places an additional barrier in an already deeply flawed system of accountability."[39] Yet this kind of "secret" warfare, as we have seen in the case of Iraq, is hardly novel to U.S. history.

NOTES

1. Andrew J. Bacevich, *The Limits of Power* (New York, NY: Henry Holt & Co., 2008), 15.

2. Jean Bethke Elshtain, *Just War against Terror* (New York, NY: Basic Books, 2003), 6.

3. Elshtain, *Just War,* 167.

4. Elshtain, *Just War,* 169.

5. Chalmers Johnson, *Nemesis* (New York, NY: Henry Holt & Co., 2006), 88–89.

6. Chris Hedges, "It's Not Going to be Okay," CommonDreams.org (February 2, 2009), www.commondreams.org/view/2009/02/02–0 (accessed July 4, 2010).

7. Sheldon Wolin, *Democracy, Inc.* (Princeton, NJ: Princeton University Press, 2008).

8. James M. Cypher, "From Military Keynesianism to Global Neo-Liberalism," *Monthly Review* (June 2007): 37–55.

9. On Melman's approach, see Seymour Melman, *The Permanent War Economy* (New York, NY: Simon and Schuster, 1974).

10. C. Wright Mills, *The Power Elite* (New York, NY: Oxford University Press, 1956), 219.

11. Mills, *Power Elite,* 223.

12. Fred Cook, *The Warfare State* (New York, NY: Collier, 1962), 100.

13. Cook, *Warfare State,* 189.

14. Cook, *Warfare State,* 354.

15. Helen Caldicott, *The New Nuclear Danger* (New York, NY: Free Press, 2002), 20.

16. Ken Silverstein, *Private Warriors* (London, UK: Verso, 2000), ix.

17. See Carl Boggs and Tom Pollard, *The Hollywood War Machine* (Boulder, CO: Paradigm, 2007), chs. 1, 2.

18. Nick Turse, *The Complex: How the Military Invades our Lives* (New York, NY: Henry Holt & Co., 2008), 33–40.

19. Turse, *Complex,* 244–70.

20. Catherine Lutz, *Homefront* (Boston, MA: Beacon Press, 2001), 3.

21. Lutz, *Homefront,* 4.

22. Mary Edwards Wertsch, *Military Brats* (New York, NY: Ballantine, 1991), 1.

23. Wertsch, *Military,* 33.

24. Wertsch, *Military,* 16.

25. Wertsch, *Military,* 15.

26. Richard Falk, "Slouching Toward a Fascist World Order," in *The American Empire and the Commonwealth of God,* eds. David Ray Griffin, et. al. (Louisville, KY: Westminster John Knox, 2006), 59–63.

27. Falk, *American Empire,* 57.

28. Falk, *American Empire,* 62.

29. Lawrence Davidson, *Foreign Policy, Inc.* (Lexington, KY: University Press of Kentucky, 2009), Introduction.

30. Tom Lantos, "Voices of Debate on Iraq," *Los Angeles Times,* October 9, 2002, http://articles.latimes.com/2002/oct/09/nation/na-excerpts9 (accessed July 4, 2010).

31. Robert Byrd, quoted in Janet Hook and Nick Anderson, "Congress Backs War on Iraq," *Los Angeles Times,* March 5, 2003, A1.

32. James Bamford, "How the Iraq War was Marketed," *Rolling Stone,* December 1, 2005, 61.

33. Mark Mazzetti and Kevin Sack, "The Challenges in Iraq," *Los Angeles Times,* December 18, 2005, A1.

34. Dilip Hiro, *Iraq: in the Eye of the Storm* (New York, NY: Nation Books, 2002), chs. 5,6.

35. Hiro, *Iraq,* 78–84.

36. Davidson, *Foreign Policy, Inc.,* ch. 5 (on Cuba) and ch. 6 (on Israel).

37. Davidson, *Foreign Policy,* 93–95.

38. John M. Mearsheimer and Stephen Walt, *The Israel Lobby* (New York, NY: Farrar, Strauss, and Giroux, 2007), ch. 2.

39. Jeremy Scahill, "The Secret U.S. War in Pakistan," *The Nation,* November 23, 2009, 18.

Chapter Three

The Security Industrial Complex

Ward Churchill

[A]s the Supreme Court has recognized in numerous opinions, the Government has a right, in fact a duty, to protect itself from destruction and to protect its institutions from violence and forcible overthrow. . . . Obviously, [this] cannot mean that before the Government may act, it must wait until the putsch is about to be executed. . . . Without a broad range of intelligence information, the President and appropriate departments and agencies of the Executive Branch could not protect our nation's security. . . .

—Deputy Assistant Attorney General Kevin T. Maroney, testimony before the House Internal Security Committee (February 20, 1974)

Translated from officialese, the above-quoted statement can be taken to mean that the function of the "domestic" or "internal" security apparatus maintained by the State is solely to ensure preservation of the socioeconomic-political status quo.[1] Stripped of Maroney's rhetorical emphasis on the supposed necessity of averting violent social upheavals, the objective by which internal security is defined centers on "neutralizing" the possibility of substantive changes to the existing order. Attainment of the desired result requires far more than mere intelligence-gathering; rather, those deemed "subversive" must be actively "disrupted, destabilized, discredited, and destroyed."[2]

The frankly antidemocratic task of constraining the range of American political expression and activity within limits demarcated by the elites whose privilege depends upon the unhampered continuation of business as usual is of necessity carried out by routinely targeting individuals and organizations guilty of no criminal activity whatsoever. Hence, there can be no defensible claim that such operations fall under the broader rubric of "law enforcement."

On the contrary, the methods employed by internal security agents and agencies in neutralizing politically objectionable targets have often been—and in many respects remain—patently unlawful.

Following a standard definition of political repression as consisting of "government[al] action which grossly discriminates against persons or organizations viewed as presenting a fundamental challenge to existing power relationships or key government policies, because of their perceived political beliefs," it is impossible to avoid the conclusion that the enterprise of "internal security" is inherently repressive.[3] Thus, insofar as the performance of internal security functions involves a form of policing, it is always and everywhere that of the political police. Indeed, it is arguable that this is an ingredient essential to the structure of the State itself.

While it is accurate to say that all States, irrespective of their stations along the spectrum running from "totalitarian" to "democratic," rely upon the mechanism of political policing to stabilize and sustain themselves, it would be untrue to contend that the impact of such policing is therefore equivalent in each instance. Notwithstanding whatever moral distinctions are to be drawn from the relative degrees of brutality evidenced by the repressive apparatus of various States at various times, a far more illuminating standard of assessment concerns the extent to which any given apparatus has proven effective in nullifying meaningful political opposition within its operational sphere.

Among the more significant considerations in this regard are the length of the period in which a State's system of political policing has been able not only to sustain itself, but to evolve; the degree of societal acceptance and consequent scope it has achieved in the process; its resulting capacity not simply to reproduce itself but to maintain its rate and trajectory of expansion in the future. Suffice it for the moment to observe that the U.S. ranks at or very near the top of the list of all States in each of these three analytical categories, that the range of permissible—that is, unpenalized—political expression is by a clear margin the narrowest of any "liberal democracy," and that for several decades the U.S. has been attempting, often with considerable success, to replicate its model on a global basis.

THE INTERNAL SECURITY MODEL

The most striking feature of the contemporary U.S. internal security system is undoubtedly the all-encompassing and seamless nature of its organizational structure. A primary signifier in this respect is the 2002 statute creating a "Department of Homeland Security" to coordinate operations conducted by relevant components of the country's military, intelligence, and police "communities."[4] It should be emphasized that far more than federal entities are at issue in this connection; the department's coordinative charge extends to the activities of specialized units lodged within state and local police forces nationwide. Similarly, it is endowed with the prerogative of enlisting "regular" police and National Guard units to provide blunt force when needed to quell generalized "civil disturbances."

Should the latter prove insufficient to "maintain public order," army/marine maneuver battalions are available for deployment in a "domestic peacekeeping" role, as they were during the so-called ghetto riots of the late 1960s.[5] Additionally, certain of the military's more esoteric formations can be utilized; for example, Delta Force, an army "surgical elimination unit," has, among other things, been used in putting down the 1987 Atlanta prison riots,[6] was present on standby status during the 1992 Los Angeles insurrection and more actively during the 1999 protests of the World Trade Organization (WTO) in Seattle,[7] and provided on-site "advisers" to assist the FBI during its extraordinarily lethal operations against the Branch Davidians near Waco, Texas, in 1993.[8]

No less noteworthy is the manner in which the constellation of governmental agencies falling within the department's purview is configured to "interface," continuously and at virtually every level, with a host of nominally private corporations. These range from "force expanding" security contractors and "intelligence consulting firms" to the providers of certain types of technology—as well "patriotic groups" drawn mainly, but by no means exclusively, from the radical right. As concerns internal security functions in the U.S., the boundaries by which the official domain has been customarily demarcated from the private have become so permeable as to render them irrelevant.[9] The result is, both for analytical purposes and in terms of practical application, an integral whole.

So well-refined is America's comprehensive domestic security model that the U.S. has long since taken to exporting it as an organizational/operational template for utilization in Latin American and other Third World client states. Since the early 1960s, when the Agency for International Development (AID) collaborated with the CIA in establishing the International Police Academy and launching the euphemistically titled Office of Public Safety program, the U.S. model has been adapted to the contexts of at least four dozen countries around the world.[10] In most cases, U.S. governmental funding, training, and equipage of the police is ongoing in these locales, and is now substantially enhanced through "consulting" provided by ostensibly private contractors.[11]

One upshot of this is that the U.S. agencies whose activities are now coordinated by the Department of Homeland Security enjoy "close professional relationship[s] with over a million police" personnel in Third World countries.[12] This provides an efficient means of maintaining close scrutiny of the activities of American citizens traveling abroad as well a ready source of intelligence on the political beliefs, associations, and activities of persons traveling or immigrating to the U.S. By the same token, interventions intended to neutralize specific targets can be—and are—requested/carried out by internal security agencies on either side of the equation (albeit, most such requests seem thus far to have been generated by the U.S.).[13]

This global reach is further extended through carefully cultivated relationships between American police/intelligence agencies with their counterparts in developed countries—especially those of the British Commonwealth, Germany, France, Israel and Japan—whose internal security systems largely resemble that of the U.S.[14] Here, in contrast to the situation in the Third World, U.S. emphasis has never been so much upon the development of infrastructure and inculcation of doctrine as it has on a sort of generalized cross-pollination. Not only is information shared among participants as a matter of course, but also technology and theoretical, technical, and tactical training.[15] In some instances, personnel from one country have even been assigned to work in an operational capacity within the security apparatus of another.[16]

Overall, the degree of interpenetration of governmental security agencies and private sector entities within the U.S., together with the ever-greater extent of their interlocks with their cohorts abroad, adds up to far more than "a system." Instead, especially when viewed in conjunction with the array of other spheres with which it directly overlaps—i.e., the military, police, judicial, penal, educational, media, and "independent" research establishments, among others—the U.S. internal security structure must be seen as constituting a whole complex of systemic enterprises.

The U.S. internal security complex is, moreover, "industrialized," not merely in the sense that one of its primary purposes—arguably the primary purpose—is to protect and further the business/economic interests of its host state, but also because its functioning has been rationalized along distinctly neo-Fordist lines (particularly those associated with the principle of "flexible specialization").[17] The burgeoning trend toward privatizing whole vectors of the enterprise also serves to propel a steadily increasing profitability for the individuals and firms offering "intelligence and security services" for a fee.[18] Such circumstances and dynamics form the basis for expectations that the complex will continue to grow in both scope and sophistication over the years ahead, becoming ever more totalizing in its repressive effects upon the global body politic.

The question obviously arises as to how and why things ever reached such a pass. A substantial part of the answer will perhaps be found in understanding that, notwithstanding the recent advent of technologies markedly upgrading the efficiency of surveillance, communications, record keeping, and other dimensions of the security process, the basic components forming the American model are nothing new. It is to be hoped that an historical examination of the origins and evolution of these components may provide deeper insight into the nature of the situation in which we presently find ourselves, thus supplying at least some of the conceptual tools necessary for turning things around.

HISTORICAL BACKDROP

In 1985, analyst Ken Lawrence published a brief but important study titled *The New State Repression*. Therein, it was observed that, "in the past, rulers and their security forces believed that the normal condition of society was stability and calm, while insurgency was thought to . . . an oddity," a reality reflected in the nature and structure of the security apparatus. What had changed in the quarter-century preceding Lawrence's writing was, in his estimation, a shift in perspective on the part of U.S. elites:

> [I]nsurgency [was no longer viewed as] an occasional erratic idiosyncrasy of people who are oppressed and exploited, but a constant occurrence—permanent insurgency, which calls for a strategy that doesn't simply rely on a police force and a national guard and an army that can be called out in an emergency, but rather a strategy of permanent repression as the full-time task of security forces.[19]

Lawrence held that this change in outlook, largely precipitated by the social and political upheavals of the 1960s, had led to adoption of an outright counterinsurgency paradigm by the U.S. internal security apparatus, and, correspondingly, its continuous engagement in the sort of "low intensity operations" taught at the Army Special Warfare School at Fort Bragg, North Carolina, as well as the Command and General Staff College at Fort Leavenworth, Kansas.[20] In support of his premise, he showcased the influence on America's political police of British counterinsurgency strategists Frank Kitson, whose credentials included a lengthy stint commanding Britain's counterinsurgency effort in Northern Ireland, and Robin Evelegh, whose specialty was extrapolating further lessons from Kitson's experiences, not only in Ulster, but in Aden, Kenya, and Cyprus.[21]

The resulting conceptual shift had already been concretized, Lawrence contended, offering several illustrations: extensive FBI "counterintelligence" operations carried out against domestic political targets under the cryptonym COINTELPRO during the 1950s and 1960s;[22] comparable initiatives carried out on the home front during the same period by the CIA under such code names as Operation CHAOS and Project RESISTANCE;[23] and a sweeping militarization of "every police force worthy of the name" through wholesale creation, beginning in 1970, of "SWAT teams, tactical squads, helicopter patrols, and the like."[24]

Another example was the California Specialized Training Institute (CSTI), established with state funds by Ronald Reagan during his final term as governor both to devise effective methods of neutralizing California's then-vibrant radical left and "to train police forces from all across the U.S. and from many other countries in counterinsurgency . . . tasks that could not, at that time, be conducted at FBI headquarters or the International Police Academy, or other federal police training institutions."[25] To head the institute, Reagan selected Louis O. Giuffrida, a former army counterintelligence officer long associated with organizations on the extreme right.[26]

Giuffrida's principle qualification for his new position was, apparently, his submission to Reagan of a series of written "scenarios" describing what he saw as the most effective approaches, both structurally and tactically, to containing—or eradicating—"civil disorder" (he seems to have served as the governor's principle advisor on terrorism and other "special topics" from 1971 onward). The curriculum with which CSTI then fulfilled its training mission closely followed the requirements set forth therein. As Lawrence pointed out, Giuffrida's scenarios, and, consequently, the CSTI curriculum, were adapted quite directly from the Kitson playbook.[27]

Lawrence went on to observe that in 1981, shortly after he became president, Reagan appointed Giuffrida to direct the Federal Emergency Management Agency (FEMA), thus positioning him to implant Kitson's counterinsurgency doctrines in the U.S. police establishment far more broadly than even his then-ongoing directorship of the CSTI had allowed.[28] Unmentioned, however, was the reality that a pair of Giuffrida's counterinsurgency scenarios, based on army contingency plans codenamed "Garden Plot" and "Cable Splicer,"[29] had already been field-tested with devastating effects by the FBI, working in concert with the army and local police and vigilante groups, against a targeted organization, the American Indian Movement (AIM), during the mid-70s.[30]

Also unmentioned was the fact that, well before *The New State Repression* was released, Giuffrida had used his station at FEMA to undertake a series of training exercises—such as "Proud Saber/Rex-82" (1982), "Pre-Nest" (1983), and "Rex-84/Night Train" (1984)—involving the military, civilian police agencies, and certain still-unidentified "citizens groups" jointly conducting simulations of Garden Plot/Cable Splicer-type operations at the regional and fully-national levels (in Rex-84, for instance, it was envisioned that "at least 100,000" U.S. citizens, pre-designated as "security threats," were to be immediately interned for indefinite periods in concentration camps already constructed for that purpose).[31]

While it was in some ways groundbreaking in its apprehension of the then-present state of affairs, Lawrence's argument was marred by other deficiencies as well. One is a misplaced emphasis deriving from his assessment of insurgency as having become a "permanent condition" in the U.S. In actuality, the brief period of domestic insurgency upon which his view was based had effectively ended a decade earlier. Hence, although there were—and still are—occasional aftershocks, U.S. internal security agencies were by 1985 far more concerned with refining their aggregate capacity to engage in counterinsurgency than with actually engaging in it. Emphasis had already shifted to its current location, i.e., maintaining a sociopolitical condition of pacification in which the conceptual/operational mode of repression is designed to preclude rather than "counter" anything resembling a genuine domestic insurgency.

A second major defect was that Lawrence virtually ignored the places/roles allotted to "patriotic organizations" and corporately-maintained security forces in fleshing out the U.S. internal security apparatus. This caused him to radically underestimate the scale, scope, and complexity of the repressive apparatus, thereby restricting the otherwise considerable utility of his analysis. Similarly, the exclusivity of his focus upon State agencies led him to an equally profound misinterpretation of the historical context from which had arisen the late-twentieth century phenomena he sought to illuminate.

Put bluntly, there was never a point during the entire century preceding the period Lawrence elected to discuss at which U.S. elites considered "stability and calm" to be the "normal condition of society" or insurgency "an oddity." Nor was there a point at which the security mechanisms correspondingly developed and employed by those elites was anywhere near so narrowly conceived or constructed as Lawrence implied. Quite the contrary. To appreciate the significance of these factors not only with regard to the nature of internal security operations during the period examined in *The New State Repression*, but, more importantly, the contemporary composition and objectives of the internal security complex, it is essential to review this deeper history.

Origins

The beginnings of what would eventually become the U.S. internal security complex date to 1855, when a young Scotch immigrant named Allan

Pinkerton founded the first of America's "private detection agencies" in Chicago. While the bulk of the services of this new enterprise were contracted by a half-dozen Midwestern railroads eager to control pilferage and incipient attempts to unionize by their employees, Pinkerton himself was also shortly commissioned to serve as a special agent of the federal government's Chicago postal facility.[32] Two of the most basic components of the contemporary U.S. internal security model—i.e., interlocks between governmental and private security agencies, as well as the structural overlaps joining corporate security interests to those of the State—were thus already apparent in embryonic form during the years preceding the Civil War.

The arrangement was firmed up considerably in January 1861, when Pinkerton and his "cinder dicks" supposedly unearthed a plot to assassinate president-elect Abraham Lincoln. Although no tangible evidence was ever produced to show that any such conspiracy actually existed—certainly, no one was ever indicted for participating in it—the very fact that Lincoln lived to take office was trumpeted as "proof" of the effectiveness with which Pinkerton techniques could and therefore should be employed to "protect the country from its internal enemies."[33] That the propaganda motif pioneered in this instance enjoys continuing employment as an official standard was evidenced by the Bush administration's constant refrain about countless nebulous "terrorist plots" ostensibly derailed because of the government's reliance upon draconian—and often illegal—methods of "maintaining Homeland security."

The short-run payoff for Pinkerton and his "operatives," as he called them, was that he was soon commissioned as an army major charged with helping to create what is today the Military Intelligence Division, while his firm was awarded a series of lucrative contracts to fulfill espionage/counterespionage functions for the Union army.[34] Plainly, this interpenetration of military and civilian domains in conducting what would now be termed counterintelligence operations—at least one friendly biographer has described certain of Pinkerton's activities as amounting even then to "counter insurgency"—gave rudimentary form to another vital component of the current U.S. internal security model.[35]

In 1871, the broader governmental reliance upon private entities to provide its "investigative capacity" was further concretized when the Pinkerton Agency was contracted to assume this role for the newly formed Department of Justice, thereby establishing a formal relationship sustained over several decades.[36] More generally, however, official needs of this sort were met by channeling requisite operations through corporate sponsors, especially the railroads, by then longtime Pinkerton clients with which federal authorities were entering into increasingly direct collaboration as a means of rapidly expanding and consolidating the U.S. transportation system on a continental scale.[37]

High on the list of priorities posited by corporate and governmental officials alike was containment of the expense entailed in their joint endeavor by forestalling a growing effort to unionize railway workers. To achieve the desired results, Pinkerton increased the number of his agency's offices/operatives dramatically and adopted the "French method" of cultivating a nationwide network of informers, thereby creating a mechanism with which union organizers and/or "sympathizers" were systematically identified and eliminated from the workforce.[38] Pinkerton's innovation in this regard unquestionably prefigured the FBI's enthusiastic utilization of the same technique (by 1972, more than 7,400 snitches were reporting to the Bureau through its "Ghetto Informant Program" alone).[39]

Even before the intelligence apparatus was fully formed, Pinkerton began to complement it with "uniformed security personnel" hired to serve as company police forces. Thus, to the threats of summary firings and blacklisting was added physical violence in the form of clubs and firearms wielded by what unionists soon referred to as "railroad bulls."[40] Moreover, given de facto, but nonetheless official, governmental policies encouraging close cooperation between local police agencies and their corporately-employed counterparts, organizers also faced the prospect of being arrested on utterly spurious charges, then fined, not infrequently imprisoned, and sometimes executed after being processed through what were at best pro forma judicial procedures.[41]

As the struggle over wages and working conditions nonetheless spread and intensified during the economic depression of the 1870s, the number of strikes and labor-related demonstrations multiplied rapidly.[42] So pervasive, sustained, and potentially destabilizing to the status quo had such industrial disruptions become before the end of the decade that U.S. elites, both corporate and governmental, had come to view them as adding up to a genuine insurgency of a sort unlikely to end in the foreseeable future—if ever.[43] Consequently, it was concluded that the institutionalization of a repressive capacity capable of going well beyond that which the Pinkertons had by then established was required.[44]

Officially, the most overt responses were a raft of statutes criminalizing syndicalist and others among the most promising approaches to union organizing, and, in 1878, creation of the National Guard Association, which coordinated formation of military units at the state level. From the outset, the primary purpose of this new system, which supplanted the old mode of

locally-organized militias, was to quell "civil disturbances," especially those
arising from "labor agitation and unrest."[45] Largely underwritten by contributions from the "business community," which displayed a particularly keen
interest in building/stocking armories,[46] the Guard had by 1892 been deployed
in more than a dozen states to forcibly break at least thirty-three strikes.[47]
Thereafter, the pace of such interventions steadily increased, a trend that did
not begin to abate until after World War II.[48]

Repressive as they were in both fact and potential, however, such governmental initiatives were greatly surpassed by those of the Pinkertons and their
corporate clientele, which expanded during the 1870s to include significant
portions of the mining, steel, lumber, textile, and other industries.[49] In 1884,
the agency added what were quite literally armies, complete with their own
arsenals, to the service package it offered any company willing to pick up the
tab. So enthusiastic was the response that not only were the Pinkertons field-
ing "more men than the U.S. Army" by 1890,[50] but scores of copycat firms had
been chartered to ply the increasingly profitable trade. [merge paragraphs?]
Twenty of the more significant imitators—among them the U.S. Detective
Agency, the American Detective Agency, the Illinois Detective Agency, the
Standard Detective Agency, and the Veterans Police Patrol and Detective
Agency—were based in Chicago alone.[51] Other heavy-hitters included the
St. Louis-based Thiel Detective Agency; Baldwin-Felts in Roanoke, Virginia;
Mooney-Boland in San Francisco; as well as the Vigilant Detective Agency
in New York. Most of these firms maintained branch offices in other cities,
where lesser agencies also flourished.

While the total number of troops ultimately contracted or otherwise hired
to meet corporate demands for "labor adjustment" is probably unknowable,
it can be said with certainty that they were decisive in transforming conflicts
over workers' rights in the U.S. into outright "labor wars."[52] As a result,
to quote labor historian Val Lorwin, "American workers had to fight [far]
bloodier battles" than their European counterparts "for the right of unions to
exist and function."[53] Even so decidedly unradical an interpreter as Richard
Hofstadter is forced to concur, observing that despite "the fact that no major
American labor organization has ever advocated violence" or, with very few
exceptions, even so much as embraced a "militant class conflict philosophy,"
the U.S., uniquely among "advanced" societies, has evidenced "a maximum
of industrial violence."[54]

Transition

It's true, as apologists declaim, that Congress passed the Anti-Pinkerton Act
of 1893 in response to widespread public outrage at the carnage ensuing

from a pitched battle between an army of 367 Pinkerton men and a much larger body of angry workers during a strike of the Carnegie steel works in Homestead, Pennsylvania, the previous year.[55] The effect was mainly palliative, however. While the federal government prohibited itself from further employment of any company offering "mercenary, quasi-military forces as strikebreakers and armed guards" for hire, thus ending the longstanding relationship between the Justice Department and the Pinkertons,[56] the prerogatives of state governments in this connection were left ambiguous. The Act was silent, moreover, on the issue of whether the corporations actually hiring such forces should suffer any penalty at all, thereby implicitly affirming their "right" to continue doing so.[57]

That being so, it is unsurprising that more than forty years later, when a subcommittee headed by Wisconsin's progressive Senator Robert LaFollette conducted an extensive investigation of private policing in the U.S., it found that the situation had worsened dramatically since the Anti-Pinkerton law had been effected. In 1939, the subcommittee reported that union busting had become an even more violent, entrenched, and ubiquitous enterprise than in the 1890s.[58] The number of contract agencies providing antiunion "services" had swollen to over 200[59]—including, in addition to those already mentioned, such more recent entries into the field as the Bergoff Brothers Strike Service and Labor Adjusters (renamed "Bergoff Brothers Services" in 1933) and a New York firm headed by James Farley (known as "King of the Strikebreakers"[60])—and there was a growing tendency among major corporations to form their own in-house guard and espionage departments "to achieve the same results obtainable through the employment of industrial detective and strikebreaking agencies."[61]

In sum, the Anti-Pinkerton Act did nothing to curtail Pinkerton-style operations in the private sphere. On the other hand, by ostensibly denying the government access to the services of contract agencies, it provided a near-perfect rationale for accelerating the construction of a State apparatus dedicated to the same purposes. At the federal level, the investigative capacity provided by the Pinkertons was replaced in 1908 by that of the Justice Department's own Bureau of Investigation (BoI, later known as the FBI).[62] By and large, the individual states emphasized increases in the number/size of National Guard units and formation of state police units to provide additional paramilitary punch.[63] Considerable weight was also placed upon building up explicitly political units—"red squads"—within municipal police departments.[64]

While this turn-of-the-century surge in the repressive capacity of the State has often been miscast as signifying something of a tectonic shift in domestic power relations—from business to government, as it were, and thence to "the people"—it was precisely the opposite: There was never a sense in which the instrumentalities of State repression were divorced from those maintained by the corporations. Quite apart from the previously noted role of business in funding the National Guard, and the Guard's subsequent role as strike-breakers, the inseparability of State and corporate police functions is readily apparent. In many states, the supposed distinction was dissolved entirely when private police personnel were deputized, individually or en masse, and thus endowed with an aura of official legitimacy/authority even though they remained on the payroll of their corporate employers and their operational responsibilities remained unchanged.[65]

In terms of local policing, LaFollette's subcommittee, although it was otherwise careful to skirt the issue of governmental involvement in anti-labor violence, was unable to avoid remarking upon the extent of corporate engagement in "the reprehensible practice of hiring municipal policemen for strike duty."[66] Still more significantly, as Frank Donner observes, the red squads were, without exception, "typified by close relations with the business community."[67] Among the more glaring examples is the Los Angeles Police Department, wherein a unit later known as the "Criminal Conspiracy Section" (CCS) served for decades as "the operational arm of the Merchants and Manufacturers Association (M&M), a confederation of over 80 percent of [the city's] business firms, whose stated purpose was to 'break the back of organized labor.'"[68]

As for the Justice Department's Bureau of Investigation, it was from 1921–24 directed by William J. Burns, founder and still owner of a Chicago-based Pinkerton clone called the Burns International Detective Agency, and included several former Burns operatives among its personnel.[69] Primarily engaged from its inception in "antisubversive" work, the BoI could by the time of Burns's tenure count among its laurels a vicious offensive against the Industrial Workers of the World (IWW, or "Wobblies," as it was often called)—by far the largest genuinely radical union in U.S. history—during World War I,[70] as well as the nationwide "Palmer Raids" targeting "alien anarchists" during the so-called Red Scare of 1919–20.[71] Under his leadership, the Bureau not only continued to target the IWW and other radical organizations, but broadened its operational scope to include such relatively conservative unions as those belonging to the American Federation of Labor (AFL).[72]

As Attorney General Harry Daugherty proudly announced after obtaining an injunction to halt a railway strike in 1922, his department could always be counted upon to "use the powers of government to prevent the labor unions of this country from destroying the open shop."[73] It is difficult to imagine a clearer or more accurate reflection than the AG's statement of the fact that those in charge of governmental police and intelligence agencies perceived their interests/purposes as being identical to those of their private sector colleagues. A transition had occurred during the early 20th century, but it was not towards "a more democratic means of maintaining public order." Instead, it embodied a vast expansion of the mechanisms of social, political, and economic control possessed by U.S. elites, all of it at public rather than corporate expense.

Tactical Continuities

Daugherty and Burns were forced to resign during the summer of 1924, when they were exposed as having ordered BoI agents to spy upon and disseminate false information about progressive legislators viewed as being "anti-business."[74] Replacing Burns as BoI director was a young man—he was only 29 at the time—who would retain the position until his death on May 2, 1972. During the course of his nearly fifty-year career as top "G-Man," J(ohn) Edgar Hoover would become the key figure in the evolution of the U.S. internal security system, and, contrary to endlessly-repeated claims that the intent behind his hiring was to "depoliticize the BoI,"[75] the direction in which he'd move it was, based on the record he'd already amassed, readily predictable.

The rise of J. Edgar Hoover was nothing if not meteoric. Initially hired as a Justice Department clerk in July 1917, he was placed in charge of the "counterradical" unit in the department's Enemy Alien Registration Section in December the same year.[76] Over the next two years, his activities became so thoroughly intertwined with those of the BoI that in early 1919 he was appointed head of the Bureau's Radical Division, which he rechristened as the General Intelligence Division (GID) a year later, meanwhile accomplishing such astonishing feats as overseeing compilation of an "index" of files on more than 200,000 supposed "subversives" in barely three months.[77] So impressive was his performance that, although he would retain immediate control of the GID until assuming the BoI directorship three years later, Hoover also served as Burns's assistant director, beginning in 1921.[78]

While much of Hoover's early success can be accounted for by his undeniable organizational skills—he's been often and quite accurately described as a "bureaucratic genius"[79]—there was far more to it than that. He was at least peripherally involved in the BoI's 48-city onslaught against the IWW in 1917,[80] as well as the so-called slacker raids, a massive cross-country dragnet to apprehend men evading military conscription undertaken a year later (ironically, Hoover himself, given his studious avoidance of active military duty, might be said to have qualified as a "slacker").[81] By 1919, Hoover's direct experience with such operations was sufficient that, according to biographer Richard Gid Powers, he "was in complete charge" of the Palmer Raids.[82] So too, the extensive counterradical/anti-labor operations conducted by the GID from 1921–24.[83]

It is commonly mentioned that among lasting effects on the FBI of Hoover's early years is that the cross-referenced filing system he created for the GID was so well-conceived that it continues to serve as the basis for the Bureau's—and, presumably, the Department of Homeland Security's—ever more expansive data storage and retrieval system.[84] Less remarked upon, or ignored altogether, are the ways in which he consciously adapted for Bureau usage a broad range of time-tested Pinkerton techniques, including many of the ugliest. In the main, these had by the 1970s become standard fare in domestic counterintelligence/internal security operations, and undoubtedly remain so today.

Allan Pinkerton was, for instance, a strong proponent of "vigilance organizations"—less elegantly referred to as "vigilantes"—which he viewed as a useful tool with which to illustrate sentiments supposedly embraced by the "law-abiding" and/or "patriotic" sectors of society, as well as an important dimension of his national intelligence network and ready source of volunteer manpower when needed to support his field operatives.[85] The BoI followed suit, issuing "police-type badges" inscribed "Auxiliary to the U.S. Justice Department" to members of the American Protective League (APL), a "patriotic citizens organization" engaged in continuous vigilante actions against those accused of "disloyalty" during and for a while after World War I.[86] These vigilante men would then also provide much of the muscle deployed by the Bureau against the IWW, during the slacker raids, and, most significantly in terms of Hoover, in conducting the Palmer raids as well.[87]

The APL was largely responsible for the speed with which Hoover was able to so rapidly assemble his subversives files in 1918; its quarter-million members had for more than a year been submitting a veritable torrent of reports on suspected radicals (as had smaller groups like the National Security League and the American Defense Society).[88] In 1919, as the wartime vigilante groups began to dissolve, Hoover solicited the newly founded American Legion to replace them as an information source, thereby establishing a nationwide network of regular informants sustained into the present moment.[89] Numerous other organizations, including the ACLU, have been drawn into similar relationships over the years.[90] Among the more recent examples is the Anti-Defamation League of B'nai Brith, which, beginning in the early 1980s, conducted intelligence operations against scores of what it for various reasons deemed to be "anti-Semitic groups and individuals," sharing the results not only with the FBI and several local police agencies in the U.S., but with the Israeli and South African intelligence services.[91]

Pinkerton is also known either to have used vigilantes as surrogates in the assassination of select targets, or to have utilized their very existence as a convenient mask with which to disguise the fact that the murders were committed by his own operatives.[92] Hoover again appears to have followed suit, as with the 1918 lynching of IWW organizer Frank Little by APL members, agents posing as APL members, or some combination of the two.[93] Similar circumstances pertain in the lynching in 1919 of another IWW organizer— and highly-decorated World War I combat veteran—Wesley Everest, although the vigilante organization involved or impersonated on this occasion was the American Legion (which went on to indulge in such an orgy of "patriotic" violence during the early 1920s that it has been seriously compared to the protonazi Freikorps in Germany).[94]

An important variation on the theme concerns what Frank Kitson termed "pseudo-gangs," i.e. ., entities created and sometimes entirely rostered by operatives under the guise of being bona fide political organizations. It seems likely that Pinkerton pioneered the technique—he implied as much in a letter written towards the end of his life—in bringing about the 1866 lynchings of the train-robbing Reno gang in Indiana.[95] Given the murkiness inherently attending such matters, it's usually difficult to discern an entirely bogus group from one co-opted by police agents. It is documented, however, that an FBI operative named Joe Burton created several phony "Maoist" organizations around the country—e.g., the "Red Star Collective" in Tampa, Florida— between 1972 and 1975.[96]

Similarly, whether they were bogus or coopted, relationships between FBI counterintelligence personnel and such extreme right wing groups as the White Knights of the Ku Klux Klan,[97] the Secret Army Organization (SAO),[98] and the Legion of Justice[99]—all of which engaged in systematic violence against dissidents targeted for neutralization by the Bureau during the 1960s and 1970s—have been demonstrated. Yet another contender in this regard was Lyndon LaRouche's "National Caucus of Labor Committees," which, as Lawrence recounted, "emerged as an ostensibly Marxist organization" during the late 1970s, then undertook a campaign to "disrupt the left with physical violence" for several years before LaRouche announced its literal embrace of "fascist" ideology.[100]

The practice of placing "labor spies" into unions for intelligence-gathering purposes was also adapted by Hoover for Bureau usage on a scale of which Pinkerton himself could only dream. One of the earliest examples began in 1919, when Hoover ordered the infiltration of Marcus Garvey's United Negro

Improvement Association (UNIA) as a means of gathering information ultimately used to deport the Jamaican-born advocate of black self-sufficiency.[101]
Among other things, the operation shows how Hoover, a virulent racist—he
allowed the hiring of no black agents until the very end of his tenure as FBI
director, while, privately, he referred to Martin Luther King, Jr., as "the bur-
rhead"[102]—was already widening the scope of the Bureau's repressive scope
to encompass not only enforcement of the status quo in terms of class relations, but of racial hierarchy as well.[103]

By the early 1960s, the latter emphasis, formalized under the heading
"Racial Matters" and assigned to the FBI's Division Five (Domestic Intelligence)—more specifically to the Division's Internal Security Section (ISS),
as the old GID had been redesignated during the 1940s[104]—had resulted in
the infiltration of virtually every black and Latino political organization in the
U.S. and Puerto Rico.[105] Nor had the ISS ignored either organized labor or the
broader left. Under a program dubbed COMINFIL, unions were infiltrated as
a matter of course[106]—albeit, the Longshoreman's Union suffered inordinate
attention from the mid-1930s through the mid-1950s, amidst a Bureau effort
to neutralize its president, former IWW member Harry Bridges[107]—while the
Communist Party USA (CP), Socialist Workers Party (SWP) and other such
organizations were literally inundated during the same period (in 1961, it was
discovered that in some locales a majority of the CP's ostensible membership
was comprised of FBI infiltrators and informants).[108]

After the so-called New Left began to materialize during the early 1960s,
the same procedure was followed, perhaps even more extensively. In 1976,
a Senate committee chaired by Idaho's Frank Church investigated the FBI's
earlier-mentioned COINTELPRO operations and concluded that literally
thousands of groups ranging from national organizations like Students for a
Democratic Society (SDS) and the National Mobilization to End the War in
Vietnam ("Mobe") to student clubs and local church groups had been infiltrated.[109] Although the Bureau claimed that COINTELPRO was terminated in
1971,[110] exactly the same pattern of infiltration and disruption was evident in
its operations against the American Indian Movement during the mid-1970s[111]
and "investigation" of the Committee in Solidarity of El Salvador (CISPES)
a decade later.[112]

An especially insidious aspect of infiltration, as is repeatedly highlighted in
memoranda written by FBI personnel involved in COINTELPRO-New Left, is
that it has the effect of inducing "paranoia" within targeted organizations, i.e.
as members become increasingly worried about whether—or which—other
members are actually police agents, the bonds of trust essential to retaining
organizational cohesion simply dissolve.[113] In such circumstances, the process

is often accelerated by utilization of a technique known as "bad-jacketing" or "snitch-jacketing" in which infiltrators actively seek to create suspicions that legitimate activists—usually those assessed as being key leaders of the organization targeted—are themselves police agents, thereby nullifying their political credibility and effectiveness.[114] The list of oppositional organizations that have disintegrated under the pressure of such tactics is staggering.

Infiltrators employing methods of this sort are no longer merely infiltrators, of course. To the extent that they engage in activities intended to disrupt the functioning of targeted organizations, rather than simply gleaning information from their presence within them, they are more accurately viewed as agents provocateurs.[115] Not infrequently, this variety of operative is assigned to go far beyond bad-jacketing and other such commonplace tactics, seeking to incite intra- or intergroup violence and/or entice bona fide activists to engage in actions which would either result in their imprisonment or serve in the public mind to justify State violence against them.[116] Once again, the Pinkertons pioneered the use of provocateurs for such purposes in the U.S.—notably against the Molly Maguires during the 1870s and the Western Federation of Miners (WFM) at the turn of the century[117]—and once again J. Edgar Hoover clearly followed their lead.

While, as with the creation of pseudo-gangs, the details of such operations are for obvious reasons a closely-guarded secret, it is known that by 1970 the FBI had inserted no fewer than forty outright agents provocateurs into the Black Panther Party alone, while others—how many is unclear—were operating within a plethora of other targeted groups.[118] The impact was devastating: provocateur Claude Hubert was instrumental in fomenting a dispute between the Black Panthers and the US organization in southern California resulting in the deaths of Los Angeles chapter leaders Bunchy Carter and Jon Huggins in January 1969, as well as at least four other Panthers over the next several months;[119] provocateur William O'Neal played a pivotal role in the December 1969 assassinations of Illinois Panther leaders Fred Hampton and Mark Clark;[120] provocateur Julius C. Butler gave false testimony during the 1971 murder trial of Los Angeles Panther leader Geronimo Pratt (Geronimo ji Jaga), a matter greatly facilitating Pratt's spending the next 27 years in prison for a crime he did not commit.[121] Many more such stories could be recited.

Structural Evolution

It is important to bear in mind that all the while Hoover was presiding over the FBI's institutionalization and refinement of the above-described Pinkerton methods, he was busily erecting the structure through which they could be employed with ever-greater comprehensiveness and efficiency. For one thing, there was the growth of the Bureau itself: when Hoover took charge, he was allotted only 441 agents and 216 clerks;[122] by the time of his death there were 8,631 agents and well over ten thousand support staff providing everything from clerical services to laboratory analyses (the latter tallies include neither the several thousand individuals contracted to perform certain functions, both mundane and specialized, nor the tens of thousands of informants and infiltrators—voluntary, paid, or coerced—upon whom the fulfillment of the FBI's mission depended).[123]

The growth of the Bureau is only part of the equation, however. From the outset, Hoover initiated a process of concretizing the interlocks between the BoI and state/local police agencies by installing picked Bureau personnel as police chiefs and state police commanders in key localities. While this entailed the BoI men relinquishing their federal positions, it was a given that relations with their former colleagues would remain intact, and that the "cooperation" of their agencies would thus be both enhanced and ensured.[124] Concomitantly, Hoover set out to gradually assume control of the International Association of Police Chiefs (IAPC), perhaps the most influential organization in the U.S. with regard to the formation of "law enforcement policy."[125] That the campaign was successful is reflected in the 1961 selection of FBI assistant director Quinn Tamm to serve as chief executive of the IACP (which counted over 6,200 members by 1970).[126]

Still deeper inroads were made when, in 1935, Hoover established the National Police Academy at the FBI's Quantico, Virginia, training facility.[127] Since then, several hundred local cops have been selected each year to undergo general training—including a serious dose of ideological indoctrination—in what the Bureau views as the proper approach to policing.[128] Specialized training sequences, mostly concerning methods and techniques applicable to the context of political repression, are also provided on a still more selective basis.[129] Thus, the FBI has systematically implanted itself over the past 75 years in every municipal police department of significance.[130] Nor have state police forces been neglected, as is evidenced in the appearance by the late-1960s of "mini-FBIs" within or adjunct to every such agency in the U.S. (e.g., the California attorney general's Criminal Investigation and Identification unit [CII]).[131]

The evolutionary capstone to this process of inculcating ever-closer working relationships between the FBI's Internal Security Section and state/municipal police Red Squads came in 1980 with formation of the first "Joint Terrorism Task Force" (JTTF),[132] an entity rostered in roughly equal measure from political intelligence personnel assigned to the Bureau's New York field office and the New York Police Department's Bureau of Special Services (BOSS).[133] Within a decade, similar arrangements had been effected by all 56 FBI field offices, located in every major city in the U.S. and it territories (the Bureau also maintains "resident agencies" in well over a hundred smaller municipalities).[134] To this has been directly coupled the proliferation of SWAT teams; the first was formed by the LAPD in 1966 and, shortly after it commenced operations targeting the Black Panther Party three years later,[135] such units were added to the FBI's inventory of repressive mechanisms.[136]

Paralleling, or even exceeding, Hoover's honing of the "sharp end" capabilities lodged in the State internal security "community" was his steady development of its capacity to collect, collate, and share political intelligence. Although it is standard Bureau lore that he suspended intelligence-gathering on radicals from 1924 until he was ordered to reinstitute it during a meeting with Franklin D. Roosevelt on August 25, 1936,[137] such operations continued without interruption throughout the period. Although Hoover refrained from assigning his agents to open any new investigations of "subversives" until the latter year, those already underway when he became director remained ongoing.[138] In addition, as historian Curt Gentry has emphasized, he'd "secretly made other arrangements which provided him with the information he desired."[139]

In part, these devolved upon the Bureau's ever-deepening liaisons with the Red Squads, as well as its cultivation of "spontaneous" reporting by the American Legion and other such groups.[140] Of at least equal significance, Hoover secured a reserve officer's commission in the army's Military Intelligence Division (MID) in 1922.[141] On this basis, he forged a back-channel relationship with those in charge of an extensive domestic surveillance program secretly run by the army, through which the FBI received a steady flow of information on "subversive activities" for the next three decades or more.[142] A similar arrangement was worked out with the Office of Naval Intelligence (ONI) at about the same time, albeit it was left to Hoover's eventual associate director, Clyde Tolson, to accept the requisite commission as a reserve naval officer.[143]

Further extending the web, Hoover began at least as early as 1923, when he engineered the placement of his own assistant, George Ruch, as head of labor espionage for the Frick Coal Co.,[144] to arrange the installation of carefully-chosen FBI personnel to direct such operations for any number of other corporations. By the time of his death, the "security chiefs of Texas Instruments of Dallas, Lockheed at Sunnyvale, California, the giant Wynn-Dixie supermarket chain, and Reynolds Metals, to name only a few, were former Hoover minions."[145] Relatedly, former agents were often assisted in starting their own detective and/or "security consulting" firms; although there are numerous examples, the most noteworthy is probably the now-giant Wackenhut Security firm, founded by ex-FBI man George Wackenhut in 1954.[146]

By 1970, the information deriving from this increasingly-vast array of sources had been compiled in files, the storage of which encumbered some 300,000 square feet of floor space at the FBI headquarters facility alone[147] (field offices and resident agencies also maintained files which were generally, but not entirely, duplicative of those at FBIHQ;[148] the tally is also exclusive of Hoover's extensive "personal" files, and an unknown but substantial quantity of "June Mail"[149] and "Do Not File" files associated with many of the Bureau's more flagrantly illegal operations[150]). Although none of this material was yet committed to electronic format,[151] relatively efficient systems were in place for sharing much of the FBI's intelligence data with other federal agencies, as well as "subscribing" police agencies across the country (undoubtedly, private agencies were also privy in some respects, but the details remain opaque).[152]

At the core of this vast, constantly growing, and intricately organized proliferation of paper remained the current versions of Hoover's original subversives files, subdivided into several cross-referenced indices.[153] Among the most significant of these were the Security Index, formally established under the heading "Custodial Detention Index" in 1939 and renamed in 1943, containing the particulars on some 26,000 individuals slated for immediate internment in concentration camps on the basis of a presidential declaration of necessity;[154] in 1971, with repeal of the Emergency Detention Act, a subpart of the 1950 Internal Security Act which afforded legal cover during the years it was in effect, the Security Index was simply rechristened the "Administrative Index" (ADEX) and maintained without interruption.[155]

Other noteworthy indices include the Communist Index, assembled in 1948 and redesignated as the "Reserve Index" in 1960;[156] this was coupled to an "Attorney General's List" of politically objectionable organizations, initially compiled during the mid-1940s and technically abolished in 1974 (actually, both the list and the index were simply recast under the rubric of "terrorism").[157] In 1967, a "Rabble-Rouser Index" was created; renamed the "Agitator Index" in 1968, it included both a "Black Nationalist Photo Album"—renamed the "Extremist Album" in 1972—and a "Key Activist Album," used in identifying prime COINTELPRO targets (in 1974, the Agitators Index was merged with the Reserve Index and thereafter maintained under another heading).[158]

Another early innovation credited to Hoover was establishment, in 1932, of the FBI's own laboratory, touted—then and now—as providing a cutting edge to "scientific law enforcement."[159] Popularly referred to as the "national crime lab," the facility was/is designed to "identify and analyze blood, hair, firearms, paint, handwritings, typewriters, inks, and other mysterious bits of evidence" gathered not only by federal investigators, but those of state/local police agencies throughout the U.S., thereby further solidifying the Bureau's working relationships in those circles.[160] Predictably, given the well-nurtured mystique attending "scientific methods" in the public perception, evidence vetted by the FBI lab has generally proven decisive in obtaining guilty verdicts against those accused of criminal activities (a result enthusiastically embraced by police and prosecutors alike)[161]

While there were always suspicions, especially among radicals, that the lab was capable not only of analyzing evidence, but of producing or falsifying it, and that it did so in certain instances—e.g., the "forgery by typewriter" attributed to the FBI in the espionage case pursued against alleged communist cum former State Department official Alger Hiss during the late 1940s[162]—it wasn't until the mid-1990s that it would finally be conclusively determined that the Bureau's forensic experts had long been tailoring their lab reports and courtroom testimony to fit the needs of police and prosecutors.[163] Not only was evidence routinely misrepresented as being inculpatory, it was sometimes manufactured outright, while exculpatory evidence was systematically withheld from defendants and their attorneys.[164]

Even when such intentional distortion was not apparent, a remarkable degree of ineptitude was shown to prevail among FBI technical personnel; in 1995, a 22 percent error rate was revealed with regard to something as basic as fingerprint identification, for instance.[165] The upshot, of course, is that thousands—more likely tens of thousands—of those comprising the vastly overburdened U.S. prison population were wrongly convicted.[166] Nonetheless, the Bureau continues to enjoy the reputation, attained during the Hoover years, of being "America's premier crime-fighting agency," its lab as being "the best of its kind in the world," and evidence carrying "the FBI seal of approval" as being iron-clad proof that accused persons are truly guilty as charged.[167]

The durability of the Bureau's image is owed primarily to the functioning of an in-house propaganda component. Called the "Crime Records Division" (CRD), this innocuous-sounding unit is best known for preparing and disseminating the FBI's annual Uniform Crime Report, and such "trade" periodicals as Law Enforcement Bulletin and, beginning in the early 1970s, Domestic Terrorist Digest.[168] A far more important purpose of the CRD was from the onset, however, to implant in the public mind a fabulous mythology concerning the supposed efficiency, integrity, and valor embodied in the Bureau.

To this end, FBI personnel, along with contract professionals like Courtney Ryley Cooper, ghostwrote well over a hundred magazine articles published under Hoover's byline in such popular venues as *American Magazine*, *American Mercury*, and *Reader's Digest*,[169] and all four of the books attributed to him.[170] Similarly, the CRD "facilitated" the writing of a lengthy string of flattering "studies" of the Bureau and its director—Cooper's *Ten Thousand Public Enemies* (1935), Frederick R. Collins's *The F.B.I. in Peace and War* (1943), Don Whitehead's *The FBI Story* (1956) and *Attack on Terror* (1970), Andrew Tully's *The FBI's Most Famous Cases* (1965), and Ralph De Toledano's *J. Edgar Hoover: The Man in His Time* (1973), to cite but six among dozens of similar screeds.[171] It also undertook production of several widely-distributed comic strips and pulp magazines like *Feds* and *G-Man*. The Bureau even sponsored a national "Junior G-Man" club, complete badges, board games, and G-Man trading cards.[172]

The deluge of print was greatly amplified through the electronic media. Beginning in 1936, Hoover personally approved the airing of weekly radio programs like *Gangbusters*, *This Is Your FBI*, and, a bit later, *I Was a Communist for the FBI*. There was also a stream of feature films, starting with *Public Hero Number One* and *G-Men* (both released in 1935), and continuing through into the 1960s with movies like *The FBI Story* (1959), over which Hoover exercised veritable veto power in terms of casting and screenplays (CRD personnel were often assigned to perform script revisions and on-location "technical consulting").[173] The same pertained to monthly shorts such as *Crime Doesn't Pay*, and, with the advent of television, weekly series like *I Led Three Lives* (1953–56)[174] and *The FBI* (1965–81), over which FBI control extended even to the questions of corporate sponsorship.[175]

Equally insidious was the CRD's penetration of the news media. Although Hoover had been cultivating relationships with selected journalists since the day he assumed the directorship, and probably earlier, the FBI's ability to use apparently objective reportage to shape public opinion never really took hold until his highly-publicized declaration of the first nationwide "War on Crime" in 1934,[176] and the opportunistic enlistment of figures like Cooper and radio newsman Walter Winchell in promoting the director himself as a celebrity.[177] By the mid-1950s, the FBI maintained a stable of at least 300 "friendly" or "cooperating" reporters at major media outlets—the real number was likely much greater at the time, and has grown steadily larger in the decades since—all of them willing to regularly publish or broadcast under their own names "news stories" produced by the CRD.[178]

The arrangement served, and continues to serve, the dual purpose of allowing the Bureau to continuously burnish its own image and to disseminate as "fact" derogatory, and often utterly false, information intended to discredit ideologically-defined targets (these are known to include congressional critics and honest journalists as well as radicals). Indeed, until at least as late as the early 1980s, when it was no doubt simply renamed, the CRD administered a formal "Mass Media Program" through which to accomplish the latter objective.[179] Small wonder, then, that the Bureau's reputation has proven well-nigh impervious to revelations such as the disclosure of its COINTELPRO operations during the mid-1970s and exposure of the crime lab's wholesale falsification of evidence twenty years later. During his tenure as FBI director, J. Edgar Hoover had built not a merely government bureau, but, as chronicler Sanford J. Ungar quite aptly described it, "a monolith."[180]

Consolidation

While it is fair to say that Hoover had put virtually all of its most vital elements in place by 1972, initiation of the process through which the structure of the U.S. internal security apparatus has been consolidated in its present form was located elsewhere. As was mentioned earlier, the influence of Louis Giuffrida was signal in this respect, especially in view of his subsequent directorship of FEMA. In many ways more significant, however, was a plan advanced in 1970 by a young White House aide named Tom Charles Huston to lift whatever restrictions remained on intelligence gathering for domestic security purposes and establish a permanent committee of ranking officials to coordinate all operations undertaken by the FBI, CIA, NSA, Military Intelligence Agency, and other such entities.[181]

Although Hoover, balking at the relinquishment of direct control over any operations in which the Bureau was involved, managed to thwart actualization of the Huston Plan in 1971,[182] and despite its being publicly savaged during Senate hearings in both 1973 and 1975,[183] the contours of what Huston proposed are immediately obvious in the structure of today's Department of Homeland Security. Moreover, the implications of Huston's role in laying out a "total package" approach to internal security went far beyond his formally-articulated plan. Even then a budding neocon—today he is, among other things, a regular contributor to the *American Spectator*—he, like fellow White House staffer Dick Cheney, was an early and influential advocate of the idea that the domestic security functions of governmental agencies should be augmented by a "maximal" program of security privatization.[184] This proposition, too, can be seen to have taken root.

In 1970, there were roughly 290,000 "regularly-employed private guards and detectives" in the U.S.[185] Today, there are at least ten times as many, and the number is growing steadily.[186] Although the Pinkerton and Burns agencies remained by far the largest firms of their sort until they were absorbed—in 1999 and 2000 respectively—by Securitas AB, a Swedish security corporation now operating in the U.S.,[187] Wackenhut better represents the industry's explosive rate of growth, mushrooming from some 3,500 employees in 1970 to more than 35,000 twenty years later (a 1000 percent increase).[188]Purchased by the Danish security firm Group 4 Falck A/S in 2002, Wackenhut has been rebranded as "G4S Secure Solutions USA" and has well over 40,000 people on its payroll.[189]

While there were fewer than a thousand contract security firms in 1970, there were over 10,000 a quarter-century later,[190] including outfits like "Fidelifacts," a 22-office operation advertising itself as being "The National Organization of Ex-FBI Agents."[191] There has even been a reappearance of firms specializing in outright strikebreaking, a business generally believed to have disappeared after the 1936 Byrnes Act made it a felony to "transport persons in interstate commerce with the intent to employ to obstruct peaceful picketing."[192] To give one egregious example, Vance International Security deployed the men of its so-called Assets Protection Team (APT) "as shock troops for the Pittston Coal Group. Inc., in its protracted and bitter struggle with the United Mine Workers" in West Virginia in 1989–90,[193] as well as the 1992 and 1996 United Auto Workers strikes at the Caterpillar plant in East Peoria, Illinois,[194] a steel workers strike at an Alcoa plant in Tennessee in 1993,[195] and a joint Newspaper Guild/Teamsters strike of Detroit's two daily papers, the *News* and the *Free Press*, in 1994.[196] All told, Vance APTs played a role in breaking more than 600 strikes between 1984 and 2003.[197]

Even the fact that there is now a force of roughly two million fielded by private entities providing various "security services"[198] doesn't really encompass the reality, excluding as it does firms offering such services in the form of an outright military capacity to both governmental and major corporate consumers. While there are now a number of such contractors, including DynCorp, Triple Canopy, and Military Professional Resources, Inc. (MPRI),[199] the most prominent by far is Blackwater Worldwide (recently renamed "Xe Security"), a multibillion dollar enterprise which claims a deployable force of 21,000, comprised largely of former members of army ranger and special forces units (including Delta Force), marine force recon and scout-sniper units, and navy SEAL teams.[200]

Best known for its lethal operations in Iraq—Blackwater gunmen were responsible for, among numerous other atrocities, the September 16, 2007 massacre of seventeen unarmed Iraqis in Baghdad's Nisoor Square[201]— the firm has also received contracts to carry out air support and combat assignments in Afghanistan,[202] to provide the sharp end capacity for an alleg-edly-canceled CIA assassination program,[203] and carry out an unknown num-ber of unspecified missions for the Departments of Defense and State as well as an assortment of other federal agencies (two-thirds of the firm's contracts have been awarded on a no-bid basis, and many of them are classified).[204] Whether such missions include provision of "expert interrogators"—i.e., specialists in torture—to "debrief" those designated as "suspected terrorists" by the CIA is presently unknown. It is clear, however, that several of Black-water's counterparts have been contracted to provide such "services."[205]

Domestically, Blackwater has been contracted to perform a range of func-tions, including the delivery of special operations training to select groups of military personnel, and the training of police SWAT units in the arts of sniping and hand-to-hand combat, as well as tactics appropriate to counterin-surgency warfare.[206] The firm also conducts hands-on operations in the U.S., as when FEMA contracted it to dispatch several combat teams at a rate of $240,000 per day to secure petrochemical and other governmental/corporate facilities in and around New Orleans in the wake of Hurricane Katrina.[207] It's worth noting that the Blackwater teams arrived immediately—several days before the first of FEMA's own personnel arrived on-scene to begin providing humanitarian assistance to people trapped in the devastated city[208]—and it is widely believed by local residents that they were responsible for the shooting deaths of an undetermined but potentially large number of civilians.[209]

While responsibility for day-to-day enforcement of the status quo has been increasingly assigned to roving patrols of rent-a-cops and fixed-position security personnel assuring the sanctity of everything from upscale shop-ping malls to gated communities,[210] state and local police forces have hardly remained stagnant. In 1970, the number of police in the U.S. was a little over 300,000;[211] by 1990, the total had swollen to a little over 554,000;[212] today, after repeated initiatives to put yet "another 100,000 cops on the street," there are more than 730,000 (adding in special police—e.g., campus cops—and federal police forces like the park rangers brings the total to nearly 837,000, second only to China's 1.78 million).[213] It has, moreover, been officially sug-gested that the number will increase by a further 99,000 or so by 2016.[214]

By-and-large, this considerable expansion of police capacity has not been devoted to protecting the citizenry from the ravages of serious crime. Instead, it has been channeled into "quality of life policing"—i.e., prevention of panhandling by the destitute, driving homeless people from public areas, enforcing parking and no-smoking ordinances, etc.[215]—and pursuing "zero tolerance" policies focusing on jaywalkers, graffiti artists, drivers exceed-ing posted speed limits, and the like.[216] At first blush, such priorities seem

inexplicable (or absurd). Viewed as part of a broader strategy of social pacification—that is, to create a thoroughly obedient, which is to say regimented,
populace—it makes perfect sense.[217]

The FBI has grown, too, reaching a total of 13,821 agents in December
2010— well over twice the number it was allotted in 1970—as well 21,751
"support professionals, such as intelligence analysts [and] information
technology specialists."[218] That it has continued to employ its time-honored
methods of eliminating political targets has been demonstrated in a number
of instances, notably by the now-proven involvement of a provocateur named
Irv Sutley in a campaign jointly undertaken by the Bureau, the Oakland Red
Squad, and at least one timber corporation to neutralize the northern California wing of the radical environmentalist organization Earth First![219] Similar
operations have been conducted more recently against such groups as the
Earth Liberation Front (ELF), Animal Liberation Front (ELF), Black Bloc
anarchists, and a variety of Muslim organizations around the country.[220]

The utilization of such methods has been greatly facilitated by passage of
the so-called Anti-terrorism and Effective Death Penalty Act of 1996 and, as a
follow-up measure, the USA PATRIOT Act in 2002. The 1996 Act in particular contains provisions that legalize many of the tactics secretly employed by
the FBI in its COINTELPRO operations.[221] Technically, legal limits still pertain to the range of techniques Bureau personnel can employ in neutralizing
political targets, but the means of circumventing such constraints have long
since been perfected. In this regard, it must be borne in mind that, although
the commission of major crimes—including murder conspiracy—by clearly-
identified FBI personnel involved in COINTELPRO has been repeatedly
proven in court, no agent has resultantly spent so much as a minute behind
bars. Indeed, the only two Bureau officials ever prosecuted for (relatively
minor) COINTELPRO-related offenses were immediately pardoned by Ronald Reagan.[222]

That the situation remains unchanged is evident in the outcome of the
above-mentioned targeting of Earth First!, which included an attempted
assassination by car bomb of key activists Judi Bari and Darryl Cherney in
1990 (both targets suffered catastrophic injuries).[223] When the extent of the
Bureau's involvement began to come out, Richard W. Held, Special Agent in
Charge of the San Francisco field office and one of the FBI's most seasoned
COINTELPRO veterans, quickly retired, reappearing shortly thereafter as
chief of security for VisaCorp.[224] No criminal charges were ever filed in the
matter, largely because Held was exempted from being called to testify before
a grand jury on grounds that he was "no longer in government service."[225]
In part, this was the rationale used to exempt him from testifying during a

successful civil suit brought by Bari and Cherney against the FBI and Oakland PD.[226]

The Bureau's ongoing capacity and willingness to engage in blunt force repression, both frontal and surgical, is therefore undeniable. In the main, however, its present station in the internal security complex is dependent neither on its conducting such operations nor increasing numbers of personnel. Exponential advances in surveillance, communications, and data processing/storage technologies over the past thirty years have made it possible for the FBI to collect intelligence in almost infinitely greater quantities, at a greater speed and from a vastly greater range of sources—literally anything posted on the World Wide Web is instantly accessible to the Bureau, as are e-mail communications, cellphone conversations, and so on—than J. Edgar Hoover, much less Alan Pinkerton, could ever have imagined. So, too, the Bureau's ability to analyze, file, and distribute such information (witness the rapidity with which the FBI recently compiled and selectively shared a million-person "Terrorist Watch List"[227]).

In this sense, the FBI might be viewed as having truly become what the Pinkerton Agency always aspired to be: "The Eye That Never Sleeps." The more so, when considered in conjunction with the welter of entities from which it receives and to which it transmits intelligence data.[228] The Bureau's primary role has thus increasingly become one of interfacing with other government intelligence/police agencies, private security firms and corporate police forces, "friendly" media outlets like Fox News, Clear Channel, and the Washington Times, and "patriotic" organizations (including quite a number that exist only in the form of right-wing bloggers or corporate astroturf).[229] It thus serves as the linchpin or, perhaps more accurately, as the essential glue that holds the whole intricate structure of the internal security system together.

CONCLUSION

As was discussed towards the beginning of this essay, the final chapter of the insurgency in the U.S., an insurgency which from an elite perspective had been sustained in one or several forms and with varying degrees of intensity since the mid-nineteenth century, was written during the 1970s. The task undertaken by the by-then highly-developed internal security apparatus, State and private, has in the years since not been to engage in counterinsurgency, but rather to prevent anything resembling a genuine insurgency from recurring. In other words, the objective is to perpetuate the sociopolitical/economic status quo by imposing the conditions necessary to maintain the overall populace in a state of sheer pacification. For this an ever more totalizing system of repression and social regimentation has been consolidated over the past forty years, the model for which has begun long since to undergo exportation to other countries (i.e., it is in the process of being "globalized").

The question of course presents itself as to what might be done about the situation in which we now find ourselves. While there is much that could and undoubtedly should be said in this regard, it will have to be said elsewhere. Constraints upon the length of the present essay—it is already too long by half—preclude anything more than the observation that the first step in the mounting of any constructive response must be to recognize the situation for what it actually is rather than pretending it's something else. To rephrase, the old dodge about how "if things keep going the way they're going, we're going to end up in a police state" is and has long been flatly untrue. The harsh reality is that we've been in a police state for the past seventy years or more. The question is not how to prevent it from happening, but rather what to do about it now that it's done.

NOTES

Ed. Note: Due to space constraints, what follows is a substantial abridgement of the annotation originally submitted for the chapter.

1. "Internal security," also referred to as "domestic security," is distinguished from "national security" in that while the objective of the former is as described in the text, the latter is primarily concerned with countering the military capacities of foreign powers. That said, it must be conceded that the two domains are overlapping, sometimes dramatically so, as in matters involving espionage and, increasingly, technology. Nonetheless, issues pertaining to national security are more properly addressed within the context of the "military industrial complex" (see Boggs in this volume).

2. The language quoted is boilerplate frequently appearing in FBI internal communications pertaining to the Bureau's domestic counterintelligence programs (COINTELPROs). For a sample memo, see Ward Churchill and Jim Vander Wall, *The COINTELPRO Papers: Documents from the FBI's Secret Wars Against Dissent in the United States* (Cambridge, MA: South End Press, [Classics ed.] 2002), 92–93.

3. Robert Justin Goldstein, *Political Repression in Modern America, 1870–1976* (Urbana, IL: University of Illinois Press, [2nd ed.] 2001), xxviii.

4. Homeland Security Act of 2002 (116 Stat. 745, 2135).

5. To my knowledge, no good study has been done on the implications attending Lyndon Johnson's deployment of the army to put down urban revolts in Newark (1967, 23 dead), Detroit (1967, 43 dead), and elsewhere. For an excellent survey of

the dynamics giving rise to the insurrections, however, see Janet L. Abu-Lughod, *Race, Space, and Riots in Chicago, New York, and Los Angeles* (New York, NY: New York University Press, 2007).

6. On Delta Force, see generally, Terry Griswold and D.M. Giangreco, *Delta: America's Elite Counterterrorist Force* (Osceola, WI: Motorbooks International, 1992). On its operations during the prison riot, see Churchill and Vander Wall, *COIN-TELPRO Papers,* xliv.

7. Robert Dreyfuss, "Spying on Ourselves," *Rolling Stone,* March 28, 2002, 34; Jim Redden, "Police State Targets the Left," in Eddie Yuen, George Katsiaficas, and Daniel Burton-Rose, eds., *The Battle of Seattle: The New Challenge to Capitalist Globalization* (New York, NY: Soft Skull Press, 2001), 139–141.

8. David T. Hardy with Rex Kimball, *This Is Not an Assault: Penetrating the Web of Official Lies Regarding the Waco Incident* (San Antonio, TX: Xlibris, 2001), 83–6, 248–51, 265–66.

9. Such "private actors" were, for example, explicitly identified as a "vital element," integral to the "National Strategy for the Physical Protection of Critical Infrastructure and Key Assets" advanced by the Bush administration in 2003. See Elizabeth E. Joh, "The Forgotten Threat: Private Policing and the State, *Indiana Journal of Global Legal Studies,* No. 357 (Summer 2006), 388.

10. This may be a considerable understatement. "The United States Government now trains at least 100,000 foreign police and soldiers from more than 150 countries each year in US military and policing doctrine and methods, as well as war-fighting skills, at the cost of tens of millions of dollars. Approximately 275 known US military schools and installations provide training, and the US trains many more in their own nations through a variety of programs. . . ." Amnesty International, USA, *Unmatched Power, Unmet Principles: The Human Rights Dimensions of US Training of Foreign Military and Police Forces* (New York, NY: Amnesty International USA, Mar. 2002), frontpapers. Also see Lesley Gill, *The School of the Americas: Military Training and Political Violence in the Americas* (Durham, NC: Duke University Press, 2004).

11. Among the major contractors are DynCorp, Military Professional Resources International (MPRI), Logicon, the Vinnell Corp., Booze-Allen & Hamilton, Texas Instruments, the Carlyle Group, BFI International, Science Applications International Corp. Amnesty International, *Unmatched Power,* 21–22. Curiously, while the activities of most of these firms have been subject to serious analysis in terms of their contracting of *military* services, including training, almost no attention has been paid to their roles as police trainers. This may be explained in part, though not entirely, by the increasing overlap between military and police functions in the countries at issue. See, e.g., P.W. Singer, *Corporate Warriors: The Rise of the Privatized Military Industry* (Ithaca, NY: Cornell University Press, 2003); Deborah D. Avant, *The Market for Force: The Consequences of Privatizing Security* (Cambridge, UK: Cambridge University Press, 2005).

12. "In 1973, Congress prohibited the use of foreign assistance funds for police training in all foreign countries in the face of mounting evidence that training and equipment provided under the Public Safety program were directly supporting

governments implicated in widespread human rights abuses, particularly in Latin America. This provision did not apply, however, to the Departments of Justice, Transportation, and Treasury, including the Federal Bureau of Investigation and the Drug Enforcement Agency, all of which are authorized and funded from budgets other than foreign assistance. Additionally, a number of exceptions were made to the 1973 law over time. . . . By 1990, the U.S. General Accounting Office was able to identify 125 countries that received police training financed by U.S. taxpayers, despite the legislative 'ban.'" Amnesty International, *Unmatched Power,* 16.

13. A prime example in the latter connection is the direct involvement of "Centra Spike," a small unit of Delta Force personnel and navy SEALs, in the operations of a U.S.-trained and -equipped element within the Columbian National Police known as the "Search Bloc" in tracking down and eventually killing drug overlord Pablo Escobar Gaviria on Dec. 2, 1993. See Mark Bowden, *Killing Pablo: The Hunt for the World's Greatest Outlaw* (New York, NY: Atlantic Monthly Press, 2001), esp. 73–82.

14. To quote one CIA analyst, the World Trade Center/Pentagon attacks on Sept. 11, 2001, prompted "recognition that combating the new threats of terrorism and the activities whereby it is funded—drug trafficking, money laundering, and organized crime—required greatly enhanced interagency communication, cooperation, and intelligence sharing on the national and international level. The ramifications of this coordination are broad, including the building of common databases, creation of intelligence clearinghouses, invention of new forms of organizational collaboration, and even institutional mergers. Paradoxically, apart from the threat that prompted it, these reforms were undertaken in perhaps the most benign security environment—in terms of traditional threats—that the United States and Western Europe had faced in over half a century." Larry L. Watts, "Intelligence Reform in Europe's Emerging Democracies: Conflicting Paradigms, Dissimilar Contexts," pg. 3 of 17 (available at www.cia.gov/library/center-for-the-study-of-intelligence/csi-publications/csi-studies/studies/vol48no1/article02.html).

15. See generally, Jack Clarke, "The United States, Europe, and Homeland Security: Seeing Soft Security Concerns Through a Counterterrorist Lens," *European Security,* Vol. 13, Nos. 1–2 (2004), 117–38.

16. See *Persona* and Victor Marchetti, "The CIA in Italy: An Interview with Victor Marchetti," Rene Backmann, Franz-Olivier Giesbert, and Olivier Todd, "What the CIA is Looking for in France," Philip Agee and *Information Dienst,* "West Germany: An Interview with Philip Agee," all in Philip Agee and Louis Wolf, eds., *Dirty Work: The CIA in Western Europe* (Secaucus, NJ: Lyle Stuart, 1978), 171, 183, 185–86.

17. "Flexible specialization" is a computer-actualized mode of systemic organization premised upon division of the workforce into "a skill-flexible core and a time-flexible periphery," both of which are perpetually changing but interacting on a continuous basis. See, e.g., Ray Kiely, "Globalization, Post-Fordism and the Contemporary Context of Development," *International Sociology,* Vol. 13, No. 1 (Spring 1998), 95–111

18. On one variety of security contractors, see note 11, above. On contractors like Total Intelligence Solutions, LLC, (a subsidiary of Blackwater Worldwide, now known as "Xe"), see Tim Shorrock, "The corporate takeover of U.S. intelligence: The

U.S. government now outsources a vast portion of its spying operations to private firms—with zero accountability," *Salon.com*, June 1, 2007 (available at www.salon .com/news/feature/2007/06/01/intel_contractors).

19. Ken Lawrence, *The New State Repression* (Chicago: International Network Against the New State Repression, 1985), 2. A slightly different version of the pamphlet was also published under the same title in *Covert Action Information Bulletin*, No. 24 (Summer 1985), 3–11.

20. For background, see Michael T. Klare and Peter Kornbluh, *Low Intensity Warfare: Counterinsurgency, Proinsurgency and Antiterrorism in the Eighties* (New York, NY: Pantheon, 1988).

21. As Lawrence observes, both men had published their ideas. See Frank Kitson, *Low Intensity Operations: Subversion, Insurgency, Peacekeeping* (London: Faber and Faber, 1971); Robin Evelegh, *Peace-Keeping in a Democratic Society: The Lessons of Northern Ireland* (London, UK: C. Hurst, 1978).

22. Lawrence, *New State Repression*, 3. For further background, see Churchill and Vander Wall, *COINTELPRO Papers;* Cathy Perkus, ed., *COINTELPRO: The FBI's Secret War on Political Freedom* (New York, NY: Monad Press, 1975).

23. Lawrence, *New State Repression*, 3. For background, see *Final Report, Book III: Supplementary Detailed Staff Reports on Intelligence Activities and the Rights of Americans; CIA Intelligence Collection About Americans: Chaos and the Office of Security* (Washington, DC: 94th Cong., 2nd Sess., Apr. 23, 1976 [available at www .icdc.com/ ~paulwolf/cointelpro/churchfinalreprtllld.html]).

24. Lawrence does not mention the emergence of SWAT units during the late 1960s, although they'd already played a significant role in the context of repression he was discussing, and had undergone a dramatic proliferation during the '70s. See Susie Bernstein, Lynn Cooper, Elliott Currie, Jon Frappier, Sidney Harring, Tony Platt, Pat Poyner, Gerda Ray, Joy Scruggs, and Larry Trujillo, *The Iron Fist and the Velvet Glove: An Analysis of the U.S. Police* (Berkeley, CA: Center for Research on Criminal Justice, [2nd ed., rev.] 1977), 93–97.

25. Unaccountably, Lawrence appears to have been unaware, or at any rate omitted mentioning, that the CIA, in concert with the so-called Office of Public Safety, had been training "police forces . . . from many other countries in counterinsurgency" techniques for at least a decade by the time the CSTI was founded. Undeniably, the facilities at which this was undertaken, situated in Texas and elsewhere, constituted "federal police training institutions," as does their successor, the now-renamed School of the Americas, at Fort Benning, Georgia. See, Bernstein et al., *Iron Fist/ Velvet Glove*, 161–68; A.J. Langguth, *Hidden Terrors: The truth about U.S. police operations in Latin American* (New York: Pantheon, 1978), esp. 52–53, 56–58, 95–96, 126–31, 225–26, 233–35, 242–43.

26. In 1970, Giuffrida, then still an active duty colonel attending the U.S. Army War College, prepared a paper calling for "the roundup and transfer of at least 21 million 'American Negroes' to 'assembly centers or relocation camps' in the event of an emergency or uprising by black citizens." He was apparently hired by Reagan on that basis a year later. Center for Grassroots Oversight, "Profile: Louis Giuffrida" (available at www.historycommons.org/entity.jsp?entity=louis_giuffrida_1).

27. Lawrence, *New State Repression,* p. 7.

28. Ibid., 6, citing/quoting California Specialized Training Institute, "Civilian Violence and Terrorism: Officer Survival and Internal Security" (Camp San Luis Obispo, CA: CSTI, rev. Aug. 1974).

29. For background on "Garden Plot," "Cable Splicer," and similar plans formulated by the army's Directorate of Civil Disturbance Planning and Operations, *circa* 1968, see Morton Halperin, Jerry Berman, Robert Borosage, and Christine Marwick, *The Lawless State: The Crimes of U.S. Intelligence Agencies* (New York, NY: Penguin, 1976), esp. 160–66; Kurt Nimmo, "Operation Garden Plot Documents Published," *Infowars,* Sept. 9, 2009 (available at www.infowars.com/operation-garden-plot-documents-published).

30. Peter Matthiessen, *In the Spirit of Crazy Horse: The Story of Leonard Peltier* (New York, Viking Press, [2nd ed] 1991), 68–69; Joan M. Jensen, *Army Surveillance in America, 1775–1980* (New Haven, CT: Yale University Press, 1991), 257–58.

31. On "Rex-84" and related FEMA exercises, see Churchill and Vander Wall, *COINTELPRO Papers,* 410–11n23. Also see Diana Reynolds, "The Rise of the National Security State: FEMA and the NSC," *Covert Action Information Bulletin,* No. 33 (Winter 1990) (available at www.publiceye.org/liberty/fema/Fema_0.html).

32. Sigmund A. Lavine, *Allan Pinkerton: America's First Private Eye* (New York: Dodd, Meade, 1963), 18–22; Frank Morn, *The Eye That Never Sleeps: A History of the Pinkerton National Detective Agency* (Bloomington, IN: Indiana University Press, 1982), 18–23, 52, 93.

33. Morn, *Eye That Never Sleeps,* 39–40.

34. The unit, formed by Pinkerton at the behest of Gen. George McClellan, was originally called the "Secret Service." See Morn, *Eye That Never Sleeps,* 43–5; James Mackay, *Allan Pinkerton: The First Private Eye* (New York, NY: John Wiley, 1996), 119–20, 149–70.

35. Mackay, *Pinkerton,* 155–7.

36. U.S. Congress, *Appropriations to the Budget of the United States of America, 1872, Section 7, United States Department of Justice* (Washington, DC: U.S. Government Printing Office, 1872); Stanford J. Ungar, *FBI: An Uncensored Look Behind the Walls* (Boston, MA: Atlantic-Little, Brown, 1976), 39.

37. "Between 1850 and 1857 [private railroad corporations] got 25 million acres of public land, free of charge, and millions of dollars in bonds—loans—from state legislatures[, in addition to which,] during the Civil War, over 100 million acres were given by the Congress and the President to various railroads, [also] free of charge." Howard Zinn, *A People's History of the United States* (New York, NY: HarperCollins, 1980), 220, 238.

38. See Whitney D. Gunter and Christopher A. Hertig, *An Introduction to Theory, Practice and Career Development for Public and Private Investigators* (International Foundation for Protection Officers, Aug. 2005), 4. The classic exposé of the Pinkerton practices in this regard is, of course, Morris Friedman's *The Pinkerton Labor Spy* (New York, NY: Wilshire Book Co., 1907).

39. U.S. Senate, Select Committee to Study Government Operations with Respect to Intelligence Activities, *Final Report, Book III: Supplementary Detailed Staff*

Reports on Intelligence Activities and the Rights of Americans; The Use of Informants in FBI Domestic Intelligence Operations (Washington, DC: 94th Cong., 1st Sess., Apr. 23, 1976 [available at www.icdc.com/~paulwolf/cointelpro/churchfinal reprtllld.html]; hereinafter cited as Senate Select Committee, *Informants*), 16.

40. This component of the agency's operations originated in 1858, with the "Protective Police Patrols" Pinkerton formed in Chicago for contract by local merchants. By the early 1870s, the operation had expanded to the point that "Pinkerton's monopolized railroad policing" nationally, while the Chicago office alone maintained an arsenal of 250 rifles, 500 rifles, and sundry other weapons. Morn, *Eye That Never Sleeps,* 58, 92–94, 104, 154; Mackay, *Pinkerton,* 93–94.

41. Pennsylvania led the way in 1865 with State Act 228, thereby imbuing select railroad personnel with official police powers. Massachusetts followed in 1871, Maryland in 1880, New York in 1890. Meanwhile, a supplement to Pennsylvania's 1865 statute extended the same authority over the corporately-funded/Pinkerton-organized "Coal and Iron Police." A decade later, the state/corporate "law enforcement" interlock in Pennsylvania had sufficiently ripened that Franklin B. Gowen, president of both the Reading Railroad and the Philadelphia and Reading Coal and Iron Company, could have himself a special prosecutor in cases he caused to be brought against the leadership of the Molly Maguires (a militant labor organization active in his coal fields). Convicted in Gowen's kangaroo court, at least twenty Mollies were executed. The Molly prosecutions were merely an extreme example of what was by 1880 a rather common phenomenon. Morn, *Eye That Never Sleeps,* 93–94; Goldstein, *Political Repression,* 23; Carl I. Meyerhuber, Jr., *Less than Forever: The Rise and Fall of Union Solidarity in Western Pennsylvania, 1914–1948* (Selinsgrove, PA: Susquehanna University Press, 1987), 152.

42. "Between 1868 and 1873, fourteen new national unions were organized, and by 1873 the union movement reached a peak of three hundred thousand members." Although there is no accurate count of the overall number, "the period 1868 to 1872 was [also] marked by a series of major strikes over the eight-hour [workday] issue, with the most spectacular . . . occurring in New York City, where one hundred thousand walked off their jobs in 1872." See Goldstein, *Political Repression,* 25–31.

43. By 1877, the wave of labor militancy had "crystallized the fear of communist revolution . . . . that had been building since [the Paris Commune of] 1871 in the minds of American elites." There was a "growing belief among businessmen and government officials that American labor was turning increasingly radical, violent, and subversive, and could only be put down with the club and the gun." Goldstein, *Political Repression,* 32, 24.

44. The army possessed such a capacity, of course, and was frequently deployed as a strikebreaking force during the 1870s. However, passage of the 1878 Posse Comitatus Act (U.S.C. § 1385)—a measure engineered by the former Confederate States, which were occupied by federal troops during Reconstruction—sharply constrained usage of the military for domestic law enforcement purposes (while freeing the South to [re]impose a Klan-enforced system of white supremacy on recently-emancipated blacks). Thereafter, each such deployment required a formal declaration of national emergency by the President and authorization by Congress. The process of "calling

out the troops" was thus not only cumbersome but, for a number of reasons, politically problematic. For an excellent, albeit unabashedly reactionary, overview of the Act, its evolution, and related legislation, see Gary Felicetti and John Luce, "The Posse Comitatus Act: Setting the Record Straight on 124 Years of Mischief and Misunderstanding before Any More Damage is Done," *Military Law Review,* Vol. 175 (2003), 86–183; on racial backdrop, see 89–90, 91–92, 100–12.

45. Authorized under Titles 10 and 32 of the U.S. Code, the National Guard was established during the late 1870s to supplant the patchwork of state/local militias until then prevailing, with the current unified system effected under the 1903 Militia Act (32 Stat. 775). Although it is technically a misnomer, the term "militia" continues to be applied to the Guard. See Jerry Cooper, *The Rise of the National Guard: The Evolution of the American Militia, 1865–1920* (Lincoln, NE: University of Nebraska Press, 1997), 23–43.

46. In 1878, "the National Guard Association was founded. The business community took an active interest in this organization, backing the establishment of armories throughout the country." Robert Mitchell Smith, *From Blackjacks to Briefcases: A History of Commercialized Strikebreaking and Unionbusting in the United States* (Athens, OH: University of Ohio Press, 2003), 3–4. It wasn't just armories. As was explained by one Illinois Guard colonel in 1881, "Our cavalry was not equipped by the state. It belongs to the National Guard, but was equipped and uniformed completely by the Citizen's Association of the City of Chicago. This association is composed of business men, who look after the best interests of our city." Quoted in Morn, *Eye That Never Sleeps,* 97.

47. Smith, *Blackjacks to Briefcases,* 3–4. The nature of these interventions is reflected by the fact that, "In 1891 Pennsylvania [guardsmen] fired on fleeing strikers, killing ten and wounding fifty." A half-dozen strikers were shot to death and scores wounded by Wisconsin guardsmen the same year. Then in 1892, the Idaho Guard simply rounded up more than 600 striking miners near Coeur d'Alene, and placed them in concentration camps. Goldstein, *Political Repression,* 45, 40, 47.

48. Goldstein, *Political Repression,* 289–90.

49. From 1877 to 1892, Pinkertons played a major role in forcibly breaking no fewer than seventy strikes. This is quite apart from the agency's extensive engagement in labor espionage and other such operations. Morn, *Eye That Never Sleeps,* 91–109.

50. Leon Wolff, *Lockout: The Story of the Homestead Strike of 1892—A Study of Violence, Unionism, and the Carnegie Steel Empire* (New York, NY: Harper & Row, 1965), 69.

51. Morn, *Eye That Never Sleeps,* 101–102; Smith, *Blackjacks to Briefcases,* 21–22, 56.

52. My use of the term "labor adjustment" in this context is not a contrivance. There was in fact a New York-based firm billing itself as a provider of "Strike Service and Labor Adjusters." Smith, *Blackjacks to Briefcases,* 56.

53. Val R. Lorwin, "Reflections on the French and American Labor Movements," *Journal of Economic History,* Vol. 17, No. 2 (March 1957), 37.

54. Richard Hofstadter and Michael Wallace, eds., *American Violence: A Documentary History* (New York, NY: Vintage Books, 1971), 19.

55. The battle left ten strikers and three Pinkertons dead, a number of others wounded on both sides, and the surviving Pinkerton men prisoners of their adversaries. Morn, *Eye That Never Sleeps*, 103; citing U.S. House of Representatives, Committee on Labor, *Employment of Pinkerton Detectives* (Washington, DC: 52nd Cong., 1st. Sess., 1893), 196.

56. The Act (5 U.S.C. § 3108), prohibits any "individual employed by the Pinkerton Detective Agency, or similar organization" from being employed by "the Government of the United States or the government of the District of Columbia." In 1977, the U.S. Fifth Circuit Court of Appeals ruled that an organization might be considered "similar" to Pinkerton's, within the meaning of the Act, *only* "if it offer[s] for hire mercenary, quasi-military forces as strikebreakers and armed guards." *U.S. ex rel. Weinberger v. Equifax* (557 F.2d 456 (5th Cir., 1977)) at 462.

57. Actually, such "rights" were repeatedly and *explicitly* affirmed by both state and federal courts over the next three decades. See Edward Levinson, "The Right to Break Strikes," *Current History*, XLV (Feb. 1937), 77–82.

58. Elizabeth E. Joh, "The Forgotten Threat: Private Policing and the State," *Indiana Journal of Global Legal Studies*, Vol. 13, No. 2 (Summer 2006), 369.

59. U.S. Senate, Committee on Education and Labor, *Violations of Free Speech and the Rights of Labor: Strikebreaking* (Washington, DC: 76th Cong., 1st Sess., 1939), 19–25, 34, 107; U.S. Senate, Committee on Education and Labor, *Violations of Free Speech and the Rights of Labor: Industrial Espionage* (Washington, DC: 76th Cong., 2nd Sess., 1938), 17–21.

60. The original "King of the Strikebreakers" was Jack Whitehead, who operated mainly out of Pittsburgh and retired in 1901. The title was thereafter bestowed upon Farley, upon Pearl Bergoff after Farley died in 1913, and there were several other contenders for the crown. All specialized in providing scab labor and mustering Pinkerton-style "armies." See Smith, *Blackjacks to Briefcases*, 40–73. On Whitehead, also see F.B. McQuiston, "The Strike-Breakers," *The Independent* (Oct. 17, 1901), 2456–458. On Farley, also see B.T. Fredricks, "James Farley, Striker-Breaker," *Leslie's Magazine* (Oct. 1905); Leroy Scott, "'Strikebreaking' as a New Occupation," *World's Work* (May 1905), 6194–6200. On Bergoff, see Edward Levinson, *I Break Strikes! The Technique of Pearl L. Bergoff* (New York, NY: McBride, 1935).

61. U.S. Senate, Committee on Education and Labor, *Violations of Free Speech and the Rights of Labor: Private Police Systems* (Washington, DC: 76th Cong., 1st Sess., 1939), 1; quoted in Joh, "Forgotten Threat," 370n77.

62. Ungar, *FBI*, 40; Fred Cook, *The FBI Nobody Knows* (New York, NY: Macmillan, 1964), 53.

63. Quite apart from private subsidies (see note 46), governmental appropriations to underwrite the National Guard more than doubled between 1903 and 1913. As for the establishment of state police forces—the "state troopers," as they're often called—Connecticut technically paved the way in 1903, but it was Pennsylvania that defined their true utility creating a unit in 1905 to provide a centralized body for "riot control" purposes, "with the policing of strikes as one of its key duties." See Cooper, *Rise of the National Guard*, 131, 64, 151.

64. Probably the best study of the origins and growth of these units is Frank Donner's *Protectors of Privilege: Red Squads and Police Repression in America* (Berkeley, CA: University of California Press, 1990).

65. In Pennsylvania, more than 7,600 commissions as "peace officers" were issued to members of the so-called Coal and Iron Police, an entirely private entity, before the practice was ended in 1931. The last known instance of a similar procedure being followed in Florida was in 1967, when it was revealed that Republican Governor Claude Kirk had deputized a team of twenty-six Wackenhut detectives contracted with state funds to gather information about area Democrats. See Meyerhuber, *Less than Forever,* 152; George O'Toole, *The Private Sector: Rent-a-cops, private spies and the police-industrial complex* (New York, NY: W.W. Norton, 1978), 32–4.

66. U.S. Senate, Committee on Education and Labor, *Employers' Associations and Collective Bargaining in California* (Washington, DC: 78th Cong., 1st Sess., 1943), 841.

67. Donner, *Protectors of Privilege,* 30.

68. Ibid., 33; citing Carey McWilliams, *Southern California Country: An Island on the Land* (New York, NY: Duell, Sloan & Pearce, 1946), 272–82, On the CCS, see Jo Durden-Smith, *Who Killed George Jackson? Fantasies, Paranoia and the Revolution* (New York, NY: Alfred A. Knopf, 1976), 118, 130–48, 163–66, 226–28, 274, 288, 291.

69. Ungar, *FBI,* 45–48, and note 59, above. For an example of Burns Agency personnel acting in a Pinkerton-style anti-labor capacity, see Melvin Dubofsky, *We Shall Be All: A History of the Industrial Workers of the World* (Chicago, IL: Quadrangle, 1969), 297.

70. It is estimated that "perhaps as many as one million workers held IWW cards" between 1905 and 1924. Patrick Renshaw, *The Wobblies: The Story of Syndicalism in the United States* (Garden City, NY: Doubleday, 1967), 22. On the BoI operation, see note 80, below.

71. In the main raid, carried out on Jan. 2, 1920, "as many as 6,000" aliens suspected of being "subversives"—i.e., anarchists or communists—were rounded up in 33 cities across the country, and held in crudely improvised detention centers, often weeks, pending deportation screening. Of these, 820 were in fact deported on the basis of their political views. See Cook, *FBI Nobody Knows,* 71–116; Richard Gid Powers, *Secrecy and Power: The Life of J. Edgar Hoover* (New York, NY: Free Press, 1987), 66–91; Curt Gentry, *J. Edgar Hoover: The Man and His Secrets* (New York, NY: W. W. Norton, 1991), 79–96.

72. One method employed was to provide "confidential" political intelligence information on radical unionists to the AFL's collaborationist president, Samuel Gompers, so that he could summarily purge them from the ranks. So thoroughly co-opted had this wing of the labor movement become by 1920 that, "When radical unions like the IWW struck for avowedly political goals . . . the moderate unions of the American Federation of Labor . . . joined business and the government in attacking them." See Gentry, *Hoover,* 104; Powers, *Secrecy and Power,* 58.

73. Quoted in "Daugherty Obtains Order: Judge Wilkerson Acts on Plea in Federal Court in Chicago," *New York Times,* Sept 2, 1922 (available at query.nytimes.com/gst/abstract.html?res=FAO714D3B5D1A7A93COA91782D85F468285F9.

74. The principle targets were Montana Senators Thomas Walsh and Burton K. Wheeler, both progressive Democrats who were playing lead roles in exposing corruption in the Republican administration of Warren G. Harding. See Cook, *FBI Nobody Knows,* pp. 126–36; Ungar, *FBI,* 47–48; Gentry, *Hoover,* 118–21.

75. In Hoover's own—uncorroborated—version of events, he took the initiative during an interview with Attorney General Stone by insisting, as a precondition of accepting directorship, that the "Bureau must be divorced from politics." Whatever the veracity of the story, Hoover's pitch was convincing enough to persuade ACLU president Roger Baldwin that he was actually "a civil libertarian" at heart (this, despite Baldwin's knowledge that Hoover maintained a "subversives" file on him, wherein Baldwin was rather absurdly characterized as "an IWW agitator"). In reality, of course, it was all a sham: "[C]ontrary to [Hoover's] pledge the Bureau never stopped collecting and filing away information on alleged radicals." See Gentry, *Hoover,* 138–42; Powers, *Secrecy and Power,* 147–48.

76. Gentry, *Hoover,* 69.

77. Cook, *FBI Nobody Knows,* 94; Gentry, *Hoover,* 79; Powers, *Secrecy and Power,* 68–69.

78. Gentry, *Hoover,* 111; Powers, *Secrecy and Power,* 131.

79. E.g.: "A substantial part of *Hoover's bureaucratic genius* was his insistence on clear lines of responsibility and a realistic conception of what he could effectively manage [emphasis added]." G. Gregg Webb, "New Insights into J. Edgar Hoover's Role: The FBI and Foreign Intelligence," *CSI Studies,* Vol. 48, No. 1 (no date) p. 13 (available at www.cia.gov/library/center-for-the-study-of-intelligence/csi-publications/csi-studies/studies/vol.48no1/article05.html).

80. See Dubofsky, *We Shall Be All,* 406–407, 438–39; Renshaw, *Wobblies,* 220; Goldstein, *Political Repression,* 117; Gentry, *Hoover,* 70–71, 96.

81. See Goldstein, *Political Repression,* 111–12; Powers, *Secrecy and Power,* 134–35; Gentry, *Hoover,* 71–73.

82. Although he "did his best to disassociate himself from the raids themselves, having the Bureau issue outright lies to minimize the importance of his role[,] Hoover was in complete charge of planning the attack on radicalism during the summer and fall of 1919." Powers, *Secrecy and Power,* 123, 66. .

83. Ibid., 137–40.

84. In this connection, it's important to bear in mind that, prior to being hired by the BoI, Hoover worked at the Library of Congress, where he his job was cataloguing new books, using "a groundbreaking new system to keep tabs on its bulging collection of over a million volumes plus hundreds of thousands of journals, manuscripts, and newspapers. Similar to the Dewey Decimal System . . . it assigned each item an index card with a unique code indicating its topic[s], title, author, and location." Having thoroughly mastered the system before leaving the library, Hoover simply adapted it to the purpose of keeping track of files, and the relationships between them, upon arrival at the Bureau. Although much evolved, the information management system he developed in 1917 remains in use today. See Kenneth D. Ackerman, *Young J. Edgar Hoover, the Red Scare and Civil Liberties* (New York, NY: Carroll & Graf, 2007), 45–46. For the basic coding involved, see Gerald K. Haines and David A. Langbart,

Unlocking the Files of the FBI: A Guide to Its Records and Classification System (Wilmington, DE: SR Books, 1993), Appendix XI: FBI Central Records Classification System, 313–19.

85. During the mid-1870s, Pinkerton repeatedly opined that vigilante "justice" would be the most effective method of dealing with the train-robbing James/Younger gang in Missouri, insinuating that the fate of Indiana's Reno gang, ten of whom were lynched by "unknown persons" during the second half of 1868, might be viewed as a useful precedent. In actuality, it appears that the Indiana vigilantes may well have been Pinkerton operatives, or were at least organized by them. In any case, one of the Pinkerton men involved in the Reno operation later threatened to go public with the details unless he was paid something on the order of $500,000. See James D. Horan, *The Pinkertons: The Detective Dynasty That Made History* (New York, NY: Crown, 1967), 199, 234.

86. On the APL, see, e.g., Goldstein, *Political Repression,* 110–13. For the most comprehensive history of the organization, see Joan M. Jensen, *The Price of Vigilance* (Chicago, IL: Rand McNally, 1968).

87. On the APL's provision of the "ground troops" necessary to carry out the raids, see Jensen, *Price of Vigilance,* 191–218; Gentry, *Hoover,* 71–72; Max Lowenthal, *The Federal Bureau of Investigation* (New York, NY: Harcourt, Brace, 1950), 26–35.

88. On APL informant reportage, see Jensen, *Price of Vigilance,* 257–75. On the American Defense Society, see Higham, *Strangers in the Land,* 199, 208, 280. On the National Security League, see Robert D. Ward, "The Origins and Activities of the National Security League, 1914–1919," *Mississippi Valley Historical Review,* Vol. 47, No. 1 (June 1960), 51–65.

89. Powers, *Secrecy and Power,* 59.

90. The key player was ACLU general counsel Morris Ernst, who not only steered the organization away from defending radicals—e.g., he "was instrumental in having the ACLU adopt the position that there were 'no civil liberties issues involved' in the Rosenberg case"—but, for decades, "reported private, sometimes privileged, conversations to Hoover [and u]nbeknownst to their authors . . . gave copies of personal letters he received from such FBI critics as I.F. Stone, the columnist Max Lerner, Congressman Wayne Morse, and FCC Chairman Lawrence Fly (who'd clashed with Hoover over wiretapping)." At one point, Ernst even offered to serve as defense attorney for accused "atomic spies" Julius and Ethel Rosenberg, "not so much to help them (he'd already decided [they] were guilty) but to assist the FBI." Gentry, *Hoover,* 234–35.

91. See Abdeen Jabara, "The Anti-Defamation League: Civil Rights and Wrongs," *Covert Action Quarterly,* No. 45 (Summer 1993), 28–33 (available at cosmos.ucc.ie/cs1064/jabowen/IPSC/articles/article0058244.html).

92. Besides the Reno case (see note 85, above), there is an unproven but nonetheless generalized belief in western Missouri that Allan Pinkerton's eldest son, William, led the "posse" that bombed the home of Frank and Jesse James's mother on the night of Jan. 25, 1875 (she lost an arm; her youngest son, eight-year-old Archie Samuel, was killed). See Horan, *Pinkertons,* 199–200; T. J. Stiles, *Jesse James: Last Rebel of the Civil War* (New York, NY: Alfred A. Knopf, 2002), 279–82.

93. On the Frank Little lynching, see Dubofsky, *We Shall Be All,* 391–92; Renshaw, *Wobblies,* 207–208.

94. On the Everett lynching, see Renshaw, *Wobblies,* 209–11; Robert K. Murray, *Red Scare: A Study in National Hysteria, 1919–1920* (Minneapolis, MN: University of Minnesota Press, 1955), 182–4. For the *Freikorps* comparison, see Powers, *Secrecy and Power,* 59.

95. On the Reno lynchings, see note 85, above.

96. See Brian Glick, *War at Home: Covert Action Against U.S. Activists and What We Can Do About It* (Boston, MA: South End Press, 1989), 27–8.

97. In his memoirs, "Wild Bill" Sullivan, the FBI associate director who oversaw Division Five (through which COINTELPRO operations were carried out), states that during the fall of 1964 his agents "merged" the three Klan factions in Mississippi—of which the White Knights were the most prominent and by far the most violent—and thereafter controlled the organization. While Sullivan claims that, "From that time on, the Klan never again raised its head in Mississippi," the reality was rather different. The violence evinced by the FBI-controlled Klan in Mississippi continued apace, averaging some 250 significant acts per year through 1970. See William C. Sullivan with Bill Brown, *The Bureau: My Thirty Years in Hoover's FBI* (New York, NY: W. W. Norton, 1975), 129–30; Kenneth O'Reilly, *"Racial Matters": The FBI's Secret File on Black America* (New York, NY: Free Press, 1989), 206, 223.

98. See Senate Select Committee, *Informants,* 24–26; David Wise, *The American Police State: The Government Against the People* (New York: Random House, 1976), 319; Frank J. Donner, *The Age of Surveillance: The Aims and Methods of America's Political Intelligence System* (New York, NY: Alfred A. Knopf, 1980), 440–46; Donald Freed, *Death in Washington: The Murder of Orlando Letelier* (Westport, CT: Lawrence Hill, 1980), 34–35, 128, 133.

99. Donner, *Protectors of Privilege,* 147–51; Donner, *Age of Surveillance,* 427–30; Margaret Jayko, *FBI on Trial: The victory of the Socialist Workers Party suit against government spying* (New York, NY: Pathfinder Press, 1988), 232–3.

100. Lawrence, *New State Repression,* 5; Donner, *Age of Surveillance,* 431–35.

101. See Theodore Kornweibel, Jr., *Seeing Red: Federal Campaigns Against Black Militancy, 1919–1925* (Bloomington, IN: Indiana University Press, 1998), esp. 100–31.

102. Quoted in David Garrow, *The FBI and Martin Luther King, Jr.: From "Solo" to Memphis* (New York, NY: W. W. Norton, 1981), 106.

103. "By the fall of 1919 the FBI had established surveillance programs aimed at blacks. Bureau field offices across the country covered 'the Negro Question' systematically, recruiting 'reliable Negroes' as informants in the 'various negro lodges and associations' and having them report on 'negro ministers' and anyone else who preached 'social equality' and 'equal rights.' The informants infiltrated every racial advancement and black nationalist group, from the moderate National Association for the Advancement of Colored People to the immoderate African Blood Brotherhood, hoping to detect 'ultra radical activities' of even 'liberal activities' . . ." O'Reilly, *"Racial Matters,"* 13. For further background, see Theodore Kornweibel, Jr., *"Investigate Everything" Federal Efforts to Compel Black Loyalty during World War I* (Bloomington, IN: Indiana University Press, 2002).

104. The GID was officially disbanded in 1924, as part of Hoover's supposed depoliticizing of the Bureau. He reestablished it in 1939, however, claiming to be acting on the verbal instructions of Franklin Roosevelt. Exactly when the GID was recast as the Internal Security Section (ISS) is unclear, but most likely in 1943, pursuant to Attorney General Francis Biddle's directive that Hoover compile a secret "Security Index" of individuals subject to extrajudicial detention in concentration camps on national security grounds (an Internal Security Division was established within the Justice Dept. at that time). Although the Bureau was reorganized during the early 1970s, the ISS was simply renamed the Internal Security *Branch,* within which its "Racial Matters" and "extremists" components were coded "IS-1." See U.S. Senate, Select Committee to Study Government Operations with Respect to Intelligence Activities, *Final Report, Book III: Supplementary Detailed Staff Reports on Intelligence Activities and the Rights of Americans; The Development of FBI Domestic Intelligence Investigations* (Washington, DC: 94th Cong., 2nd Sess., Apr. 23, 1976 [available at www .icdc.com/~paulwolf/cointepro/church finalreprtllld.html]; hereinafter cited as Senate Select Committee, *FBI Domestic Intelligence*), 9–10, 19–20, 25–28, 34, 105–107. Powers, *Secrecy and Power,* 232–33; Gentry, *Hoover,* 212–21.

105. See generally, O'Reilly, *"Racial Matters,"* 17–47. Very little has been published about FBI penetration of Latino organizations prior to 1960, but see Rodolfo Acuña, *Occupied America: A History of the Chicanos* (New York, NY: HarperCollins, [3rd ed.] 1988), 259–61; Ramón Bosque-Pérez, "Political Persecution against Puerto Rican Anti-Colonial Activists in the Twentieth Century," and "The Smith Act Goes to San Juan: La Mordaza, 1948–1957," both in Ramón Bosque-Pérez and José Javier Colón Morera, eds., *Puerto Rico under Colonial Rule: Political Persecution and the Quest for Human Rights* (Albany, NY: SUNY Press, 2006), 13–47, 59–66.

106. "A broad program was initiated during the 1950s to collect information on dissident activities under the code name COMINFIL (or Communist Infiltration). . . . Covering 'the entire spectrum of the social and labor movement' . . . this program was justified as 'fortify[ing] the government against 'subversive pressures.'" Athan Theoharis, *Spying on Americans: Political Surveillance from Hoover to the Huston Plan* (Philadelphia, PA: Temple University Press, 1978), 166. Also see Senate Select Committee, *FBI Domestic Intelligence,* 43, 59–62.

107. Goldstein, *Political Repression,* 215, 245, 251, 272, 318, 341.

108. Overall, according to a former agent who'd worked the "commie beat," of the roughly 8,500 people still listed as belonging to the CP by the end of 1961, at least 1,500 were reporting to the FBI, a ratio of one FBI operative for every 5.7 genuine party members. Other analysts have indicated that "paid up [CP] membership sank to a low of 3,474." See Cook, *FBI Nobody Knows,* 33; Michael R. Belknap, *Cold War Political Justice: The Smith Act, the Communist Party, and American Civil Liberties* (Westport, CT: Greenwood Press, 1977), 190, 197.

109. See generally, U.S. Senate, Select Committee to Study Government Operations with Respect to Intelligence Activities, *Final Report, Book III: Supplementary Detailed Staff Reports on Intelligence Activities and the Rights of Americans; COINTELPRO: The FBI's Covert Action Programs Against American Citizens*

(Washington, DC: 94th Cong., 2nd Sess., Apr. 23, 1976 [available at www.icdc .com/~paulwolf/cointelpro/churchfinalreprtllld.html]; hereinafter cited as Senate Select Committee, *COINTELPRO*).

110. As the Church Committee recounted, "On March 8, 1971, the FBI resident agency in Media, Pennsylvania, was broken into. Documents stolen in the break-in were widely circulated and published by the press. Since some documents carried a 'COINTELPRO' caption—a word unknown outside the Bureau—Carl Stern, a reporter for NBC, commenced a Freedom of Information Act lawsuit to compel the Bureau to produce other documents relating to the programs. The Bureau decided because of 'security reasons' to terminate them on April 27, 1971." *However,* as the Committee also noted, at least three—perhaps eight—otherwise unidentified "COIN-TELPRO-type operations" had continued after the supposed termination date, at least two of which were ongoing in 1975. Senate Select Committee, *COINTELPRO,* 42, 6–7.

111. See generally, Churchill and Vander Wall, *Agents of Repression;* Matthiessen, *In the Spirit of Crazy Horse.*

112. See generally, U.S. Senate, Select Committee on Intelligence, *The FBI and CISPES* (Washington, DC: 101st Cong., 1st Sess., July 1989); Ross Gelbspan, *Break-ins, Death Threats and the FBI: The Covert War Against the Central America Movement* (Boston, MA: South End Press, 1991).

113. Even when efforts to infiltrate targeted organizations were not especially successful, various techniques were employed to sow "suspicion" and "distrust" within them by creating the false impression that "the organization was infiltrated by informants on a very high level," thereby "enhanc[ing] the level of paranoia endemic to [dissident] circles," and subjecting "select[ed] top-echelon leaders" to "mental anguish." Senate Select Committee, *COINTELPRO,* 25; Goldstein, *Political Repression,* 535; Churchill and Vander Wall, *COINTELPRO Papers,* 226.

114. A stated objective of COINTELPRO-New Left, for example, was "creating the impression that leaders are 'informants for the Bureau or other law enforcement agencies." This 'snitch jacket' technique was used in all COINTELPRO programs." Senate Select Committee, *COINTELPRO,* 4–5, 13, 22, 26–27, 48n97.

115. See Goldstein, *Political Repression,* 473–77, 507–508, 512–13, 529.

116. "Approximately 28 percent of the Bureau's COINTELPRO efforts were designed to weaken groups by setting members against each other, or to separate groups which might otherwise have been allies, and to convert them into mutual enemies." Once this had been accomplished, agents sought to "capitalize on active hostility between target groups" in ways which were in many cases all but guaranteed to precipitate violence. Senate Select Committee, *COINTELPRO,* 22–24. For illustrations, see Churchill and Vander Wall, *COINTELPRO Papers,* 130–39; M. Wesley Swearingen, *FBI Secrets: An Agent's Exposé* (Boston, MA: South End Press, 1995), 79–84.

117. See Broehl, *Molly Maguires,* 230–31; MaryJoy Martin, *The Corpse on Boomerang Road: Telluride's War on Labor, 1899–1908* (Montrose, CO: Western Reflections, 2004), quote at page 10.

118. There were *at least* forty; the actual number may have been as high as 67. See Plaintiff's Brief, *Iberia Hampton et al. v. Edward Hanrahan et al.* (Nos. 70C-1384, Cons (N. Dist., Ill., 1975), 12.

119. Huey P. Newton, *War Against the Panthers: A Study of Repression in America* (New York, NY: Harlem River Press, 1996), 78–81; Ward Churchill, "'To Disrupt, Discredit, and Destroy': The FBI's Secret War Against the Black Panther Party," in Kathleen Cleaver and George Katsiaficas, eds., *Liberation, Imagination, and the Black Panther Party: A New Look at the Panthers and Their Legacy* (New York, NY: Routledge, 2001), 93–95.

120. For the most comprehensive examination, see Jeffrey Haas, *The Assassination of Fred Hampton: How the FBI and the Chicago Police Murdered a Black* Panther (Chicago, IL: Lawrence Hill, 2010).

121. See Churchill and Vander Wall, *Agents of Repression,* 87–94; Akinyele Omawale Umoja, "Set Our Warriors Free: The Legacy of the Black Panther Party and Political Prisoners," in Charles E. Jones, ed., *The Black Panther Party Reconsidered* (Baltimore, MD: Black Classic Press, 1998), 422–25.

122. Powers, *Secrecy and Power,* 148.

123. Of the more than 8,500 agents, "3 were American Indians, 15 Asian Americans, 62 Spanish surnamed, and 63 black," while "less than 10 percent" of all FBI employees were people of color. Gentry, *Hoover,* 39, 670.

124. See Ungar, *FBI,* 578–80; William W. Turner, *Hoover's F.B.I.: The Men and the Myth* (Los Angeles, CA: Sherbourne Press, 1970), xii, xiii, 331. As is noted elsewhere, by 1950, "many" members of the Red Squads in New York, Chicago, Detroit, Los Angeles, and San Francisco were former FBI agents, as were members of the campus police forces that "monitored student and faculty organizations." Gentry, *Hoover,* 408.

125. Powers, *Secrecy and Power,* 150, 154, 156; Turner, *Hoover's F.B.I.,* 220, 238–45.

126. Ungar, *FBI,* 435–37; Gentry, *Hoover,* 416–17; Turner, *Hoover's F.B.I.,* 238, 241–42.

127. Ungar, *FBI,* 428; Powers, *Secrecy and Power,* 217–18.

128. Hoover boasted that the FBI academy served as "the West Point of law enforcement." Quoted in Turner, *Hoover's F.B.I.,* 224; Powers, *Secrecy and Power,* 406.

129. During World War II, the academy began to offer specialized instruction on methods of countering espionage and sabotage to selected police personnel. Such training has evolved and expanded over the years, and now includes sequences in "counterterrorism." Federal Bureau of Investigation, *Testimony of Steven McGraw, Assistant Director, FBI, Before the House Select Committee on Homeland Security Subcommittee on Intelligence and Counterterrorism,* July 24, 2003 (available at www .fbi.gov/news/testimony/intelligence-and-counterterrorism).

130. By 1970, "Well over five thousand graduates [of the Academy had] returned to their departments imbued with the spirit of FBI-police camaraderie," with the expectation that they would "diffuse this spirit as well as their training throughout those

departments." Officially, a thousand "leaders and managers of state and local police departments, sheriff's departments, military police organizations, and federal law enforcement agencies" have been trained each year. Unofficially, the Academy has been routinely "turning out between two and three thousand FBI contacts per year" since the 1950s." See Turner, *Hoover's F.B.I.*, 225; Gentry, *Hoover*, 414–23.

131. Like the LAPD's Criminal Conspiracy Section (see note 68, above), the CII was "set up or considerably enlarged by . . . Evelle Younger, an ex-FBI agent who moved from the Los Angeles district attorneyship to the higher state post [of attorney general] under Governor Ronald Reagan's administration." During the late 1960s and early-to-mid-1970s, at least, the CII essentially functioned as a statewide Red Squad. See Durden-Smith, *Who Killed George Jackson?*, 164–65.

132. The prototype JTTF was formed in May 1980. See John Castellucci's otherwise uncommendable book, *The Big Dance: The untold story of Kathy Boudin and the terrorist family that committed the Brinks robbery murders* (New York, NY: Dodd, Mead, 1986), 244.

133. See, e.g., Peter L. Zimroth, *Perversions of Justice: The Prosecution and Acquittal of the Panther 21* (New York: Viking Press, 1974), 47–51. A class action lawsuit, *Handschu v. Special Services Division* (349 F.Supp. 766, 768–70 (F.D.N.Y. 1971)), was filed against BOSS—which was subsequently renamed the "Public Security Section"—in 1971. This resulted in a 1985 consent decree whereby the unit was constrained to acting within constitutional parameters (605 F.Supp. 1384 (D.C.N.Y., 1985). In Sept. 2002, the NYPD "sought and obtained modification of the consent decree" allowing it greater "latitude" in conducting ostensible "counterterrorism" operations. See Jerrold L. Steigman, "Reversing Reform: The Handschu Settlement in Post-September 11 New York City," *Journal of Law and Policy*, Vol. 11 (2003), 745–98.

134. As of mid-2003, there were "84 Joint Terrorism Task Forces around the United States, with participation from 25 different Federal agencies and hundreds of local and state law enforcement agencies in the 84 Task Force locations." There is also a "National Joint Terrorism Task Force located in the Strategic Information and Operations Center at [the FBI headquarters building] comprised of representatives from 35 different Federal agencies. FBI, *Testimony of Steven McGraw, Assistant Director, FBI, Before the House Select Committee on Homeland Security Subcommittee on Intelligence and Counterterrorism, July 24, 2003* (available at www.fbi.gov/news/ testimony/intelligence-and-counterterrorism).

135. On the origins of SWAT, see Bernstein et al., *Iron Fist/Velvet Glove*, 93–97. On proliferation and intensification of usage, see Peter B. Kraska and V. E. Kappeler, "Militarizing the American Police: The Rise and Normalization of Paramilitary Units," *Social Problems*, Vol. 44, No. 1 (1997), 1–18; Diane Cecilia Weber, *Warrior Cops: The Ominous Growth of Paramilitarism in American Police Departments* (Washington, DC: Cato Institute Briefing Papers, No. 50, Aug. 26, 1999).

136. The FBI's formation of designated SWAT units seems to have begun *circa* 1970, with training provided at Quantico, Virginia, by specialists such as Col. Ulrich Wegener of Germany's GSG-9. Today, each of the 56 field offices maintains a basic

42-member SWAT unit. In Sept. 2005, fourteen "enhanced SWAT teams," larger and with a more extensive array of tactical equipment, were also created. This is apart from the so-called Hostage Rescue Team (HRT), a Quantico-based "elite of the elite" formed in 1982. Although it has never actually rescued a hostage, the HRT has been frequently deployed and is rated as "the FBI's most capable and best-equipped counterterrorism team." See Ungar, *FBI*, 191-92, 236; U.S. Dept. of Justice, Office of the Inspector General, *Audit Report 06–26: The Federal Bureau of Investigation's Efforts to Protect the Nation's Seaports* (Washington, DC: U.S. Dept. of Justice, Mar. 2006; available at www.justice.gov/oig/reports/FBI/a0626/findings2.html).

137. According to Hoover, he and the President met privately on Aug. 24, 1936, at which time Roosevelt gave him verbal instructions to resume the investigation of "subversive activities." At Hoover's request, a follow-up meeting between Roosevelt, Hoover, and Sec. of State Cordell Hull was scheduled for the following day. Only when Hull told him to "go ahead and investigate the cocksuckers" during the second meeting did Hoover proceed. There is no record of what was actually said other than Hoover's own file memoranda, but, plainly, if *domestic* "subversives" were at issue, there would have been no need for *Hull's* participation/assent. See Senate Select Committee, *FBI Domestic Intelligence*, 11–12.

138. Gentry, *Hoover*, 208; Powers, *Secrecy and Power*, 161, 164.

139. Gentry, *Hoover*, 141.

140. Goldstein, *Political Repression*, 134; Powers, *Secrecy and Power*, 256; Athan Theoharis, "The FBI and the American Legion Contact Program, 1940–1966," *Political Science Quarterly*, Vol. 100, No. 2 (Summer 1985), 271–86. On Red Squad connections, see note 124, above.

141. "It is not known when Hoover and 'the father of American intelligence' [Maj. Gen. Ralph H. Van Deman] first met. What *is* known is that in 1922 Van Deman arranged for Hoover to receive a reserve officer's commission in the Army's Military Intelligence Division (by 1942, when he resigned his commission, Hoover had risen to lieutenant colonel); that Hoover worked closely with [Brig. Gen.] Marlborough Churchill, Van Deman's successor as head of MID, during the Palmer raids and thereafter." Gentry, *Hoover*, 110, 208–209.

142. This was not only through direct liaison/information sharing with the MID. As Gentry observes, "Hoover and Van Deman maintained a mutually beneficial relationship that continued until Van Deman's death in 1952," a matter devolving upon the fact that, after his retirement from the army in 1929, Van Deman established "his own nationwide network of private informants, who infiltrated the Communist party, labor unions, church groups, the ACLU, and civil rights organizations . . . amassing millions of pages of secret files." After his death, it was found that Van Deman's "private" files contained copies of myriad classified materials originating with MID, the Office of Naval Intelligence, and the FBI. Hence, it is clear that for "more than three decades, Hoover had access to, and traded information with, a privately financed intelligence network of civilian, military, and police spies." Gentry, *Hoover*, 208–209, 110.

143. Michael Newton, *Encyclopedia of American Law Enforcement* (New York, NY: Facts on File, 2007), 340.

144. Gentry, *Hoover,* 81.

145. Turner, *Hoover's F.B.I.,* 334, 329–30.

146. Turner, *Hoover's F.B.I.,* 333. Wackenhut had three partners when the firm was established. All were ex-FBI agents. In 1977, it was revealed that, among other things, the Wackenhut agency had compiled more than 2.5 million files on the political beliefs and activities of individual citizens for use by private corporations in the "pre-employment screening" of applicants. Theoharis, *Spying on Americans,* 290n1.

147. As one researcher observed during the mid-1970s, the FBI's files, which had previously encumbered an entire building in southwest Washington, D.C., took up "two and a half entire floors" of its new J. Edgar Hoover headquarters building. Ungar, *FBI,* 151–52.

148. By the early 1970s, "the volume of files became so enormous that division chiefs had to ask field offices to submit only what was necessary to have at headquarters." Ungar, *FBI,* 152.

149. "In 1949, Hoover instructed his agents to create a separate filing procedure for information from or relating to the Bureau's 'most sensitive sources' to ensure that such information would not appear in case files. Such [material] was to be sealed in an envelope marked 'June,' a codeword used because the program began in the month of June. . . . June Mail was to be used only for the most secretive sources (ELSURS [electronic surveillance] materials or surreptitious entry information). . . . In November 1978, the FBI discontinued the 'June' designation but retained the requirements for special handling and the separation of sensitive information." Haines and Langbart, *Files of the FBI,* xiii-xiv, 255–7.

150. Hoover secretly established the Bureau's parallel "Do Not File" filing system on Apr. 11, 1940, requiring that documents "on especially sensitive subjects were to be prepared on [pink or] blue paper rather than white [and] bearing no classification or serial numbers [for reference in the FBI's] General Indices. Unnumbered, they could be destroyed without leaving a telltale gap. . . . By 1942, the FBI was committing so many illegal acts that the 'do not file' system had to be expanded to hide the paper trail." See Gentry, *Hoover,* 230, 281, 707–708, 728, 731–35; Theoharis, *Spying on Americans,* 125–26, 137, 191; Haines and Langbart, *Files of the FBI,* xiii-xiv, 249–51.

151. Scanning the Bureau's fingerprint and file material into electronic format appears to have begun in mid-to-late 1974. Ungar, *FBI,* 151–52.

152. A key medium for the sharing of political intelligence between the Bureau and local police agencies has long been the "Law Enforcement Intelligence Unit" (LEIU), a corporately/federally-funded entity established in 1956 by Capt. James Hamilton of the LAPD. "[L]ocal police cadres and [SACs] routinely cooperated in assorted liaison arrangements, operational assistance, and data exchange" from the outset. At least 230 state/local police agencies were participating by 1970, a number which undoubtedly increased dramatically after the LEIU received grants from the federal Law Enforcement Assistance Administration (LEAA) to computerize its data storage and retrieval capabilities in 1974. See Donner, *Protectors of Privilege,* 79–85; Donner, *Age of Surveillance,* 426–27.

153. See note 84, above.

154. Senate Select Committee, *FBI Domestic Intelligence,* 23, 25–28, 34–35, 36–41, 52–53, 78–83, 90; Theoharis, *Spying on Americans,* 40–44; Gentry, *Hoover,* 213.

155. Senate Select Committee, *FBI Domestic Intelligence,* 98–101; Theoharis, *Spying on Americans,* 59–64; Ungar, *FBI,* 128–29; O'Reilly, *"Racial Matters,"* 338–39; Swearingen, *FBI Secrets,* 103; Haines and Langbart, *Files of the FBI,* 222–23.

156. The Communist Index was compiled as part of "a secret emergency detention program," codenamed "Portfolio," authorized in August 1948. "In a June 21, 1960, letter . . . Hoover advised special agents in charge (SACs) that henceforth the Communist Index would be renamed the Reserve Index" . . . Specifically targeted as priorities were "professors, labor union leaders and organizers, lawyers, doctors, 'individuals who could potentially furnish material financial aid,' and 'other potentially influential persons on a local or national level.'" Theoharis, *Spying on Americans,* 45–46, 55–56.

157. The Attorney General's List of subversive organizations emerged from the federal "Loyalty Program" initiated by Franklin Roosevelt in 1940 and sustained in various forms ever since. See Senate Select Committee, *FBI Domestic Intelligence,* 33–34, 95, 105.

158. Senate Select Committee, *FBI Domestic Intelligence,* 78–84, 90–91, 93; Gentry, *Hoover,* 602; O'Reilly, *"Racial Matters,"* 276–77, 286, 338–89, 340, 416n53.

159. Ungar, *FBI,* 56; Gentry, *Hoover,* 132; Turner, *Hoover's FBI,* 224.

160. Ungar, *FBI,* 56.

161. At issue is the sociopsychological phenomenon of scientism, i.e.: "a kind of logical fallacy involving improper usage of science or scientific claims," leading to "an exaggerated trust in the efficacy of the methods of natural science applied to all areas of investigation." Gregory R. Peterson, "Demarcation and Scientific Fallacy," *Zygon,* Vol. 38, No. 4 (Dec. 2003), 753.

162. Probably the best source on the matter is Morton Levitt and Michael Levitt, *A Tissue of Lies: Nixon v. Hiss* (New York, NY: McGraw-Hill, 1979), 184–209.

163. As the head of the FBI Toolmarks and Firearms Unit explained the purpose of the lab in 1995, "Sometimes [investigators are] pretty confused about what they're trying to prove. Often we can suggest a better way" of building a successful prosecution. George Washington University Professor of Forensic Science James Starrs counters with the obvious: "They're . . . starting with the hypothesis of guilt, then going out to try and prove it. That is not science. These people aren't scientists." Both quoted in John F. Kelly and Phillip K. Wearn, *Tainting Evidence: Inside the Scandals at the FBI Crime Lab* (New York, NY: Free Press, 1998), 16.

164. Apart from the Hiss case (see note 162), there are *many* examples of the FBI manipulating/fabricating physical evidence. See, e.g., *Statement of Gerald B. Lefcourt on Behalf of [the] National Association of Criminal Defense Lawyers before the Senate Judiciary Subcommittee on Administrative Oversight and the Courts Regarding Problems with the FBI Lab,* Oct. 16, 1997 (available at www.nacdl.org/TESTIFY/test0017.html).

165. Misidentification of fingerprints is only the tip of the iceberg. Earlier testing showed error-rates of 51.4 percent in paint sample identification, 68 percent in hair sample IDs, and 71 percent in IDing blood samples. Kelly Weam, *Tainting Evidence,* 32, 30.

166. As U.S. District Court Judge Gladys Kessler observed in 1997, its record of misconduct "calls into question the scientific integrity of the FBI crime lab and the thousands of prosecutions [and convictions] that rely on evidence it has produced." *Whitehurst v. FBI* (No. 96–572(GK), slip op. (D.D.C., Feb. 4, 1990)), 2.

167. For a prime illustration of how this wildly distorted image is currently peddled, see the 45-minute "documentary," *Modern Marvels: FBI's Crime Lab* (History Channel, 2010).

168. It has long since been documented that the Bureau systematically distorts its data, not only to make itself look good and ensure annual budget increases, but to shape policy, channel resources into preferred areas of enforcement and "security," and to reward collaborating police officials while punishing those critical of the Bureau. See Turner, *Hoover's F.B.I.,* 221–24; Ungar, *FBI,* 386–90; Powers, *Secrecy and Power,* 157–58; Gentry, *Hoover,* 121–22. The Bureau's *Domestic Terrorist Digest* appears to have been discontinued (under that title), but see Matthiessen, *Spirit of Crazy Horse,* 283, 307.

169. Hoover himself didn't even write the early briefs he ostensibly produced to predicate, and later to defend, the Palmer Raids. Although he signed them, they were actually written by his assistant, George Ruch. On the FBI's stable of in-house ghostwriters, see Ungar, *FBI,* p. 299; Gentry, *Hoover,* 81, 140, 448–49; Powers, *Secrecy and Power,* 343–44, 362–33. For "Hoover's" bibliography, see Richard Gid Powers, *G-Men: Hoover's FBI in American Popular Culture* (Carbondale, IL: Southern Illinois University Press, 1983), 328–36.

170. See Powers, *G-Men,* 83, 108–109; Ungar, *FBI,* 273; Gentry, *Hoover,* 448; Powers, *Secrecy and Power,* 344.

171. The extent to which the Bureau directly "shaped" these books is perhaps best reflected in Hoover's privately-expressed complaint that Whitehead was "making a fortune" from *The FBI Story* when "the FBI had done all the work" in writing it. Gentry, *Hoover,* 446–47.

172. See Powers, *G-Men,* 140–43, 146–49, 156, 158–59, 172–77, 188–206.

173. "A special squad was sent to Los Angeles to oversee filming" of *The FBI Story.* According to Mervyn LeRoy, who was personally selected by Hoover to direct the movie, "Everybody on that picture, from the carpenters and electricians right to the top . . . had to be okayed by the FBI." Gentry, *Hoover,* 447.

174. The TV series was based on the ostensibly autobiographical tract of the same title by one of the many informants inserted by the FBI into the Communist Party during the mid-1940s. Although the Bureau claimed to have had "no hand" in the series, it later admitted that its personnel "helped with" the writing of the book itself. In other words, FBI personnel were assigned to ghostwrite it. Ungar, *FBI,* 472.

175. All scripts of ABC's *The FBI* series were personally approved by Hoover before being produced. The FBI Seal appeared at the beginning of each episode along with a credit thanking the Bureau for its "assistance." Gentry, *Hoover,* 448–49, 580–82.

176. For all the fanfare accorded it both during and since, the "Crime War" of the mid-1930s was a sham from the outset, not least because the "national crime wave" the FBI was supposedly combating existed only in the Bureau's manipulations of statistics and the media. See generally, Robert M. Cipes, *The Crime War: The Manufactured Crusade* (New York: New American Library, 1967); Claire Bond Potter, *War on Crime: Bandits, G-Men, and the Politics of Mass Culture* (New Brunswick, NJ: Rutgers University Press, 1998).

177. With an estimated readership of 48 million and a weekly radio program reaching "89 out of 100 adults in the U.S.," Walter Winchell spent twenty years "broadcast[ing] the praises of his friend John Edgar Hoover" and the FBI while smearing Bureau-selected targets. To facilitate both functions, Hoover routinely provided Winchell with material from the Bureau's classified files. See Gentry, *Hoover,* 218, 386, 396, 445.

178. Kenneth O'Reilly, *Hoover and the Un-Americans: The FBI, HUAC, and the Red Menace* (Philadelphia, PA: Temple University Press, 1983), 199–200.

179. The program was begun in 1956. See O'Reilly, *Hoover and the Un-Americans,* 200; Athan G. Theoharis, with Tony G. Provenda, Susan Rosenfeld, and Richard Gid Powers, eds., *The FBI: A Comprehensive Reference Guide* (Westport, CT: Greenwood Press, 1998), 29.

180. See the chapter titled "Building a Monolith" in Ungar, *FBI,* 37–63.

181. See Theoharis, *Spying on Americans,* 13–39; Donner, *Age of Surveillance,* 263–68.

182. Donner, *Age of Surveillance,* 284–85.

183. See generally, U.S. Senate, Select Committee to Study Government Operations with Respect to Intelligence Activities, *Final Report, Book III: Supplementary Detailed Staff Reports on Intelligence Activities and the Rights of Americans; National Security, Civil Liberties, and the Collection of Intelligence: A Report on the Huston Plan* (Washington, DC: 94th Cong., 1st Sess., Apr. 23, 1976 [available at www.icdc.com/~paulwolf/cointelpro/churchfinalreportIIIm.htm]).

184. On Huston's background as a prominent member of William F. Buckley's Young Americans for Freedom (YAF) during his undergrad years at Indiana University, and subsequent period as an assistant to Patrick J. Buchanan in the Nixon White House, see Donner, *Age of Surveillance,* 155–56, 262, 331, 349.

185. Bernstein et al., *Iron Fist/Velvet Glove,* 149.

186. Data in this area is notoriously slippery. It was credibly estimated in 1990, for example, that the number of private security personnel in the U.S. had *already* reached two million. In any case, there is no doubt that by 2008 there were, at a minimum, "more than 1 million contract security officers, and an equal number of guards estimated to work directly for U.S. corporations." These numbers are exclusive of investigators, undercover operatives, consultants, and other such specialized personnel. See Terrance J. Mangan and Michael J. Shanahan, "Public Law Enforcement/ Private Security: A New Partnership?", *FBI Law Enforcement Bulletin,* Vol. 59 (Jan. 1990), 18–22; Amy Goldstein, "The Private Arm of the Law: Some Question the Granting of Police Powers to Security Firms," *Washington Post,* Jan. 2, 2007.

187. Pinkerton was acquired by Securitas AB in 1999, Burns in 2000. It then merged the two under the name "Securitas Security Services USA." In 2008, the latter entity reported 100,000 employees at $7.3 billion in revenue. See *Securitas Security Services USA, Inc.* (www.linkedin.com/companies/securitas-security-services-usa-inc).

188. By the late 1960s, "twenty-one of [Wackenhut's] forty-eight executives were former [FBI] agents or supervisors, including two former high-ranking officers in the Bureau's Domestic Intelligence Division. . . . [It] led the countersubversive private detective industry . . . boast[ing] that it owned 'one of the largest independent collections' of countersubversive files and literature in the United States, with command over 'more dossiers than any other organization in the country outside of the FBI." Donner, *Age of Surveillance,* 425.

189. See Marcia Heroux Pounds, "Danish Firm Agrees to Buy Wackenhut," *Miami Sun Sentinel,* Mar. 9, 2009.

190. Adam Walinsky, "The Crisis of Public Order," *Atlantic Monthly,* No. 276 (June 1995), 39–40.

191. Turner, *Hoover's F.B.I.,* 333–34. Wackenhut and Fidelifacts were/are hardly the only players. By 1966, nearly a hundred private security firms were run by ex-FBI or CIA agents and the number "multiplied almost exponentially" over the next decade. Among the more prominent were New York's Management Safeguards, Inc., headed by longtime FBI counterespionage specialist Saul D. Astor; retired COINTEL-man Allan Bell's Dektor Counterintelligence in Virginia; the Houston-based McCord Associates, headed by CIA clandestine operations veteran James McCord (of Watergate notoriety); and the agency of noted FBI man, turned CIA contract operative, turned private "security" specialist for Howard Hughes, Robert A. Mahue, in Las Vegas. See Jim Hougan, *Spooks: The Haunting of America—The Private Use of Secret Agents* (New York, NY: William Morrow, 1978), 63–65.

192. Smith, *Blackjacks to Briefcases,* p. 73. The Act, named after its sponsor, South Carolina Senator James Byrnes, is codified at 18 U.S.C.A § 407a (Supp. 1936).

193. See Smith, *Blackjacks to Briefcases,* p. 123–26; Mike Zielinski, "Armed and Dangerous: Private Police on the March," *Covert Action Information Quarterly,* No. 54 (Fall 1995), 46.

194. See Zielinski, "Armed and Dangerous," 46; Smith, *Blackjacks to Briefcases,* 126–27, 128; Stephen Franklin, *Three Strikes: Labor's Heartland Losses and What They Mean for Working Americans* (New York, NY: Guilford Press, 2001), esp. 96–97, 100–101.

195. See Zielinski, "Armed and Dangerous," 46.

196. See Smith, *Blackjacks to Briefcases,* 126–27; Zielinski, "Armed and Dangerous," 46.

197. The first such intervention came during the UMW's 1984 Massey Coal strike in West Virginia and Kentucky. Smith, *Blackjacks to Briefcases,* 122.

198. As of 1995, the number of such personnel in the U.S. totaled some 1.5 million, while "national labor statistics indicate[d] that more jobs [would] be added in the private security field than any other categories over the next decade," and "[i]ndustry

executives estimate[d] that the number of private guards [would] surge to 2 million by the year 2000." Zielenski, "Armed and Dangerous," p. 44. Also see note 186, above.

199. On DynCorp and MPRI, see Singer, *Corporate Warriors,* 10–11, 15–16, 119–35, 146, 152–56, 179, 208–209, 218–19, 222, 236; Avant, *Market for Force,* 9, 18–20, 101–13, 113, 117–24, 129–31, 134, 150–55, 188, 221, 234, 245. On Triple Canopy, see, e.g., Steve Fainaru, *Big Boy Rules: America's Mercenaries Fighting in Iraq* (Cambridge, MA: De Capo Press, 2008), 17–20. Also see note 11, above.

200. "Blackwater in 2006 had some twenty-three hundred private soldiers deployed in nine countries around the world and boasted a database of another twenty-one thousand additional contractors on whom it could call should the need arise." Jeremy Scahill, *Blackwater: The Rise of the World's Most Powerful Mercenary Army* (New York, NY: Nation Books, 2007), 342–43.

201. In Iraq, Blackwater personnel *initiated* gunfire on at least 163 occasions in barely three years. The UN concluded Blackwater's operatives in Iraq were functioning as mercenaries engaged in a criminal enterprise under provisions of the 1989 Mercenary Convention (which the U.S. has never ratified). See Sabrina Tavernise and James Glanz, "Iraqi Report Says Blackwater Guards Fired First," *New York Times,* Sept. 19, 2007; "Blackwater most often shoots first, congressional report says," *CNN. com/world,* Oct. 2, 2007 (available at David Johnson and John M. Broder, "F.B.I. Says Guards Killed 14 Iraqis Without Cause," *New York Times,* Nov. 14, 2007. Also see U.S. Senate, Majority Staff of the Committee on Oversight and Government Reform, Memorandum: Additional Information about Blackwater USA, Oct. 1, 2007 (available at www.graphics8.nytimes.com/packages/pdf/national/20071001121609.pdf); Karen DeYoung "Other Killings by Blackwater Staff Detailed: State Dept. Papers Tell of Coverup," *Washington Post,* Oct. 2, 2007. "WikiLeaks Iraq War Logs Expose US-Backed Iraqi Torture, 15,000 More Civilian Deaths, and Contractors Run Amok," *Democracy Now!,* Oct. 25, 2010 (available at www.democracynow.org/2010/10/25/wikileaks_iraqi_war_logs_expose_us).

202. Scahill, *Blackwater,* 43–47, 237–52, 270.

203. According to the *New York Times* and *Washington Post,* "in 2004 the CIA hired Blackwater 'as part of a secret program to locate and assassinate top operatives of Al Qaeda.' . . . Blackwater 'was given operational responsibility for targeting terrorist commanders and was awarded millions of dollars. . . . '" Jeremy Scahill, "Blackwater: CIA Assassins?", *The Nation,* Aug. 20, 2009; Mark Mazzetti, "C.I.A. Sought Blackwater's Help to Kill Jihadists," *New York Times,* Aug. 20, 2009.

204. Established in Jan. 2002, within five years "Blackwater [Worldwide had] more than $500 million in government contracts—and that does not include its secret 'black' budget operations for U.S. intelligence agencies or private corporations/individuals and foreign governments." See Scahill, *Blackwater,* pp. xix, 43, 45–7, 343.

205. The identities of two of the firms involved—Arlington, Virginia-based CACI International, and San Diego-based Titan Corp. (now rebranded as "L-3 Services" and headquartered in New York)—were revealed in connection with the 2004 Abu Ghraib torture "scandal." Predictably, no criminal charges were brought against the offenders. See David Dishneau, "Defense contractor claims immunity in Iraq torture,"

Seattle Times, Sept. 26, 2008; Scott Horton, "Security Contractors Immune from Torture Charges, Judges Rule," *Harpers,* Sep. 2009 (available at www.harpers.org/archive/2009/09/hbc-90005706).

206. The first component of Blackwater USA—the Blackwater Lodge and Training Ctr.—was incorporated in Dec. 1996 and opened for business a few months later. By 2007, demand for its services was sufficient that it began construction of two new training facilities—"Blackwater North," in Mount Carroll, Illinois, and "Blackwater West," in San Diego, California—as well as a jungle training compound at the navy's base at Subic Bay, in the Philippines. Scahill, *Blackwater,* 32–42, 151, 343.

207. "In addition to its work guarding private companies, banks, hotels, industrial sites, and rich individuals, Blackwater was quietly handed a major no-bid contract with the Department of Homeland Security's Federal Protective Service, ostensibly to protect federal reconstruction projects for FEMA. . . . By June 2006, the company had raked in some $73 million from its Katrina work for the government—about $243,000 a day." Scahill, *Blackwater,* 326–27. Also see James Ridgeway, "The Secret History of Hurricane Katrina," *Mother Jones,* Aug. 2009 (available at motherjones .com/environment/2009/08/secret-history-hurricane-katrina).

208. "The men from Blackwater USA arrived in New Orleans right after Hurricane Katrina hit on August 29, 2005 . . . beat[ing] the federal government and most aid organizations to the scene as [the first] 150 heavily armed Blackwater troops dressed in full battle gear spread out into the chaos. . . . As countless guns poured into [the] 'Baghdad on the Bayou' . . . there was a distinct absence of relief operations, food, and water distribution." Among the other firms contracted to "secure" New Orleans from the first days onward were DynCorp, Wackenhut, American Security Group, and an Israeli outfit calling itself "Instinctive Shooters International" (ISI). Scahill, *Blackwater,* pp. 321, 327–30. Also see Daniela Crespo and Jeremy Scahill, "Overkill in New Orleans," *Alternet,* Sept. 12, 2005 (available at www.alternat.org/katrina/25320/).

209. The New Orleans metro area death toll resulting from Katrina is officially listed by the State of Louisiana as having been 1,464; independent researchers have recently placed the total at more than 4,000. It has been contended that well over 500 deaths are attributable to police and private contract personnel. At this point, five New Orleans cops have been convicted or entered guilty pleas for committing and/or covering up the execution-style murders of three unarmed black men in two separate "incidents," while another trio of officers is scheduled for trial in June 2011. Several other cases, involving another dozen probable police murders, remain under investigation. See Scahill, *Blackwater,* pp. 328–30; Robert Lindsay, *Final Katrina Death Toll at 4,081,* May 30, 2009 (available at robertlindsay.wordpress.com/2009/05/30/final-katrina-death-toll-at-4081); Ewen MacAskill, "New Orleans police officers face death penalty over Katrina shootings," *The Guardian,* July 14, 2010; Lise Olsen, "Who Died in Hurricane Katrina? Hundreds of names are still a mystery—and the death toll itself is subject of controversy," *Houston Chronicle,* Aug. 31, 2010; Staff, "Henry Glover jury finds 3 officers guilty in death, burning of Algiers man," *New Orleans Times-Picayune,* Dec. 9, 2010.

210. See, e.g., U.S. Department of Justice, Bureau of Justice Assistance, *Engaging the Private Sector to Promote Homeland Security: Law-Enforcement-Private Security Partnerships* (Washington, DC: Dept. of Justice, Office of Justice Programs, 2005); Stephen E. Flynn and Daniel B. Prieto, *Neglected Defense: Mobilizing the Private Sector to Support Homeland Security* (Washington, DC: Council on Foreign Relations, Mar. 2006).

211. *Fraternal Order of Police* (Nashville, TN: Turner, 2004), 59.

212. Zielenski, "Armed and Dangerous," 44.

213. By one compilation, there were "636,396 full time state, city, university and college, metropolitan and non-metropolitan county and other law enforcement officers in the United States," as well as approximately "120,000 law enforcement personnel working for the federal government adding up to a total number of 800,000 law enforcement personnel in the U.S." as of 2006. *How many police officers are employed in the United States?* (available at wiki.answers.com/Q/How_many_police_officers_are_employed_in_the_United_states).

214. Ibid.

215. Using New York mayor Rudolph Giuliani's trend-setting "civility campaign" as a lens through which to examine what he described as an emerging "zero tolerance police state," one analyst observed in 1999 that "first [Giuliani sent the police] for the squeegee men, then the truants [and homeless]; now it is the street vendors, bus drivers, sex shops, and even protesting construction workers. . . . The police are already ticketing cabbies for violating a list of seventeen new regulations imposed by the mayor. . . . Even Manhattan office workers are under the gun for, of all things, jaywalking. To prevent this crime, police have erected metal barricades." Correspondingly, "misdemeanor arrests shot up by 73 percent" in New York between 1994 and 1997, along with complaints of police brutality, which "jumped 62 percent" during the same period. Meanwhile, the New York approach had been adopted by police departments in New Orleans, Minneapolis, Indianapolis, Baltimore, San Francisco, and other cities around the country, with similar results. Christian Parenti, *Lockdown America: Police and Prisons in the Age of Crisis* (London, UK: Verso, 1999), 83-84, 107-108.

216. The concept of "zero tolerance policing"—i.e., the proposition that maximal enforcement of even the most trivial elements of the municipal code will forestall major crime—was concocted in 1982 by the rabidly reactionary Harvard criminologist James Q. Wilson and enthusiastically pursued by former Boston police chief William J. Bratton during his tenure as head of the New York Transit Police (1990–94). Appointed New York City police commissioner by the newly elected mayor, Rudolph Giuliani, in 1994, Bratton immediately instructed the NYPD to implement the policy on a city-wide basis (albeit, quite selectively both in terms of the people targeted and with regard to which parts of the municipal code were emphasized). In 2002, Bratton was hired as chief of the LAPD, a position he held until Oct. 2009. He is now a senior executive with Altegrity, a New York-based security firm. See Parenti, *Lockdown America,* 70–72.

217. The 1994 "opening shot" in Giuliani's "pacification program" in New York "was a short, sharp war against 'squeegee operators' who, according to Giuliani, had

been 'harassing and intimidating people for years.' Their crime was offering to clean automobile windshields at street corners and at highway entrances on the Westside of the city." From there it expanded in both scope and in virulence so rapidly that, by 1997, a serious analyst would be only half-joking when he remarked upon the NYPD's "emulation of the Israeli Army's conquest of the West Bank." Parenti, *Lockdown America,* 77, 105.

218. Federal Bureau of Investigation, "Quick Facts About Us" (available at www .fbi.gov/about-us/quick-facts/quickfacts).

219. On Sutley, see Ward Churchill, "The FBI Targets Judi Bari: A Case Study in Domestic Counterinsurgency," *Covert Action Information Quarterly,* No 47 (Winter 1993–94), 4–9; Nicholas Wilson, "Judi Bari—FBI Trial Delayed As New Evidence Emerges," *Albion Monitor,* Jan. 9, 2002.

220. The rubric was set forth rather clearly in the proposed Violent Radicalization and Homegrown Terrorism Act of 2007 (H.R. 1995), which was passed in the House by a vote of 404–6 but failed in the Senate. See Jessica Lee, "Bringing the War on Terrorism Home: Congress Considers How to 'Disrupt' Radical Movements in the United States," *The Indypendent,* Nov. 20, 2007 (available at www.indypendent .org/2007/11/19/bringing-the-war-on-terrorism-home-congress-considers-who-to-'disrupt'-radical-movements-in-the-united-states/).

221. Anti-terrorism and Effective Death Penalty Act (110 Stat. 1214 (1996)). For analysis, see C. Brown Stone, "Legislating Repression: The Federal Crime Bill and the Anti-Terrorism and Effective Death Penalty Act," in Elihu Rosenblatt, ed., *Criminal Injustice: Confronting the Prison Crisis* (Boston, MA: South End Press, 1996), 100–107.

222. "Their convictions, in the U.S. District Court, on appeal at the time I signed the pardons, grew out of their good-faith belief that their actions were necessary to preserves the security interests of our country." Ronald Reagan, "Statement on the Granting of Pardons to W. Mark Felt and Edward S. Miller," Apr. 15, 1981 (available at www.presidency.ucsb.edu/ws/index.php?pid=43698).

223. See Harry Harris and Paul Grabowitz, "Pipe bomb blast: 2 Earth First! people injured; Car destroyed; People question radical group's members," *Oakland Tribune,* May 25, 1990; Lance Williams and Andy Furillo, "2 car-bomb victims arrested: Police accuse pair after blast injures them in Oakland," *San Francisco Examiner,* May 25, 1990; Paul Avery, "Earth First pair: Photos say FBI lied; Pictures to form part of suit over '90 bomb blast in car," *San Francisco Examiner,* May 25, 1993.

224. Jim Doyle, "S.F.'s Top FBI Agent Calls it Quits: Held retiring after 25 years to avoid moving family for 11th time," *San Francisco Chronicle,* May 22, 1993.

225. See Decision and Order by Judge Claudia Wilken, Plaintiff's Motion re Qualified Immunity, *Bari et al. v. Doyle et al.* (Judi Bari and Darryl Cherney v. Individual FBI and Oakland Police Officers) (No. C 91–01057 CW (N.D. Cal., Oct. 15, 1997), 23–25, 64–65 (available at www.judibari.org/immunity_decision.html.

226. "The jury in the Judi Bari and Darryl Cherney federal civil rights lawsuit against four FBI agents and three Oakland Police officers awarded the plaintiffs $4.4 million. . . . The jury found that . . . the defendants violated the First and Fourth

Amendments of the Constitution by arresting the activists, conducting searches of their homes, and carrying out a smear campaign in the press, calling Earth First! a terrorist organization and . . . the activists bombers, after the explosion of a bomb that was planted in Bari's car in 1990." Karen Pickett and Steve Christianson, "Activists Win in Judi Bari vs. FBI Trial," June 11, 2002 (available at www.judibari.org).

227. "In September 2007, the Inspector General of the Justice Department reported that the Terrorist Screening Center (the FBI-administered organization that consolidates terrorist watch list information in the United States) had over 700,000 names in its database as of April 2007—and that the list was growing by an average of over 20,000 records per month. By those numbers, the list now has over a million names on it." American Civil Liberties Union, "Terror Watch List Counter: A Million Plus" (available at www.aclu.org/technoloy-and-liberty/terror-watch-list-counter-million-plus).

228. See Federal Bureau of Investigation, *Testimony of John S. Pistole, Deputy Assistant Director, Counterterrorism Division, FBI, Before the Senate Committee on Government Affairs, July 31, 2003* (available at www.fbi.gov/news/testimony/terrorism-financing-origination-organization-and-prevention); *Testimony of Larry A. Mefford, Executive Assistant Director, Counterterrorism/Counterintelligence Division, FBI, Before the Senate Judiciary Committee, Subcommittee on Immigration and Border Security,* Sept. 23, 2003 (available at www.fbi.gov/ news/testimony/improvements-with-information-sharing-and-watch-lists); *Testimony of Carl Whitehead, Special Agent in Charge, Tampa Division, FBI, Before the House Committee on Government Reform Subcommittee on Government Efficiency and Financial Management and Subcommittee on Technology Policy and the Census,* Dec. 15, 2003 (available at www.fbi .gov/news/testimony/information-technology-enhancing-interagency-cooperation).

229. This is handled through the FBI's Office of Public Affairs (OPA), as the old CRC is now called. The OPA is responsible, among other things, for "managing daily media relations with the national and international press corps," "providing on-site assistance for major media events involving the FBI," "producing analytical and briefing products for executives" as well as their "speeches, talking points, op-eds, letters, reports, and other communications," "facilitating publicity to support operations," "responding to requests for assistance from publishers, authors, television, motion picture, and radio producers," "producing radio shows," "serving as FBI liaison to national [and] community organizations," and "organizing proactive initiatives aimed at helping members of the public to protect themselves from terrorism and crime." In effect, apart from the name, nothing has changed. See Federal Bureau of Investigation, *Office of Public Affairs* (available at www.fbijobs.gov/311178.asp).

Chapter Four

The Media-Military Industrial Complex

Toby Miller

Irresistibly enchanted by a seeming grassroots cornucopia—struck by the digital sublime—many cybertarian technophiles attribute magical properties to today's communications and cultural technologies. These beguiling toys are said to obliterate geography, sovereignty, and hierarchy in an alchemy of truth and beauty. A deregulated, individuated media world supposedly makes consumers into producers, frees the disabled from confinement, encourages new subjectivities, rewards intellect and competitiveness, links people across cultures, and allows billions of flowers to bloom in a post-political parthenon. In this Marxist/Godardian wet dream, people fish, film, fuck, and fund from morning to midnight; the mass scale of the culture industries is overrun by consumer-led production; and wounds caused by the division of labor from the industrial age are bathed in the balm of Internet love.

True believers in technological liberation from corporate domination argue that the concept of a media industrial complex is outmoded, because post-industrial societies stimulate the creative sector via small businesses and new machines permit person-to-person and person-to-population communication. These changes in the media and associated knowledges are being likened to a new Industrial Revolution and the Civil and Cold Wars. They are touted as a route to economic development as much as cultural and political expression. The First World recognizes that its economic future lies in finance capital and ideology rather than agriculture and manufacturing, and the Third World, too, is seeking revenue from intellectual property to supplement its minerals and masses.

The United States, for instance, now sells feelings, ideas, money, health, insurance, and law—niche forms of identity, aka culture. The trend is to harness the cultural skills of the population to replace lost agricultural and manufacturing employment with jobs in music, theatre, animation, recording, radio, TV, architecture, software, design, toys, books, heritage, tourism, advertising, the web, fashion, crafts, photography, gaming, and cinema. Between 1980 and 1998, annual world exchange of electronic culture grew from U.S.$95 billion to U.S.$388 billion. PricewaterhouseCoopers estimates that the U.S. culture industries generated U.S.$428 billion in 2009, putting them ahead of aerospace, automobiles, and agriculture in monetary value. They boast an expected compound annual growth rate of 3.8 percent through 2014. In 2003, culture accounted for 2.3 percent of Gross Domestic Product across Europe, to the tune of €654 billion—more than real estate or food and drink, and equal to chemicals, plastics, and rubber. Annual global growth of 10 percent is predicted.[1] But this does not represent a break with the past, either epistemologically or technologically. It is a fusion of industrial and ideological practice that draws on a century of cultural production to blend corporate and symbolic nationalism and globalization, with the United States an exemplar.

Despite much-vaunted claims that U.S. culture is uniquely independent of state support and direction, the government's violent, destructive nationalism relies on a compliant and even willing partner in the culture industries, which in turn have drawn on massive public subvention for decades. This chapter considers the links between the U.S. state and screen drama, television news and current affairs, and electronic games, focusing on propagandistic elements that develop and index U.S.-dominated corporate globalization. As a preliminary, let's think through how U.S. imperialism works in relationship to the media industrial complex.

Yanqui imperialism is quite different from the classic 19th-century model, and poses many complexities for opponents, analysts, and fellow-travelers. It has involved invasion and seizure, in the case of the Philippines and Cuba; temporary occupation and permanent militarization (Japan); naked ideological imperialism (the Monroe doctrine and Theodore Roosevelt); and a cloak of anti-imperialism (Franklin Delano Roosevelt). It's much harder to gain independence from the U.S. than was the case with its European counterparts, because U.S. imperialism is often indirect and mediated. It produces few dramatic moments of resistive nation-building as per the painful but well-defined struggles toward sovereignty that threw off conventional colonial yokes across the 20th century.

This is because Yanqui imperialism began at a well-developed stage of industrial capitalism and developed—in fact led into—the post-industrial age. It even sought to break down colonialism in order to gain access to labor and consumption on a global scale. The mature form coincided with a Cold War that favored imperial proxies over possessions, due to both prevailing ideology and the desire to avoid direct nuclear conflict with an equal. Once that conflict was over in the 1990s, the free markets that had been undermined by classic imperialism in 1914 were re-established as rhetorical tropes, confirming the drive toward a loose model of domination, with economic power underwritten by militarism rather than colonialism.

None of this means that the U.S. variety of imperialism lacks the drive or the horror of old-world imperialism—just the overt policies and colonial *rites de passage* of Spain's *conquista de América,* Portugal's *missão civilizadora,* or France's *mission civilisatrice.* The country that advertises itself as the world's greatest promise of modernity has been dedicated to translating its own national legacy, a 19th-century regime of clearance, genocide, and enslavement as much as democracy—a modernity built, as each successful one has been, on brutality—into a foreign and economic policy with similar effects and, at times, methods. But it has principally done so through an ideology of ideation rather than colonization, albeit one underwritten by callously and comprehensively self-interested military and commercial power. The Portuguese, the French, the British, and the Spanish all wanted to occupy and exemplify conduct to conquered peoples up close; the Gringos prefer to invade, then instruct from a distance. This looser model has found cultural expression in the formal and, above all, informal ties of the creative sector to propaganda and corporate globalization. This tendency is vigorously indexed in the motion picture industry, which has been a textual lodestar for ancillary domains, such as journalism, television, and gaming, and a managerial model for the pharmaceutical sector's globalization, *inter alia,* via decades of international labor exploitation.

SCREEN DRAMA

Hollywood drama exemplifies the propagandistic simulation and market distribution of U.S. culture and nationalism and the global project of corporate capital. Since the demise of Hollywood's production-line studio system of making movies, which dominated between about 1920 and 1970 but was eroding by the late 1950s, the U.S. culture industries have pioneered the flexible model of employment beloved of contemporary management: jobs are constantly ending, starting, and migrating. After World War II, location shooting across the world became a means of differentiating stories and cutting costs as color and widescreen formats became fashionable, portable recording technology was available, and technical skills proliferated. Studios

purchased facilities internationally to utilize cheap, docile labor. They were
further encouraged by the U.S. tax system to set up production companies
overseas, avoiding the cost of renting studio space in Los Angeles and paying
pension and welfare-fund contributions. By investing in overseas industries,
Hollywood avoided foreign-exchange drawback rules that prevented the
expatriation of profits, simultaneously benefiting from host-state subvention of "local" films. Other nations' screen industries, mostly built on policy
responses to external cultural domination, have enabled that domination,
because they governmentalize and commodify locations as industrial settings
of sites and services. At the same time, the messages Hollywood produces,
both domestically and internationally, frequently tell stories of nationalistic
imperialism.

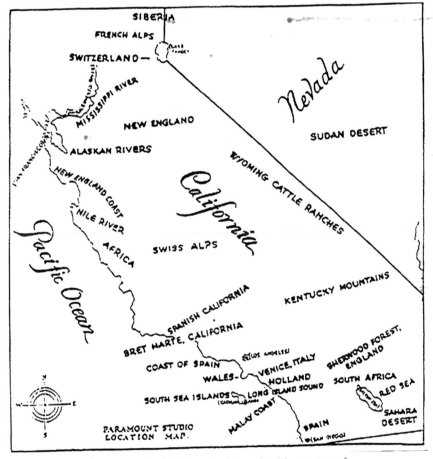

Paramount Studio's Location Map of California, 1927 [3]

The industry has long imagined its global demesne at a pictorial level. Paramount studio's 1927 map of the west coast, depicted below, is a relatively benign and amusing representation of how an industry built on fantasy manages to make dreams appear real. But it also stands for the complex geopolitical ties between U.S. imperialism and motion pictures, which are as textual as they are political-economic.

In keeping with the industry's cartographic simulation, the Federal government has a long but obscure history of participation in film production and control and industry policy based on attempts to harness and control domestic, immigrant, and foreign populations.[4] The notorious racist epic, *Birth of a Nation,* was given military support by order of the Secretary of War and endorsed by the President.[5] From the moment the U.S. entered the First World War, theaters across the country saw speakers and movies testifying to German atrocities, while films imported from the Central Powers were banned.[6] Paramount-Famous-Lasky studio executive Sidney R Kent joyously referred to cinema as "silent propaganda."[7]

As a *quid pro quo,* Hollywood lobbyists of the 1920s and 1930s treated the U.S. Departments of State and Commerce as "message boys": the State Department undertook market research and shared business intelligence, while the Commerce Department pressured other countries to grant cinema open access and favorable terms of trade. In the 1940s, the U.S. opened an Office of the Coordinator of Inter-American Affairs (OCIAA) to gain solidarity from Latin Americans for World War II. Its most visible program was the Motion Picture Division, which was headed by John Hay Whitney, co-producer of *Gone with the Wind* and future secret agent and front man for the CIA's news service, Forum World Features.[8] Some production costs were borne by the OCIAA in exchange for free prints being distributed in U.S. embassies and consulates across Latin America. Whitney accompanied Walt Disney and Donald Duck on a Good Neighbor junket to Rio de Janeiro.[9]

During the invasion of Europe in 1944 and 1945, the U.S. military closed Axis films, shuttered the industry, and insisted on the release of Hollywood movies. The *quid pro quo* for the subsequent Marshall Plan was the abolition of customs restrictions, including limits on film imports.[10] In the case of Japan, the occupation immediately changed the face of cinema. When theatres eventually reopened after the U.S. dropped its atomic bombs, local films and posters with war themes were gone, and previously-censored Hollywood texts dominated screens. The occupying troops established an Information Dissemination Section in their Psychological Warfare Branch to imbue the local population with guilt and "teach American values" through Hollywood.[11]

Once the Cold War was underway, the CIA's Psychological Warfare Workshop employed future Guggenheim Fellow and Watergate criminal E. Howard Hunt, who clandestinely funded the rights purchase and production of George Orwell's anti-Soviet novels *Animal Farm* and *1984*.[12] Around the same time as he shot a romantic rival with a gun, producer Walter Wanger trumpeted in a scholarly journal the meshing of "Donald Duck and Diplomacy" as "a Marshall Plan for ideas . . . a veritable celluloid Athens," concluding that the state needed Hollywood "more than . . . the H bomb."[13] Industry head Eric Johnston, fresh from time as a diplomat, drew up the Hollywood blacklist in order to dispatch "messengers from a free country" in the form of pro-capitalist films, which President Harry S Truman referred to as "ambassadors of goodwill."[14] The United States Information Service spread its lending library of films across the globe as part of Cold War expansion. President John F Kennedy instructed the Service to use film and television to propagandize, and his Administration funded film centers in over a hundred countries.[15] The title of a Congressional Legislative Research Service 1964 report made the point bluntly: *The U.S. Ideological Effort: Government Agencies and Programs.* Four decades later, union officials emphasized to Congress that "although the Cold War is no longer a reason to protect cultural identity, today U.S.-produced pictures are still a conduit through which our values, such as democracy and freedom, are promoted."[16]

Then there is the Defense Department. Since World War II, the Pentagon has provided technology, soldiers, and settings to motion pictures and television, in return for a jealously-guarded right to amend or veto stories that offend its sensibilities.[17] Today's hybrid of SiliWood (Silicon Valley and Hollywood) blends Northern Californian technology, studio methods, and military funding. The interactivity underpinning this hybrid has evolved through the articulation since the mid-1980s of Southern and Northern California semiconductor and computer manufacture and systems and software development (a massively military-inflected and -supported industry since Cold War II) to Hollywood screen content. Disused aircraft-production hangars became entertainment sites. Today's links are as much about technology, personnel, and collaboration on ancillary projects as story lines. Steven Spielberg is a recipient of the Pentagon's Medal for Distinguished Public Service; numerous corporations design material for use by the empire in both its military and cultural aspects; and virtual-reality research veers between soldierly and audience applications, much of it subsidized by the Federal government. This has further submerged killing machines from serious public scrutiny. Instead, they surface superficially as Hollywood props.[18]

The industry sprang into step with the state after September 11, 2001, consulting on possible attacks and forming a "White House-Hollywood Committee" to ensure coordination between the nations we bomb and the messages we export. And with NASA struggling to renovate its image, who better to invite to lunch than Hollywood producers, so they would script new texts featuring it as a benign, exciting entity? In the process, the industry's complicity with profit and power versus equality and justice was washed away by the dramatic re-enchantment of a supposedly high moral purpose expressed in national valor.[19]

Let's turn now to an example of how this worldview suffused television drama. The very week before the 2001 attacks on the U.S., the *New York Times* previewed the coming fall TV drama schedule with the headline "Hardest-Working Actor of the Season: The C.I.A.," because three prime-time shows were made under the aegis of the Agency.[20] Included in the preview was *24*, which went on to become one of the longest-running and most internationally successful Yanqui spy television shows until its 2010 cancellation. In 2009, one hundred million people watched it across 236 channels. The program was welcomed by critics as a return of high-quality network drama and a grand piece of existential philosophy, because it foregrounded a solitary figure battling untrustworthy institutions.[21]

But *24* also represents *"la suma de los miedos americanos"* [the sum of American fears].[22] John Downing has termed it *"the most extended televisual reflection to date on the implications of 9/11"* and an egregious argument in favor of the "need" for immediate and illegal action in the "public interest."[23] The show's creator, Joel Surnow, boasted of being a "rightwing nut job."[24] *24* featured cameos by his ideological *confrères* in politics (John McCain) and the news media (Laura Ingraham and Larry Elder) and was endorsed by intellectual lackeys of the Bush regime such as the *ur*-disgraced-academic John Woo, who wrote legal justifications for torture.[25] The Heritage Foundation, a reactionary, coin-operated think tank, held a press conference in 2006 to celebrate the series that featured Michael Chertoff, then the Secretary of Homeland Security, and talk-radio host Rush Limbaugh, who announced that Dick Cheney and Donald Rumsfeld were fans. The 2010 elections in California saw Republicans attack Democratic Senator Barbara Boxer by hailing fans of the show in commercials.

24 clearly endorsed torture as a means of extracting information from terrorists: it was fine for the hero, Jack Bauer, "a man never at a loss for something to do with an electrode," to deny medical assistance to a terrorist whom he had wounded, shoot another's wife in the leg, then threaten a second shot to the knee unless her husband confides in him; and fine for the U.S. President to subject a Cabinet member to electric shocks as Bauer endlessly intoned "Whatever it takes."[26] U.S. television's depiction of torture grew twenty-five-fold in the decade from 2001, led by *24*.[27] Sometimes the program went too far even for its fellow travelers: a delegation from the U.S. military's major officer training site, West Point, visited *24*'s producers in 2007 to express concern that many military recruits had adopted positive attitudes to illegal torture based on their interpolation by the series, while interrogators reported a direct mimesis with laws broken by U.S. forces in Iraqi prisons. Human Rights Watch also weighed in.[28] Thank heavens for Stella Artois's Godardian spoof of the show.[29]

TELEVISION NEWS AND CURRENT AFFAIRS

It comes as no surprise that nationalistic militarism also colors U.S. television news and current affairs. Consider the coverage of civilian casualties in imperialist conflicts since 2001. When he was called in to comment by CNN after the attacks on the U.S., Lawrence Eagleburger, a former Secretary of State, said: "There is only one way to begin to deal with people like this, and that is you have to kill some of them even if they are not immediately directly involved," while Republican-Party house intellectual Anne Coulter called on the government to identify the nations where terrorists lived, "invade their countries, kill their leaders and convert them to Christianity."[30] Coulter was also the author of the notorious rebuke on TV to a disabled veteran of the American War in Vietnam that "People like you caused us to lose that war." She proceeded to propose that the right "physically intimidate liberals, by making them realize that they can be killed too," and informed Fox News watchers and conservative magazine readers that progressives desire "lots of 9/11s," and "Arabs lie."[31] Coulter's reward for such hyperbolic ignorance was frequent appearances on NBC, CNN, MSNBC, ABC, and HBO, *inter alia*.[32]

When the assault commenced, Afghans in refugee camps were filmed by the BBC, which sold the footage on to ABC. The voiceovers to the two broadcast versions were very different: "British media presented the camps as consisting of refugees from U. S. bombing who said that fear of the daily bombing attacks had driven them out of the city, whereas U. S. media presented the camps as containing refugees from Taliban oppression and the dangers of civil war."[33]

CNN instructed presenters to mention September 11 each time Afghan suffering was discussed, and Walter Isaacson, the network's president, decreed that it was "perverse to focus too much on the casualties or hardship."[34]

As the 2003 adventure in Iraq loomed, Fox mogul Rupert Murdoch said "there is going to be collateral damage . . . if you really want to be brutal about it, better we get it done now."[35] The human impact of the invasion was dismissed by Public Broadcasting Service *News Hour* Executive Producer Lester Crystal as not "central at the moment."[36] Fox News Managing Editor Brit Hume declared that civilian casualties may not belong on television, as they are "historically, by definition, a part of war." The nature of those casualties has changed quite dramatically: a century ago, eight US soldiers were killed for every civilian in war; now that ratio is reversed. In the 1991 Gulf War, the US lost just 270 soldiers, many to friendly fire, while no NATO troops died in Kosovo. The 2001 invasion of Afghanistan saw one official US combatant killed by the opposition. But civilian suffering took second place in the U.S. to military maneuvers and odes. In the fortnight prior to the invasion, none of the three major commercial networks examined the humanitarian impact of such an action. Human Rights Watch's briefing paper, and a UN Undersecretary-General's warning on the topic, lay uncovered. Instead, a carnival of *matériel* oscillated between glorifying and denying death. Thirty-eight percent of CNN's coverage of the bombardment emphasized technology, while 62 percent focused on military activity, without referring to history or politics.[37]

More than half of U.S. TV studio guests talking about the impending action in Iraq in 2003 were superannuated white-male pundits,[38] "ex-military men, terrorism experts, and Middle Eastern policy analysts who know none of the relevant languages, may never have seen any part of the Middle East, and are too poorly educated to be expert at anything."[39] The *New York Times* refers to these has-been and never-were interviewees like this: "[p]art experts and part reporters, they're marketing tools, as well."[40] The virtually universal links between punditry and arms trading were rarely divulged, and never discussed as relevant. Retired Lieutenant General Barry McCaffrey, employed by NBC News, pointed to the *cadre*'s "lifetime of experience and objectivity." In his case, this involved membership of the Committee for the Liberation of Iraq, a lobby group dedicated to influencing the media, and the boards of three munitions companies that make ordnance he praised on MSNBC. Perhaps the most relevant factor is that General Electric, which owned MSNBC and NBC at the time, is one of the largest defense contractors in the world, receiving billions of dollars from the Pentagon each year. Disney (which owns ABC) is also a beneficiary of *largesse* from the Department of Defense.[41] Even amongst the thoroughly ideologized U.S. public, 36 percent believed the media overemphasized the opinions of these retirees.[42]

In addition to these complex domestic imbrications of the private and public sectors, the U.S. government attempted to limit the expression of alternative positions on world television. To hide the carnage of its 2001 invasion, the Pentagon bought exclusive rights to satellite photos of Afghanistan.[43] And the Associated Press Managing Editors noted, in an open protest note to the Pentagon, that "journalists have been harassed, have had their lives endangered and have had digital camera disks, videotape and other equipment confiscated" by the U.S. military.[44]

Consider the treatment of Al-Jazeera. The Qatar-owned TV news network dedicated only a third of its stories during the 2001 and 2003 invasions to war footage, emphasizing human distress over electronic effectiveness, and vernacular reportage rather than patriotic euphemism. Thousands of civilian Afghan and Iraqi deaths reported by Al-Jazeera and South Asian, South-East Asian, Western European, and other Middle Eastern news services went essentially unrecorded in the U.S.[45] Unsurprisingly, the U.S. State Department tried to disrupt Al-Jazeera by applying pressure to Qatar's Emir Sheikh Hamid bin Khalifa al-Thaniof, and the network's Washington correspondent was "detained" *en route* to a U.S.-Russia summit in November 2001.[46] Assaulted by U.S. munitions in Afghanistan in 2001 (where it was the sole broadcast news outlet in Kabul) and Iraq in 2003, Al-Jazeera was also subject to Rumsfeld's denunciation of it as "Iraqi propaganda." The Bush regime referred to the network as "All Osama All the Time." During the U.S. occupation of Iraq, staff were subject to violent assaults by U.S. soldiers, culminating in murders. Rear Admiral Craig Quigley, then U.S. deputy assistant defense secretary for public affairs, justified the attack on the network's Kabul operations by claiming that Al Qaeda interests were being aided by it. Quigley's proof was that Al-Jazeera was using a satellite uplink and was in contact with Taliban officials—pretty normal activity for a news service.[47] Quigley's next job? Vice President, Communications and Public Affairs, Lockheed Martin Naval Electronics & Surveillance Systems.

GAMES

U.S. journalists embedded with the military during the Iraq invasion likened the experience to "a video game."[48] This should not come as a surprise, since gaming has been crucial to war and *vice versa* since the late 19th century, when the U.S. Naval War College Game simulated Prussian and French field tactics. Such methods gained popularity after remarkable success in predicting Japanese strategy in the Pacific from 1942. By the late 1950s, computers were utilized to theorize and play games.[49] Game theory in 1960s and 1970s political science and warcraft sought to scientize the study and practice of crisis decision making, founded on a rational-actor model of maximizing utility that was applied to the conduct of states, soldiers, and diplomats, constructing nuclear-war prospects and counters. With the decline of Keynesianism, game theory's ideal-typical monadic subject came to dominate economics and political science more generally. Utility maximization even overtook parts of Marxism, which had tended to favor collective rather than selfish models of choice. Games were in, everywhere you looked. That notion of individuals out for themselves remains in vogue, restimulated through electronic games (which were invented for the U.S. military by defense contractors). The Pentagon established a gaming center within the National Defense University.[50]

When the end of Cold War II wrought economic havoc on many corporations involved in the U.S. defense industry in the early 1990s, they turned to games as a natural supplement to their principal customer, the military. Today's new geopolitical crisis sees these firms conducting half their game business with the private market and half with the Pentagon[51]; hence visitors to the Fox News site on May 31, 2004 encountering a "grey zone." On one side of the page, a U.S. soldier in battle gear prowled the streets of Baghdad. On the other, a *Terror Handbook* promised to explain and confront "the threat to America" under the banner: "*WAR ON TERROR sponsored by* KUMA WAR" (a major gaming company). The *Kuma: War* game included online missions entitled "Fallujah: Operation al Fajr," "Battle in Sadr City," and "Uday and Qusay's Last Stand." Its legitimacy and realism were underwritten by retired military officers who ran the firm, and the game was used as a recruiting tool by their former colleagues. Both sides benefited from the company's website, which invites soldiers to pen their battlefield experiences—a neat way of getting intellectual property *gratis* in the name of the nation.[52] The site boasted that: "Kuma War is a series of playable recreations of real events in the War on Terror. Nearly 100 playable missions bring our soldiers' heroic stories to life, and you can get them all right now, for free. Stop watching the news and get in the game!"

That form of direct address to players was vital, because the US's military-diplomatic-fiscal disasters of the period between 2001 and 2007 jeopardized the steady supply of new troops, imperiling the army's stature as the nation's premier employer of 17–24-year-old workers. At the same time as recruits to the military had decreased due to the dangers of war, recruits to militaristic game design stepped forward. Their mission, which they appeared to accept with alacrity, was to interpolate the country's youth by situating players' bodies and minds to fire the same weapons and face the same issues as on the battlefield. TV commercials depicted soldiers directly addressing gamers, urging them to show their manliness by volunteering for the real thing and serving abroad to secure U.S. power.[53] Players of the commercial game *Doom II* could download *Marine Doom*, a Marine Corps modification of an original that had been developed after the Corps commandant issued a directive that games would improve tactics. And Sony's *U.S. Navy Seals* website linked directly to the Corps' own page.

The media industrial complex is exemplified in the anecdote with which Ed Halter begins his journalistic history of computer games—the moment in 2003 when Los Angeles was occupied by U.S. Special Forces. Just two months after their ill-starred imperialist venture in Iraq had begun, these troops invaded LA's Convention Center as part of Electronic Entertainment Exposition, the annual showcase of video games. Their mission? To promote *America's Army*, an electronic game designed to recruit young people to the military via simulated first-person shooting. The game included notes to parents that stressed the importance of substituting "virtual experiences for vicarious insights"[54]—a euphemism for "cyber-boot camp."[55]

Where did this remarkably successful innovation come from? The Naval Postgraduate School's Modeling, Virtual Environments and Simulation Academic Program had developed a game called *Operation Starfighter*, based on the film *The Last Starfighter*. The next step, *America's Army*, was farmed out to George Lucas's companies, *inter alia*. It was launched with due symbolism on the Fourth of July 2002—dually symbolic, in that Independence Day doubles as a key date in the film industry's summer roll-out of features. The military had to bring additional servers into play to handle 400,000 downloads of the game that first day. *Gamespot PC Reviews* awarded it a high textual rating, and was equally impressed by the "business model." Five years later, *America's Army* remained one of the ten most-played games on line. Civilian developers regularly refreshed it by consulting with veterans and participating in physical war games, while paratexts provided additional forms of promotional renewal. Americasarmy.com took full advantage of the usual array of cybertarian fantasies about the new media as civil society, across the gamut of community fora, Internet chat, fan sites, and virtual competition. Tournaments were convened, replete with hundreds of thousands of dollars' prize money, along with smaller events at military recruiting sites. With over forty million downloads, and web sites by the thousand, its message traveled far and wide—an excellent return on the initial public investment of U.S.$19 million and U.S.$5 million for annual updates. Studies of young people who have positive attitudes to the U.S. military indicate that 30 percent of them formed that view through playing the game—a game that sports a Teen rating; that forbids role reversal via modifications, preventing players from experiencing the pain of the other; and is officially ranked first among the Army's recruiting tools.[56]

For the scholarly advocates of corporate culture who proliferate in game studies, this wasn't a problem. To quote a typical pronouncement: "games serve the national interest by entertaining consumer-citizens and creating a consumer-based demand for military technology" that is unrelated to actual violence.[57]*America's Army* was said to be "primarily a ludological construct,"[58] or to stimulate a vibrant counter-public sphere in which veterans dispute the *bona fides* of non-military players: what began as a recruitment device has allegedly transmogrified into "a place where civilians and service folk . . . discuss the serious experience of real-life war."[59] Well that's alright, then.

This sanguine outlook has its own material history in links between research schools, cybertarians, and the military. The National Academy of Sciences held a workshop for academia, Hollywood, and the Pentagon on simulation and games in 1996. The next year, the National Research Council announced a collaborative research agenda in popular culture and militarism. It convened meetings to streamline such cooperation, from special effects to training simulations, from immersive technologies to simulated networks.[60] Since that time, untold numbers of academic journals and institutes on games have enjoyed close ties to the Pentagon, generating research designed to test and augment the capacity of games to ideologize, hire, and instruct the population. The Center for Computational Analysis of Social and Organizational Systems at Carnegie Mellon University in Pittsburgh promulgates studies underwritten by the Office of Naval Research and the Defense Advanced Research Projects Agency (DARPA). DARPA is blissfully happy to use its U.S.$3.2 billion annual budget to examine, for example, how social networking uncovers "top America's Army players' distinct behaviors, the optimum size of an America's Army team, the importance of fire volume toward opponent, the recommendable communication structure and content, and the contribution of the unity among team members."[61] DARPA refers to Orlando as "Team Orlando" because the city houses Disney's research-and-development "imagineers"; the University of Central Florida's Institute for Simulation and Training; Lockheed Martin, the nation's biggest military contractor; and the Pentagon's Institute for Simulation and Training.

In Los Angeles, the University of Southern California's Institute for Creative Technologies (ICT) articulates scholars, militarists, film and television producers, and game designers under the slogan "Our innovations help save lives, resources and time." Opened by the Secretary of the Army and the head of the Motion Picture Association of America, the Institute started with

U.S.\$45 million of the Pentagon budget in 1998, a figure that was doubled in its 2004 renewal. ICT uses military money and Hollywood muscle to test out homicidal technologies and narrative scenarios—under the aegis of faculty from film, engineering, and communications.[62] ICT also collaborates on major motion pictures, for instance *Spiderman 2*, and its workspace was thought up by the set designer for the *Star Trek* franchise. The Institute produces Pentagon recruitment tools such as *Full Spectrum Warrior* that double as "training devices for military operations in urban terrain": what's good for the Xbox is good for the combat simulator. The utility of these innovations continues in combat. The Pentagon is aware that off-duty soldiers play games. The idea is to invade their supposed leisure time, weaning them from skater games and toward what are essentially training manuals. It even boasts that *Full Spectrum Warrior* "captured Saddam," because the men who dug Hussein out had been trained with it.[63]

CONCLUSION

Far from the thousand blooming flowers of cybertarianism, the culture industries are part of a perpetual virtual war, mixing hyper-masculinist action-adventure ideology, supinely celebratory military news coverage, and complicit new media to blend state violence with commercial entertainment. Their method is at once collective—we are the United States and we're here to intimidate and destroy—and individual, thanks to the immersive interpolation of narrative film, current affairs, and gaming. In addition, they model the global goals of corporate capitalism—unlike many segments of the economy, Hollywood has long gained most of its revenue internationally and has operated a global division of labor for decades. It has shown associated cultural industries the way, and has also offered a blueprint across capitalism in its nexus with the state.[64] This is the dread work of a media industrial complex.

How might we oppose this complex? I have three suggestions. First, we must challenge the hypocrisy of avowedly *laissez-faire* industries like Hollywood that in fact rely on state subsidies and are rarely if ever subjected to democratic scrutiny. Second, we need to insist that media organizations internationalize their sources and rely on experienced, cosmopolitan reporters rather than Kool-Aid-quaffing monolingual nationalists. And third, we should expose the complicity of universities with killing machines and shame our colleagues who fund their research as, effectively, coin-operated Pentagon boffins.

Each time we heard an ESPN or ABC commentator tell us in the 2010 World Cup of men's association football that his Disney employers were broadcasting to members of the U.S. military serving in 145 countries and territories, that effusive thank-you should have sent a shudder down the collective spine. That shudder was not the tingle of pleasure at our compatriots enjoying the big game; it was the unease that must accompany complicity in the complex and the way that corporate capital, state violence, and globalization ooze through each dripping drop of Disney honey. That's Hollywood.

NOTES

1. PricewaterhouseCoopers, "Fast Changing Consumer Behavior Expected to Spur New Business Models in Entertainment and Media Market Over Next Five Years," Press Release, June 15, 2010; Toby Miller, "Can Natural Luddites Make Things Explode or Travel Faster? The New Humanities, Cultural Policy Studies, and Creative Industries," in *Media Industries: History, Theory, and Method,* eds. Jennifer Holt and Alisa Perren (Malden, MA: Wiley-Blackwell, 2009), 184–98.

2. Toby Miller, Nitin Govil, John McMurria, Richard Maxwell, and Ting Wang, *Global Hollywood 2* (London, UK: British Film Institute, 2005).

3. Prospectus, "The Motion Picture Industry as a Basis for Bond Financing" (Chicago, IL: Halsey, Stuart & Co., 1927).

4. Fanning Hearon, "The Motion-Picture Program and Policy of the United States Government," *Journal of Educational Sociology* 12, no. 3 (1938): 147–62.

5. Michael J. Shapiro, *Methods and Nations: Cultural Governance and the Indigenous Subject* (New York, NY: Routledge, 2004).

6. Nick Turse, *The Complex: How the Military Invades Our Everyday Lives* (New York, NY: Metropolitan Books, 2008); Robin Andersen, "Bush's Fantasy Budget and the Military/Entertainment Complex," *PRWatch.org* (February 12, 2007).

7. Sidney R. Kent, "Distributing the Product," in *The Story of the Films as Told by Leaders of the Industry to the Students of the Graduate School of Business Administration, George F. Baker Foundation, Harvard University,* ed. Joseph P. Kennedy (Chicago, IL: A. W. Shaw Company, 1927), 203–32.

8. Frances Stonor Saunders, *Cultural Cold War: The CIA and the World of Arts and Letters* (New York, NY: New Press, 1999).

9. Hortense Powdermaker, *Hollywood: The Dream Factory: An Anthropologist Looks at the Movie-Makers* (Boston: Little, Brown and Company, 1950); E. J. Kahn, Jr., *Jock: The Life and Times of John Hay Whitney* (Garden City: Doubleday, 1981).

10. John Trumpbour, *Selling Hollywood to the World: U.S. and European Struggles for Mastery of the Global Film Industry, 1920–1950* (Cambridge, UK: Cambridge University Press, 2002); Caroline Pauwels and Jan Loisen, "The WTO and the Audiovisual Sector: Economic Free Trade vs. Cultural Horse Trading?" *European Journal of Communication* 18, no. 3 (2003): 291–313.

11. Peter B. High, *The Imperial Screen: Japanese Film Culture in the Fifteen Years' War, 1931–1945* (Madison, WI: University of Wisconsin Press, 2003).

12. Karl Cohen, "The Cartoon That Came in from the Cold," *Guardian,* March 7, 2003.

13. Walter Wanger, "Donald Duck and Diplomacy," *Public Opinion Quarterly* 14, no. 3 (1950): 443–52.

14. Quoted in Eric Johnston, "Messengers from a Free Country," *Saturday Review of Literature* (March 4, 1950): 9–12; also see Aida A. Hozic, *Hollyworld: Space, Power, and Fantasy in the American Economy* (Ithaca, NY: Cornell University Press, 2001).

15. Paul F. Lazarsfeld, "Foreword" in *Hollywood Looks at its Audience,* Leo A. Handel. (Urbana-Champaign, IL: University of Illinois Press, 1950), ix-xiv; Legislative Research Service, Library of Congress, *The U.S. Ideological Effort: Government Agencies and Programs: Study Prepared for the Subcommittee on International Organizations and Movements of the Committee on Foreign Affairs* (Washington, DC: 1964).

16. Pamela Conley Ulrich and Lance Simmers, "Motion Picture Production: To Run or Stay Made in the U.S.A.," *Loyola of Los Angeles Entertainment Law Review* 21 (2001): 357–70.

17. David L. Robb, *Operation Hollywood: How the Pentagon Shapes and Censors the Movies* (Amherst, MA: Prometheus Books, 2004).

18. Directors Guild of America, "DGA Commends Action by Governor Gray Davis to Fight Runaway Production," Press Release, May 18, 2000; Aida A. Hozic, *Hollyworld: Space, Power, and Fantasy in the American Economy* (Ithaca, NY: Cornell University Press, 2001).

19. Andreas Behnke, "The Re-Enchantment of War in Popular Culture," *Millennium: Journal of International Studies* 34, no. 3 (2006): 937–49.

20. Paula Bernstein, "Hardest-Working Actor of the Season: The C.I.A," *New York Times* (September 2, 2001).

21. Tara McPherson, "'The End of TV As We Know It': Convergence Anxiety, Generic Innovation, and the Case of *24,*" *The Oxford Handbook of Film and Media Studies,* ed. Robert Kolker (New York, NY: Oxford University Press, 2008): 306–26; Jennifer L. McMahon, "*24* and the Existential Man of Revolt," *The Philosophy of TV Noir,* ed. Steven M. Sanders and Aeon J. Skoble (Lexington, KY: University Press of Kentucky, 2008): 115–29; Paul Attallah, "A Usable History for the Study of Television," *Canadian Review of American Studies/Revue canadienne d'études américaines* 37, no. 3 (2007): 325–49; Amanda D. Lotz, *The Television Will Be Revolutionized* (New York, NY: New York University Press, 2008).

22. David Miklos, "El império en peligro," *La Tempestad* 59 (2008): 78–79.

23. John Downing, "Terrorism, Torture, and Television: *24* in its Context," *Democratic Communiqué* 21, no. 2 (2007): 62–82.

24. Quoted in Decca Aitkenhead, "One Hour with Kiefer Sutherland," *Guardian,* February 2, 2009.

25. Dahlia Lithwick, "The Bauer of Suggestion," *Slate,* July 26, 2008.

26. John Downing, "Terrorism, Torture, and Television: *24* in its Context." *Democratic Communiqué* 21, no. 2 (2007): 62–82; Dahlia Lithwick, *Slate.*

27. Jinee Lakaneeta, "A Rose by Another Name: Legal Definitions, Sanitized Terms, and Imagery of Torture in *24*," *Law, Culture and the Humanities* 6 (2010): 245–73. Also see humanrightsfirst.org/us_law/etn/primetime/index.asp#impact (accessed July 10, 2010).

28. Martin Miller, "'24' and 'Lost' Get Symposium on Torture," *Seattle Times,* February 14, 2007.

29. See guardian.co.uk/media/video/2009/mar/23/stella-artois-viral-ad (accessed July 10, 2010).

30. See *National Review Online,* September 13, 2001, old.nationalreview.com/coulter/coulter.shtml (accessed July 10, 2010).

31. Quoted in Eric Alterman, *What Liberal Media? The Truth about Bias and the News* (New York, NY: Basic Books, 2003).

32. Alterman, *What Liberal Media?;* FAIR, "*Time* Covers Coulter," April 21, 2005.

33. Douglas Kellner, *From 9/11 to Terror War: The Dangers of the Bush Legacy* (Lanham, MD: Rowman & Littlefield, 2003).

34. Kellner, *From 9/11 to Terror* War.

35. Quoted in John Pilger, "We See Too Much. We Know Too Much. That's Our Best Defense," *Independent,* April 6, 2003.

36. Quoted in J. E. Sharkey, "The Television War," *American Journalism Review,* 2003.

37. FAIR, "Do Media Know That War Kills?" March 14, 2003; Andy Deck, "Demilitarizing the Playground," *Art Context* (2004), artcontext.org/crit/essays/noQuarter (accessed July 10, 2010); James Der Derian, "Imaging Terror: Logos, Pathos and Ethos," *Third World Quarterly* 26, no. 1 (2005): 23–37.

38. FAIR, "In Iraq Crisis, Networks Are Megaphones for Official Views," March 18, 2003.

39. Edward Said, "The Other America," *Al-Ahram* (March 20–26, 2003).40.Elizabeth Jensen, "Network's War Strategy: Enlist Armies of Experts," *Los Angeles Times,* March 18, 2003.

41. Nick Turse, *The Complex.*

42. Arundhati Roy, "Do Turkeys Enjoy Thanksgiving?" *OutlookIndia.com* (January 24, 2004); Daniel Benaim, Visesh Kumar, and Priyanka Motaparthy, "TV's Conflicted Experts," *The Nation,* April 21, 2003: 6–7; Pew Research Center for the People & the Press, *Trouble Behind, Trouble Ahead? A Year of Contention at Home and Abroad, 2003 Year-End Report* (2004).

43. Norman Solomon, "Media War Without End," *Z Magazine* (December 2001); Ted Magder, "Watching What We Say: Global Communication in a Time of Fear," in *War and the Media: Reporting Conflict 24/7,* ed. Daya Kishan Thussu and Des Freedman (London, UK: Sage Publications, 2003): 28–44.

44. Associated Press, "APME Requests Pentagon Halt Harassment of Media in Iraq," November 13, 2003.

45. Justin Lewis, Terry Threadgold, Rod Brookes, Nick Mosdell, Kirsten Brander, Sadie Clifford, Ehab Bessaiso, and Zahera Harb, *Too Close for Comfort? The Role of Embedded Reporting During the 2003 Iraq War: Summary Report* (London: British Broadcasting Corporation, 2004); Vera Rich, "The Price of Return," *Index on Censorship* 32, no. 3, (2003): 82–86; Amy E. Jasperson and Mansour O. El-Kikhia, "CNN and Al-Jazeera's Media Coverage of America's War in Afghanistan," in *Framing Terrorism: The News Media, the Government, and the Public*, ed. Pippa Norris, Montague Kern, and Marion Just (New York, NY: Routledge, 2003), 113–32; Marc W. Herold, "Who Will Count the Dead?" *Media File* 21, no. 1 (2001); Laura Flanders, "Media Criticism in Mono," *WorkingForChange*, November 9, 2001; Douglas Kellner, "Media Propaganda and Spectacle in the War on Iraq: A Critique of U. S. Broadcasting Networks," *Cultural Studies Critical Methodologies* 4, no. 3 (2004): 329–38; Marco R. della Carva, "Iraq Gets Sympathetic Press Around the World," *U.S.A Today*, April 2, 2003: 1D; David Greenberg, "We Don't Even Agree on What's Newsworthy," *Washington Post*, March 16, 2003: B1.

46. International Federation of Journalists, *Les Journalistes du Monde Entier Produisent un Rapport sur les Médias, la Guerre et le Terrorisme*, October 23, 2001; Kai Hafez, "Al-Jazeera Meets CNN," *Message* (2001); Mohammed el-Nawawy and Leo A. Gher, "Al-Jazeera: Bridging the East-West Gap Through Public Discourse and Media Diplomacy," *Transnational Broadcasting Studies* 10 (2003); Noureddine Miladi, "Mapping the Al-Jazeera Phenomenon," in *War and the Media: Reporting Conflict 24/7*, ed. Daya Kishan Thussu and Des Freedman (London, UK: Sage Publications, 2003), 149–60.

47. Toby Miller, *Cultural Citizenship: Cosmopolitanism, Consumerism, and Television in a Neoliberal Age* (Philadelphia, PA: Temple University Press, 2007).

48. Marcus Power, "Digitized Virtuosity: Video War Games and Post-9/11 Cyber-Deterrence," *Security Dialogue* 38, no. 2 (2007): 271–88.

49. James Der Derian, "War as Game," *Brown Journal of World Affairs* 10, no. 1 (2003): 37–48.

50. Marcus Power, "Digitized Virtuosity."

51. Karen J. Hall, "Shooters to the Left of Us, Shooters to the Right: First Person Arcade Shooter Games, the Violence Debate, and the Legacy of Militarism," *Reconstruction: Studies in Contemporary Culture* 6, no. 1 (2006).

52. Andy Deck, "Demilitarizing the Playground"; Marcus Power, "Digitized Virtuosity"; Nick Turse, *The Complex*.

53. David Verklin and Bernice Kanner, "Why a Killer Videogame is the U. S. Army's Best Recruitment Tool," *MarketingProfs.com* (May 29, 2007); Clive Thompson, "The Making of an X Box Warrior," *New York Times Magazine*, August 22, 2004; Marcus Power, "Digitized Virtuosity."

54. Ed Halter, *From Sun Tzu to Xbox: War and Video Games* (New York, NY: Thunder's Mouth Press, 2006).

55. Timothy Lenoir, "Programming Theaters of War: Gamemakers as Soldiers," in *Bombs and Bandwidth: The Emerging Relationship between Information Technology and Security*, ed. Robert Latham (New York, NY: New Press, 2003), 175–98.

56. "AA:SF Tops 9 Million User Mark!" February 10, 2008, http://www.americasarmy.com/press/index.php?t=70#; Marcus Power, "Digitized Virtuosity"; Timothy Lenoir, "Programming Theaters of War: Gamemakers as Soldiers," in *Bombs and Bandwidth: The Emerging Relationship Between Information Technology and Security,* ed. Robert Latham (New York, NY: New Press, 2003), 175–98; John Gaudiosi, "PLAY," *Wired,* July 13, 2005; David B. Nieborg, "America's Army: More Than a Game," in *Transforming Knowledge into Action Through Gaming and Simulation,* ed. Thomas Eberle and Willy Christian Kriz (Munich, DEU: SAGSAGA, 2004); Nick Turse, *The Complex;* Kathleen Craig, "Dead in Iraq: It's No Game," *Wired,* June 6, 2006;Andy Deck, "Demilitarizing the Playground"; Noah Schactman, "Shoot 'Em Up and Join the Army," *Wired,* July 4, 2002; Clive Thompson, "The Making of an X Box Warrior," *New York Times Magazine,* August 22, 2004.

57. Karen J. Hall, "Shooters to the Left"; Marcus Power, "Digitized Virtuosity."

58. David B. Nieborg, "America's Army."

59. Henry Jenkins, *Fans, Bloggers, and Gamers: Exploring Participatory Culture* (New York, NY: New York University Press).

60. Timothy Lenoir, "Programming Theaters of War"; Mike Macedonia, "Games, Simulation, and the Military Education Dilemma," *The Internet and the University: 2001 Forum* (Boulder, CO: Educause, 2002), 157–67.

61. Kathleen Carley, Il-Chul Moon, Mike Schneider, and Oleg Shigiltchoff, *Detailed Analysis of Factors Affecting Team Success and Failure in the America's Army Game,* CASOS Technical Report (2005).

62. Andy Deck, "Demilitarizing the Playground"; David Silver and Alice Marwick, "Internet Studies in Times of Terror," in *Critical Cyberculture Studies,* ed. David Silver and Adrienne Massanari (New York, NY: New York University Press, 2006), 47–54; Nick Turse, *The Complex.*

63. Jonathan Burston, "War and the Entertainment Industries: New Research Priorities in an Era of Cyber-Patriotism," in *War and the Media: Reporting Conflict 24/7,* ed. Daya Kishan Thussu and Des Freedman (London, UK: Sage Publications, 2003), 163–75; Stephen Stockwell and Adam Muir, "The Military-Entertainment Complex: A New Facet of Information Warfare," *Fibreculture* 1 (2003); Robin Andersen, "Bush's Fantasy Budget and the Military/Entertainment Complex," *PRWatch. org,* February 12, 2007; Nick Turse, *The Complex;* Amy Harmon, "More Than Just a Game, But How Close to Reality?", *New York Times,* April 3, 2003; Arun Kundnani, "Wired for War: Military Technology and the Politics of Fear," *Race & Class* 46, no. 1 (2004): 116–25.

64. Toby Miller, Nitin Govil, John McMurria, Richard Maxwell, and Ting Wang, *Global Hollywood 2* (London, UK: British Film Institute, 2005).

Chapter Five

The Criminal (Justice) Industrial Complex

Mechthild Nagel

[L]itigation is a lot like playing the lottery—you'll win if you get lucky enough to draw the right judge.

—Jailhouse lawyer, Sam Rutherford[1]

On January 21, 2009, a constitutional lawyer was sworn in as President of the United States. Barack Obama quickly promised to restore trust in the office of the Attorney General by appointing Eric Holder who in turn promptly derided the CIA's use of torture on "enemy combatants." Among Obama's first acts was to close the internment camp at Guantánamo Bay. It seemed that the rule of law was restored in the country. Furthermore, Obama boldly declared that when he presented his first Supreme Court nominee, Sonia Sotomayor, that justice should be accompanied with a sense of compassion. It seemed for a brief euphoric moment that a new era of reform would be upon us—long overdue since the Attica rebellion of 1971, which brought some humanitarian relief measures, including the abolition of the prisoners' trustee system in the South, law libraries in prison, a modicum of prison education and the temporary abolition of the death penalty.

In April 2009, the Obama administration also signaled an end to the disparity in crack versus powder cocaine sentencing guidelines (in which crack cocaine users need only to be charged with possessing 1/100th of the amount as powder users to receive a like sentence). Along with harsh federal mandatory minimum sentences, such sentencing guidelines have historically adversely impacted communities of color. Now these (and other pressing miscarriage of criminal justice issues) may be considered by a U.S. Sentencing Commission if Congress supports Senate Bill 714 in the fall of 2010.[2] The last time a presidential commission conducted a study on Law Enforcement

117

and Administration of Justice was in 1967, when "The Challenge of Crime in a Free Society" report was produced.[3] An additional sign of hope is that punitive "three strikes and you are out" laws, as well as New York State's Rockefeller Drug Laws, have come under significant scrutiny as of late and are being increasingly supplanted by "Second Chance Act Adult and Juvenile Offender Reentry Demonstration Projects."[4]

It seems, then, that the rhetoric of fear and the need for crime control has waned somewhat. This was exemplified by Senator Jim Webb's bold move to announce a racial impact study and pilot project in ten U.S. cities to question the ethos of mass incarceration, promoted by overzealous policing and prosecution in poor neighborhoods of color. Through his gathered statistics on the subject, Webb, a white senator from Virginia, revealed that the U.S. has in fact become a prison nation: "America imprisons 756 inmates per 100,000 residents, a rate nearly five times the world's average. About one in every 31 adults in this country is in jail or on supervised release. Either we are the most evil people on earth or we are doing something very wrong."[5]

Furthermore, Webb noted that "although experts have found little statistical difference among racial groups regarding actual drug use, African-Americans—who make up about 12 percent of the total U.S. population—accounted for 37 percent of those arrested on drug charges, 59 percent of those convicted, and 74 percent of all drug offenders sentenced to prison."[6] Such figures have led civil rights advocate and litigator Michelle Alexander to conclude that an era of "New Jim Crow" has come upon us.[7] It will remain to be seen if massive decarceration will occur at the federal level and have any trickle-down effect to the states and counties.

Meanwhile, in June 2010, for the first time in almost forty years, a decline in the incarceration rate was reported by the Bureau of Justice Statistics: 2,941 fewer persons were convicted in 2009, amounting to the slightly reduced rate of 748 per 100,000 population—still, excessively high by global standards. In many states, besides New York, there seems to be a slight fatigue (by voters) to buy into the rhetoric of "war on drugs," even though overall, the imprisonment statistics don't bear witness to it yet: Over 50 percent of the 2.3 incarcerated daily by the end of 2008 were convicted of non-violent crimes, the majority thereof being drug convictions. A high percentage of those recommitted to prison are now entering on technical parole violations, prompting the "New school of convict criminology" (i.e., former convicts who have become university professors of criminology) to argue for the abolishment or curtailment of blood and/or urine testing for drug contents among other measures.

In light of the discussion above, it remains to be asked: How much of the political rhetoric of good will emanating from President Obama's first day in office has in fact found resonance in socially just political action? Congress has refused to shut down the camp at Guantánamo Bay; Attorney General Holder surmised that "terrorism suspects" need not be read the Miranda warning; the PATRIOT act continues to erode civil liberties in order to bolster the rhetoric of "War on Terror;" and suspected immigrants find themselves under siege in Arizona, not only under the xenophobic thumb of Maricopa County's infamous Sheriff Arpaio, but also under a new repressive law (SB 1070), prompting them to flee by the thousands. On a positive note, the Justice Department has sued over implementation of the law, which it considers overreaching and blatantly racist in its effect of singling out residents who appear phenotypically Latino. Nevertheless, despite Obama's promise to undertake immigration reform in his first year in office, Immigration and Customs Enforcement (ICE) officials have stepped up efforts to disappear undocumented immigrants into secret private prisons where their rights to counsel, etc., are seriously curtailed.[8]

Indeed, little mention has been made of police-ICE partnerships since September 11, 2001, and there might be none at all if it weren't for immigrant rights groups launching the "Uncover the Truth on Police-ICE Collaborations" campaign to document that cross-deputized police have had the role of border patrol all along.[9] An industrial complex of collusion between private and public interests with respect to the exploitation of immigrant labor is perhaps best witnessed in cases where immigrants decide to unionize and corporations then call ICE to raid their plants and so send a message to the undocumented workers that unionization and labor demands will not be tolerated. Furthermore, as immigrant rights advocates note, it is an uphill battle to educate the approximately 80,000 undocumented farmworkers about their tenant rights. Without the knowledge of such, local police departments often successfully collude with agribusinesses to stop labor advocates from entering work premises, even when the advocates show up with supportive letters from the state Attorney General's offices. After all, there is a huge bottom-line factor at stake. For the indentured workforce pays about $100/week per person in taxes through payroll deduction, and government services for this socially invisible group are minimal, which results in significant corporate and state profiteering—at the expense of undocumented workers and their families.[10]

GLOBALIZATION OF PENAL STRUCTURES

Modern histories of colonization and imperial conquest reveal that it was not long before penal fortresses were installed in occupied territories to subdue indigenous people who resisted enslavement and other forms of subjugation (e.g., courvée for public works projects). From the slave forts in Ghana to the first jail for Native Americans on Deer Island, New York (which today is a landfill), limiting the mobility of subjects went concomitant with the freedom of capital to move to distant shores with the help of mercenaries and the backing of nation-states. Some of the prison structures did not even need walls, as is the case of the now-closed death camp Taudenit in Northern Mali. A former salt trading post, the camp served the French and then the military regime of the neo-colonial state by imprisoning political opponents. One of its few survivors recounts that an escape into the Sahara desert would have meant certain death "by natural causes."[11] Some infamous prisons were alternatively built on small islands (e.g., Alcatraz, California, USA, and Robben Island, South Africa, both now serving as museums) to rely upon the ocean as a flight barrier.

It might be asked: in an era of human rights, have we progressed when it comes to securing "life, liberty and the pursuit of happiness" for all people the world over? Reviewing restrictions on liberty, seen narrowly, a bleak picture emerges. Just in the context of the United States prison population alone "there are nearly 2.3 million adults behind bars in jails or prisons, 4.16 million on probation, and 784,408 on parole" at the start of the 21st century.[12] Probation and parole are practices that limit the convicted persons' movement and civil rights (e.g., by being subjected to random drug tests and visits by the probation/parole officer). All told, close to seven million in the U.S. are under the supervision of the criminal justice system. How does this measure up in a global context? According to Roy Walmsley:

> More than 9.8 million people are held in penal institutions throughout the world, mostly as pre-trial detainees (remand prisoners) or as sentenced prisoners. Almost half of these are in the United States (2.29m), Russia (0.89m) or China (1.57m sentenced prisoners). A further 850,000 are held in "administrative detention" in China; if these are included the overall Chinese total is over 2.4 million and the world total over 10.65 million.[13]

Statistics are lacking for the amount of worldwide probation and parole. However it is fair to say that most nations make use of these non-carceral measures to a much larger extent than does the United States, where some 70 percent of convicted persons receive jail time. By contrast, other countries incarcerate approximately only 20 percent of those convicted of crimes and then sentence 80 percent to fines, probation, et cetera. But these numbers do not account fully for the amount of persons administrated at any given time by the global criminal (justice) industrial complex. To do so, we would need to add millions of people who are held in other facilities that resemble prisons such as asylum seekers' facilities (which can only be left with a pass from the local authorities), halfway houses, secure mental health institutions (especially placement without consent), other "civil" confinement institutions for released persons with sex-offender status (cf. *Kansas vs. Hendricks,* 1997), and schools or workplaces (such as sweatshops or the military) that mete out dire punishment for escapes. Jailing a person[14] is conducted by state actors as well as private entities, and privately-run jails, boot camps for youth, and detention facilities for immigrants have been a major growth industry in the recent decade, facilitated by the Bush administration and others on the right.[15]

THE BIG HOUSE MEETS THE SCHOOL HOUSE: THE SCHOOL-TO-PRISON PIPELINE

In *Discipline and Punish,* Michel Foucault gives us an odd juxtaposition. After a grim account of a public execution he cuts to a serene narrative of the prisoner's daily schedule not unlike those of monks, however unlike monks who freely enter the convent, convicts mark time at the will of others. Foucault explains it as a matter of contrasting penal policy in Europe and the US:

> We have, then, a public execution and a time-table. They do not punish the same crimes or the same type of delinquent. But they each define a certain penal style. Less than a century separates them. It was a time when, in Europe and in the United States, the entire economy of punishment was redistributed. It was a time of great "scandals" for traditional justice, a time of innumerable projects for reform.[16]

It was the U.S. based reform-inspired Quakers who brought us the modern prison. Students, equally, are condemned to "mark time," starting actually in kindergarten: a Brooklyn housing project playground was so inventive with preparing its population for a life in "total institutions" that it mounted a door in a jungle gym with the letters "jail" painted on it; toddlers could delight in yelling "I am locked up" for some six years till a media campaign embarrassed the housing authority to finally paint it over in Spring 2010.[17] When such "docile" children arrive in the school house, they may be forced to take legal doses of the drug Ritalin to conform to acceptable standards of civility.[18] A provocative study on public schools in California has found that schooling is an exercise of "doing nothing"—in order to prepare students for the life on the installment plan, namely prison.[19]

U.S. educators are disturbed at the high dropout rates of metropolitan schooled youth, but given the treatment of school children as potential criminals, schools resemble more prison-training grounds than institutions that present children with options to learn in a creative fashion. Passing through metal detectors, facing armed guards, counselors who tell the child that they won't amount to much, and disaffected teachers and principals—it's somewhat amazing that thirty percent of students actually stick to the regimen and graduate with a diploma. It is obvious that security industries profit by arranging for outfitting schools and since the Virginia Tech University event also colleges and universities with surveillance instruments. What is less known is the convergence of security companies with food companies such as Sodexho Alliance (formerly Sodexho Marriott), now known as Sodexo—a global outsourcing company that specializes in food and facilities management. It has managed to capture the market share from serving meals in private prisons to university food courts, which prompted a major protest campaign by university students, in particular in the U.S.[20] Sodhexho Alliance promised to divest from private prison companies, however, it is not clear to what extent the new company has followed suit.

DIFFERENCES BETWEEN THE PRISON INDUSTRIAL COMPLEX AND CRIMINAL (JUSTICE) INDUSTRIAL COMPLEX

Before outlining the finer points of difference between the politically charged terms "prison industrial complex" (PIC) and "criminal industrial complex," an interrogation is warranted of the meaning of the conventional and mainstream terminology of "criminal justice system." Jeffrey Reiman notes that the demarcation of "criminal justice" and "crime" is not all that clear cut, especially if we pursue the distinctions with the help of ethical deliberations: "Criminal justice can only be distinguished from crime if criminal justice is moral while crime is immoral."[21]. How do we know the truth of kidnapping versus arrest, of murder versus execution, or of theft versus taxation? After all, ethical standards of decency, of fairness, of proportional judgment vis-à-vis the severity of the offense, and legitimate force are important criteria that set a just system apart from a criminal system.

It is puzzling in some way that Reiman and others tend to invoke rogue nations such as Hitler's Germany or apartheid's South Africa in order to contrast them to truly democratic systems (such as the U.S. is claimed to be) that supposedly are governed under the rules of law and morality writ large. However, the more I know about the history of punishment in the U.S.

and elsewhere, I am no longer convinced by the narrative that the U.S. basically has an uncorrupted and good system in which institutional checks and balances successfully account for the all-too-human error that is otherwise ineradicable. Examples such as the 1873 Colfax massacre that paved the way of the courts' legitimation of Jim Crow,[22] the Wounded Knee massacre of 1890,[23] and the MOVE massacre that took place in 1985,[24] cannot merely be excused as unfortunate aberrations but must be considered systemic cornerstones of racial, imperial, and class injustices. Moral indecencies can also be easily chronicled across the criminal justice system that illuminate how it also works against the benefit of women, gender nonconformists, lesbians, and gay men.[25] Thus, it is hardly "truly democratic," rather the criminal justice system, U.S. style, is white supremacist—it favors the wealthy and those who are well-connected to political power or somehow can assemble a dream team of lawyers that will intimidate any prosecutor, jury, or judge. So we are hard pressed to discuss criminal justice in the mainstream way to which most criminologists casually adhere.

Criminal justice has from the beginning been set up under false pretenses in particular to disguise its charge to arrange and enforce a particular form of *capitalist* justice, leading some to indict the system as a "criminal injustice system"[26] and others to demand a new way of "abolition democracy."[27] Another astute definition comes from the new direction in critical criminology called convict criminology—informed by the perspectives of former convicts-turned-scholars such as Stephen Richards:

> The phrase "criminal justice system" is an abstract concept used in the academic literature, and refers to the intended coordination of police, courts, jails, and prisons. In fact, there is no criminal justice system; no address, phone number, or central organization. Instead, there remains a hodge-podge of numerous city, county, state, and federal agencies, jurisdictions, and facilities, operating under different authority and law.[28]

In his characterization of this system, Eric Schlosser popularized the term "prison-industrial complex" in his seminal *Atlantic Monthly* article as "a set of bureaucratic, political, and economic interests that encourage increased spending on imprisonment, regardless of the actual need."[29] He goes on to deny that there is a conspiratorial force behind all these special interest holders, which include politicians who espouse a "fear of crime" rhetoric, rural stakeholders in search of keeping their workforce, private companies in search of expanding the market share, and government officials expanding their fiefdoms. Expanding on this narrow use of the term which focuses in Schlosser's paradigm merely on corrections, Angela Y. Davis notes the "symbiotic relationship" between the prison industrial complex and the military industrial complex: "These two complexes mutually support and promote each other and, in fact, often share technologies." Davis mentions the dual use and conversion crime fighting tools of dense foam sprayed at suspects or enemies which temporarily blinds and deafens them, "smart guns," retractable barrier strips, or "smart cars," which are hooked up to mainframes in police departments.[30] The symbiosis has become even more pronounced since 2003, given the linkages between security industries (e.g., Corrections Corporation of America, Xe Services—formerly known as Blackwater, etc.) with the U.S. government for the purpose of increasing profits and securing the nation-state's imperial demands around the world.

However, the PIC term has since fallen out of favor with at least some committed penal abolitionists. Lois Ahrens, who directs the Real Cost of Prison project, explains the reasoning for such in the following way:

> I don't use the phrase the prison-industrial complex since it has become some kind of shorthand and it often seems that people who use it don't know what it means and/or it is a way of people not taking the time to actually think about its many tentacles. *The Real Cost of Prisons* was my attempt to draw attention to how many (personal, family, political, community, economic, etc.) strands there are and how they are all interconnected. I use mass incarceration but of course it doesn't include the economic cost. . . . I am not sure I know a word or words that adequately encompass the magnitude of the machine. To me, mass incarceration has an emotional impact like the words slavery and genocide.[31]

Ahrens is right to emphasize the emotional aspects of the imprisonment that PIC leaves out. Another problem with PIC is the issue of scope.

In this chapter, I wish to propose the alternative term "criminal (justice) industrial complex (CIC)" for it encompasses tentacles of punitive measures of which "prison" is only one—albeit a severe one—of many forms of social control. "Justice" is bracketed because as Elihu Rosenblatt explains, it hides the permanent element of repression that is endemic in a system geared to overempower those who exert power and domination[32] There's very little that resembles justice, accountability, fairness, the standardization of criminal sentences, etcetera, in a system that profits off of the misery of those who already have less social capital (and so get further exploited in prison in turn, as outlined by Jeffrey Reiman in *The Rich Get Richer and the Poor Get Prison*).[33]

Nils Christie, credited with coining the term "criminal industrial complex,"[34] notes that prisons are fashioned after the old work-house motive, not to produce profit but to deposit surplus labor in order to keep "free market" labor

— de emotionalyzy us leads to
mereorel Con formit.

prices down. Yet Christie is still wedded to the critique of the "big house," rather than reviewing the larger complex the system ensnares. A recent book that does a good job at framing this bigger picture is *Punishment for Sale: Private Prisons and Big Business* by Donna Selman and Paul Leighton. Therein they describe the mega-economic ascent of correctional corporations (e.g., Corrections Corporation of America, GEO Group and Cornell Companies) through the growth in community correctional facilities such as halfway houses and treatment centers:

> Between the 1970s and 1990s, the modest number of smaller businesses serving the criminal justice system morphed into a criminal justice-industrial complex. Unlike the concerns giving rise to the military-industrial complex, there is not a single event or year that ushers in a criminal justice-industrial complex. The growth in the number of businesses involved with criminal justice and the dollar volume of that commerce—not to mention politicians and communities dreaming of a prison economy—produce powerful vested interests that affect people's liberties and make crime policy something other than a tool for public safety and justice.[35]

The privatization of prisons, beginning with minimum-security prisons and federal detention centers for immigrants, has also proved to be a business opportunity in which corporations rely upon the state to subsidize infrastructure costs and guarantee insider contracts to the tune of billions of dollars. One reason why Sodexho Marriott partnered with private prison companies such as CCA is that the private prison resembles the hotel business model in managing room occupancy per diem rates.[36] As of 2009, ICE pays private prison companies which run detention centers from $200 to $272 per detainee per night.[37] Meanwhile, the same privatization interests promote themselves (falsely) as responding to court orders for systemic reform. In this way, the call for more and more prisons—and hence prisoners—is sold as a solution to the overcrowding of penitentiaries. Likewise, private prisons are marketed as being cheaper and more efficient than state-run prisons, which occludes all manner of hidden and not-so-hidden costs offset onto others in order to make this claim. Selman and Leighton also raise important critiques regarding the worrisome trends in the privatization of parole and other aspects of community corrections. Private companies note the growth market in supervising of and investing technologies in parolees and probationers with an annual yield of five million people to be disciplined. President G.W. Bush's Second Chance Act opened the floodgates of the "non-profit" sector, namely, faith-based organizations: "GEO Group, for example, recruits large numbers of religious volunteers, which provides the company with free labor and qualifies it for certain faith-based grants. CCA partnered in 2003 with Bill Glass Champions for Life, the operator of the nation's largest evangelical prison ministries program."[38] Global Positioning Systems (GPS) are being used by Big Brother, INC for electronic bracelets and are under discussion to install on youth suspected of gang activity and subject to curfew.[39]

TRANSFORMATIVE JUSTICE—BEYOND RESTORING JUSTICE?

Prison abolitionists and those who would seek to transformatively oppose the criminal (justice) industrial complex need to be vigilant about *reform* measures. It is one thing to study the racial impacts of the overcriminalization of Black young men (according to a 2009 Pew study, 1 in 11 are under criminal [in]justice supervision)[40] with an aim to reducing those numbers, and another to understand that such reforms must merely be means to the end goal of abolition of the penal system as we know it altogether. Transformative justice for those presently oppressed under the yoke of the CIC means to develop nothing short of the Marshall plan that spurred the economic miracles of post-war Germany and Japan for the underserved and socially dominated. One tends to forget that most reform measures of the past have had a punitive boomerang effect into the present. Such is certainly true of the creation of the modern prison: well-meaning Quakers in colonial America were outraged by the practice of bodily harm and executions in Europe for petty crimes. Thus they thought that constructing a building along the monastic ideal would serve offenders well who received religious instructions to repent their crimes. Ever since that fateful opening of Cherry Hill prisons in 1790, "blue ribbon" commissions the world over have lamented the failure of prisons and also the failure of reform measures to curtail recidivism amongst the convicts.[41]

So rather than outlawing *corporal* punishment and the ultimate corporal penalty, namely, capital punishment, prisons have instead become the place where both practices have become common place. Regarding corporal penalties, witness military prisons from Abu-Ghraib, Iraq to Guantánamo Bay, Cuba, where CIA agents *cum* prison wardens-who-previously-ran-private-prisons tortured prisoners and received White House clearing from counsel to do so. Since Cherry Hill's deployment of the "silent treatment," we have moved to the complex *psychological* inflictions to the incarcerated that routinely occur in places like ADX Florence, Colorado supermax prison—whose techniques against the incarcerated have withstood eighth amendment scrutiny (i.e., prisoners' accusation of cruel and unusual punishment) in the U.S. courts.[42] Such supermax prisons, tombs for the living in which prisoners remain in their cells 23 hours/day, have increasingly been replicated the world over, notoriously, in Turkey with its F-type prisons that are used to isolate political activists in prisons, which replicates the practice in the U.S. control units.[43]

Besides reform of the racism, sexism, classism, and general barbarism of the CIC, critics also need to be wary of the procedural forms of justice established within the system. The CIC has managed to make them utterly seductive in many respects, tangible evidence (it would seem) that the system follows non-arbitrary rules that adhere to evolving community standards and protocols of past precedence. But how can this be trusted in the context of an overwhelmingly inhuman industrial complex built to administer criminality for profit? As W.E.B. DuBois warned: a veritable abolition democracy has to be unearthed in order to crush the racial and class injustices—de jure!—that are embedded in the American "democratic" framework. The public may be blind to these injustices because of a naïve belief in the abstract, rights-bearing individual who, according to the criminal (justice) system itself, has full constitutional protection while under investigation or even to the very end stages of a trial.

Of the over ten million people imprisoned in 2008, the vast majority of these are remand prisoners (i.e., those *awaiting* trial). Some prisoners I met in Mali in 2003 have been in prison for *ten* years waiting for a judgment on their case. According to the President of Amnesty International in Mali, this is their major grievance—as Mali, after all, has no political prisoners (unlike the U.S.) and none of the remand prisoners there were held separately in "jails" from those who were duly convicted of an offense. Ironically, the U.S. does have a jail versus long-term prison system. Yet, even in its jails, where the majority of incarcerated youth and adults reside awaiting trial, the remand prisoners are not separated from those who are convicted on charges of one year or less. As the political prisoner Assata Shakur found out, even though she was then classified as a remand prisoner, the attending guard expected her to work nonetheless. In such cases the refusal to work means the loss of social privileges within the penal institution, as well as a trip to "the hole" (i.e., solitary confinement). It was at that point that Shakur, as have many other prisoners in her situation, found out that the U.S. constitution essentially codifies human slavery—that the thirteenth amendment, putatively written to free the enslaved population at the end of the Civil War, actually reinscribes slavery on the bodies of the nation's convicts.[44]

For these reasons, in her 10-point program on abolitionist strategies Julia Sudbury exhorts us "to live abolition NOW" by building alternative accountability forms in our communities which don't rely on "blaming, punishing or inflicting violence."[45] She extols the community organization Creative

Interventions, based in Oakland, CA, as endorsing a viable approach. Their transformative justice project advocates peaceful and non-punitive methods: "This accountability includes stopping immediate abuse, making a commitment to not engage in future abuse, and offering reparations for past abuse. Such offender accountability requires community responsibility and access to on-going support and transformative healing for offenders."[46]

Furthermore, schools can be seen as a powerful decarceration strategy. As Angela Davis notes, "Unless the current structures of violence are eliminated from schools in impoverished communities of color—including the presence of armed security guards and police—and unless schools become places that encourage the joy of learning, these schools will remain the major conduits to prisons."[47] Various abolitionists have also advocated for the importance of transforming the prison buildings themselves into productive sites. Most notably, Tiyo Attallah Salah-El, who suggests that they be turned into healing and caring centers.[48]

What seems to be undertheorized is what to do with the rest of the structures of the criminal (justice) industrial complex if its transformation is to be effected. What about the millions of personnel that would have to be retrained such as the policing, juridical, and other administrative staff? What of the buildings sustaining their jurisdictions? To take a page from my home town, Fulda, where the police headquarters (used by the Nazis for interrogation and torture) have been refashioned into modern university classrooms and offices, many rural towns could have an influx of places of higher learning, and cities, too, would benefit by transforming court houses and jails into local schools, kindergartens, assisted living facilities, and of course, colleges. Contrast the Fulda University of Applied Sciences building boom with that of northern Missouri, where penal advocates "offered to retrofit the defunct Tarkio College into a minimum security pen."[49] One way that CIC has already intersected with the Academic Industrial Complex (AIC) is the rising demand for criminal justice and justice administration programs all over the U.S.—from Pueblo Community College in the late 1990s[50] to years later at SUNY Cortland, where dozens of students signed up for Criminology within one year of establishing the major. Another little known aspect of CIC's contribution to AIC is the furniture supplied by prison industries such as New York States' Corcraft to public colleges and universities. Thus professors, students, and staff alike "benefit" from the slave labor of those confined in state correctional institutions. Undoubtedly, CIC crisscrosses all sectors of society with its $50 billion dollar yearly industry, and just as it has been difficult to derive a "peace dividend" from the end of the cold war from the Military Industrial Complex, it will equally be a tall order to demand an "abolition dividend" from CIC, however it is a struggle worth pursuing.

NOTES

1. Cited in Mumia Abu-Jamal, *Jailhouse Lawyers: Prisoners Defending Prisoners v. the U.S.A.* (San Francisco, CA: City Lights Books, 2009).

2. See www.ussc.gov/press.htm (accessed September 1, 2010).

3. See www.law.ua.edu/colquitt/crimmain/crimmisc/crime.htm (accessed September 1, 2010).

4. "Justinfo, 2010" National Criminal Justice Reference Service, www.ncjrs .gov/justinfo/jan0110.html (accessed September 1, 2010).

5. Jim Webb, "Why We Must Fix Our Prisons," *Parade,* (March, 2009), www .parade.com/news/2009/03/why-we-must-fix-our-prisons.html?index=2 (accessed September 1, 2010).

6. Jim Webb, "Why We Must Fix Our Prisons."

7. Michelle Alexander, *The New Jim Crow: Mass Incarceration in the Age of Color-blindness* (Oakland, CA: AK Press, 2010).

8. Jacqueline Stevens, "America's Secret ICE Castles," *The Nation* (December 16, 2009), www.thenation.com/article/americas-secret-ice-castles (accessed September 1, 2010).

9. Sahari Uribe, "'Secure Communities'? A Deportation Program, Deceivingly Called 'Secure Communities,' is targeting Immigrant Communities in the United States," *SOA Watch, ¡Presente!* 15, no. 2 (Summer, 2010): 3, 12.

10. Renan Salgado, "Homeland Security vs. Immigrants in New York State," Presentation at Regional Workshop "Policing, Incarceration and Militarization," Binghamton University, April 24, 2010.

11. Samba Sangare, *Dix ans au bagne-mouroir de Taoudenit* (Bamako, AF: Librairie Traore, 2001).

12. Richard S. Jones, Jeffrey Ian Ross, Stephen C. Richards and Daniel S. Murphy, "The First Dime: A Decade of Convict Criminology," *The Prison Journal* 89 (2009), 151–170.

13. Roy Walmsley, "World Prison Population List" (8th edition). International Centre for Prison Studies, 2009.

14. This paper will focus on systemic human incarceration only, and will not address zoos, etc., as confinement places for nonhuman animals.

15. Donna Selman and Paul Leighton, *Punishment for Sale: Private Prisons and Big Business* (Lanham, MD: Rowman & Littlefield, 2009).

16. Michel Foucault, *Discipline and Punish* (New York, NY: Knopf Doubleday, 1995), 7.

17. For a photo of the sign, see www.nydailynews.com/ny_local/brooklyn/ 2010/03/24/2010–03–24_See_brooklyn_housing_project_residents_say_city_tot_ lot_with_play_jail_treats_kid_li.html (accessed September 1, 2010). Residents have repeatedly protested by painting over the sign to no avail.

18. Frederick Goodwin championed the eugenically charged "Violence Initiative" in the early 1990s, which sparked a protest amidst members of the Black Congressional Caucus. Gail Wasserman and Daniel Pine's study advocates that youngsters

should be administered drugs so that they would later on avoid a life of crime. Goodwin had to resign as head of the ADAMHA for comparing the inner city with "the jungle," but the proposal lives on, having been marketed successfully by the medical-academic industrial complexes (forces of doctors, school therapists, university researchers, pharmaceutical companies, among others). Cf. Mitchel Cohen, "Beware the Violence Initiative Project—Coming Soon to an Inner City Near You," 1999, www.greens.org/s-r/19/19–07.html (accessed September 1, 2010).

19. Damien Schnyder, *First Strike: The Effect of the Prison Regime Upon Public Education and Black Masculinity in Los Angeles County, California,* PhD Dissertation, University of Texas, 2009, unpublished. I thank Ruthie Gilmore for this reference.

20. Sodexho Marriott and the For-Profit Prison Industry, 2000, www.uvm.edu/sparc/nwom/sodexho/marriott.html (accessed September 1, 2010).

21. Jeffrey H. Reiman, "Criminal Justice Ethics," in *Criminal Justice Ethics,* eds. Paul Leighton and Jeffrey H. Reiman (Upper Saddle River, NJ: Prentice Hall, 2000), 2 (emphasis by author).

22. LeeAnna Keith, *The Colfax Massacre. The Untold Story of Black Power, White Terror, and the Death of Reconstruction* (New York, NY: Oxford University Press, 2008).

23. See Dee Brown, *Bury My Heart at Wounded Knee* (New York, NY: Owl Books, 1970).

24. Karla F. C. Holloway, *Passed On: African American Mourning Stories: A Memorial* (Durham, NC: Duke University Press, 2003).

25. Julia Sudbury, "Maroon Abolitionists: Black Gender-oppressed Activists in the Anti-Prison Movement in the U.S. and Canada," *Meridians: Feminism, Race, Transnationalism* 9, no.1, 2009: 1–29.

26. Elihu Rosenblatt, ed., *Criminal Injustice: Confronting the Prison Crisis* (Boston, MA: South End Press, 2006).

27. Angela Davis, *Abolition Democracy: Beyond Empire, Prisons, and Torture* (New York, NY: Seven Stories Press, 2005).

28. Stephen C. Richards, "My Journey through the Federal Bureau of Prisons," in *Convict Criminology,* eds. Jeffrey I. Ross and Stephen C. Richards (Belmont, CA: Wadsworth, 2003), 120–149.

29. Eric Schlosser, "The Prison-industrial Complex," *The Atlantic Monthly* (1998), www.theatlantic.com/doc/199812/prisons (accessed September 1, 2010).

30. Angela Y. Davis, *Are Prisons Obsolete?* (New York, NY: Seven Stories Press, 2003), 86–88.

31. Lois Ahrens, Personal email communication, (December 24, 2009).

32. See Elihu Rosenblatt, ed., *Criminal Injustice,* 7.

33. Jeffrey H. Reiman, *The Rich Get Richer and the Poor Get Prison: Ideology, Class, and Criminal Justice* (Boston, MA: Allyn & Bacon, 2006).

34. Nils Christie, *Crime Control as Industry: Towards Gulags Western Style* (New York, NY: Routledge, 2000). I thank Paul Leighton for directing me to this aspect of Christie's work.

35. Donna Selman and Paul Leighton, *Punishment for Sale: Private Prisons and Big Business* (Lanham, MD: Rowman & Littlefield, 2010).

36. Donna Selman and Paul Leighton, *Punishment for Sale,* 93.

37. Donna Selman and Paul Leighton, *Punishment for Sale,* 162.

38. Donna Selman and Paul Leighton, *Punishment for Sale,* 166–7.

39. Donna Selman and Paul Leighton, *Punishment for Sale,* 170.

40. See realcostofprisons.org/blog/archives/2009/03/pew_study_1_in.html (accessed September 1, 2010).

41. Greg Newbold, "Rehabilitating Criminals. It Ain't That Easy," in *Convict Criminology,* eds. Jeffrey I. Ross and Stephen C. Richards (Belmont, CA: Wadsworth, 2003), 150–169.

42. Atul Gawande, "Annals of Human Rights-Hellhole. The United States Holds Tens of Thousands of Inmates in Long-Term Solitary Confinement. Is This Torture?" *The New Yorker* (March 30, 2009), tpj.sagepub.com/cgi/content/abstract/89/2/151 (accessed September 1, 2010).

43. Julia Lutsky, "Torture in our Prisons," *Partnership for Safety and Justice* (Oct. 1, 2001), www.safetyandjustice.org/node/490, (accessed September 1, 2010); Tony Samara, "Prisons, Punishment and Profiteers," *Workplace: A Journal for Academic Labor* 3, no. 2 (2000), louisville.edu/journal/workplace/issue6/samara.html (accessed September 1, 2010).

44. Assata Shakur, *Assata: An Autobiography* (Chicago, IL: Lawrence Hill Books, 1987); and see Mechthild Nagel, "Prisons as Diasporic Sites: Liberatory Voices from the Diaspora of Confinement," *Journal of Social Advocacy and Systems Change* 1 (March 2008): 1–31, cortland.edu/ids/sasc/content/prison_nagel.pdf (accessed September 1, 2010).

45. Julia Sudbury, "Building a Movement to Abolish Prisons: Lessons from the U.S." *Journal of Prisoners on Prisons* 18, nos. 1/2, (2009): 177–184.

46. See www.generationfive.org/index.asp?sec=3&pg=48 (accessed September 1, 2010).

47. Angela Davis, *Are Prisons Obsolete?* (New York, NY: Seven Stories Press, 2003).

48. Tiyo Attallah Salah-El, "A Call for the Abolition of Prisons," in *Prisons and Punishment: Rethinking Global Penality,* eds. Mechthild Nagel and Seth Asumah (Trenton, NJ: Africa World Press, 2007).

49. Christian Parenti, *Lockdown America: Police and Prisons in the Age of Crisis* (New York, NY: Verso, 1999).

50. Christian Parenti, *Lockdown America,* 216.

Chapter Six

The Revolution Will Not Be Funded

The Nonprofit Industrial Complex

Andrea Smith

In 2004, INCITE! Women of Color Against Violence learned the hard way that the revolution will not be funded. INCITE! began in 2000, with the purpose of supporting a movement of feminists of color organizing against all forms of violence—from interpersonal to state violence. When we first organized, we were generally funded through individual donations. However, by 2002, we found ourselves increasingly more successful in securing foundation grants to support our work. We took a stand against state funding since we perceived that anti-violence organizations that had state funding had been co-opted. It never occurred to us to look at foundation funding in the same way. However, in a trip to India (funded, ironically, by the Ford Foundation), we met with many non-funded organizations that criticized us for receiving foundation grants. When we saw that groups with much less access to resources were able to do amazing work without funding, we began to question our reliance on foundation grants.

Our growing suspicions about foundation grants were confirmed when, in February 2004, INCITE! received an email from the Ford Foundation with the subject line "Congratulations!" and an offer of "a one-year or two-year grant of $100,000" to cover our general operating expenses in response to a grant proposal the Ford Foundation had solicited from us. Excited about the news, we committed to two major projects, the Sisterfire multimedia tour that was organized for 2004, and the third Color of Violence conference to be held in New Orleans in 2005. Then, unexpectedly on July 30, 2004, the Ford Foundation sent another letter, explaining that it had reversed its decision because of our organization's statement of support for the Palestinian liberation struggle. Apparently, during the board approval process, a board member

133

decided to investigate INCITE! further and disapproved of what s/he found on our website. INCITE! quickly learned from first-hand experience the deleterious effects foundations can have on radical social justice movements. However, we also learned that social justice organizations do not always need the foundation support they think they do. Strapped with this sudden loss of funding but committed to organizing two major projects, INCITE! members started raising money through grassroots fundraising—house parties, individual calls, T-shirt sales and so on—and we were able to quickly raise the money we lost when the Ford Foundation rescinded its grant offer.

This story is not an isolated incident of members of a social justice organization finding themselves in a precarious state as a result of foundation funding (specifically, a lack thereof). Since the late 1970s, social justice organizations within the U.S. have operated largely within the 501(c)(3) non-profit model, in which donations made to an organization are tax-deductible, in order to avail themselves of foundation grants. Despite the legacy of grassroots, mass-movement building we have inherited from the 1960s and 1970s, contemporary activists often experience difficulty developing, or even imagining, structures for organizing outside this model. At the same time, however, social justice organizations across the country are critically rethinking their investment in the 501(c)(3) system. Funding cuts from foundations affected by the current economic crisis and increased surveillance on social justice groups by the Department of Homeland Security have encouraged social justice organizations to assess opportunities for funding social change that do not rely so heavily upon state structures.

Much of this discussion, however, tends to focus on individual foundations or nonprofits without assessing how the nonprofit system itself is part of a larger global industrial complex. That is, the problem is not individual nonprofits or foundations, but the nonprofit industrial complex (NPIC) as a whole and the way in which capitalist interests and the state use nonprofits to do the following:

- Monitor and control social justice movements;
- Divert public monies into private hands through foundations;
- Manage and control dissent in order to make the world safe for capitalism;
- Redirect activist energies into career-based modes of organizing instead of mass-based organizing capable of actually transforming society;
- Allow corporations to mask their exploitative and colonial work practices through "philanthropic" work;
- Encourage social movements to model themselves after capitalist structures rather than to challenge them.

is Cap. Safe for the World?

As this chapter will explore, the nonprofit industrial complex works in collaboration with other systems in the global industrial complex, from the prison industrial complex to the academic industrial complex, to ensure that threats to capitalism and the nation-state are managed and disciplined.

HISTORY OF THE NONPROFIT SYSTEM

Prior to the Civil War, individuals, not organizations, did most charity work. However, in the face of accelerating industrialization and accompanying social ills, such as increased poverty, community breakdown to facilitate the flow of labor, and violence, local organizations (generally headed by community elites) developed to assist those seen as "deserving" of assistance, such as widows and children. These charities focused on poverty as an individual reality rather than as a systemic outcome. Charities did not campaign for higher wages, for instance, but worked to ameliorate the impact of low wages on communities. As this charity movement spread, local charity organizations began to organize on the national level. In 1874, members of private charity organizations, religious agencies, and public officials from several northeastern states established the National Conference of Charities and Corrections to discuss mutual concerns (later renamed the National Conference on Social Welfare).[1]

This system of charitable giving increased exponentially during the early 1900s when the first multimillionaire robber barons, such as Nelson Rockefeller, Andrew Carnegie, and Russell Sage, created new institutions that would exist in perpetuity and support charitable giving in order to shield their earnings from taxation.[2] Before the 1950s, charities were generally unregulated because few states imposed taxes on corporations; only the largest foundations with the wealthiest donors required charitable deductions. The first such foundation was organized by Margaret Olivia Slocum Sage. Using the $70 million left to her by Russell Sage, who had made his fortune in the railroad industry, she started the Russell Sage Foundation in 1907, and was followed by Rockefeller in 1910 and Carnegie in 1911, respectively. By 1955, givings from individuals, foundations, and corporations totaled $7.7 billion, according to the American Association of Fund-Raising Counsel Trust for Philanthropy. By 1978, that total had grown to $39 billion. In 1998, the last year of available data, total giving had risen to $175 billion.[3]

Along with the growth in donations came a huge swell in the number of nonprofit organizations. In many cases, these foundations served as tax shelters so that corporations, under the guise of being "foundations," could avoid taxes or so that relatively privileged descendants could receive their inheritances without paying estate taxes. Early on, many of these organizations employed those who had been part of the charity movement. But, unlike their charity movement predecessors, these foundations' purviews would be general, rather than specific, and their governance would rely on private, self-perpetuating boards of trustees or directors. From their inception, foundations focused on research and the dissemination of information designed ostensibly to ameliorate social issues—in a manner, however, that did not challenge capitalism.

For instance, in 1913, Colorado miners went on strike against Colorado Fuel and Iron, an enterprise of which 40 percent was owned by Rockefeller. Eventually, this strike erupted into open warfare, with the Colorado militia murdering several strikers during the Ludlow Massacre of April 20, 1914. During that same time, Jerome Greene, the Rockefeller Foundation secretary, identified research and information to quiet social and political unrest as a foundation priority. The rationale behind this strategy was that while individual workers deserved social relief, organized workers in the form of unions were a threat to society. So the Rockefeller Foundation heavily advertised its relief work for individual workers while at the same time promoting a pro-Rockefeller spin to the massacre. For instance, it sponsored speakers to claim that no massacre had happened, and tried to block the publication of reports that were critical of Rockefeller.[4] According to Frederick Gates, who helped head the Rockefeller Foundation, the "danger is not the combination of capital, it is not the Mexican situation, it is the labor monopoly; and the danger of the labor monopoly lies in its use of armed force, its organized and deliberate war on society."[5] Thus, the development of the nonprofit industrial complex coincides with the financial industrial complex—it becomes a tool that serves as an alibi for the ravages of the financial industrial complex—presenting a humanitarian face that will provide Band-Aids to redress the harms created by financial capitalism. The irony, of course, is that the very foundations providing this humanitarian aid come from the same sources that create the need for this aid in the first place.

Even in this earliest stage of foundation development, critics noted the potential danger of large private foundations. In 1916, the U.S. Commission on Industrial Relations (also known as the Walsh Commission) filed a report on labor issues with Congress warning that foundations were a "grave menace"[6] because they concentrated wealth and power in the service of ideology which supported the interests of their capitalist benefactors. According to Samuel Gompers' testimony in the commission's report, "In the effort to undertake to be an all-pervading machinery for the molding of the minds of the people . . . in the constant industrial struggle for human betterment . . .

[foundations] should be prohibited from exercising their functions, either by law or regulation."[7]

The Walsh report called on Congress to more strictly regulate foundations, which it did not do, given the state's historic relationship with capital. However, the resulting negative publicity encouraged foundations to fund intermediaries, such as universities, rather than doing research themselves, so that the results of such research would be more convincingly objective.[8]

During the Great Depression, the societal influence of foundations was curtailed by economic crisis. However, after World War II, particularly with the emergence of the Ford Foundation (founded in 1936), foundations regained prominence, and focused on how they could further the interests of U.S.-style democracy domestically and abroad.[9] The Ford Foundation became particularly prominent, not only for philanthropic giving, but for its active involvement in trying to engineer social change and shape the development of social justice movements. For instance, foundations, particularly Ford, became involved in the civil rights movement, often steering it into more conservative directions, as the chapter from Robert Allen in this collection demonstrates. At the same time, however, this civil rights involvement also aroused the ire of the Right, particularly in the South, who then called on Congress to more strictly regulate foundations. Right-wing organizations such as the Heritage Foundation claimed that tax dollars were going to subsidize left-wing causes, while on the Left, progressives such as Allen were arguing that foundations were pushing social justice movements into more conservative directions.[10] Thus foundations earned critics from all sides.

Leading the Right's assault on liberal foundations was U.S. congressman Wright Patman of Texas, who conducted a study of foundations beginning in 1962. In reports he sent to the House of Representatives, Patman contended that economic power was consolidating in the hands of foundations; foundations were being used to escape estate taxes, compensate relatives, and pay annuities to themselves; the Internal Revenue Service (IRS) lacked proper oversight over foundations; foundations were controlling big businesses to give them a competitive advantage over small businesses; and foundations were spending too much of their money overseas.[11] In the early 1960s, foundations were growing at a rate of 1,200 per year, and financial magazines routinely promoted foundations as tax-shelter tools.[12] In response, Congress passed the Tax Reform Act of 1969, which reversed the previous state policy of only minimally regulating foundations. This act imposed a four percent excise tax on foundations' net investment income, put restrictions on the ability of foundations to engage in business operations (thus curtailing the abilities of corporations to operate tax-free as ostensible foundations), and required foundations to annually spend at least six percent of their net investment income (reduced to five percent in 1988) to prevent them from growing without serving their ostensible charitable purposes. Additionally, the act required foundations to provide more comprehensive information disclosures on their operations in annual reports to be filed with the IRS and made available to citizens at foundation offices.[13]

Notwithstanding its attack on foundations, the Right also developed its own foundations. As Michael Shuman of the Institute of Policy Studies notes, while right-wing foundations actually give away *less* money than liberal foundations, the former use their funds more effectively. Progressive funders generally give money to specific issue-oriented campaigns, whereas right-wing foundations see the need to fund the intellectual projects that enable the Right to develop a comprehensive framework for presenting its issues to the public. These think tanks, research projects, journals, etcetera, may not have an immediate short-term impact, but, in the long run, they alter the public consciousness:

This kind of investment by the Right in public policy has paid off handsomely. Its long-term support of conservative public scholars enables them to develop and promote numerous "new Ideas." . . . With ample funding, they have successfully pounded their message into heads of millions, sowing confusion, apathy, and opposition to public regulation of private corporations.[14]

Right-wing foundations pour thousands of dollars into funding think tanks such as the Heritage Foundation in order to help craft an ideological package that has fundamentally reshaped the consciousness of the public. Heritage Foundation president Edwin Feulner talks about the foresight of right-wing funders such as Richard Scaife, who saw the importance of political education. "Right-wing victories," he notes, "started more than twenty years ago when Dick Scaife had the vision to see the need for a conservative intellectual movement in America. . . . These organizations built the intellectual case that was necessary before political leaders like Newt Gingrich could translate their ideas into practical political alternatives."[15]

The rise of foundation support accompanied the rise of groups that organized as formal 501(c)(3) nonprofit organizations, because foundations could make tax-deductible donations to nonprofits, particularly after the state began to regulate foundation giving more strictly in 1969. According to the IRS, nonprofits are "religious, charitable, scientific, or educational" organizations whose receipts are tax-exempt, and whose contributions are tax-deductible for the donors. This tax-exempt status was created by Congress as part of the Revenue Act of 1913, passed after ratification of the 16th Amendment, which instituted income tax. Generally, only organizations with 501(c)(3) status can receive foundation grants, and they are prohibited from direct involvement in political advocacy. In 1953, the IRS estimated that about 50,000 organizations had received charity status. By 1978, that number had risen nearly six-fold. Today, charities number more than 730,000, according to the latest IRS count. As of 1998, there were 734,000 501(c)(3) organizations in the United States alone.[16] Today, foundations have assets of $500 billion and give around $33.6 billion annually,[17] and there are 837,027 nonprofits, excluding religious organizations.[18]

During the late 1960s, radical movements for social change were transforming the shape of the United States while Third World liberation movements were challenging Western imperialism. Foundations began to take a role in shaping this organizing so that social protest would not challenge the capitalist status quo. Robert Allen, as early as 1969, warned of the co-optation of the Black Power movement by foundations. In his germinal work, *Black Awakening in Capitalist America,* reprinted in part in this anthology, Allen documents how the Ford Foundation's support of certain Black civil rights and Black power organizations such as the Congress of Racial Equality actually helped shift the movement's emphasis—through the recruitment of key movement leaders—from liberation to Black capitalism. Similarly, Madonna Thunder Hawk describes how the offer of well-paying jobs in the nonprofit sector seduced many Native activists into diverting their energy from organizing to social service delivery and program development. As Joan Roelofs notes, large private foundations tended to fund racial justice organizations that focused on policy and legal reform, a strategy that effectively redirected activist efforts from radical change to social reform. It also helped to professionalize these movements since only those with advanced degrees could do this kind of work, thus minimizing the importance of mass-based grassroots organizing.[19] Waldemar Nielsen, in his study of the big foundations at the time, noted that funding patterns indicated that "philanthropic interest in the black [*sic*] derives from the long tradition of humanitarian concern for his [*sic*] 'plight' rather than from an ideological comment to the principle of racial equality."[20] Observing that the majority of foundation funding for racial issues went into higher education, Nielsen notes:

> Reminiscent of the ideas of Booker T. Washington, it is commonly believed that the most fruitful way to solve the problems of the blacks [*sic*] is to open educational opportunities to them; by climbing the rungs of the educational and occupational ladder, they will eventually achieve full economic, political, and social equality within the system. Moreover, once educational opportunities have been opened, the primary responsibility for his advancement rests upon the black man [*sic*]—on his own ambition, determination, and effort.[21]

So, essentially, foundations provide a cover for white supremacy. Reminiscent of Rockefeller's strategy; people of color deserve individual relief but people of color organized to end white supremacy become a menace to society.

Another strategy developed to sublimate revolutionary movements into reformist ones was "leadership training" both domestically and internationally, whereby potential organizers were recruited to develop the skills to become policy-makers and bureaucrats instead of organizers.[22] Thus, we can see how the nonprofit industrial complex works in a complementary fashion with the military industrial complex. On one hand, the military industrial complex directly represses revolutionary movements abroad. On the other hand, the nonprofit industrial complex diverts potential revolutionary leaders into the NPIC and attempts to reshape the goals of these movements through philanthropy so that they will not pose a serious threat to the capitalist world order. As Howard Dressner, secretary of the Ford Foundation, stated in 1969:

> American society is being strained at one extreme by those who would destroy what they oppose or do not understand, and at the other by forces that would repress variety and punish dissent. We are in great need of more not fewer instruments *for necessary social change under law, for ready, informed response to deep-seated problems without chaos, for accommodation of a variety of views without deafening anarchy.* Foundations have served as such an instrument.[23] [emphasis added]

Meanwhile, Robert Arnove's edited volume, *Philanthropy and Cultural Imperialism,* charged that foundations:

> Have a corrosive influence on a democratic society; they represent relatively unregulated and unaccountable concentrations of power and wealth which buy talent, promote causes, and in effect, establish an agenda of what merits society's attention. They serve as "cooling-out" agencies, delaying and preventing more radical, structural change. They help maintain an economic and political order, international in scope, which benefits the ruling-class interests of philanthropists.[24]

These critiques of the foundations and nonprofits still ring true today.

What Is the Nonprofit Industrial Complex?

Dylan Rodríguez defines the nonprofit industrial complex as "a set of symbiotic relationships that link political and financial technologies of state and owning class control with surveillance over public political ideology,

including and especially emergent progressive and leftist social movements."
He and Ruthie Gilmore argue that the NPIC is the natural corollary to the
prison industrial complex (PIC). While the PIC overtly represses dissent the
NPIC manages and controls dissent by incorporating it into the state apparatus, functioning as a "shadow state" constituted by a network of institutions
that do much of what state departments are supposed to do with tax money
in the areas of education and social services. The NPIC functions as an alibi
allowing government to make war, expand punishment, and proliferate market economies under the veil of partnership between the public and private
sectors.[25]

Christine Ahn looks more closely at the role of foundations in particular. She argues that foundations are *theoretically* a correction for the ills of
capitalism and the financial industrial complex. However, if we look at where
the actual funding goes (including who governs these institutions), we can
see that most of this country's "charity"—whether individual, corporate, or
foundation—is not directed toward programs, services, and institutions that
benefit the poor or disenfranchised, and certainly not toward effecting social
change. When wealthy people create foundations, they're exempt from paying taxes on their wealth. Thus foundations essentially rob the public of monies that should be owed to them and give back very little of what is taken in
lost taxes. In addition, their funds are derived from profits resulting from the
exploitation of labor. That is, corporations become rich by exploiting their
workers. Corporate profits are then put into foundations in order to provide
"relief" to workers whose ills are the result of corporate practices in the first
place. Rather than thinking of foundations as a source of income for which
we should be grateful, Ahn suggests, we reimagine foundations as a target
for accountability, just as we might organize to hold corporations or the state
accountable to the public good.[26]

HOW THE NONPROFIT INDUSTRIAL COMPLEX
IMPACTS MOVEMENTS

It is easy to critique the larger foundations, but what about smaller foundations that are not based on large endowments? Are large foundations the only
problem? This question is addressed by Tiffany Lethabo King and Ewuare
Osayande's work. While Ahn discusses strategies for holding foundations
accountable, King and Osayande contend that this effort to reform foundations basically serves to protect elitism within social justice movements. They
further argue that even self-described "alternatives" to foundation funding

(such as individual giving through major donors) are still based on the same logic—that wealthy people should be the donors, and thus, inevitably, the controllers of social justice struggles. Ultimately, even these funding strategies disadvantage organizations on behalf of people of color, which do not have the same access to wealthy donors as do white-dominated organizations.[27]

Thus, regardless of the intentions of particular foundations, the framework of funding, in which organizations expect to be funded by benefactors rather than by their constituents, negatively impacts social movements as well. Amara Perez explains how the initial effort of Sisters in Action for Power, a radical women-of-color organization in Portland Oregon, to become a nonprofit ultimately shifted its focus from organizing to corporate management. When Sisters in Action for Power realized the detrimental impact the NPIC had on its work, it began to explore how its organization could reject this corporate model and instead develop structures that more closely model the vision of the society it is trying to build. This step necessitated the development of organizing strategies within an integrated mind-body-spirit framework that respects organizing processes as much as outcomes. Aware that such approaches are often antithetical to foundations' requirements that focus on short-term campaign outcomes, Sisters in Action for Power explains why it nonetheless chose to engage in campaigns aiming to develop leadership in young women of color through a holistic framework.[28]

Madonna Thunder Hawk reminds us that many radical movements for change are able to accomplish much—if not more—outside the nonprofit system. Thunder Hawk was a co-founder of Women of All Red Nations (formed in connection with the American Indian Movement) that did incredible work organizing against sterilization abuse and environmental racism within Native communities without a single foundation grant. Mindful that many contemporary activists feel they cannot do their work without starting a nonprofit first, Thunder Hawk also observes that foundations only give money to more well-established NGOs who have the "expertise." But, more often than not, she warns, these purported experts are generally not part of the communities they advocate for and hence do not contribute to building grassroots leadership, particularly in indigenous communities.[29] This legacy of radical indigenous organizing has been reclaimed by Táala Hooghan, which according to their materials is an "Indigenous-established volunteer-run collective dedicated to creatively confronting and overcoming social and environmental injustices in Flagstaff and surrounding areas. We are restoring and redefining knowledge and information in ways that will be meaningful to our communities. We offer access to independent media, the arts, and alternative education, with the goal of self-development as well as empowerment for youth and the greater community into action in favor of a more just and sustainable world."

This group takes an explicit stance against the nonprofit industrial complex. Its office ground rules state the following:

> This is NOT an office. Please refrain from any activities that may be related to or directly connected to the nonprofit industry, vertical administration (hierarchy), organizational capacity building (and not community building), foundation brown-nosing, free market activism, and/or just plain capitalism.
>
> This community space respects agreements based on respect and mutual aid. They include but are not limited to: No drugs, alcohol, racism, hetero-patriarchy, colonialism, neoliberalism, hierarchy, capitalism, drama . . .

The NPIC contributes to a mode of organizing that is ultimately unsustainable. To radically change society, we must build mass movements that can topple systems of domination, such as capitalism. However, the NPIC encourages us to think of social justice organizing as a career; that is, you do the work if you can get paid for it. However, a mass movement requires the involvement of millions of people, most of whom cannot get paid. By trying to do grassroots organizing through this careerist model, we are essentially asking a few people to work more than full-time to make up for the work that needs to be done by millions.

In addition, the NPIC promotes a social movement culture that is non-collaborative, narrowly focused, and competitive. To retain the support of benefactors, groups must compete with each other for funding by promoting only their own work, whether or not their organizing strategies are successful. This culture prevents activists from having collaborative dialogues where we can honestly share our failures as well as our successes. In addition, after being forced to frame everything we do as a "success," we become stuck in having to repeat the same strategies because we insisted to funders they were successful, even if they were not. Consequently, we become inflexible rather than fluid and ever-changing in our strategies, which is what a movement for social transformation really requires. And, as we become more concerned with attracting funders than organizing mass-based movements, we start niche-marketing the work of our organization. Framing our organizations as working on a particular issue or a particular strategy, we lose perspective on the larger goals of our work. Thus, niche marketing encourages us to forward a fractured movement rather than enable us to develop mass-based movements for social change.

Suzanne Pharr notes that the move toward developing antiviolence organizations through the nonprofit system coincided with Reaganomics. At the same time Reagan was slashing government services, the women's movement organized itself into nonprofits to provide the services the government was no longer providing. Consequently, the antiviolence movement essentially became an alibi for the state.[30] The result of the influx of government and foundation funding was that the antiviolence movement focused less on grassroots organizing and more on professionalization and social service delivery. Instead of imagining domestic violence survivors who could organize on their own behalf, antiviolence organizations viewed them only as clients in need of services.

Similarly, Paula Rojas, an Austin and Chile-based activist, explains how activists in Latin America understand the NPIC. She says that we can understand our society running along a highway of colonialism and capitalism where we drive along in our gas-guzzling SUVs. The problem is that because people living in the United States live in the belly of the beast, the global industrial complex cannot afford to have them be seriously organized because it would radically transform the financial and military world orders. However, as a result of the financial industrial complex, the United States has so many resources that it can afford to pay off those who would resist the system. So, essentially, Rojas explains, the United States builds us an alternative highway that goes in a circle. We are allowed to drive on this alternative highway with our more energy efficient Toyota Prius cars. And we fail to notice that (1) we are driving around in circles, (2) the global industrial complex built the highway for us; and (3) the highway of colonialism and capitalism is continuing uninterrupted.

The impact of the NPIC on the antiviolence movement has been particularly disastrous because most of the government funding it receives has been through the Department of Justice, especially with the advent of the Violence Against Women Act. As a result, antiviolence organizations have focused primarily on criminal justice solutions to ending violence that reinforce the prison industrial complex; in fact, many antiviolence organizations are now located within police departments. Women of color, who must address both gender violence within their communities and state violence against their communities, have been particularly impacted by the direction the mainstream antiviolence movement has taken. This NGO-ization of the antiviolence movement is also actively exported to other countries, which follows a model Gayatri Spivak calls "saving brown women from brown men."[31] This NGO model tends to pathologize communities in the Third World for their "backward" attitudes toward women. The goal becomes to "save" Third World women from the extreme patriarchy in their community without looking at how patriarchy is connected to white supremacy and colonialism. Thus, for instance, mainstream feminist groups will support the bombing in Afghanistan to save Afghan women from the Taliban as if U.S. empire actually liberates women. Further analysis of the co-optation of the antiviolence movement can be found in INCITE!'s *Color of Violence: The INCITE! Anthology* (South End Press, 2006). Through the NPIC then, feminist rhetoric around violence becomes co-opted to serve the interests of the prison and military industrial complexes.

Women of color have also been particularly impacted by the role of foundations in the women's health and reproductive justice movements, which further the interests of the medical industrial complex specifically. Foundations have been active in supporting the population control movement, which blames the reproductive capabilities of women of color and Third World women for almost all social ills, including poverty, war, and environmental destruction. For instance, John Rockefeller founded the Population Council in 1952 to foster international population control policies under the notion that overpopulation causes unrest, and hence, revolution.[32] The Population Council supported mass population control efforts in Latin America during the 1960s and 1970s.[33] And in the last six months of 1976, the Population Council supported the sterilization of 6.5 million people in India through the use of police raids to round up men and women, with thousands dying from infections caused by the unsanitary conditions of the sterilizations. In one village alone, all the young men were sterilized.[34]

Today, what Betsy Hartmann terms the "population establishment"[35] spends billions of dollars each year on population programs, policy setting, and (mis)education. Certainly, Third World women/ women of color want family planning services, but many of the programs foisted upon them have been implemented without concern for their health. For instance, before Norplant, a long-acting hormonal contraceptive, was introduced in the U.S., the Population Council inserted it into nearly half a million women in Indonesia, often without providing counseling on side effects (which include menstrual irregularity, nausea, and anxiety) or notification that there had been no long-term studies on the drug's effects. Many were not told that it needed to be removed after five years to avoid an increased risk of ectopic pregnancy.[36] [Thirty-five hundred women in India were implanted with Norplant 2 in trials that began in the 1980s, without being warned about possible side effects or screened to determine if they were suitable candidates. These programs were finally discontinued due to concerns about "teratogenicity and carcinogenicity." In both cases, women who wanted the implant removed had great difficulty finding doctors who could do so.[37] (Similarly, in the U.S., many doctors can insert Norplant, but not so many know how to remove it).

The Pew Foundation, the largest environmental grant maker in the United States, spent over $13 million to increase public support for population control at the 1994 Cairo Conference on Population and Development.[38] Population control is one of Pew's top priorities; organized through the Global Steward-ship Initiative, its targeted constituencies are environmental organizations, internal affairs and foreign policy initiatives, and religious organizations.[39] In conjunction with the Park Ridge Center, in February 1994, Pew organized a forum in Chicago on religious perspectives on population, consumption, and the environment. In May 1994, it hosted a consultation that brought together thinkers from major world religions to deliberate population issues,[40] issuing a statement to contradict the Vatican's anti-choice position.[41] As a lead-in to the Cairo conference, Pew targeted churches to support a Cairo consensus on population by organizing focus groups with different constituencies, including various religious groups. It identified the "problem" constituencies as those who "accept overpopulation as a problem in terms of unequal distribution of resources and mismanagement of resources—not numbers of people."[42] Pew then targeted the "elites" of religious communities who would understand its construction of the problems of overpopulation.[43] Its efforts met with success; in 1993, a Pew survey of 30 U.S. denominations found that 43 percent had an official statement on population.[44] Church leaders in both evangelical and liberal denominations came out in support of the Cairo conference, lauding its steps forward on women's reproductive health issues. Through this work, Pew had, in the words of Hartmann, managed to "manufacture consensus" over the Cairo conference.[45] Through its vast financial resources, Pew has been able to change the agenda of environmental organizations and programs in order to suit its own vision for the world.[46] Thus, through the NPIC, the reproductive rights movement ends up furthering the financial interests of pharmaceutical companies and the medical industrial complex in the name of reproductive justice.

NONPROFITS AND GLOBAL ORGANIZING

Globally, both foundations and nonprofits/NGOs have received widespread criticism for their implicit or explicit support of First World interests and free-market capitalism. Numerous foundations and nonprofits have directly col-luded with the Central Intelligence Agency (CIA). For instance, foundations supported and continue to support CIA programs in educational exchanges with east Africa and eastern Europe to maintain a U.S. presence in these areas without the consent of Congress.[47] The CIA also employs political scientists and collaborates with professors in sponsoring university institutes. These institutes were created on the advice of foundations that assumed scholars would be more likely to cooperate with intelligence work if it were done in an academic location. These scholars also helped recruit potential allies among foreign students.[48] Additionally, the CIA directed funding through foundations to support cultural arts to recruit leftist cultural workers, and showcase U.S. cultural achievements globally. Since the State Department could not fund such activities directly, they had to be funneled through foundations.[49] Gerald Colby and Charlotte Dennett's book *Thy Will Be Done* also charges that Rockefeller funded missionary agencies that collaborated with the CIA for several decades in Latin America. These missionaries/agents would befriend indigenous peoples in Latin America, collaborate with them to translate the Bible into indigenous languages, and then use these intermediaries to funnel intelligence information to the CIA to facilitate resource extraction and destabilize leftist regimes.[50] Critics further charge that the Ford Foundation funded programs to revitalize Indian religions in India to counter the spread of communism. This tactic has the impact of defusing opposition from a leftist framework, but also fuels religious fundamentalism and the rise of Hindu Right nationalism.[51]

Foundations have also been directly involved working with the military industrial complex to squelch revolutionary movements in the Third World. The Ford Foundation was actively involved through its various programs in diverting the anti-apartheid movement in South Africa from an anti-capitalist to a pro-capitalist movement.[52] Cyril Ramaphosa, a secretary-general of the African National Congress who led a 1987 miners strike praised by the Ford Foundation,[53] signed a $900-million contract with Anglo American Corporation, a corporation that accounts for 25 percent of South Africa's gross domestic product and controls much of South Africa's gold and diamond mining. The goal of this collaboration is to bring "blacks into the mainstream economy" rather than to challenge the economic status quo.[54] These same strategies are being used by NGOs to deradicalize the struggle in Palestine and other colonized territories.[55]

James Petras make some similar arguments in his 1994 essay "NGOs: In the Service of Imperialism." Petras notes that despite claiming to be non-governmental organizations, they actually support government interests. NGOs, he writes:

> receive funds from overseas governments, work as private sub-contractors of local governments and/or are subsidized by corporate funded private foundations with close working relations with the state. . . . Their programs are not accountable to local people, but to overseas donors who "review" and "oversee" the performance of the NGOs according to their criteria and interests. The NGO officials are self-appointed and one of their key tasks is designing proposals that will secure funding. In many cases this requires that NGO leaders find out the issues the Western funding elites fund, and shape proposals accordingly.[56]

For example, he notes that NGOs direct organizing efforts away from dealing with exploitation by the World Bank to supporting microcredit projects that place the solution to poverty on individual initiative rather than changing global economic systems. He adamantly opposes even "progressive" NGOs, arguing that they divert resources from the people, they subordinate movement leadership to NGO leadership, and they do not put their lives on the lines:

> Progressive NGOs use peasants and the poor for their research projects, they benefit from the publication—nothing comes back to the movements[,] not even copies of the studies done in their names! Moreover, peasant leaders ask why the NGOs never risk their neck after their educational seminars[.]? Why do they not study the rich and powerful—why us? . . . The NGOs should stop being NGOs and convert themselves into members of socio-political movements. . . . The fundamental question is whether a new generation of organic intellectuals can emerge from the burgeoning radical social movements which can avoid the NGO temptation and become integral members of the next revolutionary wave.[57]

Reformulating the Role of Nonprofits

In contrast to Petras, Paula X. Rojas suggests alternative possibilities for understanding the proper relationship between nonprofits and social movements as informed by the role of non-profits in mass movements in other countries. Jones de Almeida and Rojas point out that in many countries, social movements are not necessarily dominated by nonprofits. Instead, movement building is funded and determined by the constituents. These movements may make strategic alliances with nonprofits or develop their own nonprofits as intermediaries to fund specific aspects of their work. But a key difference is that these nonprofits are accountable to social movements; they are not seen as part of the movement themselves. Furthermore, our goal is to sustain movements, not nonprofits that support movements[58] Eric Tang also concludes that while nonprofits can have a role in support of the movement, they cannot be a revolution. He argues that the revolution will not be funded—we must create autonomous movements. But once we develop that mass movement, nonprofits could serve as buffers that protect autonomous movements from government repression.[59] Essentially then, it is important to switch our focus from organizational survival to movement survival. In doing so, we do not necessarily have to avoid working with nonprofits. But what if we also built a strong independently funded movement that nonprofits assisted rather than attempt to build a movement through the NPIC?

Through Incite!, I was involved in organizing the Santa Barbara-based 2004 conference, "The Revolution Will Not Be Funded: Beyond the

Non-Profit Industrial Complex," which generated a volume *The Revolution Will Not Be Funded*. The conference and book helped intensify discussion within social justice organizations about the impact of the NPIC in our work. Since these events, I have learned how important it is to note the complexities around the NPIC. Precisely because the NPIC is part of a larger global industrial complex, it is important to note that it is really the tip of a larger iceberg. If we were to eliminate all nonprofits today, our organizing would not necessarily be more effective if we do not critically address how our organizing culture is shaped by all the global industrial complexes. For instance, if we will no longer be paid to do activist work, then we will have to rely on day jobs for survival. But if we do not collectivize the resources from our day jobs, then we will continue to have a class structure within our organizing whereby people with better-paying day jobs have more time and energy to do organizing work than do peoples who have low-paying jobs or who may not be able to find work at all. The impact of the financial industrial complex is that we continue to lead very privatized and individualized lives. When we think to work collectively, our collective action is confined to the public spheres of protests and other actions. But our movements do not think to collectivize the work that is seen as part of the public sphere, such as daycare, cooking and tending to our basic needs. Consequently, we build movements that are accessible to very few people and which are particularly burdensome for women who often are responsible for caretaking in the private sphere. Thus, the NPIC is a symptom of a much larger problem for social movements today—we require a radical reorientation in the way we not only do the work but how we live our lives.

In addition, if we have a critique of the NPIC without an understanding of how it relates to other industrial complexes, then we can be under the illusion that there is a politically pure place to work. But if we understand that we all live in a global industrial complex, then we see that it is almost impossible to live or survive today without being employed by the global industrial complex as a whole. What this reality suggests is that while we may be of necessity required to have one foot in either the NPIC or another manifestation of the global industrial complex, we also need simultaneously to have another foot rooted in an independently funded social movement that is accountable to its constituents. In this way, we will have more power to operate within the global industrial complex, because as New Orleans-based activist Barbara Major states: "When you go to power without a base, your demand becomes a request." We will also then have a structural relationship of accountability to a movement that can keep us more honest as we negotiate the various aspects of the global industrial complex. By being grounded in social movements that are rooted in building a stronger base of participants who are not already activists, we may then be in a better position to strategically use the NPIC to further our goals rather than have the NPIC use us to serve the interests of the global industrial complex.

NOTES

1. Sheila Slaughter and Edward Silva, "Looking Backwards: How Foundations Formulated Ideology in the Progressive Period," in *Philanthropy and Cultural Imperialism,* ed. Robert Arnove (Boston, MA: G. K. Hall and Company, 1980), 55–86.

2. James Allen Smith, "The Evolving Role of American Foundations," in *Philanthropy and the Non-profit Sector in a Changing America,* eds. Charles Clotfelter and Thomas Erlich (Bloomington, IN: University of Indiana Press, 1999), 34–51.

3. Thomas J. Billitteri, "Donors Big and Small Propelled Philanthropy in the 20th Century," *The Chronicle of Philanthropy Gifts and Grants,* January 13, 2000, philanthropy.com/free/articles/v12/i06/06002901.htm (accessed July 12, 2010).

4. Thomas Atwood, *The Road to Ludlow,* paper, archive.rockefeller.edu/publications/resrep/andrews.pdf (accessed July 12, 2010).

5. Thomas Atwood, *The Road to Ludlow.*

6. Barbara Howe, "The Emergency of Scientific Philanthropy, 1900–1920: Origins, Issues and Outcomes," in *Philanthropy and Cultural Imperialism,* 25–54.

7. Barbara Howe, "The Emergency."

8. Sheila Slaughter and Edward Silva, "Looking Backwards: How Foundations Formulated Ideology in the Progressive Period," in *Philanthropy and Cultural Imperialism,* 55–86.

9. James Allen Smith, "The Evolving Role of American Foundations," in *Philanthropy and the Non-profit Sector in a Changing America,* eds. Charles Clotfelter and Thomas Erlich (Bloomington, IN: University of Indiana Press, 1999), 34–51.

10. Waldemar Nielsen, *Golden Donors* (New York, NY: Truman Talley Books, 1985).

11. John Edie, "Congress and Foundations: Historical Summary," *America's Wealthy and the Future of Foundations,* ed. Teresa Odendahl (New Haven, CT: The Foundation Center, 1987), 43–64.

12. Thomas J. Billitteri, "Donors Big and Small."

13. Joan Roelofs, *Foundations and Public Policy* (Albany, NY: State University of New York Press, 2003).

14. Michael Shuman, "Why Progressive Foundations Give Too Little to Too Many," *The Nation* 266, January 12–19 (1998): 12

15. Karen Rothmyer, "What's Conspiracy Got To Do With It?" *The Nation* 266, February 23 (1998): 20

16. Joan Roelofs, *Foundations and Public Policy.*

17. Steve Gunderson, "Foundations: Architects of Social Change," *EJournal USA,* n.d., usinfo.state.gov/journals/itsv/0506/ijse/gunderson.htm (accessed July 12, 2010).

18. The Non-profit Congress, www.nonprofitcongress.org/sectorinfo.htm (accessed July 12, 2010).

19. Joan Roelofs, *Foundations and Public Policy*.

20. Waldemar Neilsen, *The Big Foundations* (New York, NY: Columbia University Press, 1972).

21. Waldemar Neilsen, *The Big Foundations*.

22. Joan Roelofs, *Foundations and Public Policy*.

23. Joan Roelofs, *Foundations and Public Policy*.

24. Robert Arnove, ed., *Philanthropy and Cultural Imperialism* (Boston, MA: G. K. Hall and Company, 1980).

25. Dylan Rodriguez, "The Political Logic of the Non-Profit Industrial Complex," and Ruth Wilson Gilmore, "In the Shadow of the Shadow State," both in ed. Incite!, *The Revolution Will Not Be Funded* (Boston, MA: South End Press, 2007), 21–52.

26. Christine Ahn, "Democraticizing American Philanthropy," in ed. Incite!, *The Revolution Will Not Be Funded*, 63–78.

27. Tiffany Lethabo King and Ewuare Osayande, "The Filth on Philanthrophy: Progressive Philanthropy's Agenda to Misdirect Social Justice Movements," in ed. Incite!, *The Revolution Will Not Be Funded*, 79–90.

28. Amara Perez, "Between Radical Theory and Community Praxis: Reflections on Organizing and the Non-Profit Industrial Complex," in ed. Incite!, *The Revolution Will Not Be Funded*, 91–100.

29. Madonna Thunder Hawk, "Native Organizing Before the Non-Profit Industrial Complex," in ed. Incite!, *The Revolution Will Not Be Funded*, 101–106.

30. Suzanne Pharr, plenary address, "The Revolution Will Not Be Funded" conference, University of California, Santa Barbara, April 30, 2004.

31. Gayatri Spivak, "Can the Subaltern Speak?" *Colonial Discourse and Post-Colonial Theory*, eds. Patrick Williams and Laura Chrisman (New York, NY: Columbia University Press, 1994).

32. Joan Roelofs, *Foundations and Public Policy*.

33. Reprinted in Dale Hathaway-Sunseed, *A Critical Look at the Population Crisis in Latin America* (University of California, Santa Cruz, 1979). The efforts these men supported led to 30 percent of women being sterilized in Puerto Rico and 44 percent in Brazil, despite the fact sterilization was illegal in Brazil. Betsy Hartmann, *Reproductive Rights and Wrongs: The Global Politics of Population Control* (Boston, MA: South End Press, 1995).

34. Betsy Hartmann, *Reproductive Rights*.

35. Betsy Hartmann, *Reproductive Rights*. Hartmann identifies the major players as USAID, UN Fund for Population Activities, governments of other developed countries (particularly Japan), the World Bank—(which has forced Third World countries to adopt population policies contingent upon release of structural adjustment loans), International Planned Parenthood Federation, Population Council, various consulting firms and academic centers, foundations (particularly Ted Turner and Pew Charitable Trusts) and various pressure groups (that is, Zero Population Growth and Population Action International as well as environmental organizations such as the Sierra Club).

36. Betsy Hartmann, *Reproductive Rights.*

37. Ammu Joseph, "India's Population Bomb," *Ms. Magazine* 3, no. 3: 12.

38. Betsy Hartmann, *Reproductive Rights.*

39. Pew Global Stewardship Initiative, *White Paper* (July, 1993),12.

40. Martin Marty, "Population and Development," *Second Opinion* 20 (April, 1995): 51–52. See also "Varied Religious Stands on Population," *Christian Century* 111, July 27-August 3 (1994): 714–715.

41. "Morals and Human Numbers," *Christian Century* 111, April 20 (1994): 409–410.

42. Pew Charitable Trust, *Report of Findings from Focus Groups on Population, Consumption and the Environment* (July 1993), 64.

43. Pew Charitable Trust, *Report of Findings.*

44. Pew Charitable Trust, *Global Stewardship* 1, no. 3 (March, 1994): 1.

45. Contrary to impressions left by the media, Carol Benson Holst points out that there are many people who were very critical of the Cairo program. For instance, her former organization, Ministry for Justice in Population Concerns, which was funded by Pew, issued a statement that was not allowed to be read at the plenary, calling the program "nothing but an insult to women, men and children of the South who will receive an ever-growing dose of population assistance, while their issues of life and death will await the Social Development Summit of 1995." Ramona Morgan Brown and Carol Benson Holst, "IPCD's Suppressed Voices May Be Our Future Hope," *Ministry for Justice in Population Concerns* (October-December, 1994): 1.

Consequently, Pew (which had funded the organization knowing it was concerned primarily with the relationship between social justice and population growth) defunded the organization because it "was too accommodating to people of color." *Ministry for Justice in Population Concerns, Notice of Phase-Out,* January 1 (1995). Pew's March 1994 newsletter also dismissed the concerns women of color had about the racist implications of population control as "rumor mongering." *Global Stewardship,* 3.

For another critical view of Cairo, see Charon Asetoyer, "Whom To Target for the North's Profits," *Wicozanni Wowapi,* (Fall, 1994): 2–3. She writes: "Early into the conference, it became obvious that the issues facing Third World countries such as development, structural adjustment, and capacity building was not high on the list of issues that the "Super Powers" wanted to address. It was clear that the issues facing world population were going to be addressed from the top down with little regard for how this may affect developing countries."

While it had first seemed Pew was concerned about justice issues, it became clear that they were only interested insofar as it furthered their population agenda. Other church-based organizations have privately questioned Pew's stance on this issue, but cannot do so publicly if they do not want to jeopardize their funding. Carol Benson Holst, "IPCD's Suppressed Voices."

46. Stephen Greene, "Who's Driving the Environmental Movement?" *Chronicle of Philanthropy* 6 (January 25, 1994): 6–10.

47. Barry Karl and Alice Karl, "Foundations and the Government: A Tale of Conflict and Consensus," in eds. Charles Clotfelter and Thomas Erlich, *Philanthropy and the Nonprofit Sector in a Changing America* (Bloomington, IN: University of Indiana Press, 1999), 52–72.

48. Joan Roelofs, *Foundations and Public Policy.*

49. Joan Roelofs, *Foundations and Public Policy.*

50. Gerard Colby and Charlotte Dennett, *Thy Will Be Done* (New York, NY: HarperCollins, 1995).

51. Joan Roelofs, *Foundations and Public Policy.*

52. Joan Roelofs, *Foundations and Public Policy.*

53. Joan Roelofs, *Foundations and Public Policy.*

54. Donald McNeil, "Once Bitter Enemies, Now Business Partners: South African Blacks Buy into Industry," *New York Times,* September 24, 1996, D1.

55. Andrea Smith, "The NGOization of the Palestine Liberation Movement," in ed. Incite!, *The Revolution Will Not Be Funded,* 165–184.

56. James Petras, "NGOs: In the Service of Imperialism," *Journal of Contemporaryy Asia* 29, no. 4 (1999): 429–440.

57. James Petras, "NGOs."

58. Paula Rojas, "Are the Cops in Our Heads and Hearts?" in ed. Incite!, *The Revolution Will Not Be Funded,* 197–214.

59. Eric Tang, "Non-Profits and the Autonomous Grassroots," in ed. Incite!, *The Revolution Will Not Be Funded,* 215–226.

Chapter Seven

Higher Education's Industrial Model

Cary Nelson

It is only in the last few years that advocates of public higher education in the United States began to realize that increased state expenditures on prisons often matched dollar-for-dollar decreases in state appropriations on higher education. California was a particularly telling example of the trend. Here and there across the country—because the conflict between these two priorities also reflected a long-running class war carried out economically—higher education advocates began to pose a stark alternative: "Educate the poor or plan to incarcerate them. Which is best for the country?" As a nation we have yet to confront this challenge and adopt the solution with the greater social benefits. Indeed we have yet to understand the relationship between these starkly different social options.

Meanwhile, the higher education industry has been on a steady course to emulate all other major American industries in their managerial and employment practices. This follows upon many decades in which progressive academics expressed concern about the myriad connections between the academic industrial complex and the military and corporate industrial complexes, the former a product of the cold war and the latter a fundamental feature of contemporary capitalism. These trends now have structural status. They define higher education as an industry. Though research done for the defense department represents a relatively small percentage of the national higher education budget, the academy's corporate ties are now pervasive. And earlier involvement with the DOD has been supplanted by multi-agency entanglements with the national security state.

When the former chancellor of the University of Illinois at Urbana-Champaign sent out a post-9/11 memo listing the many ways faculty members and departments could take advantage of enhanced national security funding and thus contribute to the nation's "security," cultural studies faculty members on campus asked him to add evaluating and analyzing the national security agenda as one of the ways we could contribute to a national debate. They were ignored.

Yet many academics—because their personal identities are grounded in historical and political denial—remain opposed to describing higher education as an industry compromised by its economic and political entanglements, indeed as an industry at all. My friends often write to me to ask that I use some other word than "industry," which only reinforces my sense that the term is apt and necessary.

In order to understand how higher education has evolved over the last generation it is necessary, therefore, to track two different—but increasingly intertwined—elements of the industry: the tendency to emulate corporate culture and the growing financial and administrative entanglement with corporations. The more the university behaves like a corporation, the easier it is to negotiate corporate contracts. If senior administrators can avoid the faculty oversight mandated by shared governance, they can make agreements more quickly and more easily make concessions to which faculty members might object. If administrators make hiring faculty members prepared to do product-oriented corporate research a priority, then they can incrementally redirect the university's mission toward that end. All this is easier if a top-down corporate management style is implemented.

The corporatization of higher education increasingly means that the academy is drawn into international investment patterns. Thus both American universities and those in other countries are founding satellite campuses abroad with more narrow profit-making aims than they exhibit at home. Basic rights like tenure, health care, safe working conditions, vestment in retirement systems, and the right to organize for collective bargaining can then seem merely inconvenient threats to the revenue stream. And commitments to a broad liberal education can disappear in an effort to satisfy the foreign student consumer.

These trends thus are at once economic and ideological. And they sometimes involve imitative strategies, rather than actual multi-national industry-wide agreements. Thus, for example, the International Monetary Fund began requiring that universities in countries applying for loans increase the percentage of contingent faculty not long after the increasing reliance on part-time faculty became apparent in the United States. For the IMF it was a way of assuring that universities could produce the graduates necessary to facilitate international investment in changing economies. In the U.S. it was more a matter of disempowering the faculty and directing resources elsewhere.

Similarly, efforts to defund humanities and interpretive social science programs are very much an international phenomenon, one growing out of the imitative spread of corporatist and neoliberal ideology.

To understand the current corporatized university it is also necessary to revisit its recent past, in which research funding sources were very different, but the pattern of reliance on outside funding sources steadily increased. During the cold war research universities became steadily more entangled with and dependent on the federal government. The cold war inflated Defense Department budgets, and Defense Department planners turned to faculty members to carry out an expanding program of research. Contracts were signed with the Pentagon, various units of the armed services, and with the Central Intelligence Agency. There might be a demonic bottom line, but often it was at some remove. Notoriously, the Navy reportedly funded research in dolphin intelligence and communication in part because it wanted eventually to see if these bright mammals could deliver an explosive charge to an enemy ship. The CIA funded research on AIDS epidemic modeling in Africa, in part to see if governments might be destabilized and if opportunities for intervention would arise.

Yet often enough a faculty member could ignore an agency's darker purposes. Government-sponsored research was a model of how to purchase faculty time and energy in a package designed to take advantage of faculty skill at rationalization. I can still vividly remember a Defense Department-funded political scientist in the mid-1980s gushing about what an open-minded, even visionary sponsor the Pentagon was. "They're not just financing weapons development. They're interested in long-term basic research. These are imaginative people." Indeed, and nothing like swarms of research assistants, rooms full of equipment, and a full one-third annual salary supplement to instill belief in military idealism.

There were moments of resistance—such as the heroic and successful effort spear-headed by physicists to discredit "star wars" research—but mostly the trends went the other way. Although many government agencies sponsored excellent independent research, the military-industrial complex that Eisenhower warned us about in the late 1950s within a few years encompassed part of higher education as well. Not long after that, campuses erupted in protests against the Vietnam War. By the late 1960s university participation in the research and development of the modern war machine lost all consensual grounds for rationalization. An unjust, undeclared, and pointlessly deadly war made campus military research and academic involvement with the defense industry morally abhorrent. When the makers of Napalm arrived on campus to recruit new graduates, the red carpets were occupied with protestors. Yet when the war finally ended, many government/corporate/campus links were still in place.

The 1970s saw further increases in government grants and in the federal regulation of higher education. Accounting for federal funds and justifying indirect costs meant more campus surveillance of budgets, more reporting to administrators. But in the next decade the funding balance would begin to shift to industry. Corporations in the Reagan years began to purchase faculty research time, and Reagan-era legislation facilitated corporate/university partnerships. It was often cheaper for a corporation to buy faculty time than to hire staff and operate a lab on its own. What's more, university research added an air of prestige and objectivity to corporate projects. By the early 1980s reporters were starting to write stories about the buying and selling of higher education in corporate boardrooms.

As early as 1982, historian David Noble could write in the *Nation* that "the control over science by scientists—the hallmark of the postwar pattern—is increasingly becoming the control over science by the science-based corporations that scientists serve and sometimes own or direct."[1] Six years later, in *The New Politics of Science,* David Dickson noted a still more fundamental ideological shift, arguing for a new understanding of scientists' fundamental social responsibility: "the need to help private corporations achieve their economic and political objectives."[2] As Cheryl B. Leggon outlined in an essay in *Daedalus* in 1997, "since the mid-1980s pressure has increased in Congress to shift national attention away from basic science and toward science with technological applications able to bolster declining American economic competitiveness."[3]

Over the last generation, reliance on government funding has gradually declined, and universities have turned to corporations to fund their expansion. The effective corporate purchase of individual labs or even entire departments' research functions has become common. Some labs as a result have become simple extensions of corporations. In other cases, whole departments have much of their research agenda set by one or more corporations. When the profit available from contract research becomes a department's main priority, then prestige and rewards flow to the department members bringing in the money. As institutions become more broadly addicted to the corporate finance pipeline, their whole raison d'être begins to shift. Profit-making departments become the first priority for institutional resources, and the profit-making function within those departments begins to dominate their other activities, from student recruitment to faculty hiring to curriculum design. "Excellence," that ambiguous, hyperbolic concept aptly analyzed by Bill Readings in *The University in Ruins,* gradually becomes conflated with profitability.[4]

Those departments that reach the nadir of corporatization abandon all their intellectual functions. A corporatized department can become the academic equivalent of a truck weighing station on an interstate highway. If that seems impossible, let me give the standard pattern. The devil's bargain is struck for many programs when they abandon their program of original research in favor of a corporate-directed plan. Some departments then begin shifting their time and energy away from research entirely. Toward teaching? Toward community outreach? Hardly. They become *product-testing labs.* The most thoroughly degraded corporatized university program is one that no longer does any original thinking; it simply tests products developed elsewhere by the corporation.

There are now entire programs in higher education devoted to product testing. One has difficulty thinking of them as academic units at all, but they have offices, staffs, budgets, resources, and even tenured faculty. Some are called departments. "Research" in some departments is primarily drug testing for pharmaceutical companies. They do not develop, invent, or discover the drugs. The drug companies do that. Elsewhere across the country there are agriculture programs that concentrate on testing pesticides designed by chemical companies. And so forth. Every faculty member on such campuses should be concerned about the consequences.

When faculty members are criticized for doing contract drug testing, they have a stock response: would you rather have the drug companies or universities testing their products? The question is aimed at a self-evident, common sense answer, based on an assumption about faculty independence, prestige, and integrity. Unfortunately, university researchers are as corruptible as any other human beings. When they are being well paid by the companies whose products they are testing, bias, temptation, or self-deception are endemic. If actual fraud is very rare indeed, shading interpretable results in favor of an employer (and in one's own financial interests) is relatively common, especially in nonmedical research. The companies meanwhile do their best to co-opt these saints of the laboratory, offering stock options, bonuses, and future contracts.

As federal funding for research—with its system of peer reviewing and greater independence—was replaced with corporate funding, the pressure for scholars to turn themselves into company public relations personnel increased. Indeed, it is not just income but job security and advancement that are at stake. A faculty member's record at obtaining grants or contracts can be a decisive component in a tenure or promotion decision. Keeping Sears or Goodyear or R. J. Reynolds or Smith, Kline, and French happy can make or break your career.

It can also break your budget. At the University of Illinois' National Center for Supercomputing Applications, managers seek corporate partners who gain a degree of exclusivity in a particular research area once a joint contract is signed. The corporations have limited horizons and often want to initiate and complete a project in a year or two. The university's horizon is usually much wider; it wants to develop a research area over time by hiring faculty, admitting graduate students, and making a long-term commitment. But the corporations want rapid results. The university wants to keep its business partners happy, so it tries to achieve profitable outcomes quickly. That frequently means hiring new graduate assistants or shifting personnel from elsewhere to respond to changing needs for a rapidly developing project. There never seems to be time to renegotiate the contracts fast enough to have the corporation pick up the new unanticipated expenses. So the university puts its own money into the corporation's research. Of course the university is already paying accountants, managers, secretaries, and contact negotiators out of its own pocket. As it plans new faculty lines, the campus inevitably looks to areas where corporations are interested in funding joint ventures.

The experience of contracting out its services makes it easier for a university to contract for its service needs. The focus on profit-making enterprises makes university culture accustomed to keeping its costs as low as possible. Many corporations are devoted to paying employees as little as possible. Increasingly, universities follow the same practice in many job categories, including most of their instructional work force. As Christopher Newfield writes, "financial control tends to view labor as a cost, as a site of potential savings,"[5] rather than as a resource to be valued and nurtured. In contract research units that do no original research the emphasis in faculty hiring can shift from seeking people who will make intellectual contributions to looking for people who will serve the product testing and development machine. When faculty members from more traditional units review these people for tenure, they are compelled to honor the hiring unit's debased business values. Administrators making campus-wide budget decisions may be tempted to give a high priority to their profitable units. Their "faculty" will receive salary rewards, while those who simply "cost money" may not.

We are faced, then, with several overlapping meanings for the notion of "the corporate university":

1) universities that perform contract services for corporations;
2) universities that form financial partnerships with corporations;
3) universities that design curricula and degree programs to serve corporate hiring needs;

4) universities that condone corporate influence over curriculum and program development by accepting corporate funded programs, fellowships, and faculty lines;
5) universities that adopt profit-oriented corporate values;
6) universities that adopt corporate style management and accounting techniques;
7) universities that effectively sell portions of their enterprise to corporations;
8) universities that sell faculty or staff time to corporations;
9) universities whose faculty members are co-opted by corporations that hire them as high-paid consultants and fund their research;
10) universities that engage corporations to market the products of faculty/staff labor;
11) universities that instill corporate culture in their students and staff;
12) universities whose top level of governance—boards of regents or trustees—is dominated by executive officers of corporations;
13) universities that fund or defund academic units based on their capacity to obtain profitable patents or develop marketable products.

Unfortunately, the project of both conceptualizing and confronting the corporate university necessitates dealing with all these forms of corporatization. Their penetration of university culture has, of course, been immensely enhanced and intensified by the higher education budget crisis of the last three decades and its intensification during the 2009–2011 recession. Although the effects of the crisis have been differential, that is, selective, unequal and ideologically targeted, the crisis has also transformed university culture as a whole. The exclusive focus on budgeting as the primary context for all university decision-making reached a zenith in 2010, as firings, non-renewals, and furloughs escalated and efforts to downsize or eliminate arts, humanities, and social sciences disciplines less useful to corporate managers spread across the country.

What many faculty do not realize, however, is that the "crisis" has been partly manufactured and certainly magnified by long-term administrative determination to redistribute and reinvest university funds. We have been in the construction business for decades and have eviscerated the humanities and the arts to fund the start-up and operating costs for new buildings. Aggressive capitalist initiatives on campus have thus been funded out of the salaries of less profitable disciplines and by the exploitation of lower-grade workers. Many campuses have seen comparable building programs become a priority. And they come with a whole interconnected web of increased costs. When an industrial "partnership" produces a new campus building, or an industrial park springs up nearby—with patent, royalty, rental, and research costs shared and negotiated between the university and industry—consequences ripple through the institution. New categories of administrators and managers emerge to oversee the arrangements. New staff are hired to do the work. And the supposedly consensual basis of the university's mission makes a basic shift without full faculty consultation.

The corporatization of the university has been facilitated by a fundamental shift of power on campus—away from faculty and toward managers and administrators. At the same time as the faculty has lost authority over the institution's goals, it has also come to have less and less knowledge of what the institution is actually doing. Faculty knowledge of budget issues has always been limited, but an institution devoted primarily to instruction and basic research has a fairly clear shared mission whose budgetary implications are relatively transparent. A corporate university acquires complex financial entanglements about which most faculty members know little or nothing. As the managers come to know more, they assume they also know what's best.

The institutional "cost" of cutting faculty out of the budgetary loop will only grow. The more financially ignorant faculty are, the less they can intervene intelligently and the more managers will want to keep them uninformed. Through the 1990s faculty ignorance about finances was considered a privilege. Administrators would order the paper clips, and faculty would be protected from the petty distraction of budgeting and accounting. But now finances are reshaping the university's mission, and whole new classes of expenditures have arisen. Financial secrecy in the corporate university eviscerates any notion of shared governance. Meanwhile, the relentless outsourcing, casualizing, temping, and segmenting of campus labor makes the traditional fiction of benign administrative "protection" ludicrously inapplicable. Exploited labor is not protected by its ignorance.

As a first step in shifting the balance of knowledge, faculty at all institutions should insist on complete financial transparency, including making salaries a matter of public record. Most public institutions are required to do so, though summer salaries may remain unpublished. But private universities often maintain almost complete secrecy about compensation. That practice should end. Faculty need to know not only the salaries paid to faculty and administrators in all departments, but also the wages paid graduate employees, part-timers, and cafeteria workers. Otherwise they are not only kept blind to the financial consequences of disciplinarity and to the injustice of increasing corporate-style salary polarization, but also kept ignorant of the labor exploitation carried out in their names. At the same time faculty members should demand open budgeting throughout the institution. Merely asking for open budgeting will not, of course, produce it. In the corporate university it is especially important that faculty develop their own independent sources of knowledge and structures for influence. A faculty senate too often has input without impact. Unions traditionally hire someone to do their "corporate research," to gather information about corporate finances, investments, budgets, and decision-making. Whether unionized or not, faculty and graduate students need someone doing their corporate research as well. Like unions in the industrial workplace, faculty organizations at public institutions should also hire their own lobbyist to represent their interests to the legislature and coordinate faculty/legislative interactions. A lobbyist at the state capitol often has several clients, so the cost is not prohibitive. Even faculties without collective bargaining can form organizations to research institutional finances and lobby.

The results of open budgeting can be surprising. Indeed the knowledge and insight obtained that way is the one great benefit of the spread of the accounting mentality. Perhaps the greatest revelation is that the purportedly profit-making units may not be turning a profit at all. RCM, or responsibility-centered management, for example, is an accounting and budgeting method with both risks and benefits. It redefines "income" to encompass both grants and tuition income raised by the number of students enrolled in courses. At Illinois, until 2009, a large humanities department like English turned out in that way to run a large profit overall, whereas units like the Colleges of Engineering and Agriculture run at a loss. Agriculture especially brings in significant grant money, but has relatively few students, so it generates little tuition income. Its grant receipts and tuition revenue are not enough to cover faculty/staff salaries. At the University of Illinois, then, the College of Agriculture consequently has to be heavily supported by state appropriations and by tuition income produced by departments like English. Putting both tuition and grants on the table together gives the lie to the prestige of profit. In 2009, however, the administration applied a large additional portion of central administrative costs and overhead to departmental budgets. Suddenly English was in the red and was told to cut teaching positions to cover its burden of administrative overhead.

The university's entanglement in the corporate industrial complex cannot be stopped, but it can be shaped and, where appropriate, resisted. At its worst, corporatization strips the faculty of its intellectual independence, impoverishes the teaching staff and diminishes its dignity and academic freedom, and deprives students of appropriate intellectual challenges. We are not likely to see the end of such positions as the Boeing Company Chair in aeronautics at the California Institute of Technology, the Coca-Cola Professors of Marketing at both the University of Arizona and the University of Georgia, the La Quinta Motor Inns Professor of Business at the University of Texas, the Taco Bell Distinguished Professor of Hotel and Restaurant Administration at Washington State University, the Kmart Professor of Marketing at Wayne State University, the McLamore/Burger King Chair at the University of Miami, the Lego Professor of Learning Research and the Chevron Professor of Chemical Engineering at MIT, the Federal Express Chair of information-management systems at the University of Memphis, the General Mills Chair of Cereal Chemistry and Technology at the University of Minnesota, the Coral Petroleum Industries Chair in renewable-energy resources at the University of Hawaii at Manoa, the LaRoche Industries Chair in Chemical Engineering at the Georgia Institute of Technology, the Ralston Purina endowed professorship in small-animal nutrition at the University of Missouri at Columbia, the Merck Company Chair in biochemistry and molecular biology at the University of Pennsylvania, the Sears Roebuck Chair in retail marketing at Marquette University, and several corporate funded chairs at UCLA: the Allstate Chair in Finance and Insurance, the Nippon Sheet Glass Company Chair in Materials Science, the Hughes Aircraft Company Chair in Manufacturing Engineering, and the Rockwell International Chair of Engineering. Among many others, we also have the Gerken Professor of Enterprise and Society at the University of California at Irvine, the Goodyear Professorship of Free Enterprise at Kent State, the Scott L. Probasco Professor of Free Enterprise in Tennessee, and the Mastercard International Distinguished Chair in Entrepreneurial Leadership at the University of Virginia. The right-wing Olin Foundation has endowed professorships at a dozen universities.

This kind of trend is unstoppable, but we can nonetheless organize to block major contracts that enforce corporate secrecy on campus, drain university resources, and eliminate faculty members' rights to define their own research priorities. For corporations are typically no longer satisfied with their logo on a professor's forehead. They sometimes want the faculty member to do research that benefits the corporation. The holder of the Kmart Chair spoke proudly of saving the company money with his research and summarized its view of its investment in higher education: "Kmart's attitude has always been 'What did we get from you this year?'" United Parcel Service carried on negotiations with the University of Washington not only to endow a professorship but also to name the chair's holder. Their choice just happened to be one Stanley Bigos, whose research suggested that "psychosocial factors" like "life distress" outweighed working conditions as causes of back injury claims. Good news for UPS, whose package lifting employees claim back injuries with some regularity. In the end, negotiations collapsed, but not because the university resisted UPS's demand to name the chair holder.

Of course such efforts can mushroom into entire institutes devoted to corporate-style initiatives. The key issue then is traditional faculty control of appointments and awards. Those were the problems with the effort to establish The Academy on Capitalism and Limited Government on the University of Illinois campus in 2007. Willing to sacrifice shared governance in search of funds, the Urbana-Champaign campus' chancellor negotiated a memorandum of agreement ceding control over appointments, speakers, curriculum development, and awards to a group of outside donors and board members. The faculty senate protested, and the arrangement collapsed.

Corporate funding can readily turn a purported faculty researcher into a shameless corporate flack. More than half the country's business professors receive extra income from corporate consulting. Consulting income of several hundred thousand dollars a year is not uncommon. Worse still are faculty members who offer shameless court testimony on behalf of business interests, among them University of Pennsylvania, University of Michigan, Ohio State University, and Florida State University business professors who happily testified for tobacco companies in the 1980s and 1990s, asserting that cigarette advertising did not entice people to smoke. They went on to publish pro-tobacco articles or op-ed pieces without mentioning their substantial tobacco company income.

Though such stories are disheartening, the percentage of faculty members who have effectively been bought and sold, who are seriously ethically compromised, remains relatively small. There is thus time to revive higher education by returning power to the faculty as a whole. A campaign against an individual corporate contract that promises to compromise shared governance or academic freedom is worth pursuing not only to prevent that damage from being done but also as a way of educating all members of a local higher education community about the broad dangers we face when universities model themselves after corporations.

The vast shift away from faculty eligible for tenure—66 percent in 1975, 33 percent in 2005, barely 30 percent in 2010—toward part-time teachers and full-time teachers not eligible for tenure is in part a corporatized model of a disposable work force paid as little as possible, often denied health care and retirement benefits. Add to that the growing conviction among administrators that faculty concerns block opportunities for profit and thus must be marginalized or circumvented. Then track the spreading conviction that universities exist primarily to train a corporate workforce, not to educate their graduates to be critical citizens and so to participate in the democratic process in an informed way, and you begin to see how universities are transforming themselves to fit seamlessly into the corporate industrial complex. But few signs that a university has become a corporation in the worst sense of the term are more telling than a huge spread in salaries—from a senior administrator earning hundreds of thousands of dollars annually to a contingent teacher paid $2,000 a course. Faculty members struggling to support a family on $20,000 a year, trapped in jobs that make them wage slaves or worse, begin to seem more like prison inmates than members of a viable community or profession. Yet many institutions construct a still more undercompensated workforce by hiring undergraduates at subminimum wages, thereby skirting child labor law violations. And in some ways a university that ruthlessly exploits its workers is worse than a coal mine that does the same. For a university has an educational mission. If it exploits its employees, it is effectively training the next generation of managers—its students—to do the same. And it typically touts its adherence to elevated ideals at the same time.

Although it is bizarre to have to make the argument, it must be said: faculty must try once again to occupy the center of their institutions; they must stand up for independent work everywhere on campus. To do so, faculty must be full-time and tenured. Faculty members cannot participate effectively in governance without job security and real power. Corporate university managers without actual experience in teaching and research have little understanding of the value full-time faculty add to an institution. Part-timers are vulnerable, more difficult to organize, and easily fired if they criticize administrators. The accounting mentality that likes to segment labor and quantify all tasks, then hire people as cheaply as possible to perform them, is uneasy with the deeper institutional commitment full-time faculty are able to make.

In the end only collective action can counter the ravages of corporatization. In truth faculty members collectively have the power they need to reform the corporate university. To exercise that power, however, they must adopt identities that balance narrow careerism with a sense of community responsibility. There is time and space in a life for both. Yet the available forms of collective action themselves will have to be reformed if the effort is to succeed. Unionization—the key option for faculty at public institutions— needs to embrace a broad progressive agenda, seeking living wages for all campus employees and manageable tuition for students. Only that way can unions hail other campus and off-campus constituencies. A faculty union that concentrates exclusively on faculty salaries and benefits, failing to secure academic freedom and shared governance, failing to seek better lives for all in the community, will not be a convincing agent of reform. Only by taking on all the destructive effects of a corporate ideology can a union be a compelling agent of change. Indeed only then can a faculty organization build a strong alliance with student groups and other campus workers. Where unionization is impossible, other voluntary and democratic forms of faculty organization are available. The key issues are the number of faculty members involved, the degree of solidarity they achieve, the values they promote, and the allies they gather. A campus must have different values than a corporation does if it expects to sustain public admiration and devotion.

NOTES

1. David Noble, "The Selling of the University," *The Nation,* February 6, 1982.

2. David Dickson, *The New Politics of Science* (Chicago, IL: University of Chicago Press, 1993), 104.

3. Cheryl B. Leggon, "The Scientist as Academic," *Daedalus* 126, no.4 (Fall 1997), 223.

4. Bill Readings, *The University in Ruins* (Cambridge, MA: Harvard University Press, 1997).

5. Christopher Newfield, "Recapturing Academic Business," in *Chalk Lines: The Politics of Work in the Managed University,* ed. Randy Martin (Raleigh, NC: Duke University Press, 1998), 80.

Chapter Eight

The Agricultural Industrial Complex

Vandana Shiva

INTRODUCTION: TRIPLE CRISIS

While wide-ranging wars, colonial expansion, and slavery—among other things—have long resulted in human-generated misery and destruction, never before have the actions of one part of humanity threatened the existence of the entire human species. We are now facing a triple convergence of crises, each of which threatens our survival.

- Climate: Global warming threatens our very survival as a species.
- Energy: Peak oil spells the end of the cheap oil that has fueled the industrialization of production and the globalization of consumerism.
- Food: A food crisis is emerging as a result of the convergence of climate change, peak oil, and the impact of globalization on the rights of the poor to food and livelihood.

Of the three crises, the emerging food crisis poses the most immediate threat to the survival of the poor. The food crisis emerges from two historical processes, one long term—the industrialization of agriculture and the uprooting of peasants and family farmers from the land—and one more recent—the effects of globalization and trade liberalization of agriculture on food security and food sovereignty. The impact of climate change on agricultural production, along with such false solutions to climate change as industrial biofuels, which divert food and land from the poor to the non-sustainable energy needs of the rich, further exacerbate the food crisis. We can and must respond creatively to the triple crisis and simultaneously overcome dehumanization, economic inequality, and ecological catastrophe.

169

Industrialized, globalized agriculture is at the heart of the triple crisis. It accounts for 40 percent of all greenhouse gas emissions, it uses significant quantities of non-renewable energy both to produce food and transport it, and finally it is at the root of food crisis specifically. The most significant greenhouse gas from agriculture is nitrogen-oxide. It is produced by the application of synthetic nitrogen fertilizers. According to the Intergovernmental Panel on Climate Change (IPCC) every 1000 kg of nitrogen fertilizer applied in agriculture emits 1.25 kg of nitrous oxide. Overall, industrialized, globalized agriculture promoted by corporations is a major driver of climate change. And both industrialization and globalization are driven by corporate capitalism.

An analysis of energy in the U.S. food chain found that, on average, it takes 10 calories of energy to produce 1 calorie of food. This is a net negative energy production system. A shift to ecological, non-industrial agriculture from industrial agriculture leads to a two- to sevenfold energy savings and a 5 to 15 percent global fossil fuel emissions offset through the sequestration of carbon in organically managed soil. Up to four tons of CO_2 per hectare can be sequestered in organic soils each year.

Industrial agriculture in the U.S. uses 380 times more energy per hectare to produce rice than a traditional farm in the Philippines. And energy use per kilo of rice is 80 times more in the U.S. than in the Philippines. Energy use for corn production in the U.S. is 176 times more per hectare than on a traditional farm in Mexico and 33 times more per kilo. One cow maintained and marketed in the industrial system requires six barrels of oil. A 450-gram box of breakfast cereal provides only 1,100 kilocalories of food energy but uses 7,000 kilocalories of energy for processing.

Long-distance globalized food systems, like the industrial food-production system they service, are contributing in a major way to greenhouse gas emissions. A study by the Danish Ministry of the Environment showed that 1 kilogram of food moving around the world generated 10 kilograms of CO_2. "Food miles," which measure the distance food travels from where it is produced to where it is consumed, have increased dramatically as a result of globalization. As reported by environmental journalist Dale Allen Pfeiffer:

> In 1981, food journeying across the U.S. to the Chicago market traveled an average of 1,245 miles; by 1998, this had increased 22 percent, to 1,518 miles. In 1965, 787,000 combination trucks were registered in the United States, and these vehicles consumed 6,658 billion gallons of fuel. In 1997, there were 1,790,000 combination trucks that used 20.294 billion gallons of fuel. In 1979, David and Marcia Pimentel estimated that 60 percent of all food and related

products in the U.S. traveled by truck and the other 40 percent by rail. By 1996, almost 93 percent of fresh produce was moved by truck.[1]

A study in Canada has calculated that in 2003 food in Toronto, Canada traveled an average of 3,333 miles. In the U.K., the distance traveled by food increased 50 percent between 1978 and 1999. A Swedish study found that the food miles of a typical breakfast would cover the circumference of the Earth.

The increase in food miles is related to fossil fuel and food subsidies, which allow food transported long distances to be cheaper than the food produced locally. Thus, India imported 5.5 million tons of wheat in 2006, based on the argument that it was cheaper to import wheat from Australia and the U.S. than to transport it from Punjab in the North to Kerala and Tamil Nadu in the South. We should be reducing food miles by eating biodiverse, local, and fresh foods, rather than increasing carbon pollution through the spread of corporate industrial farming, nonlocal food supplies, and processed and packaged food. We need to reduce CO_2 emissions by moving toward economic localization and satisfying our needs with the lowest carbon footprint. Economic globalization, on the other hand, only serves to increase CO_2 emissions. This total disconnect between ecology and economics is threatening to bring down our *oikos,* our home on this planet.

RISING FOOD PRICES/INCREASING HUNGER/ RISING PROFITS

Rising Food Prices

Food prices started to rise as a result of connecting India's domestic market to global markets, especially the edible oil and wheat import markets. At first, in the early days of globalization, the agribusinesses that dominate trade lowered prices to grab markets. The dumping of soy in the 1990s is a prime example. Now that global corporations like Cargill have created import dependency, they are increasing prices. Additionally, speculation through futures trading is driving prices upward. Climate change and the diversion of foods to biofuels are also adding an upward pressure on international prices. The increase in international prices highlights the need to focus on food sovereignty. It makes both political and economic sense to focus on self-reliance in food and agriculture.

	Wheat	*Rice*	*Soya Oil*
2008	U.S.$ 343	U.S.$ 580	U.S.$ 1423
↑	↑	↑	↑
2005	U.S.$ 152	U.S.$ 207	U.S.$ 545

Rising International Food Prices [2]
(Units U.S.$ per metric ton)

At the end of December 2008, the UN's FAO estimated that 33 countries were experiencing severe or moderate food crisis. Global prices increased by around three and a half times between January 2007 and June 2008.

Increasing Hunger

Hunger has become the biggest commodity market. Money is first being made through the creation of hunger. And it is being made again through the production of false solutions to this hunger.

Where are the hungry? [3]

India	214 m
Sub Saharan Africa	198 m
Asia/Pacific	156 m
South America	56 m
China	135 m

Who are the hungry?

Farm Households	400 m
Rural Landless	160 m
Urban Households	64 m
Herders, Fishers & Forest Dependent	56 m

Ironically, it is the technologies and economic systems that are offered as solutions to hunger that are actually creating hunger.

How Industrial Agriculture Creates Hunger and Malnutrition

Industrial agriculture, sold as the Green Revolution and 2nd Green Revolution to Third World countries, is a chemical-intensive, capital-intensive, fossil fuel-intensive system. It must, by its very structure, push farmers into debt, and indebted farmers everywhere are pushed off the land, as their farms are foreclosed and appropriated. In the poor countries, farmers trapped in debt for purchasing costly chemicals and non-renewable seeds sell the food they grow to pay back debt. That is why hunger today is a rural phenomenon. The debt-creating negative economy of high cost industrial farming is a hunger-producing system, not a hunger-reducing system. Wherever chemicals and commercial seeds have spread, farmers are in debt and lose entitlement to their own produce. They become trapped in poverty and hunger. This is why the Gates and Rockefeller foundations' initiative, Alliance for a Green Revolution in Africa (AGRA), is misguided as to the food programs it promotes. Such food programs create more hunger and famine than they do to reduce them.

A second way in which industrial chemical agriculture creates hunger is by displacing and destroying the biodiversity that provides nutrition. Thus the Green Revolution displaced traditional crops such as pulses (legumes yielding edible seeds, as beans, peas, or lentils), which are important sources of proteins as well as oil seeds. It therefore *reduced* nutrition per acre, not increased it. Monocultures do not produce more food and nutrition. They use up more chemicals and fossil fuels, and hence are profitable for agrichemical companies and oil companies. They produce higher *yields* of individual commodities, but a lower output of food and nutrition.

The conventional measures of productivity focus on labor (and the direct labor on the farm at that) as the major input and externalize many other energy and resource inputs. This biased productivity pushes farmers off the land and replaces them with chemicals and machines, which in turn contribute to greenhouse gases and climate change. Further, industrial agriculture focuses on producing a single crop that can be globally traded as a commodity. The focus on "yield" of individual commodities creates what I have called a "monoculture of the mind." The promotion of so-called high-yielding varieties leads to the displacement of biodiversity. It also destroys the ecological functions of biodiversity. The loss of diverse outputs is never taken into account by the one-dimensional calculus of productivity. When the benefits of biodiversity are taken into account, biodiverse systems have higher output than monocultures. And organic farming is more beneficial for the farmers and the earth than chemical farming.

Industrial chemical agriculture creates hunger and malnutrition in a third manner—by robbing crops of nutrients. Industrially produced food is a nutritionally empty mass, loaded with chemicals and toxins. Nutrition in food comes from the nutrients in the soil. Industrial agriculture, based on the "NPK" mentality of synthetic nitrogen-, phosphorous-, and potassium-based fertilizers leads to depletion of vital micronutrients and trace elements such as magnesium, zinc, calcium, and iron.

David Thomas, a geologist turned nutritionist, discovered that between 1940 and 1991, vegetables had lost—on average—24 percent of their magnesium, 46 percent of their calcium, 27 percent of their iron and no less than 76 percent of their copper. Carrots had lost 75 percent of their calcium, 46 percent of their iron, and 75 percent of their copper. Potatoes had lost 30 percent of their magnesium, 35 percent calcium, 45 percent iron and 47 percent copper. It can be concluded from such research that, to get the same amount of nutrition, people will need to eat much more food. The increase in "yields" of empty mass does not translate into more nutrition. In fact it is leading to malnutrition.

Healthy soil produces healthy food. The most effective and low cost strategy for addressing malnutrition is through organic farming. Organic farming enriches the soil, and nutrient-rich soils give us nutrient-rich food.

When I carried out research on the Green Revolution in Punjab, I found that after a few years of bumper harvests, crops failures at a large number of sites were reported despite liberal applications of NPK fertilizers. The failure came from micronutrient deficiencies caused by the rapid and continuous removal of micronutrients by "high-yielding varieties." Plants quite evidently need more than NPK, and the voracious high-yielding varieties drew out micronutrients from soil at a very rapid rate, creating deficiencies of such micronutrients as zinc, iron, copper, manganese, magnesium, molybdenum, and boron. With organic manure these deficiencies do not occur, because organic matter contains these trace elements, whereas chemical NPK does not. Zinc deficiency is the most widespread of all micronutrient deficiencies in Punjab.

Earthworm castings, which can amount to 4 to 36 tons per acre per year, contain 5 times more nitrogen, 7 times more phosphorus, 3 times more exchangeable magnesium, 11 times more potash, and 1½ times more calcium than soil. Their work on the soil promotes the microbial activity essential to the fertility of most soils. Soils rich in micro-organisms and earthworms are soils rich in nutrients. There products too are rich in nutrients. Organic foods, on average have been found to have 21 percent more iron, 14 percent more phosphorous, 78 percent more chromium, 390 percent more selenium,

63 percent more calcium, 70 percent more boron, 138 percent more magnesium, 27 percent more vitamin C, and 10–50 percent more vitamin E and beta carotene. This low cost, decentralized strategy for addressing malnutrition serves the people. It does not serve the industry that first created malnutrition through chemical fertilizers and now wants to turn malnutrition into the next market through industrial fortification and genetic engineering.

The corporate answer to malnutrition is not organic farming and biodiversity. It is industrial and chemical fortification, mimicking the industrial/chemical model of farming which created the nutritional deficiencies in the first place.

Hunger has become the biggest market commodity. Money is first being made through the creation of hunger. And it is being made again through false solutions to hunger.

The Global Alliance for Improved Nutrition (GAIN) has been part of "an innovative response to malnutrition" by the Bill and Melinda Gates Foundation. GAIN is giving economic incentives to Kraft, Proctor & Gamble, H.J. Heinz and Roche to fortify foods with micronutrients. GAIN works closely with the International Life Sciences Institute whose members include Bayer, Coca Cola, Dow, DuPont, Exxon Mobil, McDonalds, Merck, Monsanto, Nestle, Novartis, PepsiCo, Pfizer and Proctor & Gamble.

An example of the kind of high cost, high risk "fortification" proposals these corporate leaders regularly promote is the "Golden Rice" genetically engineered to be a fortified Vitamin A food source for supposedly nutritionally deficient regions. Yet, the genetically modified (GM) rice provides some 70 times less Vitamin A than Vitamin A-rich sources of biodiversity such as coriander, fenugreek, curry leaves, and drumstick-plant leaves. In addition, since genetic engineering is based on the use of antibiotic resistance markers and viral promoters, it introduces new and unnecessary health risks. Further, GM rice is a high-cost solution. The golden rice is patented, and patents generate royalties. That is the objective of patents. Even if, in introducing golden rice, the seeds will be subsidized as chemical fertilizers were first subsidized, in the long run the idea is to generate profits. Governments might themselves pay for these high-cost, high-risk options—but public money is public money. Instead, it could be used to promote biodiversity-based organic farming as an ecological fortification strategy. Corporate greed, along with the industrialization of food and agriculture, has delivered to us a hunger and malnutrition crisis. Corporate greed and the more intensive industrialization of food through artificial fortification of nutrients is not the answer to malnutrition. It will make it worse. Greed robs the poor of food. It is at the root of hunger.

Rising Profits

While millions go hungry, corporate profits have increased. Cargill saw profits increase by 30 percent in 2007; Monsanto's profits increased by 44 percent. These profits will increase as corporate monopolies deepen. Monsanto increased the price of corn seed by $100 per bag to $300 per bag. For a 1,000-acre farm in the U.S., this means an increased cost of $40,000. Still, since the second half of 2008, the global economy has been characterized by a financial meltdown. Trillions have been spent by governments to bail out failing banks and financial institutions. Yet the bailouts are not working. Like Humpty Dumpty, who had a great fall and "all the kings' horses and all the kings' men could not put Humpty Dumpty together again," the financial collapse is symptomatic of deeper cracks which can't be fixed by Band-Aids or bailouts.

If the symptoms are treated as the disease, then the solutions offered for each crisis will make the other crisis worse. We have two choices: we can make a nature-centered, people-centered transition to a fossil fuel-free future, with meaningful work and decent and dignified living for all; or we can continue on our current path toward a commodity market-centered future, which will make the crisis deeper for the poor and the marginalized, and provide a *temporary* escape for the privileged.

This chapter will focus on agriculture and first deal with the pseudo-solutions to the triple crisis; the second part of the chapter will offer equitable and lasting solutions that center around non-fossil fuel-based, locally adopted forms of organic agriculture.

PSEUDO-SOLUTIONS TO THE TRIPLE CRISIS

Corporations are rushing to turn the triple crisis into a capitalist market opportunity. In this way, they are driving policy responses to the climate, energy, and food crises, offering false solutions which in turn aggravate the crises further.

First False Solution: A New Corporate-led Green Revolution Based on Chemicals, Patents on Seeds and GMOs (Genetically Modified Organisms)

Chemical and GMO-based agriculture is being introduced on a global scale, even though the original Green Revolution has failed to deliver food security and is implicated in climate change.

The "Green Revolution" was in fact the name given to U.S.-styled industrial agriculture hewn seeds bred to respond to agricultural chemicals. It was introduced through heavy coercion in India. The occurrence of drought in 1966 caused a severe drop in food production in India and an unprecedented increase in food grain supply from the U.S. In short, food dependency was used to set new policy conditions for India. The U.S. President, Lyndon Johnson, put wheat supplies on a short tether in order to maximize leverage for industrial agricultural interests. In this way, he refused to commit to providing food aid beyond one month in advance until an agreement to adopt the Green Revolution package was signed between the Indian Agriculture Minister, C.S. Subramaniam, and the U.S. Secretary of Agriculture, Orville Freeman.

Lal Bahadur Shastri, the Indian Prime Minister in 1965, had raised caution against rushing into an agriculture paradigm based on new varieties of crops. Upon his sudden death in 1966, the Green Revolution strategy became easier to introduce. Importantly the Planning Commission, which approves all large investment in India, was also bypassed since it was viewed as a bottleneck by Green Revolution supporters.

Rockefeller Foundation agricultural scientists saw Third World farmers and scientists as unable to improve their own agricultural basis. Relatedly, they believed that the answer to Third World nutrition issues lay in establishing greater crop productivity, and that such productivity was afforded only by the American-styled agricultural system. However the imposition of the American model of agriculture did not go unchallenged in the Third World (or even in America). Edmundo Taboada, who was head of the Mexican office of Experiment Stations, maintained, like K.M. Munshi who was the Agriculture Minister in the 1950s in India, that ecologically and socially appropriate research strategies could only evolve with the active participation of the peasantry:

> Scientific Research must take into account the men that will apply its results . . . Perhaps a discovery may be made in the laboratory, a greenhouse or an experimental station, but useful science, a science that can be applied and handled must emerge from the local laboratories of . . . small farmers, ejidatorios [communes] and local communities.[4]

Together peasants and scientists searched for ways to improve the quality of "criollo" seeds (openly pollinated indigenous varieties) which could be reproduced in peasant fields. However, by 1945, the Special Studies Bureau in the Mexican Agriculture Ministry, funded and administered by the Rockefeller Foundation, had eclipsed the indigenous research strategy and started to export Green Revolution techniques to Mexico. In 1961, the Rockefeller-financed center took the name of CIMMYT (Centro International de Mejoramiento de Maiz Y Trigo, or the International Maize and Wheat Improvement Center). The American industrial strategy, first reinvented in Mexico, then came to the entire Third World.

The Green Revolution approach to agriculture is flawed both from the perspective of participatory development and that of science. It is led by external experts, thus discounting the centuries of knowledge of breeding and farming in agrarian societies and peasant communities. It leaves out the experts of local agriculture, the farmers. You cannot begin with researchers, if you are designing a sustainable agriculture system. You have to begin with the land, with indigenous biodiversity and indigenous knowledge. Unfortunately, the Green Revolution strategy is based on destroying the very foundation of sound farming.

The Green Revolution strategy is scientifically flawed because it is reductionist. It fragments and reduces agro-ecosystems. Reductionism allows false claims to be made about yields and the productivity of chemical monocultures compared to biodiverse organic systems which build on indigenous knowledge and resources.

As mentioned, the Rockefeller and Gates foundations have more recently set up an alliance for a Green Revolution to come to Africa. The acronym chosen for this is AGRA. However, AGRA will not create a Taj Mahal for Africa's agriculture because the new Green Revolution for Africa is in fact the old Green Revolution for Asia. And, as the Punjab experience shows, the Green Revolution in Asia (as elsewhere) was neither "green" in terms of ecological sustainability and the conservation of natural capital in the forms of soil-water-biodiversity, nor revolutionary in terms of increasing equality and promoting justice for small and marginal peasants. This not-so-green revolution is the same now being proposed as a solution for hunger and poverty in Africa.

AGRA has a $150 million "Program for Africa's Seed System" (PASS) and a fertilizer access program. The programs assume that "improved seed" and chemical fertilizers are necessary for augmenting Africa's farm productivity. To accomplish this, strategies based upon the promotion of private seed companies and the commercialization of the seed supply have been undertaken. AGRA has also sought to increase the sale of chemical fertilizer. As Gary Toenniessen of the Rockefeller Foundation (and head of AGRA) writes in *Securing the Harvest* (2001), " . . . no matter what efficiencies genetic enhancement is able to build into crop plants, they will always draw their nutrition from external sources" and "no alternatives to the use of inorganic nitrogen currently exist for densely populated developing countries."[5]

This ignores the successes in Asia, Africa, and Latin America of doubling and tripling farm productivity through biodiverse organic farming based on farm breeding, biodiversity conservation, and agro-ecology. Fertilizer advocates also ignore how the rising cost of oil affects fertilizer prices. Imported fertilizer costs from Rs 55,000 to Rs 60,000 per ton and is sold at Rs 9,350 per ton. Rs 45,000 per ton is paid through taxes collected to cover the subsidies. In India, the shift to chemical agriculture has created the need for 4 to 4.8 million tons of synthetic Diammonium phosphate (DAP). As only around 2 million tons are produced in India, the rest must be imported.

Fertilizer protests took place in Karnataka, where a farmer was killed when police opened fire on hundreds of farmers waiting for fertilizers. This was an entirely unnecessary tragedy. Similar incidents have occurred in Amrati, Vidarbha, Latur, Marathwada, and Maharashtra. First the Green Revolution made Indian farmers addicted to chemical fertilizer. Now globalization is making them dependent on imports. While the soil and farmers die, agribusiness corporations like Cargill are making a killing. Cargill's fertilizer profits doubled from 2006 to 2007, with India paying 130 percent more for fertilizers and China 227 percent more for fertilizers during that period.

Nitrogen fertilizers contribute to emissions of nitrogen oxide, a greenhouse gas three times more responsible for climate change than carbon dioxide, molecule for molecule. According to the Intergovernmental Panel on Climate Change (IPCC) every 1000 kg of nitrogen fertilizer applied in agriculture emits 1.25 kg of nitrous oxide.

Overall, the industrialized, globalized agriculture currently promoted by corporations contributes some 40 percent of the greenhouse gases that lead to climate change. And both industrialization and the globalization of agriculture are driven by corporate capitalism.

GMOs: A False Solution

The agrichemical corporate giants are now additionally the gene giants peddling genetically engineered, patented seeds as a solution to both food insecurity and climate change. However, on both counts GMOs are a false promise. Monsanto has been distributing an ad across the world that says:

9 billion people to feed.
A changing climate
Now what?
Producing more. Conserving more. Improving farmers lives.
That's sustainable agriculture. And that's what Monsanto is all about.

All the claims that the ad makes are untrue. Firstly, GM crops do not produce more. While Monsanto claims its GMO Bt cotton gives 1500 kg/ acre, the average is actually 300—400 Kg/acre. Secondly, Monsanto's GMOs, which are either Roundup Ready crops or Bt toxin crops, do not conserve resources. They demand more water, they destroy biodiversity, and they increase the amount of toxics used in farming. For instance, pesticide use has increased 13 times as a result of the use of Bt cottonseeds alone. Thirdly, Monsanto's GMOs do not improve farmers' lives. They have pushed farmers to suicide. 200,000 Indian farmers have committed suicide in the last decade. Eight-four percent of the suicides are linked to debt created by Bt cotton. For GMOs are non-renewable, while the openly pollinated varieties that farmers have bred are renewable and can be saved year to year. The price of cottonseed was Rs 7/kg. Bt cottonseed price was Rs 17,000/kg. This is neither ecological, economical, nor social sustainability. It is ecocide and genocide. There is no place for Monsanto's GMOs in sustainable agriculture.

Monsanto is also using Roundup as a "conservation" technology for "mitigating" climate change. The false argument is that by spraying Roundup and killing weeds tillage can be avoided, which prevents carbon from escaping from the soil into the air. However, recent reports from the U.S show how Roundup has led to the invasion of farms with Roundup-resistant weeds. Farmers are therefore spending more on herbicides, or totally abandoning farming.

Second False Solution: Industrial Biofuels

Industrial biofuels are being promoted as a source of renewable energy and as a means to reduce greenhouse gas emissions. However, there are two ecological reasons why converting crops like soy, corn, and palm into liquid fuels can actually aggravate the CO_2 burden and worsen the climate crisis, while also contributing to the erosion of biodiversity and the depletion of water resources.

First, deforestation caused by expanding soy and palm oil plantations is leading to increased CO_2 emissions. The FAO estimates that 1.6 billion tons, or 25 to 30 percent of the greenhouse gases released into the atmosphere each year, comes from deforestation. According to Wetlands International, destruction of Southeast Asian forests for palm oil plantations is contributing to 8 percent of global CO_2 emissions. By 2022, biofuel plantations could destroy 98 percent of Indonesia's rainforests. Every ton of palm oil used as biofuel releases 30 tons of CO_2 into the atmosphere, ten times as much as petroleum does. Ironically, this additional burden on the atmosphere is treated as a beneficial Clean Development Mechanism (CDM) by the Kyoto Protocol. Still, the reality is that biofuels are exacerbating the same global warming that they are supposed to reduce.

Biofuels: A Greenhouse Threat

Two important studies published in February 2008, in the journal *Science,* reveal that biofuels cause more greenhouse gas emissions than conventional fuels if the full emissions costs of producing these "green" fuels are taken into account. The studies follow a series of reports that have linked ethanol and biodiesel production to increased carbon dioxide emissions, destruction of biodiverse forests, and air and water pollution. The destruction of natural ecosystems, whether rainforests in the tropics or grasslands in South America, not only releases greenhouse gases into the atmosphere, but also deprives the planet of natural sponges to absorb carbon emissions. The new cropland, the study reports, also absorbs far less carbon than the rainforests or even scrubland it replaces. Together the two studies offer sweeping conclusions: taken globally, the production of almost all biofuels resulted, directly or indirectly, intentionally or not, in new lands being cleared. Whether that land was rainforest or scrubland, the greenhouse gas contribution is significant.

Joseph Fargione, an author of one of the studies and a scientist at the Nature Conservancy, says, "The clearance of grassland released 93 times the amount of greenhouse gases that would be saved by the fuel made annually on that land.["] In Indonesia and Malaysia, palm biodiesel, one of the most controversial biofuels currently in use, because of its connection to rainforest deforestation in these countries, has a carbon debt of 423 years. Soybean biodiesel in the Amazonian rainforest has a debt of 319 years. Until the carbon debt is repaid, biofuels from converted land have greater greenhouse gas impacts than the fossil fuels they displace. A "carbon debt" refers to the CO_2 released during the first fifty years from the land conversion. "People don't realize there is three times as much carbon in plants and soil than there is in the air. While we cut down forests, burn them, churn the soil, we release all the carbon that was being stored," says Dr. Fargione.[7]

According to Dr. Fargione, the dedication of so much cropland in the United States to growing corn for ethanol has caused indirect land-use changes far away. Previously, Midwestern farmers had alternated growing corn and soy in their fields, one year to the next. Now many grow only corn, meaning that soy has to be grown elsewhere. The studies show that the purchase of biofuels in Europe and the United States leads indirectly to the destruction of natural habitats far afield. This has also been proven by the Navdanya study on food versus fuel, which found that the grasslands and common lands are being destroyed in Chhattisgarh and Rajasthan to grow jatropha for biofuel.

David Pimentel and Ted Patzek, professors at Cornell and Berkeley, respectively, have shown that all crops have a negative energy balance when converted to biofuels—it takes more fossil fuel energy input to produce biofuels than the resultant biofuels can generate. It takes 1.5 gallons of gasoline to produce one gallon of ethanol. For each fossil fuel unit of energy spent producing corn ethanol the return is 0.778 units of energy, 0.688 units for switchgrass ethanol, and 0.534 for soybean diesel. Pimentel and Patzek were criticized by the U.S. government for including the energy used for building new refineries. However, these are new energy investments that do generate emissions, and Pimentel and Patzek are right to include them when calculating the overall energy balance.

In 2006 the U.S. used 20 percent of its corn crop to produce 5 billion gallons of ethanol, which only substituted for 1 percent of its oil use. If 100 percent of the corn crop were used to make ethanol, it would be able to substitute for 7 percent of the total oil used. Even if all U.S. soy and corn were converted to fuel it would only substitute for 12 percent of the gasoline and six percent of the diesel. To satisfy the entire current oil demand of the U.S. with biofuels would take 1.4 million square miles of corn for ethanol or 8.8 million square miles of soy for biodiesel, which is more than all the agricultural land in the U.S. All the solar energy collected by every green plant in the U.S. in 2006—including agriculture, forests, and lawns—is only half as much as the fossil fuel energy consumed in that year. This is clearly not a solution to either peak oil or climate chaos.

In fact, ethanol is a source of other crises when you look at all the resources it demands. It takes 1,700 gallons of water to produce a gallon of ethanol. Corn uses more nitrogen fertilizer, more insecticides, and more herbicides than any other crop. Ethanol constitutes 99 percent of all biofuel production in the U.S.: In 2004, there were 3.4 billion gallons of ethanol produced and blended into gasoline, amounting to about 2 percent of the nation's gas consumption.

There has been a flood of subsidies in the West for production of biofuels. The cost of support of ethanol varies from $0.29 to $0.36 per liter in the U.S. and $1 per liter in the EU. Support for biodiesel varies between $0.20 per liter in Canada and $1 in Switzerland. In 2007 U.S. taxpayers provided $6 billion to ethanol producers through subsidies. In 2008, the government introduced a tax credit of $0.51 per gallon on ethanol and mandated a doubling of the amount of ethanol to be used in gasoline by 2012, to 7.5 billion gallons. The total cost to the consumer of subsidizing corn ethanol is $8.4 billion per year.

Subsidization of biofuels is creating a deep impact on the demand for foodstuffs from the United States. In 2007, for example, the increase in ethanol production will account for more than half of the global increase in the demand for corn. Much the same is true in the U.S. and EU for soybeans and rapeseed used in biodiesel. The rising price of food is good for producers. It is dreadful, however, for consumers, particularly for those in poor, food-importing countries. Increased production of biofuels also adds stress on existing land and water supplies.

These subsidies will distort agriculture policy and encourage farmers to divert their crops from food to fuel. They promote monocultures and industrial agriculture, which contribute to climate change. In effect, industrial biofuels will increase climate instability, rather than mitigate it. According to Patzek, "the United States has already wasted a lot of time, money, and natural resources pursuing a mirage of an energy scheme that cannot possibly replace fossil fuels. The only real solution is to limit the rate of use of these fossil fuels. Everything else will lead to an eventual national disaster."[8]

For Italy to meet the EU requirement to have 5 percent of its gas and diesel be biofuel by 2010 will require 69 percent more land to be farmed than is available in the entire country and require 102 percent more water and 40 percent more chemicals. The UK has set targets of 2.5 percent of fuel to be biofuel by 2008, rising to 5 percent by 2010. Compulsory biofuels are thus a recipe for disaster. It is a case of the cure being worse than the disease.

The planet and the poor are losing; the rainforests—the lungs, the heart, the liver of the planet—are being bulldozed to plant soy and palm. In Brazil, 22.2 million hectares have been converted to soy plantations, producing in 2004–2005 over 50 million tons. Brazil will clear an additional 60 million hectares of land due to the gold rush for soy. Since 1995 in Brazil, soy cultivation has been increasing at 3.2 percent (320,000 hectares) per year. Twenty-one percent of Brazil's cultivated area is now soy, and 300,000 people have been displaced in Rio Grande do Sul. Since January 2003 nearly 70,000 kilometers of the Amazon rainforest have been cleared for biofuels production. Corporations like Cargill, ADM, and Bunge are at the heart of the destruction of the Amazon, according to Greenpeace. Since 1990, Indonesia has destroyed 28 million hectares of rainforest for palm plantations. The poor are losing

because land and water that would have produced food for the hungry is being
used to run cars.

Third False Solution: Carbon Trading

Carbon trading is not working to reduce emissions and stop global warming.
Polluting the atmosphere is an enclosure of the commons. What was once a
resource available to all, the atmosphere, has been privatized by the oil and
coal companies, the automobile and power companies, as a place to dump
their pollutants. The buildup of carbon dioxide from coal and oil has deprived
humans and other animals of their share of a clean, unpolluted atmosphere.
It is the poor, those who have contributed the least to the degradation of the
atmosphere and the destruction of its capacity to recycle carbon, who bear
the heaviest costs.

In the wake of the first privatization of the atmosphere, we now face a
second privatization—this one offered as a "solution" to the first. The second
enclosure is the carbon and emissions trading schemes that were the main
outcomes recommended by the Kyoto Protocol and the Stern report. In one
of the most widely read and discussed economic assessments of global warming, Sir Nicholas Stern, a one-time chief economist at the World Bank, stated,
"The very basis of emissions trading is assigning property rights to emitters,
and then allowing these to be traded."[9] Larry Lohmann, the author of *Carbon
Trading,* shows how market solutions to climate change, whether embodied
in U.S. pollution trading programs, the Kyoto Protocol, or the EU Emissions
Trading Scheme, give "property rights" to the atmosphere "to a selection of
historical polluters—wealthy countries and companies—for free."[10] Indiana
law professor Daniel Cole notes, "The allocation of marketable pollution
permits constitutes a form of limited privatization as the government conveys
to private parties limited entitlements to use the public atmosphere."[11] PricewaterhouseCoopers, notorious for working with the World Bank to priva-
tize Delhi's water (a move defeated by a massive mobilization of Citizens
Against Privatization through the Water Democracy Movement), itself states
that "trade in CO_2 emissions is equated with the transfer of similar rights
such as copyrights, patents, licensing rights and commercial and industrial
trademarks."[12]

The Kyoto Protocol allows industrialized countries to trade their allocation
of carbon emissions among themselves (Article 17). It also allows an "investor" in an industrialized country (industry or government) to invest in an eligible carbon mitigation project in a developing country and be credited with
Certified Emission Reduction Units that can be used to meet its obligation to

reduce greenhouse gas emissions. By developing greed abroad, corporations get credits that allow them to pollute at home. This is referred to as the Clean Development Mechanism (CDM) under Article 12 of the Kyoto Protocol. The Kyoto Protocol gave emissions rights to the 38 industrialized countries that are the worst historical polluters. The European Union Emissions Trading Scheme (ETS) rewarded 11,428 industrial installations with carbon dioxide emissions rights.

Through Emissions trading, Larry Lohmann observes, "rights to the earth's carbon cycling capacity are gravitating into the hands of those who have the most power to appropriate them and the most financial interest to do so." That such schemes are more about privatizing the atmosphere than preventing climate change is made clear by the fact that the emission rights given away in the Kyoto Protocol were several times higher than the levels needed to prevent a 2 degree Celsius rise in global temperatures. Just as patents generate super profits for pharmaceutical and seed corporations, emissions rights generate super profits for polluters. The ETS granted allowances of 10 percent more than 2005 emission levels; this translated to 150 million tons of surplus carbon credits, which with the 2005 average price of $7.23 per ton translates to $1 billion in free money. The UK allocations for British industry added up to 736 million tons of carbon dioxide and required no commitment to reducing emissions. Since the restrictions being put on Northern industrial polluters do not call for a reduction in emissions, they will continue to pollute and there will be no reduction in CO_2 emissions.

Market solutions in the form of emissions trading run counter to the bedrock environmental principle that the polluter should pay. Through emissions trading, private polluters are getting more rights and more control over the atmosphere, which rightfully belongs to all life on the planet. Emissions trading "solutions" pay the polluter.

Carbon trading is based on inequality because it privatizes the commons and because it claims the resources of poorer people and poorer regions as "offsets." In the global market it is considered to be 50 to 200 times cheaper to plant trees in poorer countries to absorb CO_2 than to reduce emissions at the source. And the *Stern Review* states, "Emissions trading schemes can deliver least cost emissions reductions by allowing reductions to occur wherever they are cheapest."[13] In other words, the burden of "clean up" falls on the poor. In a market calculus, this might appear efficient. In an ecological calculus, it would be far more effective to reduce emissions at the source. And from an environmental justice perspective, it is perverse to burden the poor twice— first with the externalized costs and climate disasters caused by the pollution

ınd then with the burden of remediating the pollution of the rich
ʌwerful.

Only 2 percent of the CDMs of the Kyoto Protocol cover renewable energy
projects. Seventy-two percent of the projects are based on carbon capture
and 21 percent on biomass. Solving the problem of air pollution has thus
translated into a land grab. As Lohmann points out, "The new carbon dumps
that large polluters need usually have to appropriate someone else's land,
someone else's water or someone else's future."[14] Since the land and biomass
that carbon traders seek to appropriate performs life support and livelihood
functions for local communities, emissions trading is not just based on the
theft of the air as commons, it is also based on the theft of people's land and
biodiversity. This is what is happening in India with biofuels plantations. First
the poor lost climate security, now they are losing their livelihood security
through market solutions to climate change.

The *Stern Review* is clear on the severity of climate change: "Climate
change is a serious global threat, and it demands an urgent global response."[15]
However, the "urgent global response" Stern proposes is emissions trading:
"Expanding and linking the growing number of emissions trading schemes
around the world is a powerful way to promote cost-effective reductions in
emissions and to bring forward action in developing countries: strong targets
in rich countries could drive flows amounting to tens of billions of dollars
each year to support the transition to low-carbon development paths."[16]

There are two flaws in this response. Firstly, the *Stern Review* continues
to depend on market solutions, when market failure has helped create the
crisis. Second, by simply focusing on "carbon" the report fails to differentiate
between the dead carbon in fossil fuels and the living carbon of biodiversity
and renewable resources. It focuses on carbon emissions, rather than addressing the health of the carbon cycle more broadly. It does not differentiate
between the high carbon dioxide buildup when fossilized carbon is burned
and the recycling of carbon fixed through photosynthesis in plants and the
food chain. And the limited focus on carbon emissions allows eco-logically
unsustainable technology such as nuclear energy and hydroelectric energy
based on large dams to be offered as a "low carbon development path."

The *Stern Review* is focused on what is good for business, not what is
good for the planet and the poor. It therefore proposes business as usual for
the rich and powerful. The carbon allocations of the ETS are allocations to
companies. They are not allocations to all human beings. Stern has called the
ETS the "world's largest greenhouse gas emissions market."

Creating a global market in pollution is ethically perverse. Some things
should not be tradable—water and biodiversity are too valuable to be

reduced to marketable commodities. Other things, like toxic waste and greenhouse gases, should not be generated. To turn them into tradable commodities ensures that they will continue to be produced. Instead of putting a value on clean air, emissions trading schemes have put a value to pollution. The European market for carbon trade pollution is estimated at U.S. $115 billion over a three-year period from 2005–2007. Instead of defending the rights of all citizens to clean air and climate security, emissions trading defends the rights of corporations to continue to pollute the atmosphere and destabilize the climate, leaving it to someone else, somewhere else to pollute less. Someone else not polluting cannot ethically be equated with a corporate polluter reducing its own industrial pollution when the polluter continues to pollute.

Market fundamentalists are so committed to defending and enlarging the capitalist marketplace that even when it is clear that climate change demands radical change in our ways of thinking and patterns of production and consumption, their preoccupation is with protecting market mechanisms, not protecting Gaia's ecological processes. They are busy creating a supermarket of pollution while glaciers and ice caps melt, hurricanes and tornadoes tear apart coastal ecosystems and communities, and temperatures rise. As Larry Lohman observes "carried to its logical extreme, trading in credits from 'offset' projects would result in a world in which all the coal, oil and gas had been burned up. That calls up the image of a landscape full of wind farms, solar stations, and the carcasses of biofuel plantations and hydroelectric dams, all baking in an atmosphere hot enough to boil water."[17]

Not only is carbon trading ethically perverse, it is also ecologically perverse as a solution to climate change. Climate change demands that we adopt post-fossil fuel, post-industrial pathways for production and consumption of goods and services. Emissions trading and carbon trading promote fossil fuel dependence and industrial patterns of production instead of ecological patterns.

Carbon trading is based on carbon credits. On the one hand it allows polluters to keep polluting by buying credits. On the other hand credits are linked not to the least polluting activity or pathway available but tiny reductions in heavily polluting activity. The trade in emissions is based on so many tons of carbon dioxide (or the equivalent in other greenhouse gases) not being emitted by the seller and therefore allowable for emission by the buyer. Factories and plants that pollute too much are required to buy more allowances (not cut their pollution). Those that become less polluting can sell their allowances.

Carbon trading is ecologically-speaking a false solution at many levels. It does not begin with policies and laws that protect and support non-polluting patterns of production, distribution, and consumption. In fact, ecological options disappear from the "carbon market" altogether. The "trade" is between polluters—those who continue to pollute, and those who have reduced pollution partially. The non-polluters are excluded.

The second reductionism involved in carbon trading is the shift to finance and the disappearance of nature's economy and peoples' sustenance economies. The ethical and ecological problem of reducing our carbon footprint has been transformed into a financial opportunity to make billions. The carbon market is now worth $30 billion and could grow to $1 trillion within a decade. "Carbon will be the world's biggest commodity market, and it could become the world's biggest market overall," according to Louis Bradshaw of Barclays.[18] Shell has called carbon "a new alien currency." Nature's economy has been forgotten. Carbon more and more circulates in Wall Street, not in a carbon cycle.

The solution to climate chaos is not an energy shift from fossil fuels to nuclear, biofuel, and Big Hydro. The solution is a paradigm shift:

From a reductionist to a holistic worldview based on interconnections;
From a mechanistic, industrial paradigm to an ecological one;
From a consumerist definition of being human to one that recognizes us as conservers of the earth's finite resources and co-creators of wealth with nature.

A people- and planet-centered paradigm identifies laws to live by other than the laws of the market. These are the laws of Gaia and the universe, the laws of physics, of energy and entropy, the laws of evolution and emergence, and the laws of justice, which offer equity on a finite and fragile planet. It is these ecological and natural laws that provide the real basis for human action and human transformation. And it is these laws that are being violated by the corporate-driven, globalized, high-energy economy that defines how we produce, what we produce, how we consume, what we consume, how we live, and if we live.

Soil Not Oil: Making a Transition to Biodiverse, Organic, Local Agriculture and Food Systems

How can agriculture contribute to resolving global warming? How can it address the food and energy crises? Centralized knowledge systems falsely promote standardized, corporate-sector-led (IPR-based) chemical-and-energy intensive techno-fixes which are unsustainable. The sustainable solution to the triple crisis resides in biodiverse, decentralized, ecological food-systems.

Reductionism seems to have become a habit of the contemporary human mind. We are increasingly talking of "the carbon economy" and the context of climate change. We refer to "zero carbon" and "no carbon" as if carbon exists only in a fossilized form under the ground. We forget that the cellulose of plants is primarily carbon. Humus in the soil is mostly carbon. Vegetation in the forests is mostly carbon. Carbon in the soil and in plants is living carbon. It is part of the cycle of life.

The problem is not carbon per se, but our increasing use of fossil carbon as coal, oil and gas—which were formed over millions of years. Today the world burns 400 years worth of this accumulated, biological matter every year, 3 to 4 times more than in 1956. While plants are renewable resources, fossil carbon is not one. When it is burnt, this carbon cannot be renewed as coal, oil, or gas for millions of years.

Before the industrial revolution, there were 580 billion tons of carbon in the atmosphere. Today there are 750 billion tons. It is the burning of fossilized carbon and its accumulation in the atmosphere that is leading to the problem of climate change. This is the problem humanity needs to solve if humanity is to survive. And it is the other carbon economy, the renewable carbon embodied in biodiversity, which offers the solution to climate change throughout many sectors of human activity—especially in the production of food.

With our dependence on carbon in the form of fossil fuels, we have broken out of nature's cycle of renewable carbon. We have fossilized our thinking through creating an economic dependence on carbon in its fossilized form. But the real miracle of energy is in plants fixing carbon in the cycle of life and in the relationship between plants and animals.

The organic farming pioneer, Albert Howard, in his typical way, captures well in words the dynamic energy of living carbon: "But how does life begin on this planet? We can only say this: that the prime agency in carrying it on is sunlight, because it is the source of energy, and that the instrument for intercepting this energy and turning it to account is the green leaf."

This wonderful little example of Nature's invention is a battery of intricate mechanisms. Each cell in the interior of a green leaf contains minute specks of a substance called chlorophyll and it is this chlorophyll which enables the plant to grow. Growth implies a continuous supply of nourishment. Now plants do not merely collect their food; they manufacture it before they can feed. In this they differ from animals and man, who search for what they can pass through their stomachs and alimentary systems, but cannot do more; if they are unable to find what is suitable to their natures and ready for them, they perish. A plant is, in a way, a more wonderful instrument. It is an actual food factory, making what it requires before it begins the processes of feeding and digestion. The chlorophyll in the green leaf, with its capacity for intercepting the energy of the sun, is the power unit that, so to say, runs the machine. The green leaf enables the plant to draw simple raw materials from diverse sources and to work them up into complex combinations. Thus from the air it absorbs carbon dioxide (a compound of two parts of oxygen to one of carbon), which is combined with more oxygen from the atmosphere and with other substances, both living and inert, from the soil and from the water which permeates the soil. All these raw materials are then assimilated in the plant and made into food. They become organic compounds, ie., compounds of carbon, classified conveniently into groups known as carbohydrates, proteins and fats; together with an enormous volume of water (often over 90 percent of the whole plant) and interspersed with small quantities of chemical salts which have not yet been converted into the organic phase, they make up the whole structure of the plant—root, stem, leaf, flower and seed. This structure includes a big food reserve. This life principle, the nature of which evades us and in all probability always will, resides in the proteins looked at in the mass. These proteins carry on their work in a cellulose framework made up of cells protected by an outer integument and supported by a set of structures known as the vascular bundles, which also conduct the sap from the roots to the leaves and distribute the food manufactured there to the various centers of growth. The whole of the plant structures are kept turgid by means of water.

The green leaf, with its chlorophyll battery, is therefore a perfectly adapted agency for continuing life. It is, speaking plainly, the only agency that can do this and is unique. Its efficiency is of supreme importance. Because animals, including man, feed eventually on green vegetation, either directly or through the bodies of other animals, it is our sole final source of nutriment. There is no alternative supply. Without sunlight and the capacity of the earth's green carpet to intercept its energy for us, our industries, our trade, and our possessions would soon be useless. It follows therefore that everything on this planet must depend on the way mankind makes use of this green carpet, in other words on its efficiency.[19]

The green carpet, the biodiversity, is the alternative to fossil carbon. Everything that we derive from the petrochemicals industry has its alternative in biodiversity. The synthetic fertilizers and pesticides, the chemical dyes, the sources of mobility and energy, have sustainable alternatives in the plant and animal world. In place of nitrogen fertilizers, we have nitrogen-fixing leguminous crops and biomass recycled by earthworms (vermicompost) or microorganisms (compost). In place of synthetic dyes, we have vegetable dyes. In place of the automobile, we have the camel, the horse, the bullock, the donkey, and the elephant.

The problem of carbon pollution leading to climate change is a consequence of the transition from biodiversity-based renewable carbon economies to a fossil-non-renewable carbon economy. This was the transition called the industrial revolution. It was made possible with the ability to burn coal and oil through the internal combustion engine and transform it into useable energy, thereby making the labor of humans and nonhuman animals replaceable.

While climate change, combined with peak oil and the end of cheap oil is creating an ecological imperative for a post-oil, post-fossil fuel, and post-industrial economy, the industrial paradigm is still the guiding force for the transitional search for a pathway beyond oil. This is in part related to the fact that industrialization, which materially was based on the transition from a biodiversity economy of renewable carbon cycles to a fossil fuel economy of non-renewable carbon use, has also become a cultural paradigm for measuring human progress. Therefore, we problematically seek a de-addiction to oil without further desiring a de-addiction to capitalist industrialization as a key measure of human development. We want a post-oil world but do not have the courage to envisage a post-industrial, post-capitalist world. As a result, we cling to the infrastructure of the energy-intense fossil fuel economy and try to run it on substitutes such as nuclear energy and biofuels. Dirty nuclear power is being redefined as "clean energy." The non-sustainable production of biodiesel and biofuel is being welcomed as a "green" option.

Humanity is playing these tricks with itself and the planet because we are locked into the industrial paradigm, which was built on the use of fossil fuels and the programmatic forgetting of biodiversity's potential to meet our needs and provide a good life. Our ideas of the good life are based on production and consumption patterns that resulted directly from the use of fossil fuels. And we cling to these patterns without reflecting on the fact that they have become only a human addiction, developed primarily over the past fifty years, and that this short-term, non-sustainable pattern of living has the risk of wiping out millions of species and destroying the very conditions of human survival on the planet if it is allowed to continue for another fifty. Spatially, we are reducing the capacity for well-being to a privileged class of humans, neglecting the well-being and rights of other species or those who are socially marginalized. Temporally, we are reducing well-beingo another fifty years of human "affluenza," sacrificing the welfare of future generations and the future of the human species on behalf of an addiction to the industrial paradigm.

To move beyond oil, we must move beyond the addictions associated with it, including the addiction to a certain model of human progress and human well-being. To move beyond oil, we must move beyond spatial and temporal exclusion. To move beyond oil, we must re-establish our partnership with other species. And economies of partnership with other species are the other carbon economy—the renewable economies based on biodiversity.

Renewable carbon and biodiversity redefine progress. They redefine development. They redefine being "developed," "developing," and "underdeveloped." To be developed in the fossil fuel paradigm is to industrialize—to industrialize food and clothing, shelter and mobility, ignoring the social costs of displacing people from work and the ecological costs of polluting the atmosphere and destabilizing the climate. To be underdeveloped in the fossil fuel paradigm is to have non-industrial, fossil-free systems of producing our food and clothing, and providing shelter and mobility.

In the biodiversity paradigm, to be developed is to be able to leave ecological space for other species, for all people and future generations of humans. To be underdeveloped is to usurp the ecological space of other species and communities, to pollute the atmosphere and threaten the planet. This cultural transformation in ideas of progress and well-being is at the heart of making an energy transition to an age beyond oil. What blocks the transition is a cultural paradigm, one which perceives industrialization as progress combined with false ideas of productivity and efficiency. We have been erroneously made to believe that the industrialization of agriculture is necessary to produce more food. This is not at all true. Biodiverse ecological farming produces more and better food than the most energy and chemical intensive agriculture. We have been incorrectly made to believe that cities designed for automobiles provide more effective mobility to meet our daily needs than cities designed for pedestrians and cyclists.

Vested interests who gain from the sale of fertilizers and diesel, cars and trucks have brainwashed us to believe that chemical fertilizers and cars translate into social progress. Our humanity has been reduced such that we have become mere buyers for non-sustainable manufacturers rather than creators of partnerships of cooperation and sustainability, within human society, and with the greater biodiversity of the planet.

The biodiversity economy is the sustainable alternative to the fossil fuel economy. In addition, creating biodiversity economies is necessary for the mitigation of and adaption to climate change. The shift from fossil fuel-driven to biodiversity-supported systems reduces greenhouse gas emissions by emitting less and absorbing more CO_2. But above all, because the impacts of atmospheric pollution will continue even with reduction of emissions, we need to create biodiverse ecosystems and economies because only they offer the potential to adapt to an unpredictable climate. And only biodiverse systems provide alternatives that everyone can afford. We need to return to the renewable carbon cycle of biodiversity. We need to create a carbon democracy so that all beings have their just share of useful carbon, and no one is burdened with carrying an unjust share of climate impacts due to carbon pollution. Every step in building a living agriculture sustained by a living soil is a step toward both mitigating and adapting to climate change.

Over the past 20 years, I have built Navdanya, India's biodiversity and organic farming movement. Increasingly, we are realizing that there is a convergence between the objectives of biodiversity conservation, the reduction of climate change impact, and the alleviation of poverty. Biodiverse, local, organic systems produce more food and higher farm incomes while they also reduce water use and risks of crop failure due to climate change. Increasing the biodiversity of farming systems can reduce vulnerability to drought. Millet, which is far more nutritious than rice and wheat, uses only 200–300mm water, compared to the 2500mm needed for Green Revolution rice farming. India could grow four times more food using millet. However, global trade is instead pushing agriculture to GMO monocultures of corn, soya, canola and cotton, worsening climate vulnerability.

Biodiversity offers resilience to recover from climate disasters. After the Orissa Super Cyclone of 1998, and the Tsunami of 2004, Navdanya distributed seeds of saline-resistant rice varieties such as "Seeds of Hope" in order to rejuvenate agriculture in lands with reentered saline by the sea. We are now creating seed banks of drought-resistant, flood-resistant, and saline-resistant seed varieties to respond to climate extremities. Climate chaos creates uncertainty. Diversity offers a cushion against both climate extremes and climate uncertainty. We need to move from the myopic obsession with monocultures and centralization, to diversity and decentralization.

Diversity and decentralization are the dual principles to build economies beyond oil and to deal with the climate vulnerability that is the residue of the age of oil. While reducing vulnerability and increasing resilience, biodiverse organic farming also produces more food and higher incomes. As David Pimentel has pointed out, "Organic farming approaches for maize and beans in the U.S. not only use an average of 30 percent less fossil energy but also conserve more water in the soil, induce less erosion, maintain soil quality and conserve more biological resources than conventional farming does." [20] After Hurricane Mitch in Central America, farmers who practiced biodiverse organic farming suffered less damage than those practicing chemical agriculture. The ecologically farmed plots had on average more topsoil, greater soil moisture and less erosion, and experienced less economic loss.[21]

Navdanya's work over the past twenty years has shown that we can grow more food and provide higher incomes to farmers without destroying the environment and killing our peasants. Our study on "Biodiversity based organic farming: A new paradigm for Food Security and Food Safety" has established that small biodiverse organic farms produce more food and provide higher incomes to farmers. There is an alternative. The alternative is in lowering the costs of production while increasing output. We have done this successfully on thousands of farms and have created a fair, just, and sustainable economy. The epidemic of farmer suicides in India is concentrated in regions where chemical intensification has increased the costs of production and farmers have become dependent on nonrenewable seeds and cash crop monocultures—which leads to a decline in prices and income due to globalization. In this way, the global agricultural industrial complex is leading to debt and suicides around the world for those marginalized to its monetary benefits. The high costs of production it institutes are the most significant reason for rural indebtedness. Simply put: High Cost Seeds + Chemicals = Debt = Suicides.

Yet, biodiverse organic farming addresses all these problems:

- Falling incomes for farmers;
- Rising costs for consumers;
- Increasing pollution of our food.

Biodiverse organic farming creates a debt-free, suicide-free, productive alternative to industrialized corporate agriculture. It leads to an increase in farm productivity and farm incomes, while lowering the costs of production. It establishes fair and just trade, and thereby lowers costs for consumers. And it provides for pesticide and chemical-free production and processing, bringing safe and healthy food to communities. We must protect the environment, farmers' livelihoods, as well as public health and people's right to food. We do not need to go the Monsanto way. We can go the Navdanya way. We do not need to end up in food dictatorship and food slavery. We can create our food freedom.

NOTES

1. Dale Allen Pfeiffer, *Eating Fossil Fuels: Oil, Food and the Coming Crisis in Agriculture* (New York: New Society Publishers, 2006), 24.

2. See www.fao.org/es/esc/prices/CIWP QueryServlet (accessed September 1, 2010).

3. See www.developmenteducation.ie/issues-and-topics/hunger/hunger-geography .html (accessed September 1, 2010).

4. Quoted by Gustavo Esteva in "Beyond the knowledge power syndrome: the case of the Green Revolution," Paper presented at the UNU WiDER Seminar, Karachi (January, 1989), 19.

5. Joseph DeVries and Gary H. Toenniessen, *Securing the Harvest: Biotechnology, Breeding, and Seed Systems for African Crops* (New York, NY: CABI Publishing, 2001).

6. Joseph Fargione, Jason Hill, David Tilman, Stephen Polasky, and Peter Hawthorne, "Land Clearing and the Biofuel Carbon Debt," *Science* 319 (2008): 1235–1238.

7. Joseph Fargione, et al., "Land Clearing."

8. David Pimentel and Ted Patzek, "Ethanol Production Using Corn, Switchgrass, and Wood; Biodiesel Production Using Soybean and Sunflower," *Natural Resources Research* 14, no. 1: 65–76.

9. Nicholas Stern, "What is the Economics of Climate Change?" Stern Review on the Economics of Climate Change (January 31, 2006), London.

10. Larry Lohmann, "Carbon Trading: A Critical Conversation on Climate Change, Privatization and Power," *Development Dialogue* 48 (September, 2006): 73.

11. Daniel H. Cole, *Pollution and Property: Comparing Ownership Institutions for Environmental Protection* (Cambridge, UK: Cambridge University Press, 2002), 86.

12. United States Department of Energy, Energy Information Administration, "Analysis of S.139, the Climate Stewardship Act of 2003: Highlights and Summary," Washington, as quoted in Larry Lohman, "Carbon Trading" (note 68).

13. Nicholas Herbert Stern, *The Economics of Climate Change: The Stern Review* (Cambridge: Cambridge University Press, 2007), 371.

14. Larry Lohman, "Carbon Trading," 167.

15. Nicholas Herbert Stern, *The Economics of Climate Change,* xv, 643.

16. Nicholas Herbert Stern, *The Economics of Climate Change,* 643.

17. Larry Lohman, "Carbon Trading," 141.

18. James Kanter, "Carbon Emissions Open New Market Internationally," *Herald Tribune,* June 21, 2007, 1.

19. Albert Howard, *The Soil and Health: A Study of Organic Agriculture* (Greenwich, CT: Devin Adair Company, 1947), 20–21.

20. David Pimentel, Paul Hepperly, James Hanson, David Douds, Rita Seidel, "Environmental, Energetic, and Economic Comparisons of Organic and Conventional Farming Systems," *BioScience* 55, no. 7 (July, 2005): 573–582.

21. Gemenez E. Holt, "Measuring Farmers' Agroecological Resistance After Hurricane Mitch in Nicaragua: A Case Study in Participatory, Sustainable Land Management Impact Monitoring," *Agriculture Ecosystems and Environment,* 93 (2002): 87–105.

Chapter Nine

Origins and Consequences of the Animal Industrial Complex

David Nibert

The modern animal industrial complex, a massive network that includes grain producers, ranching operations, slaughterhouse and packaging firms, fast food and chain restaurants, and the state, has deep roots in world history. Historically, the treatment of both devalued humans and other animals has been characterized by exploitation and violence, and the fates of the two groups have been deeply entangled. From the time humans first captured, confined and controlled the reproduction of such animals as cows, pigs, sheep, goats and horses—which largely benefited powerful elites—in turn [those activities] facilitated human social stratification, domination, and widespread violence.

For example, for thousands of years in Eurasia violent conquerors such as Genghis Khan and Attila the Hun sat atop the backs of horses and launched deadly invasions, massacring or enslaving millions of people. This bloodshed was materially driven, prompted by the gains to be secured from the expropriation of land and water necessary to sustain large numbers of animals, the theft of precious metals and manufactured goods and the capture of humans and other animals as slaves and resources. Some societies, like the warlike nomadic pastoralists from the Eurasian steppe, were largely migratory. Other, more settled societies such as Rome that depended on the labor of exploited animals for extensive agricultural production were able to carry out distant and extended invasions only because of the exploitation of horses, mules, donkeys and cows. Enormous numbers of cows were forced to accompany Roman military campaigns, where they were treated as a food resource. Areas of the world without populations of such large, social animals, such as the pre-Columbian Americas, simply did not experience anything like the widespread violence and destruction that the exploitation of animals promoted and

enabled—nor did these areas see millions die from zoonotic diseases transmitted, if not created, through the capture and confinement of large numbers
of animals.

Elites in Eurasia used oppressed animals to support their deadly invasions
of other parts of the world, such as the ferocious foray into the Western
Hemisphere by the Spanish conquistadors, whose use of horses gave them a
significant advantage over indigenous peoples. Once the Spanish colonizers
were entrenched in Latin America, they reaped profits from the skins, hair
and flesh of ranched animals, and their successful mining and agricultural
operations were possible only because of their exploitation of animals. Millions of indigenous peoples perished from zoonotic diseases introduced by
the Spanish. Countless others, who were not killed outright, were displaced
or enslaved in ranching and mining operations or on sugar plantations;
their lands were expropriated for the creation of vast ranching empires. The
oppression of each group, exploited humans and other animals, supported the
oppression of the other.

The oppression occurring in colonized areas around the world brought
wealth to European investors and merchants, in the form of silver and gold
expropriated from Latin America and the trade in sugar and the skin of cows
ranched and killed there. By the early 18th century, Europe's new rich, flush
with profits from the exploitation of humans and other animals, promoted an
economic system free of management by the state as they sought to throw off
the forms of control that had long served the interests of the old aristocracy.
As this rising capitalist elite challenged aristocratic control of state power,
however, they needed the support of the masses to actually overthrow the old
system. Slogans like "liberty, equality and fraternity" and "give me liberty or
give me death" served to seduce people who were exploited by the aristocracy
into supporting the capitalists' struggle for ascendancy. However, the freedom
actually sought by the capitalists was their freedom to accumulate private
profit with little government restriction—but with considerable government
assistance. After their rise to power, the new capitalist elite created militias
to protect their increasing control of property and wealth from challenges by
exploited workers and the dispossessed.

Not surprisingly, capitalism turned out to be every bit as violent and
oppressive as the social systems dominated by the old aristocrats. However, the capitalist system contained an additional and pernicious peril—the
necessity for continuous growth and expansion. In his book *Against Empire*,
scholar and activist Michael Parenti observes:

A central imperative of capitalism is expansion. Investors will not put their
money into business ventures unless they can extract more than they invest.

Increased earnings only come with growth in the enterprise. The capitalist ceaselessly searches for ways of making more money in order to make still more money.[1]

For capitalist elites to maintain such substantial economic and political control—in societies ostensibly based on freedom and democracy—their efforts required considerable finesse. They exerted a significant level of ideological control for the purpose of explaining and rationalizing state policies and obtaining, if not public support for their dominance, then at least public acquiescence.

One example of insidious capitalist expansion that was driven by profit, supported by the state and legitimated by ideological control was the killing and displacement of indigenous peoples and animals in North America. The creation of ranching operations, first by the British colonists and then under the U.S. republic, began in the East and then expanded into the South and the Midwest. From the start, the invading Europeans' reliance on large numbers of exploited animals led inevitably to intrusions onto Native American lands, widespread violence and displacement. In the 19th century, the massacre of millions of buffalo on the Great Plains, and the violent subjugation of indigenous peoples by the U.S. military, occurred largely so the plains could be populated by cows and sheep to be raised for profit. Both the government and contemporary newspapers promulgated racist ideology to legitimate in the public mind the expropriation of indigenous peoples' lands. The financial cost of the U.S. military violently subduing and confining Native Americans to permit the expansion of ranching enterprises was socialized—that is, paid for by the public—but the proceeds of this entangled oppression did not benefit the public, instead becoming the personal profit of the elites who "owned" the ranches and farmed animals. Growing numbers of oppressed animals were raised on lands once populated by Native Americans and free-living animals, leading to the growth of the railroads that brought animals eastward, and in turn leading to the expansion and concentration of slaughterhouse operations. Smaller slaughterhouses were bought out, or driven out of business, and soon a small number of Chicago slaughterhouses dominated the industry.

Slaughterhouse companies' profits also were increased through the exploitation of a vulnerable workforce, composed largely of recent immigrants. Slaughterhouse workers were over-worked, poorly housed, undernourished and frequently sick. The nature of the work was macabre, as assembly-line-style carnage was made even more horrific by the deafening squeals, bellows and bleating of terrified animals being forced to their final, violent destination. The force of the state, only recently used to clear much of the nation of indigenous peoples, now was brought to bear against slaughterhouse workers who tried to improve their wages and working conditions, through a legal system that labeled unionization efforts as criminal conspiracies and military and police forces that repressed demonstrations and help businesses break strikes. The Chicago slaughterhouses became major forces of the commercial and marketing expansion in the Midwest and were significant economic powers in early 20th century. The giant Chicago slaughterhouse firms like Swift, Armour and Morris were famous for the cruel, rapid-paced killing and disassembly of enormous numbers of animals. Indeed, the emerging automobile industry copied the slaughterhouse system of overhead rails and gravity power in the creation of a production process involving multiple unskilled, assembly line jobs that made individual workers interchangeable and easily replaced.

The profits obtained from land expropriation, worker exploitation, and the enslavement and brutal killing of millions of animals built even more enterprises that, in turn, both facilitated and capitalized on the oppressive practices. Ranchers, land speculators, railroad companies, railroad holding-yard operations, corn and other grain producers, commission agents who managed the sale of animals, packinghouse buyers, market news services, railroads and trans-Atlantic shipping firms, commercial retail operations, marketing firms and advertising and legal and banking services—all were among the ventures that formed an early version of what Barbara Noske in her work Beyond Boundaries aptly called the "Animal Industrial Complex."[2]

In 1929, due to what John Kenneth Galbraith called a "great speculative orgy," the capitalist system crashed under the weight of greed and cupidity. During the Great Depression that ensued, millions in the United States and around the world fell victim to hunger and poverty. Capitalism survived, in part, because of the influence of British economist John Maynard Keynes who advocated government intervention as a means of regulating, and partially mitigating, the more destructive practices of a profit-driven society. The privation, fear and suffering of the Great Depression, and the Keynesian policies that followed, would lead to further deterioration of the treatment of animals under capitalism—especially those relegated to the socially constructed position of "farm animal."[3] Their treatment was to become so wretched as to seem diabolical.

Seeking to stabilize farm revenues, one aspect of the Roosevelt Administration's New Deal economic reconstruction policies was to reduce surpluses of corn and other grains. The government created price supports for corn, soy, and other commodities and placed controls on the production of agricultural goods by paying farmers to reduce the acreage planted. However, the program backfired. Seeking ways to increase their incomes, farmers started investing in "Green Revolution" technologies—including the use of chemical pesticides and herbicides, synthetic fertilizers, and hybrid seeds—to maximize production on the limited acreage they planted. These strategies turned out to be environmentally unsound, and anything but "green" as the term is used today. Farmers with the capital to "modernize" began producing much greater yields per acre and soon generated the very surpluses the government had attempted to end. The organization representing large farming operations, the American Farm Bureau Federation, defended the practice and argued that government policy needed to change in order to utilize the surpluses and maximize agribusiness gains. As Bill Winders notes in the article Expanding the Surplus, the Federation:

> Opposed further supply management policies and argued that the answer was to increase the demand for and consumption of agricultural goods. Controlling production effectively stifled the expansionary tendency in capitalism and potentially limited profits, which was not in these organizations' interests. The solution was obvious: increase 'meat' consumption.[4]

The solution, promoted by agribusiness and embraced by the government, was to use the surplus corn and soy as feed for animals and to increase the numbers of animals raised, killed, and profitably promoted as food. State-funded land grant colleges and other public institutions used taxpayer funds to develop ways to breed and raise animals economically and to force them to grow more rapidly. Factory farming was born. Large confined animal feeding operations (CAFOs) were created that allowed enormous numbers of animals to be raised in small areas, with minimal expenditures of labor.

As increasingly intensive confinement of animals destined to become "food" developed, an early critique of the "monstrous" effects on the animals came in 1964 in Britain in the book *Animal Machines: The New Factory Farming Industry* by Ruth Harrison. Detailing the intensive confinement and violent treatment of chickens, cows, pigs and rabbits, Harrison noted, "if one person is unkind to an animal it is considered to be cruelty, but where a lot of people are unkind to animals, especially in the name of commerce, the cruelty is condoned and, once large sums of money are at stake, will be defended to the last by otherwise intelligent people."[5] While Harrison's book evoked some calls for reform, because of agribusiness's great influence over the state, only modest reforms for animals on factory farms resulted in Britain. In the United States, other than a weak and largely unenforced "humane" slaughter law, other reformist pieces of legislation specifically excluded "animals raised for food" from any legal protection.

Capitalism—especially in the United States—had been revived after the Great Depression by a horrific world war among competing capitalist nations, with wartime military production spurring industrial production and employment. U.S. capitalism stayed afloat after the war in part because of the perpetual Cold War military spending that followed—a policy promoted by powerful corporate, military, and government officials that Dwight Eisenhower forebodingly referred to as the "Military Industrial Complex." Wartime destruction had been so extensive in other capitalist nations that in the 1950s the United States also became the world's primary source for many manufactured commodities, further buttressing U.S. capitalism. With reduced competition and substantial profits, capitalists in the middle part of the 20th century capitulated to some worker demands, creating a period of relatively decent wages and improved workplace conditions for many workers and the expansion of the middle class in the United States.

Also during this period, capitalists recognized that the new broadcast media constituted a powerful tool for controlling information and creating a consumer culture—while simultaneously distracting the masses with ideologically compatible entertainment. As the public airways were being expropriated by large corporations, the automobile industry, growing in tandem with the steel, rubber and oil oligopolies, was undermining public transportation systems in the United States and promoting individually owned cars. Both government policies and the advertising power of television helped build the ultimately destructive and unsustainable, but initially profitable, car culture.

By the 1950s, an increasingly mobile public was being prompted to eat while on the go in their cars by a plethora of businesses hawking take-out "hamburgers" and related fare. Such enterprises as White Castle, McDonald's, Burger King, and Big Boy restaurants came to dominate the restaurant industry and created extensive adverting campaigns, with many of the advertisements targeted to children. "Meat" consumption also was boosted in 1956 when the agribusiness-promoting U.S. Department of Agriculture launched its "four food groups" nutritional education campaign, which became a mainstay of family and school nutrition education for decades. The first food group largely was "meat," and the second was "dairy." The consumption of cow flesh alone in the United States increased from 69.4 pounds per capita in 1942 to 104.7 pounds by 1965. This socially constructed "consumer choice" in diet was the result of several factors including: the expropriation of Native American land for ranching and the development of factory farming practices; the pressure from large agribusiness to convert surplus grain to highly profitable "meat;" the emergence of fast food chains that used the power of mass media advertising to promote and sell "meat" products; and government practices that fostered increased production and sales.

Increasingly, in the later 20th century the U.S. animal industrial complex was going global, best exemplified, perhaps, by its reach into Latin America.

Increasing consumption of cows as food in the United States, especially as "hamburgers," prompted the fast-food industry in the 1950s to search for more and cheaper supplies of grass-fed cows. This goal was advanced in 1960 when the Kennedy Administration, confronted with the success of the Cuban revolution, created a foreign "aid" program for Latin America in an attempt to bolster U.S.-friendly social and economic development—and to suppress anti-capitalist movements. The Kennedy program, called the "Alliance for Progress," largely promoted Latin American compliance with U.S.-endorsed economic and political structures, both of which facilitated increased exports to the United States.

A fundamental part of the Alliance program was the promotion of "beef" exports. The Alliance provided "aid" in the form of U.S. loans at prevailing market rates. The loans were controlled by the newly created U.S. Agency for International Development (USAID), the U.S. Export-Import Bank, and the Inter-American Development Bank. However, the Alliance's goals of fully integrating Latin America into the U.S.-dominated, global capitalist system were promoted most effectively by loans issued by the International Bank for Reconstruction and Development (the World Bank), based in Washington D.C. and subject to considerable control by the U.S. government. Increasingly, U.S.-controlled "aid" in Latin America served U.S. corporate interests by requiring and financing the establishment of a "cattle" infrastructure. When not funding the production of animals directly, the complex system of international financial organizations supported the construction of roads and bridges that facilitated the expansion of ranching into tropical forests. The value of "beef" exports just in Central America grew from $9 million in 1961 to $290 million in 1979, and the amount exported increased more than eight-fold. By the 1970s, Central America had 28 modern "meat"-packing plants authorized to export to the United States. Most of this "beef" went into the corporate fast-food machine; Burger King alone purchased 70 percent of the "beef" exports from Costa Rica.

In South America between 1970 and 1987, the World Bank Group issued loans for the development of "cattle" projects in Bolivia, Ecuador, Uruguay, Paraguay, Colombia, Chile, and Brazil totaling more than $283 million. Another $180 million in loans went to agricultural projects with substantial "cattle" elements. Between 1978 and 1988, in Brazil alone, approximately $5 billion in various international loans and tax incentives promoted the expansion of "cattle" production. The purpose of these loans and other inducements was to make Brazil a major supplier of "beef" to Europe and the United States. Moreover, in 1971 the U.N. Food and Agricultural Organization recommended that Latin American nations begin cultivating feed grains for export, and the U.S. tied food aid to feed-grain export production. U.S. corporations such as Cargill and Ralston Purina received low-interest government loans to facilitate feed-grain production in Latin America.

The consequences of these decades of activity of the animal industrial complex, in conjunction with other complex industrial systems, such as the military industrial complex, global international banking systems and global media conglomerates, have been cataclysmic. In Latin America, for example, subsistence farmers who resisted forcible removal from the land—displacement usually caused by the influx of international loans to expand ranching, feed-crop cultivation, and related enterprises—were subjected to violent repression and death by governments backed by the United States government and commonly by soldiers trained at the U.S. School of the Americas. Many subsistence farming families were forced to migrate to urban areas where they were transformed into proletarians and became vulnerable to transnational corporations seeking exploitable workers.

The use of so much land for the production of "meat" instead of grain for human consumption is a leading cause of malnutrition, hunger, and famine around the world. In Central America alone, by the late 1980s, 45 percent of the arable land was used to graze cows—while half of all of Central Americans did not have their minimal nutritional needs met. By the end of the 20th century, the use of land for grazing or to raise feed for animals destined to become "meat" for the affluent had crowded out essential food production for the poor in Brazil, Colombia, Mexico, Peru, Venezuela, and other periphery countries. In 2002, the Director of the U.N. Food and Agricultural Organization—the same organization that had promoted some of the underlying policies 30 years earlier—announced that 54 million people in Latin America and the Caribbean suffered from chronic malnutrition. What is more, while global supplies of fresh water are decreasing, leaving millions with insufficient or contaminated supplies, enormous amounts of water are spent in raising intensively confined animals and irrigating feed crops.

As urban centers in Latin America expanded from these migrations, increasing numbers of people experienced profound deprivation. Funding for social services was sparse because, ironically, after so much effort to create ranching and slaughterhouse enterprises in the region, with so much attendant suffering and destruction, U.S. ranchers successfully lobbied "voluntary quotas" so that supplies of Latin American "beef" would not significantly undercut their profits. The quotas, coupled with wide fluctuations in the global "beef" market, made the enterprises in Latin America only marginally profitable and contributed to the accumulation of enormous debt in the region. The International Monetary Fund presented Latin American countries with debt restructuring programs that required the implementation of structural adjustment programs that cut government expenditures for health care, education and other public services, while pushing privatization and other neoliberal-friendly policies. Already limited social, education and medical services became more difficult to obtain.

People in Central America and Mexico fleeing repression and deprivation by seeking employment in the United States find, ironically, that the likely jobs open to them are in slaughterhouses and "meat"-packing facilities, operations that offer only low wages and ghastly, dangerous working conditions. These contemporary versions of Upton Sinclair's *Jungle* are strikingly similar to the Chicago slaughterhouses of the early 20th century—both in the horrific nature of the work and in the oppressive treatment of both the animals and the workers. One difference, however, is that the contemporary disassembly line moves much faster. Another difference is the location of most operations. Seeking to avoid unionization efforts, in the 1980s industry giants like Cargill, ConAgra, and Tyson moved slaughterhouses to rural areas, particularly in the U.S. South, for two profitable reasons. First, killing animals closer to where they are raised cut transportation costs and reduced the weight loss and illness in the animals caused by crude, and cruel, transport and treatment. Second, operating in more isolated, rural areas in states historically unfriendly to labor unions reduced the possibility that workers would organize for better pay and conditions.

The slaughterhouse firms are especially welcoming to immigrants from Mexico and Central America because they are largely without economic resources—and therefore both desperate and insecure—and their mere presence plays into existing racism and xenophobia, further reducing the odds of solidarity and organizing among workers. A few giant firms control most of the industry and wield enormous influence over the regulatory agency, the U.S. Department of Agriculture, reducing outside controls that would moderate the drive for profit. Therefore, the death and disassembly lines at these facilities move at an extremely fast pace, causing stress and frequent injury to workers. What is more, the giant slaughterhouses are notorious for sexual harassment and assault against workers; and women of color are particularly at high risk.

Environmental destruction is another consequence of the animal industrial complex. Raising large groups of cows and sheep has long been tied to deforestation and desertification in many parts of the world. In Central America, for example, between 1950 and 1990 the most significant change in land in the region was the destruction of forests for the purpose of creating pasture. Tropical forests in the area fell from 29 million hectares to 17 million during the period. In all of Latin America the conversion of tropical forests into pastures and ranches for raising cows for food is responsible for more defor- estation than all other production systems combined. The creation of pasture accounts for roughly 75 percent of global deforestation.

In the United States, for decades the government has permitted ranchers to pasture cows on public lands at bargain costs. Millions of acres of public lands have been profoundly damaged and made desert-like. After grazing cows on public lands, ranchers transport them to feedlots where they are fed large amounts of taxpayer-subsidized corn and soy to add body weight before they are killed. These feedlots, frequently packing 100,000 or more cows into small areas, generate massive amounts of manure that pollutes U.S. streams and rivers, kills fish, and contaminates drinking water with bacteria, chemicals and pharmaceuticals. While feedlots confine cows who are bred, raised, and killed primarily for their flesh and other body parts, contempo- rary CAFOs primarily are packed with "dairy" cows, pigs, and chickens. In addition to being the primary source of water pollution in the United States, animals intensively confined in feedlots and CAFOs also generate toxic gases such as ammonia, hydrogen sulfide, and methane that pollute the air. Again, due to the influence agribusiness exerts over the government, regulation of the environmental and public health effects of feedlots and CAFOs generally is patchy and casual.

Feedlot operations, CAFOs, and giant slaughterhouses are rapidly expand- ing into Third World nations, where environmental and labor regulations largely are nonexistent or weak and unenforced. The magnitude of the envi- ronmental damage caused by raising other animals for food was recognized in a 2006 report by the United Nations' FAO, which stated:

> The livestock sector emerges as one of the top two or three most significant con-
> tributors to the most serious environmental problems, at every scale from local
> to global. . . . [I]t should be a major policy focus when dealing with problems
> of land degradation, climate change and air pollution, water shortage and water
> pollution and loss of biodiversity. [Italics added][6]

The FAO report noted that the processes involved in raising animals as food create more greenhouse gases than all forms of transportation combined. It is clear that tremendous environmental damage, expropriation of land and exploitation of people in the Third World and the horrific oppression of other animals are caused by pursuit of profits generated by creating "meat" for the affluent.

The practice of "meat" and "dairy" consumption also takes a fatal toll on those encouraged to do so by government, agribusiness, restaurants, and other corporate interests. In addition to the public health problems created by feedlots and CAFOs, thousands are sickened every year, and some die, from "meat" contaminated with salmonella, E. coli, and listeria, while others go undiagnosed with mad cow disease (Creutzfeldt-Jakob disease), whose symptoms often are mistaken for Alzheimer's. Consuming other animals and their secretions as food causes cardiovascular disease, the leading cause of death in affluent nations such as the United States, and places consumers at higher risk for type-2 diabetes and some forms of cancer. And the system of factory farming underlying the animal industrial complex has the potential for even graver public health catastrophes. The increasingly intensive confinement of animals in CAFOs is responsible for the mutation and spread of deadly microbes such as the H1N1 influenza virus. The continued operation and expansion of CAFOs unquestionably will allow for further mutations of deadly microbes and threatens the emergence of a global flu pandemic like the one that ravaged the world in 1918.

The animal industrial complex also is intertwined with the medical industrial complex, as the treatment of the conditions and diseases stemming from the socially manufactured, "meat"-based diet results in billions of dollars in profits. Indeed, television advertisements for drugs to treat high cholesterol, hypertension and diabetes are now almost as common as commercials for the fast-food chains and other retailers that helped give people those conditions. Instead of promoting disease prevention, the medical industrial complex largely is focused on highly profitable treatments. To further this aim, the pharmaceutical arm of the animal industrial complex subjects tens of millions of animals every year to industrialized forms of vivisection. Increasing numbers of physicians view animal testing as a deeply flawed means of conducting medical research applicable to humans, but it continues at an astounding level.

Even without the horrendous health, environmental, and human rights consequences of the animal industrial complex, the horrific treatment of other animals that it produces is in itself a powerful and compelling reason to resist and reject the system. Sentient beings who have preferences and desires, who are capable of profound social relationships and who have inherent value apart from their ill use by the Complex, are treated essentially as inanimate objects, as "biomachines." Most of these individuals, experiencing torturous confinement in CAFOS, have no opportunity for normal activity or stimuli, and many are kept in darkness for long periods. Their bodies often are crudely and painfully mutilated to facilitate growth or to mitigate the pathological behavior produced by overcrowding. Some animals are so intensively bred and genetically manipulated that they have difficulty standing. Animals are roughly handled and cruelly prodded when transported to slaughterhouses;

once there, they are beaten and forced with electric prods onto the slaughter-house floor, where many are still conscious when the "disassembly" begins. In just the United States, more than ten billion individuals suffer inexpressible horror every year in the name of "food" production.

The profound cultural devaluation of other animals that permits the violence that underlies the animal industrial complex is produced by far-reaching speciesist socialization. For instance, the system of primary and secondary education under the capitalist system largely indoctrinates young people into the dominant societal beliefs and values, including a great deal of pro-capitalist and speciesist ideology. The devalued status of other animals is deeply ingrained; animals appear in schools merely as caged "pets," as dissection and vivisection subjects, and as lunch. On television and in movies, the unworthiness of other animals is evidenced by their virtual invisibility; when they do appear, they generally are marginalized, vilified, or objectified. Not surprisingly, these and numerous other sources of speciesism are so ideologically profound that those who raise compelling moral objections to animal oppression largely are dismissed, if not ridiculed.

Thus, the entangled and violent oppression of humans and other animals, which began when animals first were captured and enslaved, has expanded under contemporary capitalism into the monstrous animal industrial complex. This complex—a predictable, insidious outgrowth of the capitalist system with its penchant for continuous expansion—is so profoundly destructive as to be the contemporary equivalent of Attila the Hun. Like Attila, the animal industrial complex is in constant pursuit of water and land to raise animals whose bodies are its source of material wealth.

The world's human population is expected to reach nine billion by 2050, and the animal industrial complex is predicting a 40 percent increase in "meat" production by that date. Just by 2020, it is projected that 80 percent of the world's agricultural land will be used for pasture or for feed crop production. Despite the public health, environmental, and social consequences, the World Bank continues to promote "meat" consumption among the more affluent and states "the developing world is projected to be the most important supplier to this growing market."[7] Such a policy will only increase violence, repression, environmental destruction, landlessness, poverty, hunger, and death.

An essential part of any successful plan for the promotion of global justice must be a campaign for the elimination of the practice of oppressing other animals, especially as sources of food. As we work for a democratic global economy, we must transform the system that uses increasingly precious land and water for profitable "meat" production into a truly "green" form of agriculture organized to provide nutritious plant-based food where it is needed throughout the world—and to parts of the world where many have few alternatives to exploiting animals. In a more just global economy, with plant-based diets that require much less land than is now used for "meat" production, land would be available to resettle millions trapped in urban squalor. Land also could be set aside as sanctuaries for other animals—with whom humans must learn to peacefully co-exist. Such change will take more than just a challenge to the animal industrial complex; it will require the development of a social-economic alternative to capitalism as it has developed across multiple fronts of social antagonism.

NOTES

1. Michael Parenti, *Against Empire* (San Francisco, CA: City Lights Publishers, 1995), 3.

2. See Barbara Noske, *Beyond Boundaries: Humans and Animals* (New York, NY: Black Rose Press, 1997).

3. Words and expressions that are disparaging to other animals and euphemisms that tend to disguise the reality of oppression (such as the term "meat," which disguises the reality that other animals' dead bodies are used for food) are placed in quotation marks. If such language is used in quoted material, the devaluative terms are placed in italics. While this may make the text somewhat awkward at times, it is much preferable to using smoother language that implicitly supports oppressive arrangements. See David Nibert, *Animal Rights/Human Rights: Entanglements of Oppression and Liberation* (Lanham, MD: Rowman & Littlefield, 2002), xv.

4. William Winders and David Nibert, "Expanding the Surplus: Expanding 'Meat' Consumption and Animal Oppression," *International Journal of Sociology and Social Policy* 24, no. 9 (2004): 80.

5. Ruth Harrison, *Animal Machines: The New Factory Farming Industry* (London, UK: Vincent Stuart Ltd., 1964).

6. Henning Steinfeld, et al., *Livestock's Long Shadow: Environmental Issues and Options* (Rome: Food and Agricultural Organization of the United Nations, 2006).

7. Cornelis de Hahn, et al. *Livestock Development: Implications for Rural Poverty, the Environment, and Global Food Security* (Washington, DC: The World Bank, 2001).

Chapter Ten

Bad For Your Health

The U.S. Medical Industrial Complex Goes Global

Asif Ismail

Since the late industrial period, a steady stream of remarkable inventions and scientific discoveries has had twin effects upon medicine and health care. On the one hand, the introduction of new medicines, methods, and technologies in the treatment of diseases has expanded the frontiers of health care. At the same time, it has also led to the growth of an industry that monetizes those breakthroughs to grow bigger and bigger, now accounting for a dominant share of both national and global economies.

The impact of innovations such as the electrocardiogram (1903), penicillin (1928), heart transplants (1967) and magnetic resonance imaging, or MRI (1973), on public health was profound. Diseases that were considered terminal became curable; conditions that once condemned a significant section of the population to a perpetually painful existence became treatable. Epidemics that hitherto claimed tens of millions of lives could now be contained. Advances in preventive medicine have helped save entire populations from dreaded diseases. Overall, these gains have lead to significant rise in life expectancy in many parts of the world, especially in developed nations.

Yet, shamefully, the fruits of the breakthroughs of the past several decades were not distributed equitably. According to the World Health Organization, more than a third of the world's population still has no access to essential drugs.[1,2] A University of California study found that a baby born in Swaziland is nearly 30 times more likely to die before the age of five than an infant born in Sweden, and a child in Cambodia 17 times more likely to die in its first five years than one in Canada.[3] Inequalities exist not just between countries, but within them, too. In the developing world, the rich have access to better health care, while the poor in many rich nations are left to fend for themselves. In the United States, where approximately 17 cents of every dollar spent is on health care products and services, more than a seventh of the population does not have health insurance.

Ironically, a big reason quality health care remains a mirage for much of humanity, despite all the scientific and technological progress made in conquering diseases and other health challenges in the past century, is the second development mentioned at the beginning of this chapter. The European and American transnational corporations that turned most scientific innovations into profitable products, along with their allies within governments and outside, dominate the global health policy-making process and distribution system, and also control most of the global health resources. Their vast network, the global medical industrial complex, operates solely on free market principles: it runs health care, first and foremost, like a business and views public health as a for-profit activity, with investments made only in areas where substantial returns are guaranteed. Across the geographies, the market-driven policy it has dictated has led to the commodification of health. The results: quality care is limited to only those "consumers" who can afford to buy it; also, importantly, it has "medicalized" much of the industrialized world to such an extent that medical goods and services have become an integral part of the society.

Like other global industrial complexes, the medical industrial complex consists of two elements that are bound together by common economic interests. One part of it is the businesses surrounding health products and services industry, such as pharmaceutical and medical-device manufactures, hospitals, health insurance corporations, doctors and other health care professionals, drug and device advertising and marketing machinery, as well as medical schools, among others. Public institutions, including the legislative and executive branches of governments, health departments and agencies that are charged with administering public health services and deliveries, as well as their employees, constitute the other. In most cases, national governments, besides enacting policies conducive to its sustenance and growth, are also the global medical industrial complex's single largest client. For instance, the U.S. federal government alone spends a trillion dollars on health care, much of which ends up in the pockets of big corporations. The Patient Protection and Affordable Care Act, enacted in March 2010 after a vigorous campaign by President Obama and the House Democratic leadership, further expanded the role of the government in health care delivery.

The abundance of taxpayer dollars and an exponential rise in consumption of pharmaceutical and other health products and services over the decades— a result of years of brilliant marketing and sales campaigns by the industry—have made the medical industrial complex one of the largest industrial complexes. It is bigger than even the military industrial complex. The health care economy of the United States alone is more than $2.2 trillion (translating to nearly $7,500 per every American); in comparison, global defense spending was roughly $1.5 trillion in 2008.[4]

Businesses belonging to the medical industrial complex are also among the most profitable globally. In 2008, for example, Johnson and Johnson, the world's largest health care products maker, posted profits of nearly $13 billion, the sixth-most profitable company on the Fortune 500 list.[5] Pfizer, the No. 1 drug-maker, was 11th with a profit of more than $8 billion,[6] while Merck was 13th, with a profit of more than $7.8 billion.[7] Seven of the top 50 Fortune 1000 companies are from within the health care sector.[8] Overall, nearly 13 percent (129) of all companies on Fortune's list of top 1000 corporations belong to this sector. They include 17 medical facilities, 14 insurance and managed care companies, nine pharmacy and other services, 16 food and drug stores, 26 life and health insurance corporations, 18 medical products and equipment makers, and 21 pharmaceutical companies, and seven wholesale health care companies.[9]

While the companies and their executives posted such dizzying profits, patients (including the elderly in particular) have seen the cost of essential medicines go up constantly. The huge growth in consumption of drugs, meanwhile, has had very little effect on public health. The United States, which spends more money on drugs than any other country, lags behind most other industrialized countries in life expectancy at birth, while in many sub-Saharan African countries, life expectancy is at a stage where America was at the dawn of the 20th century.

U.S. ORIGIN

Like most other industrial complexes, the medical industrial complex first grew in the United States, and to this day, the country remains its epicenter. Having originated under the same historical circumstances that led to the possibility of other industrial complexes across society, the medical industrial complex shares with them a number of social factors that led to its own growth and evolutionary trajectory.

Different industries within the medical industrial complex have existed in one form or another for centuries. Among pharmaceutical companies, Merck, for example, traces its origin to 1668. Pfizer, the world's largest drug company, was established in 1849. Johnson and Johnson, a pharmaceutical and health products giant, was founded in 1886. Drug companies such as

Parke-Davis, Lilly, Squibb, Abbott, and Upjohn & Searle and Bayer also came into existence in the 19th century. Many of these corporations were transnational in nature even then. Merck, a German company, had U.S. operation by the late 1800s.

The modern hospital system, with physicians and surgeons, began emerging in the eighteenth century in Europe. Similarly, the concept of insurance has existed for more than a hundred years, even though coverage of hospital and medical procedures is a relatively newer trend. The government involvement in health care, as we see it today, began with the introduction of a welfare system in Europe in the late 19th century in Europe and gained speed in the early 20th century.

The eventual consolidation of the medical industrial complex—the coming together of these various players—was aided by three factors. The first, of course, was the flurry of inventions and discoveries that began pouring in after the industrial revolution. One such breakthrough that was turned into an enormously profitable product was the miracle drug penicillin, discovered by Scottish scientist Alexander Fleming in 1928. When the U.S. government needed large volumes of the antibiotic for its troops during World War II, the obvious choice for the mass production was Pfizer. The company worked round the clock to supply large doses of the drug to the Allied forces in combat zones. (That collaboration was a significant moment in the history of the medical industrial complex; it also foretold the shape of things to come.) Across the industry, there were many similar innovations that were turned into mass products. Drug manufacturers and other companies that provided raw materials to them profited from these breakthroughs, and began thriving in Switzerland, Germany, Italy and Britain, as well as the United States, among other countries.

The second factor was the emergence of a new global order after World War II. At the end of the destructive war, the United States and other victorious nations set up a system of rules and institutions to regulate the global economy. The idea was promoted that a regulation-free market and globalized capital would not only create more wealth for everyone but also prevent future conflicts. At the heart of this enterprise were two newly created institutions: the International Monetary Fund and the World Bank. The policies they pursued would eventually trigger modern globalization. The "free" flow of capital and the creation of "free market" objectives would inevitably lead to transnational corporations becoming an integral (if not defining) part of the global economy. Many of them grew big and powerful enough to be able to influence—and in many cases dictate—policies of national governments.

Many pharmaceutical and other health products manufacturers and service providers thrived under this new post-War economic regime and a majority of the global drug production came under the control of Euro-American capital. Drug giants such as Pfizer established operations on several continents during the period.

The third major milestone in the history of the medical industrial complex was the Reagan-Thatcher policies of the 1980s. Deregulation (removal or loosening of many governmental rules that governed the operation of businesses) and privatization of public enterprises were two pet ideas the two conservative leaders promoted tirelessly on both sides of the Atlantic. This was also the period the United States increasingly began using intellectual property rights as an instrument of its trade and policies. The gradual birth of a global intellectual property regime would, in turn, lead to a rapid rise of the medical industrial complex internationally.

There are many reasons why America midwived this phenomenon, not least being the fact that it is the most dominant capitalist economy in the world. Additionally, it is the largest prescription drug market, accounting for nearly 38 percent of global sales.[10] For the same reason, many of the top corporations in the health care sector are based in the country—of the top 15 global pharmaceutical corporations, seven are U.S.-based[11]—and almost all leading non-state players in health care have a presence in the United States.

The United States also runs the most expensive health programs in the world. Total U.S. federal government budget for health care for the current year is more than $1 trillion. Just two programs alone, Medicare and Medicaid, are projected to cost nearly $750 billion this year.[12] In fact, the creation of these two well-funded programs in 1965—to help senior citizens and low-income Americans—was a significant development in the growth of the complex. They dramatically increased government spending in the field, propelling the U.S. health industry from the periphery of the national economy to a more central position.[13] From 5.2 percent of the gross domestic products in 1960, health care expenditures rose to 16.2 percent of the GDP in 2007.[14] According to the National Health Expenditure Accounts (NHEA), which measures spending on health care goods and services, public health activities, private insurance, research and other health care expenditure, the size of the health care economy more than tripled in the past five decades.

In addition to the Medicare and Medicaid programs, the U.S. government also spends tens of billions more for the health insurance of its employees and in health care expenses to veterans, making it the single largest client of the health care industry. The American government also bankrolls the most expensive medical research infrastructure through the National Institutes of

Health, the Food and Drug Administration and other agencies within the Department of Health and Human Services and the Department of Defense, among other branches of government. States also have huge health budgets, running into tens of billions of dollars.

The existence of all these programs at the federal and state levels means the presence of a huge bureaucracy to administer them. As with other industrial complexes, the economic interests of these public servants are tied to that of the corporations they are regulating and doing business with, since their jobs are linked to the sustenance of the industry. Similarly, the hundreds of thousands of health professionals employed at the more than 15,000 small and large hospitals in the country, tens of thousands of faculty member researchers at medical schools and research institutes, the pharmacists who dispense billions of prescriptions annually, all have similar stake in a durable medical industrial complex.

The U.S. political system, which allows business and other interests to influence policies directly and indirectly through lobbying and campaign contributions, is another reason the phenomenon thrives in the country. Its lobbying rules permit corporations to spend unlimited resources to influence government officials, and the electoral system lets them infuse millions of dollars to the campaigns of their favored candidates. The medical industrial complex runs one of the largest and most expensive lobbying operations in Washington. The health sector has spent more than $3.2 billion to influence government officials between 1998 and 2009, according to the Center for Responsive Politics, a Washington, D.C.-based watchdog. Similarly, it has given more than $824 million campaign contributions to various candidates running for offices at the federal level.[15] In return for such extravagance, the industry gets a series of favorable legislation decisions and policies enacted that add to its bottom line.

The fact that the health industry offers lucrative jobs, as lobbyists and consultants, to many of these officials once they leave the government is an incentive for them to take care of the interests of businesses while in office. A 2005 Center for Public Integrity study found that more than a third of the 3,000 lobbyists the pharmaceutical and other health products manufactures hired from 1998 to 2004 were former federal officials, and that included 75 former members of the U.S. Congress.[16] The long list of individuals who have gone through the revolving door between the industry and the government includes former Congressman Billy Tauzin and former Secretary of Defense Donald Rumsfeld. Tauzin joined the Pharmaceutical Research and Manufacturers of America, the industry lobbying arm, as its president and CEO barely months after stepping down as the chairman of the powerful House Energy and Commerce Committee. Just months before leaving the powerful committee he had overseen the passage of the Medicare Modernization Act, which had several sweetheart deals to drug companies. In between his two stints as the Secretary of Defense, Rumsfeld headed the pharmaceutical firm G. D. Searle & Company (which is now part of Pfizer) and served as chairman of Gilead Sciences, the developer of the antiviral drug Tamiflu. When the fear of a bird flu epidemic in 2005 led to an increase in Tamiflu sales, Rumsfeld reportedly had made a profit of at least $1 million from his Gilead shares. The Defense Department itself was one of the biggest buyers of the drug. Officially, the secretary recused himself from all decision pertaining to Gilead.[17]

It is no coincidence that the medical industrial complex first consolidated in the United States in the 1960s, the decade the Medicare and Medicaid programs were launched. With corporations increasingly driving health policy, American health care became a commodity by the end of the decade, like any other product—highly industrialized and monopolized. There were winners and losers. While the quality of care deteriorated in small towns and rural areas, big cities were filled with high-tech medical centers.[18]

Another indication of the burgeoning corporate takeover of the health care in the country during the period was the birth of investor-owned hospital chains. Historically, America's hospitals were run as nonprofits; most of them were owned and operated by religious groups or universities. On the forefront of this new development were Hospital Corporation of America and Tenet, the two largest hospital chains today.

By the 1970s, the foundation for a pervasive medical industrial complex was in place throughout the country. One of the first to warn about its negative impact was Barbara Ehrenreich. She cautioned people of the "expanding medical empires" that rely "more and more on government money to nurture their development" and warned that "they are themselves becoming essentially private 'governments of health.'" She saw the emergence of a "single, American, Medical-Industrial Complex," with two interdependent components, the "health products industry and health services industry." She also documented the nexus between its various strings:

Executives of the health products companies sit on the boards of medical schools and medical centers and on prestigious commissions to study health policy. Research physicians consult eagerly and profitably for the health products industry. Health products industry executives are showing an increasing interest in expanding into the still largely nonprofit health care delivery system.[19]

Soon even those within the health care field were sounding the alarm bell. In an essay in the October 1980 issue of the *New England Journal of*

Medicine, Dr. Arnold Relman, then editor of the publication, wrote that a new medical industrial complex had emerged in the United States in the preceding decade. The new phenomenon had as much "potential for influence on public policy" as the military industrial complex, he argued.[20]

The complex, already in ascendancy, would get a shot in the arm with the Republican Ronald Reagan capturing the White House. Marcia Angell, another former editor of the *New England Journal of Medicine* would later call Reagan's election in 1980 "perhaps the fundamental element in the rapid rise of big pharma."[21]

With the new president and his administration going on a deregulation spree, the country's health care system was part of the many public institutions turned over to corporations. When there was money to be made, Wall Street wasn't far behind. As investigative reporters Donald L. Barlett and James B. Steele pointed out, what made the health sector a fertile field for deal-making was its fragmented nature, with separate parts ranging from hospitals and insurers to drug companies and pharmacies.

"Best of all, the amount of money flowing through the various entities was growing exponentially, on its way to becoming a multitrillion-dollar marketplace, with a solid, guaranteed chunk of the cash coming from the federal government's Medicare and Medicaid programs, or more precisely, taxpayers. What's more, there was little likelihood of a downturn. After all, disease and sickness—and equally important, the fear of both—were as certain as death and taxes.[22]

Many of the largest health care service providers such as HealthSouth, which operates more than 200 facilities, were founded during the 1980s. Several health maintenance organizations, or HMOs, which were nonprofit until then, were turned into for-profit corporations, and even doctors were organized into large networks of corporations.

Another big development that strengthened the emerging medical industrial complex in the United States was the landmark 1980 legislation, known as the Bayh-Dole Act, after its sponsors, Senators Birch Bayh and Bob Dole. It promoted the commercial licensing of federally funded inventions, thus allowing pharmaceutical companies to tap universities and other taxpayer-supported facilities for inventions and turn them into profitable products. (Since then, some of the drugs developed with public-funded research have become blockbusters, earning billions of dollars for companies. Taxol, a best-selling cancer drug manufactured by Bristol-Myers Squibb Company, was developed by researchers from the National Institutes of Health and Florida State University. From 1993 to 2002, Taxol's worldwide sales exceeded $9 billion.)[23] What the Bayh-Dole act accomplished was making America's institutions of higher education a cog in the wheel of the medical industrial complex. Today, many of the nation's top universities are in effect acting as research arms of corporate America.

GLOBAL GROWTH

Because of economic logic, at the beginning, the focus of the medical industrial complex has been rich nations and their citizens who have the money to spend on expensive care. But outside of the United States and Europe, it began to spread its influence in the 1980s—the high noon of the free market creed. With Reagan and Thatcher making cases for unfettered and unregulated capitalism in the United States and Britain, the belief that a global market and global free trade would be better for everyone began to gain currency with leaders worldwide.

Historically, national governments have been the biggest player in health care in the developing world. The United Nations agencies also played a crucial role by coordinating on significant health issues and policies. But beginning in the 1980s, multinational businesses started assuming a more dominant position in global health policy-making, thereby reducing the role of public institutions.[24]

What gave the global health business interests a foothold in many countries were the policies of the International Monetary Fund and the World Bank. Tough economic conditions, along with corruption and bad governance, had nearly bankrupted several developing countries. In order to avoid financial default and economic collapse, many of these states had to approach the IMF and the World Bank, the so-called lenders of last resort. But loans from these two institutions came with a catch. Since the 1950s, they have attached stringent conditions on nations that sought loans. Those conditions, known as structural adjustment programs (SAPs), included reducing social spending (in areas such as health and education), and augmenting trade liberalization and the privatization of state-owned enterprises.

The consequences of slashing health budgets became quickly evident. As early as 1987, UNICEF had raised concerns about the impact structural adjustment programs were having on many countries. In a study, *Adjustment with a Human Face,* the organization documented that "the growing economic imbalances, in particular, the decline in household incomes and/or government expenditure experienced in the 1980s by 70 per cent of the developing countries in Latin America, Africa and the Middle East have led to a widespread and sharp reversal in the trend toward the improvement in standards of child health, nutrition, and education."[25]

The World Health Organization, itself part of the global multilateral hierarchy, also pointed out the effects of structural adjustment programs on the countries on whose throats they were forced down.

In health, SAPs affect both the supply of health services (by insisting on cuts in health spending) and the demand for health services (by reducing household income, thus leaving people with less money for health). Studies have shown that SAP policies have slowed down improvements in, or worsened, the health status of people in countries implementing them. The results reported include worse nutritional status of children, increased incidence of infectious diseases, and higher infant and maternal mortality rates.[26]

A second wave in the global spread of the medical industrial complex occurred in the 1990s, when a multilateral trade regime that had been gradually evolving since World War II took on a concrete form with the creation of the World Trade Organization in 1994. The mission of the newly created body was to liberalize and regulate trade, and a condition for any country wishing to join it was the ratification of Trade-Related Intellectual Property Rights. The agreement, better known as TRIPS, guarantees intellectual property rights to drug companies and other multinational corporations in the global arena.

 What WTO and TRIPS made possible was the multinational health interests' long-cherished goal of establishing a worldwide market that would guarantee patents for drugs and other products on a global scale. Not being able to sell the same product for the same price everywhere was one of their old grievances. Drug companies were among the first to lobby to make intellectual property rights an important part of the U.S. trade and foreign policies[27] and they were also one of the most vociferous advocates of instituting a global patent regime. Therefore, the emergence of TRIPS as an essential part of global trade was a huge victory for them. Within years of TRIPS becoming an internationally binding agreement, its colossal negative impact was in evidence in South Africa, when the global drug giants used it against that country. By the turn of the last century, the HIV-AIDS epidemic was wreaking havoc in Africa, especially in the sub-Saharan part of the continent, which was home to more than two-thirds of the global infected population. One of the countries hit hard by the crisis was South Africa, which had the world's largest HIV-infected population. Drug prices in that country, where U.S. companies were controlling half the prescription drug market, were among the highest in the world. When South Africa decided, in 1997, to provide its citizens greater access to antiretroviral drugs and other essential medicines, by allowing the importation of cheaper drugs from nations such as India, the global pharmaceutical industry let loose all its fury on its government.

The multinational drug giants and Western governments—in perhaps the first-ever joint public appearance of the medical industrial complex on the global stage—claimed that the South African move to import drugs violated pharmaceutical trademark rights guaranteed by TRIPS.[28]

Stunningly oblivious to or uncaring for the public health realities on the ground—people dying by the thousands without having access to essential drugs—the industry mounted a well-orchestrated campaign against South Africa on many fronts. It enlisted the U.S. Congress and the White House to pressure the African nation with threats of trade sanctions. Then, in February 1998, more than three dozen global pharmaceutical giants sued the South African government. The industry eventually retreated in the wake of a massive public relations backlash worldwide. Yet, its attempt to utilize powerful national governments and to collude strategically as a corporate sector in order to maximize global profits, even if this meant denying essential medicines to impoverished patients during one of the gravest health crises of recent decades, was illustrative of the way industrial complexes operate.

Another big expansion battle waged by the global medical industrial complex was in India, a nation of more than a billion people and hence a potentially lucrative market for global industry. When the country opted to join the WTO, like many other developing states, it was given 10 years—until 2005—to make its national law TRIPS-compliant, meaning to "strengthen" its patent laws in order to offer more intellectual property protections to the products of multinational corporations. The previous law had allowed Indian companies to reverse-engineer brand name drugs, keeping pharmaceutical prices in that country substantially low. That law was largely responsible for the growth of a strong local generic drug industry, a world leader, which supplied life-saving drugs to poor nations at a very low cost. In fact, Indian generic companies were credited with bringing down the average annual cost of antiretroviral drugs in Africa from more than $10,000 to about $300. The global pharmaceutical giants had been waging a campaign against the Indian generic drug industry for years, accusing it of infringing on their patents, and thereby making their products less competitive in India and in other parts of the world such as Asia-Pacific and the Middle East. Now the WTO and TRIPS provided an opportunity to eliminate the competition. But there was huge resistance to amending the Indian patent law from groups within civil society who argued that such change will severely limit the ability of the Indian generic drug industry to produce future generations of important medicines, such as antiretrovirals, or that it would otherwise make them prohibitively expensive. India itself has a substantially large HIV-infected population, estimated at more than 2.3 million. Concerned that the new law would also deprive patients in other Third World countries of low-cost drugs, many international access-to-medicine activists joined the debate. In the end, after an acrimonious political struggle, the Indian parliament passed the new patent law which offers stronger protections to multinationals. Then, in one stroke, the drug giants were able to expand their presence within the growing Indian health care market and weaken competition from the domestic generic industry that had undercut its profit.

In India and elsewhere, the drug industry has not been coy about its ultimate goal of reshaping the health care systems everywhere on the model of the highly market-oriented U.S. system.

Inevitably, the new global legal and juridical apparatus put in place by WTO would increase the prominence of legal and state bureaucracies that assist the medical and other industrial complexes in navigating intellectual property-related issues worldwide. They mostly operate out of world capitals and financial centers such as Washington, London and New York, and Geneva, where WTO and the World Intellectual Property Organization—a United Nations agency—and a number of other international groups are headquartered. This network of bureaucrats, lawyers and industry professionals work across borders to craft and implement policies that affect a good part of humanity, in partnership with various industries. An important part of this network is the Office of the United States Trade Representative (USTR), a nearly five-decade old agency that has done more to advance the "Intellectual Property regime" worldwide than any other entity. The agency releases annual reports recommending actions against countries that don't offer adequate patent protection to U.S. companies. Historically, USTR has been an ally of the pharmaceutical industry. The agency routinely heeds the recommendation of the industry while including countries on its watch lists.

CONSEQUENCES OF ITS INFLUENCE

As mentioned earlier, one of the main consequences of the huge sway the medical industrial complex has over global health policy is the disparity in distribution of health care. It is natural that when public health is run as a business, diseases become nothing more than opportunities for making money. Thus, over the past half-century, we have seen most of the top research and development dollars going to the discovery of those illnesses that affect the rich. Because they are not likely to provide a high net return, a whole range of diseases that mostly affect people in the least developed world are ignored.

It is the reason some of the greatest public health challenges of our era, such as HIV and malaria in the developing world, remain unmet. It is also why there is such a big difference in life expectancy between the global north and south. Infectious diseases such as HIV/AIDS, malaria and tuberculosis that primarily affect people in the least developing world continue to cause heavy human toll, as adequate resources are not invested in treating them. These three illnesses account for nearly 1 in 10 deaths globally.

AIDS is, in fact, a classic example of how the lack of resources and access to medicine can be the difference between life and death. Since its onslaught in the 1980s, the epidemic has been largely contained in the Western world through sex education and antiretroviral therapy. However, in poor countries, especially in Africa, it is a different story. According to the WHO, a vast majority of more than 33.4 million people living with HIV/AIDS worldwide in 2008 were in low- and middle-income countries. In those countries, only about 4 million had access to antiretroviral therapy.

Similarly, that malaria, an eminently treatable illness, is still a huge menace in Africa has to do with the lack of access to medicine. Caused by a parasite called Plasmodium that is transmitted via the bites of infected mosquitoes, malaria affects anywhere from 350 million to 500 million every year. The World Health Organization says the disease kills a child every 30 seconds. The prevalence of malaria is so great that it consumes up to 40 percent of public health expenditures.[29] Malaria is one of the most preventable and curable diseases; yet drug companies do not seem to be in a hurry to invest in the eradication of the disease. This is despite having a huge pool of humanity as potential customers. Approximately half the world (3.3 billion people) is at risk of getting malaria. But, they happen to be the poorer half of the world.

The first malaria vaccine is unlikely to hit the market before 2015. According to the global Malaria Vaccine Initiative program, there isn't adequate funding to "get a malaria vaccine across the finish line."[30]

Cures for many other diseases largely affecting poor nations are similarly ignored. The region most affected is Africa, a global area still largely outside the radar of the medical industrial complex. It is no surprise that, of the 39 countries where life expectancy is below 60 years, all but one (Afghanistan) are African nations.[31]

In fact, many illnesses such as diarrhea, one of the most common causes of death in those countries, can be tackled by adopting a commonsensical approach. Increasing potable water coverage would absolve the need for medical treatment for several mortal illnesses and save millions of lives annually.

Meanwhile, the patent system now in place under the WTO has led to a rise in medicine and other health care costs in rich as well as poor countries. World Health Organization estimates show that pharmaceuticals account for up to 30 percent of health spending in transitional economies and anywhere from a quarter to two-thirds in developing countries. "In some developing countries, medicines are the largest health expense for poor households," according to the agency.[32]

The global inequality in the distribution of health care is just one the many consequences of the stranglehold this complex has on the health policy worldwide. If in the South, its influence is reflected in the lack of access to medicines, in much of the North, it results in over-prescription and increasing "medicalization" of every human trait, behavior and condition.

In his 1976 manifesto, *Medical Nemesis,* Austrian philosopher and priest Ivan Illich subjected modern medicine to scathing criticism. He detailed how technological medicine and medical intervention are having a detrimental effect on public health. Illich and other influential critics of the modern medical profession have documented how "medicalization"—the process by which everyday behavior has been turned into medical conditions—has been used as an instrument of control by those within the health care profession. Even when diseases can be cured without expensive medicines and technological intervention, patients are subjected to these methods, turning Illich's worst nightmare into a reality.[33]

Australian journalist Ray Moynihan and pharmaceutical policy expert Alan Cassels describe, in their book *Selling Sickness,* how more and more people are turned into patients by making the "ups and downs of daily life" mental disorders and transforming routine complaints "into frightening conditions":

> With promotional campaigns that exploit our deepest fears of death, decay and disease, the . . . pharmaceutical industry is literally changing what it means to be human. Rightly rewarded for saving life and reducing suffering, the global drug giants are no longer content selling medicines only to the ill. Because as Wall Street knows well, there's a lot of money to be made telling healthy people they're sick.[34]

Today, the "medicalization" of rich societies is so complete and thorough that prescription drugs have become part and parcel of the lives of a significant section of their populations. Over-prescription and over-medication lead to not just physical harm to patients, they also are a strain on their bottom line. Similarly stretching the individual and public resources is the practice of administrating a large number of tests—that are often deemed unnecessary—and other procedures on the healthy as well as the ill. Dan Merenstein, an assistant professor in the Department of Family Medicine at Georgetown

University, the lead author of a 2006 study conducted by researchers from Georgetown University Medical Center and Johns Hopkins University, argues that avoidable tests, besides costing millions (or even billions) of dollars, may also cause unnecessary patients stress and other harmful effects.[35]

Harmful and unnecessary, they may be. But they are good for the economic health and social power of the global medical industrial complex. In their book, *Critical Condition,* Donald L. Barlett and James B. Steele brilliantly illustrate how every segment within the medical industrial complex profits by making people sick. Browsing through various estimates of different ailments and conditions Americans are supposedly suffering from, as touted by the media, drug company commercials and studies by medical foundations, as well as universities and others in the health care community, the two legendary reporters point out that, if such numbers were true, there were more than 1.5 billion sick people in America—or five times the U.S. population. For instance, the American Heart Association says a third of the country's population has excessive cholesterol; Johns Hopkins Medical Institutions claim that 35 million Americans have irritable bowel syndrome. Other diseases include genital herpes: up to 60 million; GERD, or gastroesophageal reflux disease: 60 million; Incontinence: 25 million; hypertension: 50 million; sleep disorder: 70 million; obesity: 60 million; and restless legs syndrome: 12 million. These numbers, gross exaggerations as they are, serve the best interest of everyone, everyone except the public, Barlett and Steele write.

For drug companies that offer multiple pills for every affliction, real or imagined, they mean billions of dollars for their shareholders, which helps explain why pharmaceuticals are the country's most profitable businesses year in and year out. For doctors and hospitals, those inflated numbers mean billions more in revenue. For Madison Avenue, newspapers, magazines, television, and radio, they translate into billions in advertising dollars and commissions, as well as increased ratings and sales. For testing laboratories and manufacturers of expensive diagnostic equipment, such as MRI machines, they also result in billions more in sales. For special-interest groups, they reap billions of dollars as well in permanent funding for a bloated health care bureaucracy. For members of Congress, the diagnosis of mass affliction across society ultimately leads to campaign contributions and positive press as lawmakers appear to wage a perpetual crusade on behalf of the sick. For celebrities raising funds for their favorite disease, the medicalization of society means endless publicity and generous fees.[36]

The result of well-orchestrated propaganda tools like these studies that Barlett and Steele describe in their book, besides fattening the belly of the medical industrial complex, is that entire populations, especially in the developed world, are drugged from cradle to grave. They have managed to deeply entrench in people's psyches the dictum "A pill for every ill," which entails a continuous rise in drug sales. The phenomenon is most visible in the United States, where drug sales as a percentage of GDP tripled in the past 20 years. Pharmacists dispensed a staggering 3.8 billion prescriptions[37] in the country in 2008, which is more than 12 prescriptions for every man, woman and child in the country that year. This is in addition to the countless vitamins and other nutritional supplements Americans are consuming on a daily basis. But again, it's not just Americans that are consuming drugs like there is no tomorrow. Global drug sales have also been increasing steadily. They doubled to $773 billion in 2008 from $393 in 2001, according to the pharmaceutical industry research firm IMS Health.[38]

Of course, the administration of drugs into the human body in such huge quantities is not without consequences of various kinds. Thus, a recent report by the Florida Medical Examiners Commission concluded that more Americans die by prescription drugs than illegal drugs. The organization analyzed 168,900 autopsies in Florida in 2007 and found that the number of people killed by legal drugs was three times more than by cocaine, heroin and all methamphetamines put together.[39] But such findings that go against the grain of the conventional wisdom perpetuated by the health care industry hardly find any takers. The economic rationale behind the medical industrial complex dictates that drug consumption is encouraged, no matter at what cost, whether human or economic.

ANTITHETICAL TO PUBLIC HEALTH

Like other global complexes, the medical industrial complex is inherently structured to act against the common good. If one needs any proof of that, Exhibit A is the multitrillion dollar United States health care system. After the corporate health care interests ran it lock, stock and barrel for decades, the world's largest health care system is in shambles today. Despite the country spending $2.2 trillion on health care (which is more than the 2009 nominal gross domestic product of any other country on the planet, except Japan, China, Germany and France)[40], more than 46 million Americans remain uninsured in the country.[41] As many as 5 million of them have "pre-existing conditions," or medical conditions that would exclude them from having insurance under the commercial insurance system. Individuals with "pre-existing conditions," unlike the relatively healthy, will almost certainly cost insurance firms a lot of money; hence the companies routinely decline to insure them. (Though the health care legislation signed by President Obama last March tried to address this issue, many have pointed out that the new law doesn't stop insurance firms from limiting coverage claims.)

Two demographic groups with substantial numbers of uninsured are the working poor and the unemployed. In 2007, one-third of people under 65 years of age with a family income below 200 percent of the poverty line were uninsured for at least part of the 12 months, the U.S. Department of Health and Human Services' 2009 annual report on trends in health statistics revealed.[42] (For an average family of five, 200 percent of federal poverty threshold in 2007 was just over $50,000; the poverty threshold for a family of that size for that year was $25,080)[43] Among ethnic groups, Hispanics, American Indians and African Americans have been and remain the most affected. Almost one-third of the Hispanic population and almost two-fifths of American Indian and Alaska Native persons were uninsured in 2007.[44]

What being uninsured in America means is that one is less likely to receive health services. The report found that more than a fifth of the uninsured population had not received needed medical care.[45] Studies have shown that uninsured people not only receive less preventive care but often are diagnosed at more advanced disease stages, and even when they are diagnosed, they receive less therapeutic care than those with insurance coverage. A study published in the November 2009 issue of the *American Journal of Public Health* found that a lack of health insurance contributed to nearly 45,000 deaths in the country each year (or one death every 12 minutes).[46] Higher uninsurance rates are reflected in a higher rate of mortalities among black Americans.[47] High uninsurance rates have societal costs, too. In communities with high rates of uninsurance, public resources for disease prevention and surveillance programs are diverted to pay for uncompensated medical care.[48]

Another result of the medical industrial complex driving health care policy is high health care costs. From prescription drugs to hospital visits to lab tests, almost every aspect of U.S. health care has become prohibitively expensive, driving up the overall price of maintaining one's health. Home to the largest drug industry in the world, every year U.S. taxpayers further bankroll drug research to the tune of billions of dollars. Yet, Americans pay more for their medicines than people anywhere else in the world. The culprit is the U.S. free-market health care system. Because there are no price regulations (unlike some other industrialized nations) on pharmaceutical products, companies are able to sell their drugs at costs that they alone determine to be fair.

Inefficiency is another hallmark of U.S. health care. Often advocates of capitalism take pride in the system's efficiency. But "efficiency" is one of the last words one would associate with American health care. The Congressional Budget Office, the agency tasked with supplying economic data to Congress, estimates that "nearly 5 percent of GDP—or roughly $700 billion each year—goes to health care spending that cannot be shown to improve health outcomes."[49] These are just a few of the many symptoms of the seriously ailing American health system.

In the run-up to the passage of the recent Patient Protection and Affordable Care Act, the country was subjected to one of the most bitter and divisive legislative debates in its history. Even though there was hardly a soul in the country who thought the health care system was not broken and didn't need fixing, President Obama's attempt to overhaul it was met with huge resistance at the grassroots level. Much of this opposition was orchestrated by those health care interests that feared that the new law would affect their profit margin and their right-wing allies. In the end, the legislation, which would expand health insurance coverage to poor and lower middle-class Americans, was a watered-down version of what Obama initially proposed. One of the provisions dropped was a proposal to set up a government-run agency that would compete with private health insurers. If created, such an agency would have had the effect of stabilizing health insurance costs, but it was killed by the champions of insurance industry within Congress. The White House also made similar concessions to the drug industry and the influential American Medical Association, which represents physicians and medical students. Invariably, the law, touted as the most far-reaching social legislation of the past half a century, contained plenty of goodies to these groups. To begin with, by ensuring that millions more are insured, it is set to expand their markets significantly.

Nevertheless, the fact that a U.S. president had dared to take on part of the medical industrial complex caused him to suffer politically, at least in the short term. Obama, however, was not the first American politician to find that attempting to fix health care has political costs. Bill Clinton experienced it at the beginning of his presidency in the early 1990s, when his attempt to reform health care damaged his presidency. .

What the perennially broken U.S. health care system and the recent, acrimonious legislative attempt to reform it once again reveal is this: if America offers a compelling case for weakening, or even dismantling the medical industrial complex, it also presents documentary evidence of how deeply ensconced the complex is and how difficult it would be to defeat it on a global stage.

NOTES

1. World Health Organization, "Infectious diseases are the biggest killer of the young," www.who.int/infectious-disease-report/pages/ch1text.html (accessed February 23, 2010).

2. Essential medicines, as defined by WHO, are "those that satisfy the priority health care needs of the population." There are well over 300 drugs on the agency's current list. But those who advocate a community-based health care paradigm

health care co. profit b/c its $ gne
For Profits Not Care.

challenge the WHO framework which focuses more on "essential" pharmaceuticals and medical technologies and prescribes more or less the same remedy that the medical industrial complex sells. They call for more participatory and alternative modes of medicine that have greater community integrity.

3. "UC Atlas of Global Inequality," ucatlas.ucsc.edu/health.php (accessed February 23, 2010)

4. Sam Perlo-Freeman, Catalina Perdomo, Elisabeth Sköns and Petter Stålenheim, "Military expenditure," *Stockholm International Peace Research Year Book 2009*, www.sipri.org/yearbook/2009/05 (accessed February 23, 2010).

5. "The Fortune 500's Biggest Winners," *CNN*, money.cnn.com/galleries/2009/fortune/0904/gallery.f500_mostprofitable.fortune/6.html (accessed February 23, 2010).

6. "The Fortune 500's Biggest Winners," *CNN*.

7. "The Fortune 500's Biggest Winners," *CNN*.

8. They are Cardinal Health (18th), CVS Caremark (19th), Johnson and Johnson (29th), WellPoint (32nd), Walgreens (36th), Medco Health Solutions (45th), and Pfizer (46th), *CNN*, money.cnn.com/magazines/fortune/fortune500/2009/full_list/ (accessed February 23, 2010).

9. Fortune 500 Annual Ranking of America's Corporations, money.cnn.com/magazines/fortune/fortune500/2009/industries/ (Accessed February 23, 2010).

10. "Top Therapeutic Classes by U.S. Sales, *IMS Health*, www.imshealth.com/deployedfiles/imshealth/Global/Content/StaticFile/Top_Line_Data/2008_Top_Therapy_Classes_by_U.S._Sales.pdf (accessed February 23, 2010).

11. "Top 15 Global Corporations," *IMS Health*, www.imshealth.com/deployed files/imshealth/Global/Content/StaticFile/Top_Line_Data/Global-Top_15_Companies .pdf (accessed February 23, 2010)

12. See www.gpoaccess.gov/USbudget/fy10/pdf/summary.pdf (accessed July 15, 2010).

13. Barbara Ehrenreich, "The Medical-Industrial Complex," *The New York Review of Books* 15, no. 11 (December 17, 1970).

14. "National Health Expenditures Aggregate, Per Capita Amounts, Percent Distribution, and Average Annual Percent Growth, by Source of Funds: Selected Calendar Years 1960–2008," www.cms.hhs.gov/NationalHealthExpendData/downloads/tables.pdf (accessed February 23, 2010).

15. Center for Responsive Politics, www.opensecrets.org/ (accessed February 23, 2010).

16. M. Asif Ismail, "Drug Lobby Second to None," projects.publicintegrity.org/rx/report.aspx?aid=723 (accessed February 23, 2010).

17. Nelson D. Schwartz, "Rumsfeld's growing stake in Tamiflu," money.cnn.com/2005/10/31/news/newsmakers/fortune_rumsfeld/ (accessed July 14, 2010).

18. Barbara Ehrenreich, "The Medical-Industrial Complex."

19. Barbara Ehrenreich, "The Medical-Industrial Complex."

20. Dr. Relman's use of the term was very narrow. What he meant by "the medical industrial complex" was "a large and growing network of private corporations engaged in the business of supplying health-care services to patients for a profit—services

heretofore provided by nonprofit institutions or individual practitioners." He specifically excluded drug and medical equipment manufacturers and suppliers from it, arguing that they "have been around for a long time, and no one has seriously challenged their social usefulness." Ehrenreich, on the other hand, considered a whole gamut of private and public enterprises from doctors to hospitals, from drug and device-makers to insurance firms, and even health systems and consulting and accounting firms, part of the medical industrial complex.

21. Marcia Angell, "The Truth about the Drug Companies," *The New York Review of Books* 51, no. 12 (July 15, 2004).

22. Donald L. Barlett and James B. Steele, *Critical Condition: How Health Care in America Became Big Business and Bad Medicine* (New York, NY: Doubleday, 2004), 76–77.

23. "NIH-Private Sector Partnership in the Development of Taxol," *GAO Report,* www.gao.gov/htext/d03829.html (accessed February 23, 2010).

24. Eeva Ollila, "Global Health Priorities—Priorities of the Wealthy?" *Globalization and Health,* www.globalizationandhealth.com/content/1/1/6 (accessed February 23, 2010).

25. Giovanni Andrea Cornia, Richard Jolly, Francis Stewart, eds., *Adjustment With a Human Face* (New York, NY: Oxford University Press, 1987), 34.

26. "Structural Adjustment Programmes (SAPs)," World Health Organization, www.who.int/trade/glossary/story084/en/index.html (accessed February 23, 2010).

27. Pfizer was one of the co-founders of the Intellectual Protection Committee, a business coalition formed in 1986 to lobby on patent issues. Merck was also part of the coalition, which was instrumental in making intellectual property rights a key part of U.S. trade policy. Pfizer, in fact, claims credit for the existence of a global intellectual property regime. "Pfizer, together with other members of the Intellectual Property Committee (IPC), worked very closely with U.S. negotiators, the Congress, and with our private sector counterparts in Europe and Japan to develop a GATT agreement that would contain adequate and effective intellectual property protection," the company's senior assistant general counsel, Peter C. Richardson, said in a May 1994 congressional testimony.

28. The WTO, though, does allow parallel importation—the importing of products from another country without the approval of the intellectual property owner—and the compulsory licensing of drugs during public health emergencies. (Under the latter, a national government can force a drug company to hand over a particular entity for large-scale production during crises.) But in the eyes of Big Pharma and the U.S. and other Western governments that backed it, the epidemic was not a public health emergency.

29. "Malaria," World Health Organization, www.who.int/mediacentre/factsheets/fs094/en/index.html (accessed February 23, 2010).

30. "The need for a vaccine," Malaria Vaccines Initiative, www.malariavaccine.org/malvac-need-for-vaccine.php (accessed February 23, 2010).

31. "Country Comparison: Life Expectancy at Birth," *CIA World Fact Book,* www .cia.gov/library/publications/the-world-factbook/rankorder/2102rank.html (accessed February 23, 2010).

32. "Facts on essential medicine," World Health Organization, www.who.int/ features/factfiles/essential_medicines/essential_medicines_facts/en/index1.html (accessed February 23, 2010).

33. Ivan Illich, *Medical Nemesis* (New York, NY: Pantheon, 1976).

34. Ray Moynihan and Alan Cassels, *Selling Sickness* (New York, NY: Nation Books, 2005), ix-x.

35. "Millions Squandered in Unnecessary Tests Ordered in Routine Doctor Visits," explore.georgetown.edu/news/?ID=15536&PageTemplateID=295 (accessed February 23, 2010).

36. Donald L. Barlett and James B. Steele, Critical Condition: How Health Care in America Became Big Business and Bad Medicine (New York, NY: Doubleday, 2004), 195–198.

37. Top Corporations by U.S. Dispensed Prescriptions," *IMS Health,* www .imshealth.com/deployedfiles/imshealth/Global/Content/StaticFile/Top_Line_ Data/2008_Top_Corp_by_U.S._RXs.pdf (accessed February 23, 2010)

38. "Global Pharmaceutical Sales, 2001—2008," *IMS Health,* www.imshealth .com/deployedfiles/imshealth/Global/Content/StaticFile/Top_Line_Data/Global_ Pharma_Sales_2001–2008_Version_2.pdf (accessed February 23, 2010).

39. Damien Cave, "Legal Drugs Kill Far More Than Illegal, Florida Says," *New York Times,* www.nytimes.com/2008/06/14/us/14florida.htm (accessed February 23, 2010).

40. "GDP (official exchange rate)," *CIA World Fact Book,* www.cia.gov/library/ publications/the-world-factbook/fields/2195.html (accessed February 23, 2010).

41. "Income, Poverty, and Health Insurance Coverage in the United States: 2008," *U.S. Census Bureau,* www.census.gov/prod/2009pubs/p60–236.pdf (accessed February 22, 2010).

42. U.S. Center for Disease Control, *Health, United States, 2009,* www.cdc.gov/ nchs/data/hus/hus09.pdf (accessed February 22, 2010).

43. US Census Bureau website, www.census.gov/hhes/www/poverty/data/ threshld/thresh07.html (accessed July 13, 2010).

44. U.S. Center for Disease Control, *Health, United States, 2009.*

45. U.S. Center for Disease Control, *Health, United States, 2009.*

46. "45,000 American deaths associated with lack of insurance," *CNN,* www.cnn .com/2009/HEALTH/09/18/deaths.health.insurance/ (accessed February 22, 2010).

47. U.S. Center for Disease Control, *Health, United States, 2009.* It was revealed herein that overall mortality was 25 percent higher for black Americans than for white Americans in 2007. The age-adjusted death rates for African Americans exceeded those for whites by 48 percent for stroke, 31 percent for heart disease, 21 percent for cancer, 113 percent for diabetes, and 786 percent for HIV disease; www.cdc.gov/ nchs/data/hus/hus09.pdf#highlights (accessed July 15, 2010).

48. National Center for Biotechnology Information, "News and Notes: Community Consequences of Lack of Health Insurance," www.ncbi.nlm.nih.gov/pmc/articles/ PMC1497563/pdf/12884852.pdf (accessed February 22, 2010).

49. Peter R. Orszag, "Opportunities to Increase Efficiency in Health Care" (statement at the Health Reform Summit of the Committee on Finance, United States Senate, on June 16, 2008), 4, www.cbo.gov/ftpdocs/93xx/doc9384/06–16-HealthSummit. pdf (accessed February 22, 2010).

Chapter Eleven

College Sports

It's All about the Money!

Earl Smith and Angela Hattery

Spending on sports at the average school in the NCAA's top-tier Football Bowl Subdivision went from a little more than $31 million in 2004 to $42.2 million in 2007, the most recent year covered in the report.[1]

INTRODUCTION

The contemporary institution of intercollegiate sport is all about money. Money has become central to the administration and sustainability of intercollegiate athletics. Athletic directors make salaries on par with university presidents (or higher) and coaches in the high profile sports of football and men's basketball make 5, 10, and even 20 times more than the average college professor on the same campus. College and university athletic budgets are exorbitant and stretch into all aspects of sport, but especially coaching salaries, stadiums, and recruiting. We refer to this as the Athletic Industrial Complex (AIC).[2]

THE ATHLETIC INDUSTRIAL COMPLEX

We use the term Athletic Industrial Complex (AIC) in the same manner that sociologist C. Wright Mills and former President Dwight Eisenhower used the term "Military Industrial Complex."[3] The term AIC refers to the fact that intercollegiate athletics is now firmly embedded into other economic institutions, from the hotel and entertainment industry to construction to clothing and transportation. We argue here that the primary mechanism that drives the

233

exploitation of student athletes, the mechanism that plants them firmly in the "periphery" of the economics of intercollegiate sport, is the AIC. The AIC is about more than just the exploitation of student athletes, however. It is an institution embedded in both higher education and the global sports economy and as such it has the power to shape hegemonic ideology and collude with other institutions in the enterprise of sports. For example, every Memorial Day weekend in the United States NASCAR partners with the military to recognize the contributions of military personnel. Similarly, on Thanksgiving and Christmas the sports programs often "advertise" that the NFL or NBA games we are watching while we eat our turkey or unwrap our gifts are being broadcast through the generosity of sports networks like ESPN to our troops in Iraq and Afghanistan. This collusion furthers both the dominance of the ideology of the AIC as well as the expansion of global sports markets. Perhaps the most compelling case comes from the story of Pat Tillman who left his "job" as a professional football player and enlisted in the military to serve his country after 9/11. Tillman was killed in Afghanistan in what would become a highly controversial event, primarily because the military lied about the details of his death only revealing after significant pressure from his family the fact that Tillman was killed by "friendly fire" by a unit in which his brother was serving. The Tillman family claims that the government has still not been totally honest about the circumstances surrounding his death. Perhaps what makes the "sting" even greater is the fact that the U.S. government, including then President George Bush, hailed Tillman's courageous decision to leave sports and enter the military. His picture and story were plastered everywhere, and his family now feels that he was taken advantage of in life and ignored in death.[4]

One of the key features of the AIC is the global expansion of both professional and intercollegiate sports. For a variety of reasons—our status as professors on a college campus who witness aspects of the AIC in higher education nearly every day as well as our belief that the college sports are often diametrically opposed to the primary mission of colleges and universities—our chapter will focus primarily on intercollegiate athletics and provide evidence for invoking the term "Athletic Industrial Complex" when referring to intercollegiate sport. That said, before we dive in to this discussion it is important to note, albeit briefly, the fact that the AIC's power and influence stretches from little league sports programs all the way through the ranks of professional sports. And, it is in the professional ranks where the vastness of the AIC is witnessed. For example, at the time of the writing of this chapter there is a debate in the United States over the fact that the 2014 Super Bowl will be played in New York—actually in New Jersey. Because the Super

Bowl will be played in February, opponents of this decision argue that fans won't want to come and spend money because Super Bowl fans—especially those from the populous northern cities like New York and Chicago—look forward to attending the Super Bowl somewhere in the sunbelt where they will be assured warm, sunny weather. The proponents of the decision argue that the decision is not about anything other than money and that (1) the majority of viewers of the Super Bowl who the advertisers pay to reach will not attend the game anyway, they'll be watching it on TV in the comfort of their own homes, and (2) corporations will continue to pay for luxury boxes for their executives regardless of the weather and location of the Super Bowl. And, proponents suggest that the rental of luxury boxes will be enhanced by the fact that the game will be played in a new, billion dollar stadium, with luxury boxes outfitted with all of the latest amenities. Furthermore, we can speculate that the NFL's interest in promoting interest in American football abroad—particularly in Western Europe where they stage exhibition games every year—may be tied to the decision to hold the Super Bowl in New York. Europeans who have been courted and cultivated by the NFL would likely see the chance to combine a vacation to New York City with the opportunity to attend the Super Bowl as a "win-win" and thus the NFL may boost the attendance of wealthy Europeans and thus open additional doors of opportunity to expand interest and viewership in Europe.

When it comes to understanding intercollegiate sports and the issues of money, we argue that Immanuel Wallerstein's World Systems Theory, modified slightly herein, is useful in helping us to understand the global expansion of intercollegiate athletics and other aspects of the AIC, including stadiums and locker rooms, recruiting, and coaches' salaries. Finally, we conclude with an analysis of the relationship between the AIC and winning championships by examining football expenditures on Division 1 campuses (the Football Bowl Subdivision) and the likelihood of winning the national championship or playing in a BCS (Bowl Championship Series) bowl. We begin with a brief overview of the theoretical lens we employ for this discussion: Wallerstein's World Systems Theory.

THEORETICAL LENS: WORLD SYSTEMS THEORY

In 1974, Immanuel Wallerstein published his revolutionary grand theory which he termed "World Systems Theory." In short, Wallerstein's theory divides up the world into three parts, the "core," the "semi-periphery" and the "periphery." The relationships among these three groups of countries shape everything from geo-politics (war) to the movement of goods and services and even people. As a neo-Marxist theory, World Systems theory assumes that these relationships are based on inequality, particularly with regards to power and resources, and just as was the relationship between Marx's bourgeoisie and proletariat, this relationship is characterized by exploitation of those nations in the semi-periphery and periphery by those nations in the core.

So, briefly, the U.S. has oil interests in the major producing oil nations in the Middle East. Relations between the U.S. and a semi-peripheral nation, such as Saudi Arabia, may involve exploitation that is focused on managing the flow of oil toward the U.S. and away from other nations. Relations between the U.S. and peripheral nations, such as Iraq, are not only highly exploitative, but the U.S. government is confident in waging war with a peripheral nation like Iraq and seeking an occupational arrangement in order to increase exploitation through augmenting its own access to oil while limiting the access of semi-peripheral nations such as China. Finally, the countries in the semi-periphery may exploit those in the periphery—Saudi Arabia is able to dictate much about the implementation of conservative Islamic law in nations such as Pakistan and Afghanistan. Yet, when it was threatened by Iraq during the invasion of Kuwait, core nations such as the U.S. and many European Union (EU) nations stepped up its defense. In this model, exploitation is unidirectional. These different strategies, U.S.-Saudi Arabia and U.S.-Iraq and configurations, Saudi Arabia's relationship with its neighbors, can be understood using Wallerstein's model.

We argue that a modification of Wallerstein's theory, in which the "core" is the NCAA, the "semi-periphery" are the individual athletic departments at colleges and universities, and the "periphery" are the student athletes themselves, allows us to understand with more precision the role of money in intercollegiate athletics and the explosion of the AIC.

With this basic overview of Wallerstein's World Systems theory and our adaptation of it, we turn now to the empirical evidence that in fact the AIC exists, that it is increasing, and that it has in effect hijacked the university—or university athletics at a minimum—such that money and profit are the key motives driving intercollegiate athletics.

GLOBAL EXPANSION

There are at least three key ways in which intercollegiate athletics, shepherded by the NCAA, has become part of the global economy: (1) recruiting

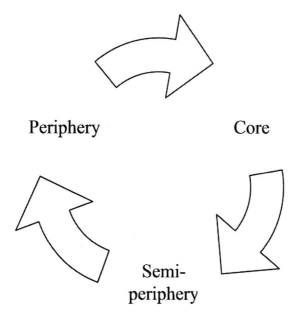

Periphery   Core

Semi-
periphery

Figure 11.1. Wallerstein's Model of World Systems Theory

international athletes, (2) playing contests abroad, and (3) extensive television broadcasts that allow for games to be carried all over the country and indeed the world. Here we address each separately.

Recruiting International Athletes

Recruiting international athletes has been going on since at least the 1970s, and though it has increased over time—according to the NCAA more than 16,000 international student athletes compete in American colleges and universities, more than 70 percent in Division 1 institutions—its effect is felt mostly in non-revenue generating sports like tennis, golf, and track & field. However, in the last ten years, the rosters of intercollegiate basketball teams have swelled with international athletes.[5, 6]

Recruiting international athletes (rather than international students) undermines the mission of the university because these students receive admission and funding that would otherwise go to American students. This is particularly important for state and land-grant universities that have as their mission the education of the citizens of the state. As such, they are required, in most

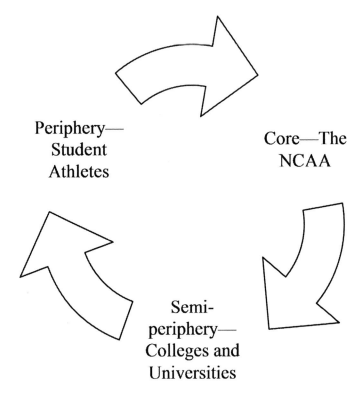

Periphery—
Student
Athletes

Core—The
NCAA

Semi-
periphery—
Colleges and
Universities

Figure 11.2.   Smith-Hattery's Intercollegiate Systems Theory

cases, to admit at least 80 percent of their freshman class from residents of the state and the tuition for out of state students is generally set at twice the rate charged to in-state students. Thus, when international students are admitted and counted against the remaining 20 percent that is open for out of state there are fewer seats available for out of state American students. In addition to the issue of admissions, there is also the matter of funding, in this case athletic scholarships. The genesis of the controversy in the 1970s was located in NCAA track and field. One of the most recent debates has centered on American universities recruiting international tennis players—who played on the international tennis circuit and earned a living doing so—and giving them scholarships to play tennis as "amateurs."[7] This matter came to the attention of the first author recently when one of the students enrolled in his class on immigration was complaining about the number of international students on the golf team. As a member of the team she had a bird's eye view of the resources she witnessed going to international golfers who had

(1) made money as professionals before coming to college, (2) in her words could not even really speak English, and (3) thus had no interest in a college education but only wanted to play intercollegiate golf as a stepping stone in their golf careers. Meanwhile she lamented the fact that there were many American golfers from her own state who would have been grateful for a college scholarship and the opportunity to get a college education at a prestigious university but to whom offers did not come because the spots on the teams were already filled by international student athletes. Popp, Hums and Greenwell studied 174 international student athletes from 49 different countries and confirm that though some were highly motivated by the educational opportunities made available to them in the universities they attended, their motivations for and expectations of playing sports in an American university were markedly different than their native born counterparts'.[8]

The argument here is not an ethnocentric one. We are not suggesting that the intellectual climate of the university would not be enhanced by the presence of international students. We believe it would be. But, these student athletes—who play a variety of sports but most often tennis and golf—are not necessarily here to engage and enrich the intellectual climate. They are here to participate in intercollegiate sports, an activity that dominates their time and energy. In fact, as professors we see this played out each and every semester. Though we have international student athletes in our classes and perhaps their very presence enriches the intellectual climate, in our experience we note that they are rarely if ever involved in international issues or clubs on campus, they are not present at events highlighting international issues, and so on. Additionally, though most people assume that the students missing the most class are those playing the high profile sports of football and men's basketball, in fact it is the tennis and golf players who miss the most class primarily as a result of the extensive and often international travel associated with their teams. For example, in the fall of 2009, the women's golf team at Wake Forest traveled for two weeks (missing 10 class days) to Japan to play a tournament. This extensive travel more or less prohibits any golfer—American or an international athlete—from participating in the central mission of the University. And, the money we spend to bring these athletes here is money we cannot spend to bring international *students* into our colleges and universities, a move that most certainly would enhance the intellectual climate on campus.

Furthermore, the recruiting of international athletes to play golf, tennis, and basketball depletes resources and undermines the primary mission of the university: which for public universities is to provide access to higher education for the state's population[9]. The logic behind recruiting international athletes is simply to increase the odds of winning a championship, thus increasing the money that flows into the athletic department, not serving the higher education needs of the states' citizenry. Popp, Hums and Greenwell note that recruiters who are increasingly recruiting internationally would be more successful if they understood some of the differences between sports in the United States and sports in most other countries. For example, their promise of winning a Big 10 or ACC championship—which is often highly persuasive for American students—is generally more or less meaningless for international athletes. However, emphasizing the opportunity to train in top facilities with top coaches in preparation to represent their home countries in the next Olympics would be a successful pitch for many international athletes.

Intercollegiate Contests Abroad

Two schools, the University of Wisconsin and Michigan State, several hours apart by bus and separated by just a short airline flight, traveled to Tokyo in 1992 to play a regular season football game that could have been played in either Madison or East Lansing. There are no club or professional "American football" teams in Japan—in fact, the Japanese do not even play American-style football. Why then would two Big Ten schools travel 10,000 miles during the academic year to play a football game? The most compelling explanation is that the NCAA is interested in increasing its fan base and TV market, so they concoct these international games in places as far away as Japan.[10] Though perhaps there is some argument to be made that a global presence enhances the reputation or image of a university or perhaps appeals to alumni living abroad, these goals are generally achieved through others means including featuring study abroad programs and international research in alumni magazines, hosting international alumni travel tours and so on. Athletic departments stand to make the most money when they host home games, particularly against rivals or as was the situation in this case in competing for a conference title and a bowl berth. In these cases they sell out stadiums, they sell concessions, they sell team paraphernalia and they generate donations from their alumni who were unable to attend the contest but watched it eagerly on television. Thus, it appears that the driving force behind this decision was the NCAA—which controls all of the scheduling of competitions—rather than the two individual institutions.

This globalization of sports follows the model of corporate expansion,[11] thus wresting even more control of intercollegiate athletics away from the institutions and placing that control in the hands of marketing and advertising executives who are not interested in higher education but rather are only intent on increasing profits from sports.

We note that there are many noble reasons for taking student athletes abroad that are in line with the educational mission of the university: cultural exchange and study abroad are now key elements of many institutions of higher learning. However, the Tokyo Bowl, typical of international intercollegiate contests, bears little resemblance to any study abroad program. While in Tokyo, the athletes were required to attend practice, eat the food ordered by the coaching staff, and prepare for the football game.[12] In this case, the game had special importance because it determined the Big Ten champion and a berth in the Rose Bowl. Thus, there was little, if any, educational value in this experience. Furthermore, we note that the football game took place during the final exam period at the University of Wisconsin and as a result, individual faculty were required to reschedule exams for the football players in their classes—yet another example of the athletic department setting the schedule for the university.

Television Contracts[13]

A critical part of global expansion and the AIC is the relationship that the NCAA and various athletic conferences, such as the Big Ten, Big East, and ACC, have with the media. The right to televise an athletic contest, specifically football and men's basketball, brings millions of dollars to the "core." Beginning a decade or so ago, the contracts between media outlets and the "core" institutions (NCAA and power conferences) began to spiral out of control. By 2002, the multi-year contract between CBS and the NCAA for the exclusive rights to broadcast the men's basketball tournament, March Madness and the Final Four, rose to $8 billion, an increase of nearly *$1 billion per year.*

The contracts are so lucrative that the media are allowed to exercise control over the athletic schedule. For example, it is the television contracts that dictate that men's basketball games will be played, and thus televised, nearly every night of the week. As a consequence, student athletes miss class to travel to and from games. Though some coaches, including Lloyd Carr (formerly at Michigan) and Bobby Knight (formerly at Indiana University and Texas Tech), have resisted the scheduling of weeknight games and games that interrupt the academic schedule, the contracts are just too lucrative to be denied.[14] This is yet another example of the way in which intercollegiate athletics, in this case via the direction of the NCAA, has influenced the university calendar. This is in line with the type of relationship Wallerstein describes. Just as Saudi Arabia exerts influence over Islamic law in Afghanistan, and many women and children have seen their rights erode as a result, the NCAA exhibits control over the university calendar and it is most often the student athletes themselves who suffer. Finally, we conclude this section by noting that part of what drives the lucrative television contracts and their influence over universities is the global expansion of sports markets. We turn now to an examination of a set of relationships among the NCAA, athletic departments, and a series of institutions that together constitute the AIC.

Consistent with the search for student athletes globally and the need to build international audiences for college sports—which often work in tandem—is the necessity for athletic programs to adopt a corporate model to upgrade facilities (such as locker rooms and stadiums) to compete in the highly competitive recruitment "game" in which sophisticated student athletes are well aware of their needs for special amenities. Second, in order to respond to, expand, and retain a fan base that has become accustomed to luxury accommodations, athletic departments must build and remodel stadiums and other facilities to meet the needs of the demanding customers. For example, the University of Maryland plays football at Chevy Chase Bank Field at Byrd Stadium per a 25-year, $20 million naming-rights agreement that helped finance new luxury suites and other upgrades to the stadium.[15] Moreover, the customers for such amenities are no longer the students of the university who have come to cheer on the team; they are members of the local business and professional classes who attend the games and then donate from their coffers to the ever needy athletic department, not the university more widely.[16] For example, at our university the student section at the football stadium remains where it has always been; the $42 million dollar "upgrade" to the stadium created luxury boxes and suites paid for by local entrepreneurial magnets who are also big donors to the university. We can guess that most students have never been in the Flow Lexus Suite though many a student's parents have purchased vehicles from this donor mogul. These multiple concerns fuel the increasingly competitive AIC.

For instance, many Division 1A institutions have instituted or undertaken new stadium building projects.[17, 18] Though the trend follows the mantra that bigger is better, a new strategy has emerged: building and remodeling stadiums to seat *fewer* spectators. Why would an athletic department want a facility that seats fewer spectators? For programs that struggle with low attendance, such as Princeton and Stanford, reducing the seating in the stadium accomplishes two goals: (1) it makes the stadium "feel fuller" and (2) it drives up the demand for the seats, thus allowing the athletic department to sell more season tickets and to charge more for each ticket. The cost to "downsize" the Stanford stadium: $100 million.[19]

Recent data[20] illustrate the average costs of facilities (stadiums and locker rooms) for Division 1A football programs.[21] Though several teams report spending nothing on facilities, other programs report spending in the millions, with Ohio State leading the pack at more than $13 million spent on football facilities in 2006. The average in the highest spending conference, the Big Ten, was nearly $3 million. Finally, the ratio (computed by dividing the highest costs by the lowest, for each conference) reveals that there are enormous discrepancies in spending on facilities by conference, including in the Big Ten.[22]

Facilities construction (stadiums and locker rooms) provides a clear illustration of the ways in which the AIC is at work. Athletic departments are no longer building or remodeling stadiums with attention to the needs of the university or student body. Rather, these construction projects, funded in part by university funds, are focused entirely around the needs of the athletic department. Specifically, athletic departments are approaching stadium building with an eye for appeasing donors and potential donors as well as with a focus on making money. We can assume, for example, that shrinking the size of the Stanford stadium will have a negative impact on the number of seats available for students, who are largely non-paying and non-donating (at least until they become alumni).

This clearly illustrates not only the focus of the athletic department *away* from the needs of the university and its mission but also illuminates the fact that athletic departments are organized almost entirely like businesses that seek to maximize profit regardless of the impact on the university. We also note that on our own campus, faculty and staff who want to hold events in the meeting and dining facilities in the new $42 million dollar football stadium must pay fees that start at several hundreds of thousands of dollars. In contrast, academic units are not allowed to charge fees to other academic units, administrative units, or even the athletic department when they want to hold meetings in our seminar spaces and classrooms. Finally, we note that these building projects pour literally tens of millions of dollars into the local construction economy, thus further embedding athletics into the wider institutional complex, the AIC.[23]

The Costs of Travel and Hosting Home Games

Athletic contests "on the road" obviously cost the institutions financially. Airline fares, hotels, and food for coaches and athletes are a major portion of the athletic department's budget. In fact, on *our own campus,* the cost of the charter plane for the men's basketball team is approximately $35,000 *per round-trip flight.* Adding the cost of hotels and food, we estimate the cost of each away game for men's basketball at $40,000 minimum. With 10 away games per year this cost alone accounts for nearly a half a million dollars.[24] Clearly the cost of away games for the football team is significantly higher, despite the fact that they are far more likely to travel using commercial airlines or busses, because the team is significantly bigger. At least 75 people, players, coaches, other staff, athletic department "friends" and family members travel to each away football game. We note that during the year we spent teaching in a non-BCS Division 1 school, in response to the recession that began in late 2007 and early 2008, the athletic director issued a missive in which he severely limited the costs associated with travel by requiring all teams to cut their travel squads, to travel on the smallest vehicles possible—for example using vans instead of buses—and sleeping 4 rather than 2 student athletes per hotel room. This move reinforces the argument that travel costs contribute significantly to the burgeoning athletic budgets and these costs can be cut, presumably with little impact on the competitive nature of the teams; this is precisely the type of issue that is at the core of our argument regarding the AIC.

Furthermore, consistent with the AIC, many football teams have adopted a policy of housing the football team off campus in hotels the night before *home games.* The estimated cost of housing football teams for home games can run in the range of $6,000 per home game or upwards of $50,000 to $65,000 for the home game portion of the season.

When this practice is questioned, the explanations tend to fall into two main themes: social control and bonding. The social control rationale is that football players will get into trouble the night before the game if they are not separated from the campus-at-large and monitored. The bonding rationale is that segregating the team from the rest of the campus and housing the players together is necessary for team bonding, sort of like when 7th grade girls or boys get a chance to stay in a hotel together as part of a birthday party or club sport. We note that most of the football players live together anyway, sharing dorm rooms and apartments off campus, so we are not certain why this special type of bonding experience is needed before the Saturday home game. And, apparently others are beginning to question the practice as well. In the financial crisis of the last few years, with universities suffering in excess of 20 percent losses in their endowments, and universities regularly demanding across-the-board 5 percent budget cuts, some athletic departments have decided to suspend this practice. To our knowledge, this is limited to teams in the mid-major conference, and is not a phenomenon found in the major football conferences or at the powerhouse programs. The data confirm that athletic departments spend millions of dollars in travel and on the cost of hosting home football games. At the high end, Ohio State spent $2.75 million on football team travel and $7.8 million on football game expenses for a total of $10 million in 2005.

We have argued in this section that athletic departments are now deeply embedded in other social institutions and that this web can be characterized as the Athletic Industrial Complex similar to the Military Industrial Complex described by C. Wright Mills and former U.S. President Dwight Eisenhower. Intercollegiate athletics has moved away from a mission that is focused on providing athletic outlets for college students to a mission that is simply about making money. We turn now to a discussion of the ways in which the NCAA and athletic departments ("the core") have come to resemble a colonizer that has invaded a "host" country (the college or university) and is extracting resources from it and exploiting its "labor" (the student athletes).

THE PRICE OF THE COACH

Also included under the rubric of the AIC are the buying, selling and trading of coaches. Prior to Steve Spurrier leaving Florida (1989 to 2001), there were approximately two $1 million dollar NCAA football coaches.[25] Today, according to estimates, there are a sizeable number of football coaches making over two million dollars a year, many of whom are at programs that will never make the Bowl Championship Series or break into the top 25 national rankings.[26] And, the coaches at the highest-profile programs often command salaries in the $3–4 million per year range.

The data reveal some striking numbers related to coaches' salaries. In the data reported here, coaches' salaries are aggregated so that we cannot examine individual salaries, but we can see the inflation of salaries, particularly in certain programs and conferences. Auburn University reportedly spent nearly $5 million on football coaches' salaries in 2005 and the mean for the Big Twelve conference was $3.2 million.

We also note that when coaches are compensated at rates higher than the president of the university and ten to twenty times more than the full-time faculty, something is out of balance. Athletics has reached a point such that we argue it now threatens to replace the primary mission of the university. The relationship between the academic side of the university and the athletic side of the university is fraught with deep tension not dissimilar to the tensions that arise in semi-peripheral countries when core countries attempt to control trade, law, political elections, and so forth.[27] For example, in December 2009 University of Texas coach, Mack Brown, received a contract extension making him the highest paid football coach ever, earning an average of $5 million per year through 2016. The faculty on campus signed a petition decrying the huge discrepancy between coaches' salaries and faculty salaries. Similarly, at the end of his career as the head football coach at the University of Southern California (USC), Pete Carroll was reportedly the highest paid individual in all of *private* colleges and universities; his salary exceeding even those of Nobel laureates and top-ranked physicians.

RECRUITING

Recruiting is also a central part of intercollegiate athletics, involving trips to campus, hostess squads, and meetings with parents. It is during these meetings with parents that the "promise" of a chance at a professional career and earning a degree from the institution of higher learning are made. We suggest that if as much time and money were spent helping students graduate as was spent recruiting them, then the institution of intercollegiate sport could be transformed from exploitative to something honorable and fair. Recruiting is a key feature of the AIC and involves a large package of inducements.

The data reveal that at the high end, the University of Tennessee spent more than $800,000 in 2005 on football recruiting; and the teams in the ACC averaged $433,000. All of this, we note, to fill perhaps 25 spots on the roster. Thus, at a typical ACC school, an average of more than $17,000 is spent to recruit a single football player. The illogic of the situation is that many of these athletes will never play in a regulation game because of limited talent, injury, academic ineligibility, or trouble with the criminal justice system. For example, consider the cases of high profile athletes like Maurice Clarett and Marcus Vick, who have the talent but end up cutting short their intercollegiate careers because of trouble with the criminal justice system. In the end, you never know what you are getting once the recruiting is over. It is a bit like gambling: there is no guarantee on your investment.

Here is a description provided by then 17-year-old high school football star recruit Willie Williams:

> . . . after flying to Tallahassee in a private jet, he was taken to the best restaurant in the city by a Florida State University coach. After ordering a lobster tail at $49.95 and a steak at market value, he then saw that there was no restraint by others at the table. He called the waiter back and made his order four lobster-tails, two steaks, and a shrimp scampi. There were a dozen other recruits at the table. In Miami at the Mayfair House Hotel Willie's room, *The Paradise Suite,* featured a Jacuzzi on the balcony. He said he felt that he was living like King Tut and concluded that he would major in business so this lifestyle would continue.[28]

The description of Willie Williams's recruiting visit illustrates the excesses to which recruiting has ballooned.[29] The cost of recruiting has come to constitute a major portion of athletic department budgets and as with all other costs associated with big-time college sports, it has the effect of limiting other ways in which this money might be spent. For example, this money could be spent instead on recruiting and providing scholarships for female student athletes (who are often on partial scholarship)[30] and non-athlete students. In addition, athletic recruiting also contributes to some of the same problems we have highlighted above. One of the most significant problems is that it supplants the mission of the university by working in virtual isolation from the admissions office. No other unit in the university can recruit and admit its own student body, yet for athletic departments this is routine business. Though many student athletes do meet the admissions requirements of the university or college they attend, most universities have special "slots" set aside that the athletic department can use to admit students who otherwise do not qualify for admission.[31]

During the first months of 2006, a series of stories broke in the *New York Times* that uncovered the fraud of "sports high schools" that offer athletes who could not graduate from high school or who did not pass enough core classes to be eligible for a chance to get the credentials necessary to satisfy the NCAA's requirements. Most of the schools that were identified in the scandal had no faculty, the players admitted attending no classes, but at the end of the year they had earned Bs in 6 to 8 core classes, which is more than double the credits in core classes that an honors student would earn in a year of high school. When athletic departments were questioned about admitting players from these high schools, they all indicated that they rely on the NCAA for accreditation. These students never went through the "front door" of the admissions office and many are now attending prestigious colleges, including George Washington University.[32]

The outcome for the student athletes may be that they associate the university exclusively with the athletic department, it is where they were recruited and admitted, it is where they receive tutoring and advising, it is where they receive help with everything from opening a checking account at a local bank to navigating a health care system if they get sick or injured, and thus for student athletes the athletic department can displace the mission of the university and many of its offices. Additionally, the recruiting process is a "lie." During recruiting, when parents and their sons (this is true in men's sports more so than women's) are wooed to the university, coaches assure these young men and their families that they will have an opportunity to earn a degree from a major university. Yet, with fewer than 50 percent of student athletes graduating in men's basketball and football, this part of the recruitment is an untruth that further undermines the mission of the university.

The essence of the AIC as explained by the World Systems paradigm is that institutions must expand in order to remain competitive. That is, they must seek better ways of recruiting "blue-chip" athletes to their institutions, they must develop better relationships with fans and boosters, many of whom must be financially able, and they must at all times maintain a high level of facility upkeep that continues to lure both the student athletes as well as the fans. The expenditures are not voluntary; they are a must to remain in big time sports.[33]

THE BOTTOM LINE

The bottom line for our discussion of the AIC can be captured by considering two key relationships: (1) the relationship between football revenue and football expenditures (does football make or lose money for the university) and (2) the relationship between football spending and bowl and national championship appearances.

Does Football Make Money for the University?

The claim of most athletic directors, boosters, football coaches, fans, and other defenders of big spending in football is that football pays for itself, it makes money for the university, and it pays for non-revenue generating sports programs such as baseball and women's volleyball.

The data reveal that with only two exceptions (Atlantic Ten and Mountain West), at least one team in every football conference lost money in 2005, and in many cases these losses exceeded a million dollars. In the SEC, the University of South Carolina, Steve Spurrier's team, lost $2.6 million. Topping the losses was the University of California-Berkeley, losing nearly $8 million in 2005. When we consider these losses relative to the excesses in stadiums and facilities, coaches' salaries, recruiting and so on, these spending practices are increasingly difficult to defend.

Does Football Spending Translate into Bowl and National Championship Experiences?

The second claim that defenders of football spending practices make is that the exorbitant spending on travel, recruiting, coaches' salaries, scholarships, and facilities is necessary to increase the probability of playing in bowl games and/or for the national championship. In order to test this claim, we used correlation coefficients to examine the relationship between spending in various areas and the likelihood of participating in bowl games or the national championship. We limited the analysis to the time period 1998–2006, based on the beginning of the Bowl Championship Series (BCS) in 1998. Second, we restricted the analysis to teams that have actually appeared in a BCS bowl or played for the national championship. The data were restricted in this manner because most teams never compete in post-season play thus acting like a "constant." In order to measure BCS bowl and national championship appearances, we simply counted each appearance as reported on the NCAA website.

The data in Table 11.1 reveal some troubling findings. Overall, there is no statistically significant relationship between playing in a BCS bowl or for the national championship and money spent in any category of spending in the football budget. Though we might not have expected a relationship between some categories of spending (for example, facilities) and post-season play, most defenders of the excess spending in college sports point to several key variables: (1) coach's salary, (2) travel, (3) scholarship, and (4) recruiting as money that is "well spent" in the pursuit of a national championship. And yet, our data from nearly a decade disconfirm these claims. No area of spending in the football budget, including coach's salary, team travel, scholarship, or recruiting were significantly related to the number of appearances in BCS bowls or national championship games.

We note that the overall football budget was also not correlated with post-season play. And, this lack of a relationship between spending and post-season appearances held for teams that *have* competed in BCS bowls and for the national championship. This raises the even more important question for teams like Mike Price's University of Texas El-Paso (WAC), that spent nearly $7 million in total operating budget on football (Florida State's total operating budget is $11 million), or the University of Hawaii (WAC), which reported a $2 million deficit in their football budget. Neither team, Hawaii or Texas at El-Paso, will *ever* be eligible to compete in a BCS bowl or for the national championship because they are in mid-major conferences.[34] So, how can they justify these exorbitant expenditures?

Lastly, we note that some defenders of big spending in football point to the financial rewards dispersed by the NCAA. Yet, the data in Table 11.1 demonstrate that conference membership is a far better determinant of NCAA distribution than is program spending. The bulk of NCAA distributions are paid to the BCS conferences, with only small distributions going to the remaining conferences. Within those non-power conferences, the majority of the distribution goes to just one team. This leads us to wonder why the mid-major and minor conferences would be willing to pay the heavy fees associated with NCAA membership when most will never receive any money back from the NCAA.

AN AGENDA FOR THE FUTURE IN THE NEW MILLENNIUM

Our description and analysis of the AIC shows that it is an interlocking web of relationships, full of contradictions that appear illogical. As noted above, much of what ends up taking place at so many individual institutions are unintended consequences based mostly on poor decision making[35]

For example, what successful college or university would jeopardize its academic standing and national reputation for an unknown basketball player? Yet that is exactly what happened in the case of St. Bonaventure, where moral sacrifices were made in the name of basketball glory. A player named Jamil Terrell with no academic credentials (he had a junior college certificate in welding) was admitted by President Robert J. Wickenheiser, who overruled the compliance officer in admitting Terrell. Why would a good Catholic liberal arts university lower its academic standings for one student? The answer to this question is complicated but falls in the range of the following: the student could play basketball.

This was also the situation at the University of Missouri. In 2002, Missouri basketball under coach Quin Snyder recruited Rickie Clemmons from a junior college to play for Missouri. Clemmons played a year and during that time he was arrested for domestic assault on his girlfriend Jessica Bunge, a Missouri student who accused Clemons of choking her and detaining her in his Columbia, Missouri apartment against her will.

Bunge also contends in allegations that Clemmons received cash, shoes and clothing and improper academic help while he was playing basketball for Missouri. Clemmons, in the jailhouse tapes of several conversations he had with coaches, friends, and the wives of administrators including Carmento Floyd, the wife of Chancellor Elson Floyd, confirms that he, along with two other players, did receive money, shoes and clothing from Coach Snyder out of the trunk of his car. These allegations cost Snyder his job. Clemmons was kicked off the team.

At Baylor University, basketball coach Dave Bliss "coached" several of his players to lie about the death of Patrick Dennehy, who was shot by his teammate Carlton Dotson. Dennehy had been missing and his badly decomposed body was later found at a gravel pit near Waco, Texas. Dennehy was shot in the head. During the investigation period, Bliss asked his players to lie about Dennehy and asked that they portray him as a drug dealer. Later it was found that Dotson shot Dennehy. To cover up other allegations (e.g., paying for Dennehy's SUV, paying players cash money, etc.), Coach Bliss tampered with the collection of evidence. These charges cost Bliss his job at Baylor and Dotson is serving a prison term of 35 years.

These examples (and there are many) help support the logic of World Systems theory wherein those athletic departments, whether at the top, in the mid-range, or struggling from the bottom, all claw and fight to have a chance at the "golden egg." That struggle begins and ends with the recruitment and retention of student athletes.

All of this, from recruiting strategies to overpay for mediocre coaches to undermining the academic system in place at many of the institutions, falls into the category of the complicated web of ambivalence and unintended consequences so carefully defined and explained by Merton (1976), and more recently by Fine (2006).

In a recent dialogue on these issues, University of Texas Classics Professor Thomas G. Palaima *underscores the point that money going into athletics is money that does not go to academics.* He put it thus:

Sports funding is not separate from overall funding. When our many skyboxes are rented out, each one has a $44,000 to $60,000 tax-deductible donation to an institution of higher education attached. Little to none of that money goes to higher education. If we encourage people to contribute to the sports programs through tickets and mandatory Longhorn Foundation fees, we are siphoning off millions of dollars that could be directed to improve student education. Every one of those sky box rental 'donations' could cover the full costs of an undergraduate year at UT for three students. When UT regents and UT Austin administrators sign off on a plan to use donated funds to increase the multimillion-dollar salary of our football coach by about $400,000, they are saying to the people of Texas, this is where we want our money spent, not on improving education on the 40 Acres.[36]

Athletics on academic campuses must be taken seriously.[37] Sports are a mirror reflection of the society we live in. It is only in the United States that sports are embedded within the structure of higher education, thus deeply impacting the quality of the education at institutions that offer full-blown athletic programs.[38] Yet, intercollegiate sports today, and not only at the Division 1A level, have become a massively commercialized industry based on activities that are often irrelevant and in direct competition with the educational mission of the institutions under whose name they are played.[39]

Some of the more lucrative sports are purely a "farm-system." They are a route to professional sports participation, without cost to the professional teams but at a high cost for the colleges and universities that sponsor them. Other sports merely exist to satisfy federal legislation (e.g., gender equality dictated by Title IX) and are poorly funded, if funded at all. Add to this the "flight" of some institutions to other conferences, often causing massive destruction to what were natural alignments, and it becomes clear that the nature of the game has changed considerably in just the last decade.[40]

When conferences re-align, when some schools are allowed into the prestigious Bowl Championship Series (BCS) post-season games, and others are not, when at least a dozen college football coaches earn a base pay of $2 million dollars (and several like Mack Brown at the University of Texas earn $3 million), and when the payout for BCS post-season play is in the neighborhood of $185 million dollars, it becomes easier to define intercollegiate sports as a central part of the entertainment industry driven by the crass dominance of commercial TV, and very often funded by the advertising of alcoholic beverages despite the fact that college sports are played mostly by people under the legal drinking age, used to advertise alcohol. It is important to re-state that intercollegiate sport is now big business.

From the first intercollegiate competition in New Hampshire between rowers to the January 4, 2006, Rose Bowl, where Texas upended the University of Southern California, can we still call these contests amateur intercollegiate sport competitions between men? Athletics is supposed to be the other half of education, not the better half, and conceived wisdom has it that it is surely time to turn down, or turn back, the building of the AIC and return the role of athletics to be in line with the real mission of higher education.[41]

Intercollegiate Athletics has become too important to be treated with benign neglect. As a nation, we are reeling in the abyss of being unable to solve major social problems. The federal deficit has been predicted by the Congressional Budget Office to be at $2 trillion dollars[42] and rising. Medicare and Medicaid programs are not meeting the needs of American citizens and on any given day, or night, tens of thousands of American citizens are groping for a place to eat and sleep for they are homeless. In the fall of 2008 there was a rapid decline in all areas of the economy but most severe in the world's financial markets and banking. Behemoth banks like Washington Mutual and IndyMac went under. Large international banks like Lehman Brothers, a global investment bank serving the financial needs of corporations, institutions, governments and high-net-worth investors worldwide, collapsed. Giant insurance companies like American International Group (AIG), a supplier of international insurance and financial services, and automaker General Motors[43] were recipients of portions of the first U. S. federal government bailout funds—a total "package" hovering around $900 billion and officially titled the Troubled Asset Relief Program. Even as comparisons to the Great Depression abounded, each of the aforementioned companies received *billions* of dollars, painting a picture of an unprecedented collapse of the American economic structure.[44] The second "stimulus" package, at $787 billion dollars, is just more of the same. Along with the collapse of both Wall Street and the housing market, many Americans lost their 401K retirement funds and their homes—home foreclosures numbering in the millions—and job loss and unemployment have reached highs not seen in 25 years. When it's all over, economists predict 5 million jobs will have been lost and unemployment may reach 20 percent.[45] In this context it seems that sports[46], games once relegated to the edge of campus and played in order to maintain a healthy balance of body and mind, have become more important than is reasonable.

What we have provided is a different theoretical lens through which to see the ways in which these issues, namely the effects of capitalism on intercollegiate athletics and the exploitation of student athletes, are not random. They are systematic. It is in fact is the institutionalization of the commercialism within intercollegiate athletic programs, effectively removed from the governance structures in their respective institutions of higher learning that allows these injustices to continue. Indeed, Wallerstein's World Systems paradigm allows us to see this clearly. Institutions of higher learning are not at the core of intercollegiate athletics. Their administrations do not control the beast. Rather, at the core, where the power and control lies, is the NCAA, *an unregulated cartel* that adjusts athletic schedules to meet television contracts, moves games from the Midwest to Tokyo, and in all other ways controls the entire system of college athletics.

To be sure, universities are thus relegated to the semi-periphery, much like colonized countries, where their resources (athletes and athletic contests) can be mined for global sale and consumption. Finally, we find the student athletes themselves on the margins. They are exploited for their talents and discarded like diamond miners in South Africa once they outlive their utility.[47] In sum, we argue that athletics has a place, and a very important place at that, on college campuses but that athletics needs to be "put in its place" so that it is integrated into the university rather than subsuming it. College athletics is a prized endeavor and one that enriches the experience of college students. The question should not be "at what price athletics" but rather how to structure athletic programs that *serve both the student athletic interest and the greater goals of liberal arts institutions.*[48]

EPILOGUE

Across the spring and summer of 2010, as this chapter was going to production—we thank the editors for allowing us an extended deadline to address this issue—the BCS conferences engaged in a complicated dance of conference re-alignment that at its inception appeared to threaten the very underpinnings of college football, but as it continued dissipated to the extent that the only major change will be a remarkable increase in the revenues for several schools in the Big 12.

We summarize the "dance" here because it lays bare the truth behind college sports—at least football—and that is money! In the late spring of 2010 the PAC 10 and the Big 10 (which already had 11 teams) began to talk about the possibility of expanding their conferences. Simultaneously, Boise State, a team that has had a great deal of football success in the last decade but who has been undervalued and even with an undefeated record found itself fighting for a birth in a BCS bowl, voiced its desire to move to a BCS conference which would bring it the kind of visibility and respect it desired—and we would argue deserved—and ultimately during successful seasons a birth to a BCS bowl.

Inside of one week, led by the PAC 10, there was serious speculation that the Big 12 would be robbed of its most powerful football teams with as many as 6 teams going to the PAC 10 and Nebraska going to the Big 10. By week's end, both Colorado and Nebraska had signed contracts to move. Most everyone suspected that these moves were like a canary in a mine and shortly after, the University of Texas, the powerhouse of the Big 12 would leave for the PAC 10 as well, taking with it the "Texas" teams and leaving behind, like the girls no one wanted to dance with, Kansas, Kansas State, Iowa State and Baylor along with the challenge to save the Big 12 or find conferences into which they could be absorbed.

What came as a surprise to most everyone was the decision the University of Texas made *not* to migrate to the PAC 10 and instead to use its power and influence to bolster the Big 12. How and why did this dance that seemed to have so much momentum suddenly shift gears? David Ubben, writing for ESPN.com argued that just as the interest in expanding conferences was driven by the greed of the PAC 10, the decision the University of Texas made to stay in the Big 12 was even more blatantly just about the money! "We may not know the details and motives until Tuesday, but Texas wouldn't have stayed in the Big 12 if it didn't believe in what the commissioner was selling: more money."[49]

And, Andy Katz, also writing for ESPN.com, reported that the move to keep Texas in the Big 12, which revolves ultimately about guaranteeing Texas $20–25 million dollars annually in television revenues, and promises of another $14–17 million per every other Big 12 school, was also politically motivated. Because of the importance of the data we quote Katz extensively here:

An NCAA source with direct knowledge of what occurred told ESPN.com that the aggressiveness of the Pac-10 caused various factions of the collegiate sports world to coalesce. They then worked to slow and try to stop the pace of moves that would have left a number of schools searching for a new conference home. The source said the people involved were business executives, conference commissioners, athletic directors, network executives with ties throughout college athletics, administrators at many levels throughout the NCAA membership and a "fair number of them without a dog in the hunt." According to the source, this collection of interested and influential people made phone calls, visited in person and held conference calls with the Big 12 schools that were being pursued, including Texas, as well as Big 12 commissioner Dan Beebe. The influential group also helped broker the new television deal between Texas (and the other schools considering leaving the conference) and Beebe, who represented the remaining Big 12 schools. According to the source, there was a growing sense that the Pac-10 was taking an approach inconsistent with the best interests and values of the schools impacted, both positively and negatively.[50]

Deconstructing this dance we argue that three key findings that demonstrate the power of the AIC emerge. (1) It is all about the money. (2) It is all about college football. The conference re-alignment proposals and TV contracts that kept the Big 12 intact were all about BCS bowl games and football telecasts. Indeed David Ubben pointed out that a secondary benefit to Texas for staying in the Big 12 was a "clear path" to the BSC bowl (with Nebraska having moved to the Big 10). Additionally, everyone agrees that the movement of Nebraska, Colorado and Boise State have no impact on March Madness because none of these schools have fielded a successful men's basketball team in years. And, if it were about basketball there would never have been talk of stranding Kansas, who won the national championship as recently as a year ago. (3) It has nothing to do with higher education. Andy Katz makes it clear that the conference alignment decisions were influenced by NCAA officials——whose concern was about the athletic programs not the educational missions of the member schools—athletic directors, politicians, and business men, some of whom he argued didn't even have a dog in the fight. Thus, this dance of conference re-alignment lays bare the truth behind college athletics: it is nearly completely divorced from the educational mission of the universities and its affiliation with universities is merely nominal. The name of the game is money and clearly there is much money to be made and the stakes are very high for those with financial interests in college athletics.

CONCLUSION

We conclude by reminding the reader of the powerful role that college athletics plays not only on college campuses but in the larger realm of the AIC. The

Table 11.1   Correlations Between "Winning" (BCS and National Championships) and Sources of Football Revenues and Football Expenditures

		Total BCS & Championship Appearances
Total FB Operating Budget	Pearson Correlation	.259
	Sig. (2-tailed)	.202
	N	26
Revenue Budget	Pearson Correlation	.019
	Sig. (2-tailed)	.927
	N	26
Contributions	Pearson Correlation	.048
	Sig. (2-tailed)	.816
	N	26
NCAA Distributions	Pearson Correlation	-.036
	Sig. (2-tailed)	.863
	N	26
Athletic Scholarships	Pearson Correlation	-.109
	Sig. (2-tailed)	.595
	N	26
FB Guarantees	Pearson Correlation	.196
	Sig. (2-tailed)	.338
	N	26
Coaches Salaries	Pearson Correlation	.355
	Sig. (2-tailed)	.075
	N	26
Recruiting Costs	Pearson Correlation	.182
	Sig. (2-tailed)	.374
	N	26
Game Expenses	Pearson Correlation	-.136
	Sig. (2-tailed)	.507
	N	26
Facilities Costs	Pearson Correlation	.315
	Sig. (2-tailed)	.117
	N	26
Travel	Pearson Correlation	.168
	Sig. (2-tailed)	.401
	N	27

** Correlation is significant at the 0.01 level (2-tailed).
 * Correlation is significant at the 0.05 level (2-tailed).

frenzy that surrounds events like the College Football National Championship and "March Madness" contributes to the development and perpetuation of a global hegemonic ideology of sports that elevates this institution far above its appropriate place. For example, during the month period between June 11, 2010 and July 11, 2010 the FIFA World Cup may provide relief from the stresses associated with the global recession, but it will also render invisible the fact that many if not most of the countries competing in the World Cup have unemployment and poverty rates that leave the vast majority of their citizenry unable to provide themselves and their families with stable housing and nutritious food let alone bask in the luxury that is expressed poignantly in the globally televised FIFA World Cup.

Finally, while there is much, much more to be said about the Athletic Industrial Complex, we end here noting that for all the excesses documented above in intercollegiate athletic spending, it is the Knight Commission, of all organizations, calling on Congress to come in and help athletic departments weather the fiscal crisis of 2008–2009. Knight Commission co-chairman William E. (Brit) Kirwan said, "While we generally don't believe that Congressional action is necessary to regulate intercollegiate athletics, we are not ready to dismiss any proposals that could provide effective means to address our challenging financial problems." We are reminded it is this Commission that came into existence in 1989/1990 to reform college athletics.[51]

NOTES

1. Steve Wieberg and Steve Berkowitz, "NCAA report: College Sports Spending Keeps Skyrocketing," *USA Today*, April 29, 2009, www.usatoday.com/sports/college/2009–04–29-college-athletic-spending-report_N.htm (accessed July 12, 2010).

2. Earl Smith, *Race, Sport and The American Dream*, 2nd edition (Durham, NC: Carolina Academic Press, 2009).

3. Dwight D. Eisenhower, "Military-Industrial Complex Speech," The White House, January 17, 1961. The Avalon Project at Yale Law School, www.yale.edu/lawweb/avalon/presiden/speeches/eisenhower001.htm (accessed July 12, 2010); C. Wright Mills, *The Power Elite*. (New York, NY: Oxford University Press, 2000), 1035–40.

4. J. Krakauer, *Where Men Win Glory: The Odyssey of Pat Tillman* (New York, NY: Doubleday, 2009).

5. This is also true in the NBA. See Earl Smith, "Race Matters in the National Basketball Association," *Marquette Sports Law Journal* 9, no. 2 (1999): 239–252.

6. The biggest impact that international recruiting has had in contributing to the unbridled growth of intercollegiate athletics is its influence on recruiting

more generally. We will discuss recruiting and its role in the AIC in the section on "recruiting."

7. Joe Drape, "Foreign Pros in College Tennis: On Top and Under Scrutiny," *New York Times,* April 11, 2006.

8. N. Popp, M.A. Hums, and T.C. Greenwell, "Do International Student-Athletes View the Purpose of Sport Differently than United States Student-Athletes at NCAA Division I Universities?" *Journal of Issues in Intercollegiate Athletics* 2 (2009):93–110.

9. In the United States private universities are not bound by this mission. And, indeed at many of the most prestigious including Harvard, Yale, and Princeton we see significantly higher rates of international students than we do in public universities.

10. Richard Sandomir, "Sports, Media and Business: The Network Cleans Up in Overtime," *New York Times,* March 29, 2005.

11. This global expansion is also evident in the National Football League (NFL). The NFL started the American Bowl on August 3, 1986. The first game was between the Chicago Bears and the Dallas Cowboys, played at London's Wembley Stadium. Chicago won, 17 to 6.

12. Michael Hunt, "Everything Comes Up Roses in Tokyo," *Milwaukee Sentinel,* December 4, 1993.

13. We don't discuss the details of the multi-year TV contract between NBC and Notre Dame in this chapter. The recent extension of the contract runs out in 2015, making it a 25-year deal.

14. Coach Lloyd Carr's views are contained in Tim Griffin, "Alamo Bowl Sets Game Day in Familiar December Spot," *San Antonio Express-News,* June 22, 2006, 3C.

15. See www.umd.edu/umnews/chevy_chase_bank_field.html (accessed July 12, 2010).

16. It is important to note that the student athletes themselves are making demands that they play for teams that get TV time, that they have bigger locker rooms and better weight room facilities and that they play in state-of-the-art stadiums. For an overview of this problem see Doug Lederman, "A Better Look at Sport Budgets," *Inside Higher Education,* June 23, 2006, insidehighered.com/news/2006/06/23/ncaa (accessed July 12, 2010).

17. For a description of some of the more expensive projects, including at our home institution, contact the authors.

18. The big-business aspect of the Athletic Industrial Complex is so big that it has spurned a newsletter for construction industry entitled "New & Expanding Athletic Facilities," a semi-monthly newsletter providing profiles on hundreds of new and expanding fitness centers, gymnasiums and athletic facilities nationwide. See www.athleticleads.com/projects/default.asp?provider_id=1000&UID={2F0C2A89–5838–4EFB-82A8–9BBBB84B134B} (accessed July 12, 2010).

19. Jonathan Glater, "Stanford Shrinking Football Stadium to Boost Ticket Sales," *New York Times,* March 1, 2006.

20. Data not shown. For copies of the tables please contact the authors.

21. Data referenced here comes from a database compiled by Mark Aleysia, a columnist at the *Indianapolis Star.* Analyses of the data were performed by the authors. For more information on this data, which is available for most of the NCAA Division Member Institutions, contact the authors.

22. For data on individual teams, please contact the authors.

23. It is interesting that there is even a construction site (and newsletter) that allows you to look at the bids for athletic facilities buildings. See www.constructionwire.com/projects/ (accessed July 12, 2010).

24. Note: We use this data from our own campus because this specific data is nearly impossible to get and thus we relied on contacts inside the athletic department to supply it.

25. Coaches are expensive. They not only demand million dollar salaries, they must have full access to facilities in the summer months to house their camps. In addition, they negotiate contracts that have "appendages" such as a certain number of game tickets, airline tickets to travel (Dick Bennett formerly at Wisconsin), and shoe endorsements that provide income above and separate from annual salaries (NIKE, Adidas, Puma, etc.). Before he was fired from UNC-Chapel Hill, Matt Doherty had a base salary of $150,000 but had a "shoe deal" with NIKE worth $500,000.

26. In football and basketball, there are approximately five coaches that make over $3 million a year in base salary alone.

27. The escalation of coaches' salaries is starting to compare to those of corporate CEO's. While not as egregious, they are fast approaching these disparities. In fact, studies of CEO salaries and employee salaries demonstrate that in 1950, the average CEO earned 15 times as much as the average employee. By 2005, that ratio had grown to 531 times. See, especially, Anderson, Sarah, John Cavanagh, Chris Hartman and Betsy Leonard-Wright, "Executive Excess 2001, Layoffs, Tax Rebates, The Gender Gap," Institute for Policy Studies & United for a Fair Economy (2001), www.faireconomy.org/press/2005/EE2005_pr.html (accessed July 12, 2010).

28. Richard Crepeau, *Sport and Society for H-ARETE,* February 23, 2004, www.h-net.org/~arete/ (accessed July 12, 2010).

29. It is important to note that Williams wrote a "recruiting diary" prior to his accepting a scholarship at the University of Miami. Williams's time at Miami was unrewarding. He left Miami in August, 2006, to enroll at West Los Angeles College, a junior college in California, where it is reported he will play football. See Susan Degnan, "Williams Clears Probation Early," *Miami Herald,* August 18, 2006.

30. See our paper, Angela Hattery, Earl Smith and Ellen Staurowsky, "They Play Like Girls: Gender Equity in NCAA Sports," *The Journal for the Study of Sports and Athletes in Education* 1 (2008): 249-272.

31. On most campuses, including our own, there are slots referred to as "special admits." See William Bowen and Sarah Levin, *Reclaiming the Game: College Sports and Educational Values* (Princeton, NJ: Princeton University Press, 2003).

32. "Betraying Student Athletes," Editorial, *New York Times*, March 2, 2006; Mark Schlabach, "A Player Rises through the Cracks[:] Academic History of GW's Williams Reveals Flaws in NCAA Process," *Washington Post*, Sunday, March 5, 2006, A01.

33. University of Connecticut has just entered into Div. 1A football. To do so they had to seek $100 million in bonding for a new 35,000-seat arena. Another example shows that Texas, Texas A & M, Nebraska, North Carolina State, Arkansas and others are playing the game of football by playing the game of "keeping up with the Joneses." In a report about new stadium scoreboards we have learned that scoreboards only ten years old are being replaced with new, high tech scoreboards that cost $8 million dollars. The new scoreboard at Texas, for example, is 134 feet wide, 55 feet tall, with the nickname *Godzillatron*. The features that stand out are that *Godzillatron* requires 40 five-ton air conditioners to keep it cool and it can capture high definition (HD) signals. It has light emitting diodes (LED) so that you can see it at all times, in all types of weather, and it has surround sound. *Godzillatron* covers a total area of 7,370 square feet.

34. In the fall of 2006, much debate raged over the exclusion of Rutgers from a BCS bowl despite their outstanding record against BCS teams. Rutgers' membership is in the Big East Conference.

35. R. K. Merton, *Sociological Ambivalence and Other Essays* (New York, NY: Free Press, 1976).

36. Thomas Palaima, "Put Academics before Athletics," *The Daily Texan*, February 24, 2006, www.dailytexanonline.com/media/paper410/news/2006/02/24/Opinion/Put-Academics.Before.Athletics1636217.shtml?norewrite&sourcedomain=www.dailytexanonline.com (accessed July 12, 2010).

37. Elliott J. Gorn and Michael Oriard, "Taking Sports Seriously," *Chronicle of Higher Education*, March 24, 1995.

38. A good reason for this is that athletics at the university affects the type of student applicant pool. This evidence is strong. See McCormick and Tinsley, "Athletics versus Academics: Evidence from SAT Scores," *Journal of Political Economy* 95 (1987): 1103–1116.

39. Consider the massive case that unfolded at Baylor, a mid-level basketball power in Texas, wherein not only was a basketball player killed by another jealous basketball player, but also the chain reaction when the coach attempted to organize a systematic cover up of the whole ordeal. Baylor University is now known for these incidents worldwide instead of for the fine academic curriculum it produces.

40. See especially Mike Mitchell, "College Football Landscape Will Change Drastically with Realignment for 2005," May 18, 2005. Mitchell shows clearly that with the Atlantic coast Conference (ACC) wooing Boston College, Miami and Virginia Tech to the conference beginning with the 2005 football season it started a ripple effect throughout the country, www.collegefootballpoll.com/2005_conferences.html (accessed July 12, 2010).

41. We never used to talk about the AIC impacting high-school-level athletics. Now it has invaded all levels of sport, including those that fall under the category of

"little league" sport programs. An example of this is found in Seattle, Washington, where there is a scandal involving the recruitment of young girls to sport teams away from their assigned schools. Coaches have been fired and law suits have been filed. See Christine Willmsen and Michael Ko, "Ex-Sealth Coaches to Get Jobs Back?" *Seattle Times,* July 11, 2006.

42. Edmund L. Andrews, "Budget Office Forecasts Record Deficit in '04," *New York Times,* January 27, 2004; Jackie Calmes, "Budget Gap Is Revised to Surpass $1.8 Trillion," *New York Times,* May 11, 2009, www.nytimes.com/2009/05/12/business/economy/12budget.html?hpw (accessed July 12, 2010).

43. AIG: $90 billion; General Motors: $5 billion.

44. Michael Lewis and David Einhorn, "The End of the Financial World as We Know It," *New York Times,* January 3, 2009.

45. According to Smith, *Race, Sport and The American Dream:* 8 percent nationally and 634,000 filed for unemployment as of January 2009, and a total of 2 million jobs were lost in 2008.

46. In professional baseball there is something else going on, concomitant with the worst economic downturn in American history. The New York Yankees professional baseball team paid over $423.5 million for two pitchers and one first baseman inside of a two-week period. While the contracts varied, CC Sabathia received a $161 million, seven-year contract and A.J. Burnett an $82.5 million, five-year contract, with first baseman Mark Teixeira netting a $180 million, eight-year contract. The Yankees also open their 2009 season in a brand new, $1.3 billion ball park; ironically, several of the corporate sponsors whose signs hang in Yankee Stadium—including the largest single sponsor, Bank of America—received millions in "bailout" money as well. Meanwhile, across town, the New York Mets open the 2009 season in their new billion-dollar ballpark "Citifield," named for sponsor CitiBank, which also took millions of dollars in tax-payer financed federal bailout money; see Earl Smith, *Race, Sport and The American Dream* .

47. The best example for all of this and how the NCAA works to make life difficult for student athletes is the case of former University of Colorado football player and champion skier Jeremy Bloom. Bloom, a championship skier with six straight World Cup victories and a participant in the 2006 Olympics, sought to collect endorsement and prize money for his skiing prowess. The NCAA stepped in and declared that this was illegal and would render Bloom no longer an amateur student athletes or eligible to play football. Bloom sought to fight this injunction by advocating for his and others eligibility rights but was unable to convince the NCAA of his perspective. He recently signed a 4-year, $1.8 million dollar contract with the Philadelphia Eagles. See Lynn Zinser, "Pro Football: Olympian Bloom Now Tries to Be an Everyman," *New York Times,* June 5, 2006.

48. Amy Campbell, "Division III Intercollegiate Athletics," Paper Commissioned for the book *Reclaiming the Game: College Sports and Educational Values* (Princeton, NJ: Princeton University Press, 2002), 1–2.

49. See espn.go.com/blog/Big12/post/_/id/13424/texas-got-what-it-wanted (accessed July 12, 2010).

50. See sports.espn.go.com/ncaa/news/story?id=5286816 (accessed July 12, 2010).

51. See www.knightcommission.org/index.php?option=com_content&view=article&id=295:may-12–2009-knight-commission-urges-college-leaders-to-consider-bold-innovative-solutions-to-address-fiscal-health-of-college-sports&catid=22:press-room.

Chapter Twelve

Driving to Carmageddon

Capitalism, Transportation, and the Logic of Planetary Crisis

Michael Dawson

In *The Communist Manifesto,* Marx and Engels quipped that capitalism's advance means that "all that is solid melts into air."[1] They might have added that, because profit seekers also remake what they devour, the reign of capital also means that *all that was air becomes solid.* Because of its need for "a constantly expanding market for its [constituent firms'] products," capitalism drives its players "over the whole surface of the globe," observed Marx and Engels, driving them to "nestle everywhere, settle everywhere, establish connections everywhere."[2] So long as it survives, capitalism presses for its own growth, regardless of the wider human and ecological situation. Though anarchic and partially compatible with democracy, business society is, therefore, inherently totalitarian, recognizing no limits to its own requirements, accepting no sphere or aspect of life as off-limits.

The claim of this chapter is simple: Once it fell within the scope of capitalism, transportation—the field of human arrangements for moving people and things from one place to another under given conditions—became an industrial complex[3] that serves not just to move people and things, but to extend and deepen capitalists' drive to commercialize and commodify human activities. As this complex has evolved, its operational requirements, business logic, and ideological impact have become deeply enmeshed with those of the military, energy, housing, financial, and entertainment industrial complexes, with ramifications that reach across the whole of the planet. The overall result has become not only immensely profitable to investors, but also profoundly and pressingly dangerous to the human future.

CAPITAL AND HUMAN MOBILITY: THE BROAD HISTORY

All parents labor long and hard to help their able-bodied children learn to walk. Once that deed is done, however, we tend to take moving from one spot to another for granted. In doing so, we overlook much.

Bipedal locomotion, of course, was deeply essential in Homo sapiens' momentous and wildly unlikely emergence from the tree of life.[4] Walking upright on two feet "is as much of a biological imperative as any aspect of our species's behavioral repertoire, and appears in conjunction with numerous specializations of the axial skeleton and lower limbs."[5] Though the fastest quadrupeds can easily outrun the fastest human, bipedalism facilitated other advantages, such as taller and more flexible visual fields and the refinement of specialized upper limbs, aka arms and hands. The emergence of hominid bipedalism not only gave our direct ancestors "the most powerful and tenacious and yet the most delicate and precise manipulatory forelimbs in the animal kingdom," but it allowed them to "do something on the ground that no other creature had ever done so much of or done so well: use hands to make and carry tools, and use tools to satisfy daily needs."[6] Combined with our large, complex, 100-billion-cell brains, two-legged walking and the hominid hand also made us the only species capable of consciously understanding, planning, and refining our methods of travel.

This is not to say we humans have yet taken full advantage of our capacity for rational transportation design and provision. For the vast majority of time in biologically modern humanity's 150-or-so millennia of existence, walking and running were supplemented only with various vessels for hand-carrying small amounts of goods, plus the eventual, occasional use of small boats and wheel-less sleds. Even today, when immense, dense, exorbitantly costly networks of high-technology travel infrastructure and machinery interweave the globe, the degree to which our transportation arrangements stem from democratic control and truly rational calculation is far smaller than either prevailing propaganda claims or socio-technical possibility suggests. At least arguably, most of what gets built and used today remains, despite its sophistication, a result of non-optimal and even irrational forces, including institutional inertia, a general historical pattern of bumbling intensification of established production habits, and, the self-serving, socially reckless command-and-control powers of entrenched socio-economic interests.[7]

Macro-historical sleepwalking and the rise of ruling social classes have not prevented progress, of course. Indeed, there have been many moments at which people's accumulating knowledge has produced new, epoch-making transportation innovations. In the pre-capitalist world, major breakthroughs included several phases of improvement in boats, the domestication of animals, and the much joked-about but quite real "invention of the wheel."

The first great leap forward in human transportation history may have been the boats that facilitated human arrival in Australia from Southeast Asia 30,000 to 40,000 years ago. Jared Diamond describes the significance of this travel:

> During the Ice Ages, so much of the oceans' waters was locked up in glaciers that worldwide sea levels dropped hundreds of feet below their present stand. As a result, what are now the shallow seas between Asia and the Indonesian islands of Sumatra, Borneo, Java and Bali became dry land. The edge of the Southeast Asian mainland then lay 700 miles east of its present location. Nevertheless, central Indonesian islands between Bali and Australia remained surrounded and separated by deep water channels. To reach Australia/New Guinea from the Asian mainland at that time still required crossing a minimum of 8 channels, the broadest of which was 50 miles wide. Most of these channels divided islands visible from each other, but Australia itself was always invisible from even the nearest Indonesian islands, Timor and Tanimbar. Thus the occupation of Australia/New Guinea is momentous in that it demanded watercraft and provides by far the earliest evidence of their use in history.[8]

More recently but equally momentously, in phases running from about 10,000 to 5,000 years ago, various societies mastered or adopted animal domestication, leading to a quantum leap in the muscle power available for travel, cargo-carrying, and land-plowing activities. Diamond again provides an apt statement of the significance:

> Big domestic animals further revolutionized human society by becoming our main means of land transport until the development of railroads in the 19th century. Before animal domestication, the sole means of transporting goods and people by land was on the backs of humans. Large [domesticated] mammals changed that: for the first time in human history, it became possible to move heavy goods in large quantities, as well as people, rapidly overland for long distances.[9]

Next, toward the end of humanity's initial species-domestication period, pottery wheels were turned 90 degrees and explored as a new travel aid. Though experts remain unsure of the exact time and place of the "invention" of the wheel as a transportation technology, evidence of transport-wheel use becomes clear and overwhelming in the 500 years following the rise of the ancient Sumerian city-state of Uruk in Mesopotamia about 6,000 years ago.[10] No Jared Diamond required here: Anybody who has ever pulled a wagon or ridden a bicycle knows how profoundly wheels have affected human transit possibilities.

The final major breakthrough in pre-capitalist travel was actually the one that catalyzed the transition to capitalism: This was "the parallel fusion" of naval navigation techniques rooted in Arab astronomy and mathematics with greatly improved ship construction methods in the Mediterranean and the Iberian Peninsula.[11] This fusion began the process of knitting the world's various cultural networks "into a single, global one."[12] It also provided Western Europe's competing mini-kingdoms with the means of reaching and plundering the host of societies that saw their labor and raw materials become "primitive accumulation" of proto-capitalist wealth back in Europe, from whence the wealth-seeking conquistadors sailed.

Once capitalism took hold, its inherent commercialization-and-commodification drive quickly began engulfing pre-existing cultures and technologies, progressively remaking transportation activities according to the logic of the endless competitive expansion of private profit seeking. On the production side, beginning with the sea-faring breakthroughs that facilitated the conquistadors' infamies, new machines and geographical knowledge opened vast new stores of land, energy, raw material, and labor to capitalist exploitation. On the sales side, commerce and rapid urbanization generated a host of new opportunities for selling new transportation goods and services.

In the capitalist era, four transportation technologies have been epoch-making, in that they have both altered the possibilities of travel and opened huge new investment fields for profit seekers. Historically, the first of these epoch-makers was the seaworthy cargo ship. The second was the railroad, which so famously sprang from and extended the Industrial Revolution. The third was the automobile. The last was the airplane.

Each of these technologies has been the subject of a mini-industry of historical research. Study of these mini-industries reveals important and sometimes surprising results. In the United States, for example, despite their eventual domination by private investors, historians have shown that the initial construction of the nation's railroads was largely accomplished by the public sector, through investment subsidies and major deployments of the U.S. Army Corp of Engineers, which "engaged in a wide range of activities that promoted and directed . . . the industry's growth."[13]

Without minimizing the importance of knowing the micro-histories, it remains true that virtually all of what has been said about the transportation industrial complex remains just that—"micro," detailed, narrow, technical—in its level of analysis. As a result, little attention has been paid to the three most important large-scale consequences of capitalism's ongoing transformation of human mobility.

CONSEQUENCE #1: RADICAL COMMODIFICATION

Sociologically speaking, commodification is the process through which human activities come to employ, or to employ more intensively than before, products produced for sale, not immediate use.[14]

In the capitalist production-and-sales process, commodities, which can be either goods or services, are the means to attaining the ultimate aim of private businesses—the generation of profits for investors. To the extent business owners can discover ways to hire employees to make goods or provide services whose sales price exceeds the owners' costs of having the goods or services made and delivered to buyers, profits can ensue. Because every capitalist firm aims to maximize its shareholders' returns-on-investment and also to grow them over time, searching for ways to sell new commodities, or larger quantities or more complex versions of existing ones, is always on the business agenda. The result is a socio-economic order in which the dominant institutions strive mightily and constantly to find ways to commodify more and more aspects of life, particularly in regions where substantial popular purchasing power exists.

The transportation industrial complex has advanced this fundamental process of the capitalist epoch both directly and indirectly.

Indirect Commodification

From the beginning, capitalism has generated an intense demand for new methods and capacities for transporting goods and workers from place to place. As businesses have created new varieties and rising quantities of salable products, they have needed means of both gathering laborers and raw materials and sending out finished items. Roughly speaking, under capitalism, economic growth means a growing flow of people and materials, which in turn requires a growing infrastructure for moving the people and things drawn into and sent out of the commercial process. To draw an analogy, as the body of capitalism grows, so must its circulatory system. That circulatory system is the sub-sector of the transportation industrial complex devoted to moving raw materials, employees, and finished commodities: the shipping and commuting systems, in other words.

As we have already seen, shipping came first, as the means of conquering and plundering the great bolus of precious metals, raw materials, and new-to-Europe products that facilitated capitalism's take-off as a self-sustaining process. "By the mid-1530s," writes maritime historian Timothy R. Walton, Spain's "treasure fleets were carrying over one million pesos per year" in gold and silver.[15] According to Eduardo Galeano, by 1660, the physical mass of such shipments registered in the single port of Seville, Spain was 407,000 pounds of gold and over 37 million pounds of silver.[16] As the world was "molded into a commercial and financial system that operated on European terms," both the range of items being shipped and the rate at which ships themselves were being enlarged and refined exploded.[17]

More notable, if less infamous, the invention of the steam-powered railroad locomotive in the 1790s unlocked yet another great leap forward in the progress of capitalism and commodification. At a time when coal was the cutting-edge industrial fuel and transporting mined coal was as much of a labor as digging it from the Earth, the Stockton and Darlington Railway, having been authorized by an Act of Parliament in 1821, opened in 1825 in England's northeastern coal mining region. By 1828, the Stockton and Darlington had halved the cost-per-ton of moving coal, while doubling the speed of its transport.[18] A huge boom in railway construction and overall industrial activity ensued, as the new transport capacity cheapened and expanded energy inputs. "In 1825," notes a British rail history museum, "there were only 25 miles of public railroad open in the world. 50 years later this had grown to 160,000 miles and continued at an amazing pace thereafter. In 1825 there were only 2 locomotives available for use on a public railway, by the turn of the [19th] century, this had increased to 70,000."[19]

The two transport revolutions of the twentieth century—the rise of the automobile and air flight—were also important breakthroughs for the freight-moving sector of the capitalist transportation industrial complex. Air freight not only opened new means of rushing people and objects to far-distant points, but has come to carry a disproportionate share of the most expensive and fragile commodities. By the year 2007, "[t]he value of what was moved by air was about a third of the value of all freight moved [in the world], even though in terms of ton-kilometers, air freight was less than 0.5 percent of total freight movement."[20] Also by 2007, trucking had slightly surpassed rail in its ton-kilometers share of the world's annual freight movement, though motor vehicle-based shipping still carried less than one-fifth the freight ton-kilometers of shipping via water.[21]

Meanwhile, beyond its role in shipping and commuting, the automobile has provided other enormous indirect contributions to capitalism's commodification of life. First, the rise of the car has spurred suburbanization and detached, low-density housing. Any population that moves from cities to suburbs is going to purchase more goods and services. Basement laundromats are urban; laundry rooms in individual houses are suburban. Likewise, suburban living generates new markets for things like yard-care products, while also requiring vastly more construction of both public streets and infrastructures and houses themselves. Without the spread of the personal car, the degree of suburbanization that has happened in capitalism's core societies over the past century would have been far smaller, and the housing industrial complex of at least the United States would have evolved much differently.

Especially in the United States, where cars-first transportation policies have prevailed for more than a century, automobiles have also made huge indirect contributions to the medical, legal, and financial industrial complexes. According to the National Highway Traffic Safety Administration, in the year 2008, automotive collisions killed 37,261 people in the United States.[22] That's 102 a day; 717 a week; 3,105 a month. And 2008 was no anomaly: 37,261 is very close to the average annual death toll for the prior half-century, during which well over *2 million* individuals perished in U.S. car crashes.[23] In typical years, the number of people "severely or critically" injured, but not killed, in U.S. car crashes surpasses the number killed, and the number of people with moderate and minor car-crash injuries runs into the millions per year.[24] Automobiles also contribute to air pollution and, by discouraging walking and cycling, to physical deconditioning and caloric imbalances between dietary intake and exercise burn-off—all with gigantic negative health consequences. Of course, from the point of view of the hospital, the pharmaceutical corporation, the doctor, the lawyer, and the insurer, it all means a greatly enlarged pool of business and potential profits.

Such general stimulus of business opportunities has long been a central motive among planning elites. Lucius D. Clay was a four-star general who had served as Dwight D. Eisenhower's chief deputy during the Second World War. Later, in August of 1954, Eisenhower appointed Clay to serve as chair of the President's Advisory Committee on a National Highway Program. Charged with developing the plans that soon led to passage of the Federal-Aid Highway Act of 1956, Clay, who at the time was also a member of the Board of Directors of General Motors, recalled to his biographer that his committee advocated construction of the vast, visible-from-space U.S. interstate highway network not merely for the reasons of military and civilian mobility promoted to the public, but also because they knew "we needed them for the economy, not just as a public works measure, but for future growth."[25]

Direct Commodification

The transportation industrial complex has not just provided new and improved means of circulating commodities (and thereby indirectly aiding commodification). As capitalists have progressively commodified travel itself, the results of such efforts have comprised a growing chunk of the transportation industrial complex. Indeed, though it may have been coincidence that automobiles and corporate capitalism emerged at roughly the same time, the latter has long since been institutionally addicted to promoting the ascendance of the former. To adapt Voltaire, if the car didn't exist, it would have been necessary for big business investors to invent it.

The first reason for this dependency is capitalism's inherent tendency toward economic maturity. When the system was young, few commodities were being mass produced, and the opportunities for inventing and selling new goods and services were comparatively vast. The main business problem was acquiring the money and the workforce to invest in producing items that were rather easy to sell, once produced. But now, after 500 years of past competitive commodification and the rise of giant conglomerate corporations conducting increasingly elaborate marketing operations, the field for producing easily-sold new products is much less obvious to the naked eye than it used to be. As capitalism advances, "markets"—meaning opportunities for new, expanded rounds of profitable investment in commodity production and sales—tend to become saturated, by capitalism's own prior successes.

This problem is compounded by corporate capitalism's tendency to accumulate more investable capital for major investors than major investors can easily re-invest in expanded commodity production. Originally formed as a means of tamping down price competition, modern giant corporations have not only succeeded in achieving that goal, but have also provided their shareholders with expanding power within markets, politics, and the spheres of mundane human experience that determine the quality of both product production and product usage.[26] As investor incomes consequently grow as fast or faster than popular buying power, the resulting macro-economic climate not only encourages increasing non-productive forms of investment[27] (fueling the explosive growth of the financial industrial complex), but makes finding new buyers a cardinal problem.

Normalcy now means that, in the words of corporate marketing consultant Regis McKenna, "production systems have undergone vast improvement, to such an extent that almost every manufacturing-based industry can outproduce their market demand."[28] Within particular corporations, macro-economic maturity and sustained radical income inequalities (both forms of capitalist success) press top executives to seek managerial responses. "The hard part," runs one typical behind-the-scenes admission by a corporate vice-president, "is saying, OK, we've got this whole production facility and we want to produce at an economic rate—how do we get the sales at a productive rate? That's not . . . so easy."[29]

In this situation, there is a premium on discovering how to sell what I call "maximum commodities"—goods or services complex and commercially friendly enough to provide the basis for new sales opportunities that are deep and wide enough to form the basis for a self-perpetuating capitalist industrial complex.

To serve as a possible maximum commodity, a good or service must simultaneously possess several special characteristics. These include:

- *Salability:* Oxygen, though a primary requirement of life for all humans, is ordinarily not a salable product. Except in hospitals and laboratories, where its concentrated and controlled use is required, it is a free gift from nature. Hence, capitalists enjoy no "oxygen industrial complex."
- *Labor Intensity:* Since business profits derive largely from the difference between the final value of a product and the expenses incurred in arranging for waged or salaried employees to produce it, it follows that, other things being equal, the more chances there are to build such financial differentials into a given product, the more potential there is to realize a larger profit upon final sale. Due to the simplicity of its function and simplicity of its construction, there is only so much potential for making big money selling dining spoons. Railroad locomotives, on the other hand, are, thanks to their size, potentially highly profitable.
- *Complexity:* Simpler objects are easier to build, fix, and find substitutes for. More complex objects are harder to build, fix, and find substitutes for. Hence more complicated goods and services provide opportunities for charging higher prices and selling more related services.
- *Fragility:* Products that break more frequently require more repairs and more frequent replacement. Other things being equal, fragile products make better capitalist commodities than durable ones.
- *Fetishizability/Marketability:* Products that can be more successfully promoted to individuals on the basis of their styling, color, and superficial amenities are both easier to sell and more likely to be replaced for non-mechanical reasons.
- *Secondary Business Implications:* Candles imply candleholders and matches or lighters. Automobiles imply a much vaster range and scale of allied goods and services, from road building, to insurance, to parking facilities. The greater the secondary business opportunities implied by a particular commodity, the greater will be its macro-economic stimulating effects, the number and range of its partner businesses, and its political clout.
- *Practical Necessity:* Contrary to the first premise of neo-classical economic orthodoxy, individuals' comparative desire for particular products is not the sole result of abstract calculations and pristine personal preferences.[30] Both biological requirements and practical exigencies shape people's calculations

and preferences, and hence, their product choices. If biology or the built environment encourages acquisition and use of a particular product, its sales potential is higher than products that remain more biologically or socially optional.

This chapter is not the place for a full examination of the car's near-perfection as a maximum commodity. I provide an extended examination of this topic elsewhere[31], and trust that readers of this book can also readily understand and explore the point. For now, I will merely note the extreme labor intensity (and hence profit-making opportunity) inherent in the private automobile.

It would be hard to imagine a product that contains more and more precisely interrelated parts than an automobile. "The major subsystems of a car," write industry consultants Graeme P. Maxton and John Wormald, "are the body, the chassis, the driveline, the electrical power subsystem, and the command, control, and communication subsystem. Each subsystem divides into a set of functional areas, [each of which] further subdivides into a set of specific functions . . . assembled from a set of individual components." Maxton and Wormald list 66 varieties of such individual components, many of which, in their "individuality," themselves include intricate sub-assemblages: compressors, airbags, shocks, struts, wishbones, master cylinders, pumps, catalysts, camshafts, batteries, radiators, displays, and sensors.[32] For capitalists, each and every one of these many hundreds of precision components and sub-components is a profit-bearing commodity.

All in all, the extent to which using an automobile for daily travel is a triumph of commodification can be roughly comprehended in three ways. The first way is to ponder the sheer volume of raw materials involved in automobile production. According to Maxton and Wormald, the automotive-production industry "uses 15 percent of the world's steel, 40 percent of the world's rubber, and 25 percent of the world's glass."[33] A second way to appreciate the commodity-intensity of the personal automobile is to think not just of its material bulk, but of the volume of time that individual cars typically sit parked and unused: According to UCLA Urban Planning Professor Donald Shoup, "the average car spends about 95 percent of its life parked."[34] Finally, there is the sheer financial flow: Residents of the United States alone now spend well over a *trillion* dollars every single year buying, equipping, fixing, fueling, parking, insuring, and road-building for their cars.[35]

In the small but percolating anti-car movement, such realities are why activists frequently point out that driving a personal car for everyday travel is akin to slicing bread with a chainsaw. From an economical and ecological perspective, the automobile is stupendously wasteful. From a capitalist perspective, however, it is a dream come true, a source of system-sustaining lifeblood, the basis for an industrial complex.

CONSEQUENCE #2: TRANSPORTATION INEQUALITY

In public, elite assertion and conventional thought have always portrayed the capitalist transportation industrial complex as an equalizing and democratizing phenomenon. In standard accounts, technological improvements in the speed, comfort, and flexibility of travel are not only held to be excellent compensations for life's harshnesses and unfairnesses, but access to them is commonly treated as if they were easily available to almost all.

This has been especially true of conventional claims about the spread of automobiles. From the beginning, corporations and allied planners and politicians have promoted the automobile with large doses of syrupy propaganda about its overwhelming wonders and benignity. This wave of dogma routinely includes paeans to the automobile's allegedly democratic and egalitarian nature. According to Rutgers University transportation engineer James A. Dunn, for example, not only does "the auto provide a kind of individualist equality that is particularly well suited to American values," but owning and driving cars "unites [Americans] across class, racial, ethnic, and religious lines as few other aspects of our society can."[36]

Alas, Dunn seems not to have examined the most basic data on the distribution of automobiles in the United States, to say nothing of the world. If he had bothered to do so, he might have discovered that, contrary to long-running industry intimations and intellectual pre-suppositions, both transportation and cars are, in fact, among the most *unequally* distributed product categories in the United States.

As Table 12.1[37] shows, as of 2008, on average, the richest fifth of U.S. households spent 4.6 times more money on transportation than did the poorest fifth. In the case of new vehicle purchases, the ratio for these two groups was 12.3-to-1. Such is the reality that professional experts and conventional pundits studiously ignore, all while making *a priori* claims about how cars-first transportation "unites [Americans] across class, racial, ethnic, and religious lines as few other aspects of our society can."

Though the topic is equally ignored, *qualitative* experiences with transportation and automobile acquisition also differ immensely as one descends the pyramid of social stratification in the United States.

For the private jet set, the travel world is luxurious and comparatively full of fun. CNBC reports that, as of 2008, "Private jet travel [was] the fastest growing luxury market segment. Over 15 percent of all flights in the U.S.

Table 12.1   Average Per-Household Income and Spending United States, 2008

	Richest Quintile	*Poorest Quintile*	*RQ/PQ Ratio*
Pre-Tax Income	$158,652	$10,263	15.5
Expenditures:			
Tobacco	$268	$268	1.0
Healthcare	$4,391	$1,624	2.7
Food	$10,982	$3,473	3.2
Housing	$30,791	$8,900	3.5
Apparel	$3,490	$962	3.6
Transportation	$15,614	$3,430	4.6
Passenger Fares	$1,335	$220	6.1
Vehicle Purchases	$5,457	$845	6.5
- Used	$1,997	$492	4.1
- New	$3,183	$258	12.3
Entertainment	$5,673	$1,082	5.2
Insurance & Pensions	$15,126	$532	28.4

Source: Consumer Expenditure Survey, 2008.

are by private jet. There are more than 1,000 daily private jet flights in key markets such as South Florida, New York and Los Angeles."[38] In between Asian and European shopping junkets, trips to exotic beaches, and retreats to country homes, the super-rich commonly maintain mega-garages full of extravagant, specialized cars and trucks, each of which serves the need or mood of any particular moment. "The typical Ferrari customer, for example, orders $20,000 to $30,000 of options, reports CNN, noting that "most Ferrari owners have more than one—a half-dozen or so is common."[39]

At the bottom of American society, experiences are different. In 2001, when 11.7 percent of U.S. households received incomes below the official poverty line, those same households accounted for only 6.1 of all automotive miles traveled in the United States.[40] The last time the U.S. Department of Transportation conducted its National Household Transportation Survey, it found that:

> Households without a vehicle are not spread uniformly across the population. For example, households with an annual income of less than $25,000 are al-most nine times as likely to be a zero-vehicle household than households with incomes greater than $25,000. Not only is income related to the availability of household vehicles, but it is also related to the age of the vehicle. For example,

households with a household income of $100,000 or more had a vehicle with an average model year of [5 years old], while households with a household income of less than $25,000 had a personal vehicle [when they had one] with an average model year of [ten years old].[41]

At a purely logical level of analysis, seeing a car critic such as the present author draw attention to inequality in the distribution of automobiles might strike some readers as a case of forgetting the lesson of the old joke in which the diner complains that "The food in this restaurant is awful, and the portions—so small!" Yet, however awful cars-first transportation may be, it remains true that, once it exists, access to one's own automobile can be a major determinant of the quality of life.

Indeed, in her extensive interviews with welfare recipients in the United States, family sociologist Karen Seccombe has found that automobiles are a very deep dilemma in their lives. Seccombe summarizes what she learned:

> It . . . became clear in the interviews that transportation was a major structural barrier to women getting or keeping jobs. Past recipients . . . report that the lack of affordable transportation presents a barrier even more serious than the lack of childcare to securing employment. Women on welfare cannot afford to buy reliable automobiles. . . . Most women who had cars . . . [almost always] owned older models that were in a constant state of disrepair. . . . Obviously, [despite a widely-known political trope to the contrary] women on welfare are not driving Cadillacs. . . . While offhand it is easy to say, "You can walk to work," reality may dictate something else. . . . Walking can add an hour or two to childcare bills, and may necessitate being away from one's children for 9, 10, or 11 hours a day instead of the usual 8. . . . In many communities, walking to work can be more than just inconvenient. It can be dangerous.[42]

Of course, this reality is immensely worse at the global level. The most basic statistics about worldwide disparities in access to transportation are stark. In the United States, there are now about 765 motor vehicles per 1,000 residents, and these vehicles operate on more than 4.2 million miles of paved, dedicated roadways. Meanwhile the number of motor vehicles per thousand residents is 19 in Guatemala, 8 in Pakistan, and less than 1 in both Afghanistan and Malawi.[43]

CONSEQUENCE #3:
GLOBAL SOCIO-ECONOMIC ENDANGERMENT

Anti-car activists' observation that driving an automobile for everyday personal mobility is like using a chainsaw to slice bread may prove to have been an understatement. Strong evidence is mounting that capitalism's transportation industrial complex and its cars-first sub-component are deeply implicated in twenty-first-century humanity's burgeoning, multifacetedaceted socio-political crisis.

The most intractable dilemma may be the mismatch between capitalist priorities and the planet's energy supplies. Petroleum, the primary fuel for the world's existing cars-first infrastructures, is almost certainly a one-of-a-kind substance in terms of its advantages as an automotive fuel. "Oil," observes urban critic James Howard Kunstler:

> Is an amazing substance. It stores a tremendous amount of energy per weight and volume. It is easy to transport. It stores easily at regular temperature in unpressurized metal tanks, and it can sit there indefinitely without degrading. You can pump it through a pipe, you can send it all over the world in ships, you can haul it around in trains, cars, and trucks. You can even fly it in tanker planes and refuel other airplanes in flight. It is flammable but has proven to be safe to handle with a modest amount of care. . . . It can be refined by straightforward distillation into many grades of fuel . . . and innumerable useful products. . . . It has been cheap and plentiful.[44]

According to leading geologists, "peak oil," the point at which half the Earth's original stock of petroleum has been extracted, has either already arrived, or will very soon.[45] When it does, we will have used up not just half, but the "easy half," of Earth's oil reserves. Thereafter, obtaining more petroleum will be increasingly difficult, expensive, energy intensive, and ecologically destructive.[46]

Meanwhile, many Americans, swallowing the claims of speculators and, increasingly, the automotive industrial complex itself, believe one or more "alternative fuels" can replace petroleum as an adequate energy basis for cars-first transportation. For a host of reasons related to Kunstler's point about the uniqueness of pre-peak petroleum, this is likely to prove a pipedream.

Consider the example of one of the first popular proposals for replacing petroleum but keeping autos-über-alles: hydrogen cells. Problems abound here. First of all, contrary to what you may have gleaned from their promoters, hydrogen cells are merely a new kind of battery, not a new energy source. As such, the energy they might make available to cars must come from somewhere outside the hydrogen cells themselves. And producing hydrogen is both expensive and energy-intensive. "Extracting useful quantities of hydrogen from water requires a massive amount of energy—energy that typically comes from burning oil or coal," reports Fox News.[47] Indeed, advocates of "the hydrogen economy" now concede that the only "solution to large-scale hydrogen production lies in using renewable electricity to extract hydrogen."[48] But where will we get all the new "renewable electricity" it would take to produce enough sequestered hydrogen to run the U.S. Automotive fleet? Hydrogen's boosters, now a dwindling corps, don't say. All in all, surveying the range of hydrogen cells' costs and technical problems, physicist Joseph Romm concludes: "Seriously—how many fatal flaws does the technology need? Hydrogen cars were apparently killed in the drawing room by the knife, revolver, lead pipe, rope, *and* candlestick."[49]

Converting cars to natural gas is another possibility. But, again, there are huge, basic problems. Like hydrogen, natural gas is just that—a gas, not a liquid or a solid. As such, it is much harder than petroleum to contain and move. In order to ship natural gas across oceans, for instance, the gas must first be liquified, then loaded onto tankers, sailed without spills, and finally de-liquified and contained after off-loading. Doing this on a vast-enough scale to run even a small chunk of the U.S. auto fleet would mean building, maintaining, and defending a large amount of extremely expensive and energy-intensive new infrastructures at both the shipping and receiving ends. And, shipping is less than half the problem. How dangerous and expensive would an adequate national network of natural gas car-filling stations be? How dangerous would leaking natural gas be in both car crashes and garaged, aging vehicles? Nobody knows, but the physical properties of natural gas don't suggest happy answers.

And then there is also the supply problem: As in the case of petroleum, Earth's natural gas supply is finite. Indeed, many experts believe we will hit "peak natural gas" in the very near future.[50] Hence, even if it were possible, converting autos-über-alles to natural gas would likely be an extremely Pyrrhic victory. As energy scholar Richard Heinberg puts it, "in view of the precarious status of North American gas supplies, it seems . . . likely that any attempt to shift to natural gas . . . would simply waste time and capital in the enlargement of an infrastructure that will soon be obsolete anyway—while also quickly burning up a natural resource of potential value to future generations."[51]

What about plant-derived "biofuels" such as ethanol, methanol, and bio diesel? Alas, despite the enthusiasm of their promoters, making biofuels also requires very large up-front energy inputs. These include heavy use of petroleum-based fertilizers and pesticides to grow the plants, highly mechanized harvesting and crop-transport operations, and complex extraction, distillation, refining, and fuel-distribution processes. Even for the most economical of the existing bio-fuels—corn ethanol—research shows that "[e]thanol production using corn grain require[s] 29 percent more fossil energy than the ethanol fuel produce[s]" when burned.[52]

Making biofuel from leaves, wood, grasses, or algae is also possible. But these processes involve even more complex and expensive processes for growing, gathering, processing, and disposing of plant inputs than does making automotive fuel from a naturally sugary grain like corn. In fact, thanks to their added complexity and expense, both cellulosic ethanol and algae-derived oils remain commercially unavailable on any scale, while even boosters publicly continue to wonder "Is it doable?"[53] Even heavily subsidized demonstration plants struggle to meet a fraction of their goals. "[I]t is clear that we cannot count on demonstration plants to produce at or near capacity in 2010, or in their first few years of operation for that matter," admitted the Environmental Protection Agency in early 2010.[54]

Even if scientists someday find a way to coax net energy surpluses from biofuels, mass producing them on a scale adequate to running autos-über-alles would have truly radical impacts on both agriculture and ecospheres. Gathering enough wild wood, grass, or leaves to make our car fleet go would make present rates of forest, wetland, and grassland destruction look like a tea party. Likewise, growing enough corn to power 200 million cars would require shifting huge tracts of cropland away from food production. Experts who have studied this issue find that converting the whole U.S. car fleet to corn ethanol would, by the year 2012, require "all the available cropland area" in the United States. "[B]y the year 2036, not only the entire US cropland area but also the entire land area now used for range and pasture would be required. Finally, by 2048, virtually the whole country, with the exception of cities, would be covered by corn plantations."[55] And this is the situation for the most promising of the biofuel candidates. Imagine a nation of shore-to-shore scum-ponds for growing algae.

There is one other geologically given, energy-rich fuel that remains in somewhat more optimistic supply: coal. Predictably, some who won't allow themselves to question the transportation status quo suggest that coal could keep present arrangements going smoothly for several more decades. But fueling the U.S. auto fleet on either liquefied coal or electricity made from stepped-up rates of coal-burning would require construction of a forest of new coal processing plants, and getting "the coal which would have to go into these plants would involve the largest mining operation the world has ever seen."[56] Worse, processing and burning coal is much dirtier than processing and burning either petroleum or natural gas. "[T]he coal-fired power plant," reports *The New York Times,* "burns the dirtiest, most carbon-laden of fuels, and its smokestacks belch millions of tons of carbon dioxide, the main global warming gas."[57]

Even solar-electric collectors, if they could ever be made compact, lightweight, and quick-charging enough to power road-worthy automobiles, will likely always require uneconomical amounts of up-front energy "embedded in the manufacture of . . . solar panels."[58] Furthermore, sunlight energy is inherently diffuse and variable. As a result, with even the very best (i.e., extremely expensive) current solar technology, it takes a massive, raw-materials-intensive contraption to gather enough of the Sun's radiation to compete with the gas can in your garage. According to its lead builder, Cal Tech chemist Nathan S. Lewis, this whole cutting-edge solar-electric structure (see Figure 12.1) produces only "the energy equivalent of about one gallon of gasoline"[59] per day.

Meanwhile, energy supply is but one dimension of the iceberg of the world's emerging transportation-related social crisis. There are also serious matters of pollution. In the United States, the largest source of carbon dioxide emissions comes "from fossil fuel combustion, the largest share of any end-use economic sector," with cars and trucks accounting for seven-eighths of "the transportation sector."[61] The U.S. automotive fleet, in other words produces more greenhouse gases than do all the nation's industrial production facilities; all the nation's retail stores; all the nation's personal residences.[62] In February of 2010, NASA scientists examined worldwide evidence, and concluded that, of all economic sectors of the world economy, "motor vehicles emerged as the greatest contributor to atmospheric warming now and in the near term. Cars, buses, and trucks release pollutants and greenhouse gases that promote warming, while emitting few aerosols that counteract it."[63]

The problem here, as almost everybody now knows, is that current-scale human hydrocarbon combustion may be causing or speeding global warming. We know Alaska's glaciers are retreating 100 feet a year, as its northernmost villages sink into rising seas.[64] Scientists also point out that the famines and wars wracking Africa's Sahel Zone, including the supposedly "cultural" civil

Figure 12.1[60]

war in Darfur, Sudan, probably stem as much from agricultural problems induced by wind-born air pollution and global-warming-induced soil drying as from the more famous problems of overgrazing, population growth, and ethno-religious zealotry.[65] Meanwhile, even the Pentagon has begun to worry about the "possibility that [even] gradual global warming could lead to a relatively abrupt slowing of the oceans' thermohaline conveyor, which could lead to harsher winter weather conditions, sharply reduced soil moisture, and more intense winds in certain regions that currently provide a significant fraction of the world's food production. With inadequate preparation, the result could be a significant drop in the human carrying capacity of the Earth's environment."[66]

Finally, and perhaps most dangerously, there are almost certainly deep and conscious behind-the-scenes links between major capitalist interests, the existing transportation industrial complex, elite military policies, and the danger of future wars.

Consider the example of former Iranian Prime Minister Mohammad Mossadegh. In the eyes of the powers-that-be in the United States, Mossadegh was the ultimate Middle Eastern enemy—a secular oil-state democrat. *Time* magazine's "Man of the Year" for 1951, Mossadegh wanted to re-focus Iranian politics on oil revenues and domestic democracy. Appointed Prime Minister in 1951 by Iran's democratically-elected parliament and backed by a clear majority of Iranians, Mossadegh quickly moved to nationalize Iran's previously British-dominated oil industry, so that Iranians could henceforth retain most of Iran's oil revenues for the primary use and benefit of themselves. Mossadegh's repayment? To stamp out this expression of sane, secular independence atop "our" Middle Eastern oil, the CIA overthrew Mossadegh in an August 1953 coup d'etat. His U.S.-selected replacement? Reza "the Shah" Pahlavi, the "king" who, having signed the "royal order" that removed Mossadegh from office and put the CIA's coup in motion, fled to the safety of Rome. Days later, after the CIA's minions had imprisoned Mossadegh, the Shah flew home and proceeded, over the next 25 years, to re-impose one-party rule, jail and/or kill a huge percentage of Mossadegh's political allies and supporters, and fill his own personal coffers with kickbacks and payoffs from the U.S. government and transnational oil corporations, whom the Shah welcomed back to their traditional dominant places.[67]

This massive, momentous (and, in the United States, still virtually unknown) international crime was merely the beginning of the United States' ruthless and unwavering opposition to secularity, democracy, and independence in petroleum states.[68] Cutting the sweetheart deals they can probably only get from kings and autocrats, and using warring Jewish and Islamic theocrats to keep the Middle East's masses otherwise occupied, top U.S.

policy makers have consistently been willing to risk whole populations—not excluding that of the United States itself—in order to preserve the corporate elite's dominance over the extraction and deployment of nature's one-time gift of petroleum.[69] The ensuing horrors and perversions of life in the Middle East have been vast and obvious. As they persist, so does the likelihood of further blowback.

In the United States, which was itself once the world's leading oil exporter, domestic production of petroleum entered permanent decline in the early 1970s, just as M. King Hubbert, the original "peak oil" theorist, had predicted. If cars-first transportation continues to exist in the United States, progressively increasing dependence on imported hydrocarbons is assured. Meanwhile, current oil-exporting nations will themselves face trouble, as their domestic supplies peak and their populations grow. The ensuing tensions are sure to heighten the risk of new oil wars. In a fractious, ideologically zealous, heavily armed world, shouldn't this give us the ultimate pause? After all, it was none other than Albert Einstein who once said that, while he wasn't sure what weapons would be used in World War III, he was quite sure World War IV would "be fought with sticks and stones."[70]

CONCLUSION

In his magnum opus, *Capital: A Critique of Political Economy,* Karl Marx elaborated his and Friedrich Engels' previous thoughts on capitalists' intense institutional interests in the radical commodification of life. "'After me, the flood!,'" Marx noted in a classic passage, "is the watchword of every capitalist and every capitalist nation. "Capital is reckless of the health or length of life of the laborer, unless under compulsion from society. To outcries about physical and mental degradation, premature death, the torture of overwork, it answers: "Ought these to trouble us, since they increase our profits?"

The evidence, for those willing to see it, is powerful and frightening. If the human race is to survive the twenty-first century still in possession of the social and ecological basis for continued science-aided, culturally complex and egalitarian living, we will almost certainly have to examine capital's continuing heedlessness to "premature death." The transportation industrial complex, constructed under the stern logic of the world's dominant institutions and individuals, embodies this heedlessness in especially deep and urgent ways. While its continued operation threatens to trigger global ecological and energy-supply catastrophes, its unexamined collapse would also deal a severe blow to capitalism, and, thereby, existing processes of social sustenance and reproduction. In the face of this conundrum, either society will rise up and protect itself from the multiple, profound attending threats to our and our children's chances at further advancing life, liberty, and the pursuit of happiness, or we may very well see ourselves driven into the land of Mad Max.

NOTES

1. Karl Marx and Friedrich Engels, *The Communist Manifesto.* (New York, NY: Monthly Review Press, 1964), 7.

2. Karl Marx and Friedrich Engels, *The Communist Manifesto.*

3. I would define "industrial complex" as a group of qualitatively related activities large and functionally important enough to be necessary for the continued operation of a particular socio-economic order.

4. In *Full House: The Spread of Excellence from Plato to Darwin,* Stephen Jay Gould argued that, "If we could replay the game of life again and again," some high-complexity lifeforms would always emerge, "but the inhabitants of this region of greatest complexity would be wildly and unpredictably different in each rendition—and the vast majority of replays would never produce (on the finite scale of a planet's lifetime) a creature with self-consciousness."

5. J. Marks, "Genetic Assimilation in the Evolution of Bipedalism," *Human Evolution* 4, no. 6 (December 1989): 493.

6. Marvin Harris, *Our Kind: Who We Are, Where We Came From, Where We are Going* (New York, NY: Harper Perennial, 1989), 2–3.

7. On bumbling intensification and its connection to social stratification, see Marvin Harris, *Cannibals and Kings: The Fates of Human Cultures* (New York, NY: Vintage Books, 1974); John H. Bodley, *The Power of Scale: A Global History Approach* (Armonk, NY: M. E. Sharpe, 2002); and Jared Diamond, *Collapse: How Societies Choose to Fail or Succeed* (New York, NY: Viking, 2004).

8. Jared Diamond, *Guns, Germs, and Steel: The Fates of Human Societies* (New York, NY: W. W. Norton, 1997), 41.

9. Jared Diamond, *Guns, Germs, and Steel,* 90–91.

10. David W. Anthony, *The Horse, The Wheel, and Language: How Bronze Age Riders From the Eurasian Steppes Shaped the Modern World* (Princeton, NJ: Princeton University Press, 2007), 73–74.

11. J. R. McNeill and William H. McNeill, *The Human Web: A Bird's-Eye View of World History* (New York, NY: W. W. Norton, 2003), 164.

12. J. R. McNeill and William H. McNeill, *The Human Web,* 163.

13. Robert G. Angevine, *The Railroad and the State: War, Politics, and Technology in Nineteenth-Century America* (Stanford, CA: Stanford University Press, 2004), 227.

14. For more on the sociology of commodities, see Karl Marx, *Capital: A Critique of Political Economy, Volume I* (New York, NY: Vintage, 1977), and Marvin Harris, *Why Nothing Works: The Anthropology of Daily Life* (New York, NY: Touchstone, 2000).

15. Timothy R. Walton, *The Spanish Treasure Fleets* (Sarasota, FL: Pineapple Press, 2002), 21.

16. Eduardo Galeano, *Open Veins of Latin America: Five Centuries of the Pillage of a Continent* (New York, NY: Monthly Review Press, 1997), 188.

17. Timothy R. Walton, *Spanish Treasure Fleets*, 22.

18. Maurice W. Kirby, *The Origins of Railway Enterprise: The Stockton and Darlington Railway 1821–1863* (Cambridge, UK: Cambridge University Press, 2002), 65, 67.

19. John Metcalfe, Age of Steam, www.railcentre.co.uk/ (accessed July 12, 2010):

20. John Metcalfe, Age of Steam.

21. John Metcalfe, Age of Steam.

22. U.S. Department of Transportation, "U.S. Transportation Secretary Ray LaHood: Overall Traffic Fatalities Reach Record Low," Press Release Number DOT 93–09, July 2, 2009, www.nhtsa.dot.gov (accessed July 12, 2010).

23. See NHTSA annual releases. For a useful single-page view of the data for 1957 through 1997, see "Annual US Street & Highway Fatalities from 1957," www.publicpurpose.com/hwy-fatal57+.htm (accessed July 12, 2010).

24. L. Blincoe, A. Seay, E. Zaloshnja, T. Miller, E. Romano, S. Luchter, and R. Spicer, "The Economic Impact of Motor Vehicle Crashes, 2000," U.S. DOT Technical Report 809446, www.nhtsa.dot.gov (accessed July 12, 2010), 9.

25. Jean Edward Smith, *Lucius D. Clay: An American Life* (New York, NY: Henry Holt and Company, 1990), 619.

26. For a fuller review of these trends, see Chapter 2, Michael Dawson, *The Consumer Trap: Big Business Marketing in American Life* (Urbana, IL: University of Illinois Press, 2003).

27. See John Bellamy Foster and Fred Magdoff, *The Great Financial Crisis: Causes and Consequences* (New York, NY: Monthly Review Press, 2009).

28. Regis McKenna, *Total Access: Giving Customers What They Want in an Anytime, Anywhere World* (Boston, MA: Harvard Business School Press, 2002), 2.

29. John W. Howell, February 5, 1987 Tape-Recorded Interview, conducted by Barbara Griffith, Alka-Seltzer Oral History and Documentation Project, Smithsonian Institution, Center for Advertising History, National Museum of American History—Archives Center, Washington, DC, Collection Number 184.

30. See Thorstein Veblen, who coined the phrase "neo-classical" and observed that, among its practitioners, "[t]he categories employed for the purpose of knowing this economic conduct with which the scientists occupy themselves are not the categories under which the men at whose hands the action takes place themselves apprehend their own action at the instant of acting. Therefore, economic conduct still continues to be somewhat mysterious to the economists." In Thorstein Veblen, "The Preconceptions of Economic Science III," *Quarterly Journal of Economics*, Volume 14, no. 2 (February 1900): 269.

31. Michael Dawson, *Courting Carmageddon: Capitalism, Transportation, and the Crisis of the United States* (New York, NY: Monthly Review Press, forthcoming).

32. Graeme P. Maxton and John Wormald, *Time for a Model Change: Re-Engineering the Global Automotive Industry* (Cambridge, UK: Cambridge University Press, 2004), 137–139.

33. Graeme P. Maxton and John Wormald, *Time for a Model Change*, 3.

34. Donald C. Shoup, *The High Cost of Free Parking* (Chicago, IL: Planners Press/American Planning Association, 2005), 6.

35. Vehicle-purchase, equipment, fuel, repair, parking, and roadway figures are reported in *National Income and Product Accounts of the United States*, Table 2.4.5. (lines 3, 34, and 62) and 3.15.5 (line 13), all available at www.bea.gov. Insurance expenditures calculated from 2002 data reported by the Insurance Information Institute, *III—Auto Insurance*, www2.iii.org/media/facts/statsbyissue/auto/ (accessed July 12, 2010).

36. James A. Dunn, *Driving Forces: The Automobile, Its Enemies, and the Politics of Mobility* (Washington, DC: The Brookings Institute Press, 1998), 1.

37. Consumer Expenditure Survey, 2008, Table 1: Quintiles of Income, U.S. Department of Labor, Bureau of Labor Statistics, ftp://ftp.bls.gov/pub/special.requests/ce/standard/2008/quintile.txt (accessed July 12, 2010).

38. "Untold Wealth: The Rise of the Super-Rich," CNBC special report, www.cnbc.com/id/25013054/ (accessed July 12, 2010).

39. Peter Valdez-Dapena, "How the Super-Rich Go Car Shopping," *CNN*, April 6, 2006, www.cnn.com/2006/AUTOS/04/04/rich_car_shopping/index.html (accessed July 12, 2010).

40. See Census Bureau, "Poverty Rate Rises, Household Income Declines, Census Bureau Reports," CB 02–124, www.census.gov/Press-Release/www/2002/cb02–124.html (accessed July 12, 2010); U.S. Energy Information Administration, "Table A7. U.S. Vehicle-Miles Traveled by Family Income and Poverty Status, 2001" www.eia.doe.gov/emeu/rtecs/nhts_survey/2001/tablefiles/table-a07.pdf (accessed July 12, 2010).

41. U.S. Department of Transportation Statistic[s], "Household, Individual, and Vehicle Characteristics," 2001 National Household Travel Survey, www.bts.gov/publications/highlights_of_the_2001_national_household_travel_survey/html/section_01.html (accessed July 12, 2010).

42. Karen Seccombe, *"So You Think I Drive a Cadillac?": Welfare Recipients' Perspectives on the System and Its Reform* (Boston, MA: Pearson/Allyn & Bacon, 2007), 92–93.

43. Figures are United Nations Environment Programme data, as reported by www.nationmaster.com/graph/tra_mot_veh-transportation-motor-vehicles (accessed July 12, 2010).

44. James Howard Kunstler, *The Long Emergency: Surviving the Converging Catastrophes of the Twenty-First Century* (New York, NY: Atlantic Monthly Press, 2005), 31.

45. For up-to-date access to such professional opinion, see "Peak Oil Primer," www.energybulletin.net/primer.php (accessed July 12, 2010).

46. See, for example, Clifford Krauss, "In Canada's Wilderness, Measuring the Cost of Oil Profits," *The New York Times* (National Edition), October 9, 2005, 3.

47. "Hydrogen Fuel May Not Be So 'Clean,'" January 24, 2005, www.foxnews.com (accessed July 12, 2010).

48. "The Car of the Perpetual Future," unsigned editorial, September 4, 2008, www.economist.com/science/tq/displaystory.cfm?story_id=11999229 (accessed July 12, 2010).

49. Joseph Romm, "*The Economist* Agrees With Me on Hydrogen," September 14, 2008, gristmill.grist.org/story/2008/9/12/11056/3834 (accessed July 12, 2010).

50. John Mills, quoted in www.peakoil.net/headline-news/shell-vice-president-peak-gas-could-come-earlier-than-we-think (accessed July 12, 2010).

51. Richard Heinberg, *The Party's Over: Oil, War and the Fate of Industrial Societies*, Second Edition (Gabriola Island, BC, 2005), 143.

52. David Pimentel and Tad W. Patzek, "Ethanol Production Using Corn, Switchgrass, and Wood; Biodiesel Production Using Soybean and Sunflower," *Natural Resources Research* 14, no. 1 (March, 2005): 65.

53. On unavailability, see American Petroleum Institute, "Ethanol Fact Sheet," www.api.org/aboutoilgas/otherfuels/upload/Ethanol_Fact_Sheet_Final.pdf (accessed July 12, 2010); Michael Kanellos, "The Challenge of Algae Fuel: An Expert Speaks," August 23, 2007, news.cnet.com/8301–10784_3–9765452-7.html (accessed July 12, 2010).

54. Beth Evans, "Cellulosic Shortfalls of Two Companies Led to RFS Target Cut: EPA," February 5, 2010, www.platts.com/RSSFeedDetailedNews.aspx?xmlpath=RSSFeed/HeadlineNews/Oil/6787243.xml (accessed July 12, 2010).

55. Marcelo E. Dias De Oliveira, Burton E. Vaughan, and Edward J. Rykiel Jr., "Ethanol as Fuel: Energy, Carbon Dioxide Balances, and Ecological Footprint," *Bioscience* 55, no. 7 (July, 2005): 600.

56. Walter Youngquist, *Geodestinies: The Inevitable Control of Earth Resources Over Nations and Individuals* (Portland, Oregon: Halcyon House/National Book Company, 1997), 224.

57. Steve Lohr, "The Cost of an Overheated Planet," December 12, 2006, www.nytimes.com/2006/12/12/business/worldbusiness/12warm.html (accessed July 12, 2010).

58. See Dmitry Podborits, "High Noon in the Desert," December 20, 2005, www.livejournal.com/users/dpodbori/3590.html (accessed July 12, 2010).

59. Nathan S. Lewis, "Powering the Planet," *Engineering & Science,* Number 2, 2007, 23, eands.caltech.edu/articles/LXX2/lewis-web.pdf (accessed July 12, 2010).

60. Frontal View of SAIC Dish, National Renewable Energy Laboratory, Courtesy of DOE/NREL, Credit—Warren Gretz.

61. U.S. Environmental Protection Agency, "Inventory of U.S. Greenhouse Gas Emissions and Sinks: 1990—2006," April 15, 2008, www.epa.gov/climatechange/emissions/downloads/08_CR.pdf (accessed July 12, 2010): 3–8.

62. See U.S. E.P.A., "Inventory of U.S. Greenhouse Gas," Figure 3–9: 3–8.

63. See "Road Transportation Emerges as Key Driver of Warming in New Analysis from NASA," February 18, 2010, www.nasa.gov/topics/earth/features/road-transportation.html (accessed July 12, 2010).

64. Timothy Egan, "The Race to Alaska Before It Melts," travel2.nytimes.com/2005/06/26/travel/26alaska.html (accessed July 12, 2010), June 26, 2005.

65. See Tim Flannery, *The Weather Makers: How Man is Changing the Climate and What It Means for Life on Earth* (New York, NY: Atlantic Monthly Press, 2006), 125–126.

66. Peter Schwartz and Doug Randall, *An Abrupt Climate Change Scenario and Its Implications for United States National Security: A Report Commissioned by the U.S. Defense Department* (Washington, DC: Environmental Media Services, October 2003), 1.

67. Stephen Kinzer, *All the Shah's Men: An American Coup and the Roots of Middle East Terror* (New York, NY: John Wiley and Sons, 2004).

68. See Noam Chomsky, *Failed States,* 110–165.

69. Robert Baer, *Sleeping With the Devil: How Washington Sold Our Soul for Saudi Crude* (New York, NY: Three Rivers Press, 2004).

70. See en.wikiquote.org/wiki/Albert_Einstein (accessed July 12, 2010).

Afterword

Peter McLaren

Mit der Dummheit kämpfen Götter selbst vergebens.
("With stupidity even the gods struggle in vain.")

—Friedrich Schiller on Germany

Yes, of course it's nice to have a president who speaks in complete sentences. But that they're coherent doesn't make them honest.

—John R. MacArthur, publisher of Harper's Magazine

Struggle exposes us to the simple form of failure (the assault did not succeed), while victory exposes us to its most redoubtable form: we notice that we have won in vain, and that our victory paves the way for repetition and restoration. That, for the state, a revolution is never anything more than an intervening period. Hence the sacrificial temptations of nothingness. For a politics of emancipation, the enemy that is to be feared most is not repression at the hands of the established order. It is the interiority of nihilism, and the unbounded cruelty that can come with emptiness.

—Alain Badiou

The conflict between private appropriation and the social needs of humanity has reached a juncture of the most extreme exigency. It is no exaggeration to assert that the survival of humanity is at stake. The task to transform the alienation and suffering that has afflicted humanity for centuries into social relations of substantive equality, reciprocity and sustainable development seems today more daunting than ever. And while the credulousness of the transnational capitalist class is in serious jeopardy as never before, the neoliberal consensus that blankets the globe like the industrial flatulence from the

Great Smog of London has caused those most hurt by it to remain at a standstill. The popular majorities who remain ensepulchured in a culture of silence stare ahead, as if they are watching a blank screen, their lives unspooling like a film in an empty projection room. Almost all of the options put on the table by the politicians simply reboot the same conditions that fomented the crisis.

This is the case, in part, because many critics of the current crisis of capital place the blame on the creditor class and its bubblemeisters, on the banking system of widespread negative equity (which included gangster capitalists who headed Citigroup as well as master manipulators who ran hedge funds attached to investment banks such as Lehman Bros. and Bear Stearns), on over-mortgaged real estate, or on over-indebted corporations. Yet it has become increasingly clear, even to those uninitiated in the grand mysteries of neoliberal economics, that financialization is not just a mistake made by greedy corporate executives, but is part of capital unleashed, part of the unrestrainment of capital.

Our lives are organically interrelated in a mighty, entangled, supersensible ensemble of social relations. Clearly in this enmeshment, those who control capital control the government, forcing governments to become part of a corporate superstructure, overseeing capital's base. And there has been an accompanying corporate colonization of civil society as well, effectively stifling any ameliorative function that might be offered by new social movements, those very pragmatic organizations that have become a more capital-friendly substitute for revolutionary manifestos of groups bent on overthrowing the regime of capital. U.S. bankers are set for record compensation for a second consecutive year, shattering both the illusion of pay reform and the expectation that bank bonuses would be tempered while the U.S. economy remains weak.

With U.S. companies garnering record amounts of cash, they have decided not to hire workers or build factories or spend their profits on job-generating activities but instead have vigorously engaged in buying back (by some estimates $273 billion of) their own stock shares to prop up their own share prices. A share buyback is a quick way to make a stock more attractive to Wall Street. It improves a closely watched metric known as earnings per share, which divides a company's profit by the total number of shares on the market. Such a move can produce a sudden burst of interest in a stock, improving its price.

Speculative expansion under the banner of extreme free market ideology and monopoly finance capital has boosted capital accumulation, but in doing so it has increased both income and wealth inequality. This polarization and its attendant antagonisms has signaled the inevitable decline of civilization. It is not so much a question of oversupply and underconsumption as it is the

Real Wealth
vs
Speculative Wealth

frictionless logic of capital in which we witness production occurring today solely for the benefit of capital in order to generate profit or surplus value, a process that effectuates the co-propriety of capital and power. We can see with much greater transparency the egregious inequalities between the social classes and between countries, between the agrarian workers in the so-called Third World, the unemployed and the unemployable in the slums of our major cities, and the middle classes of the so-called "developed" nations. We can see, too, that these conditions have been accompanied by boundless planetary ecological destruction. The current capitalist system cannot impose limits to the growth necessary to sustain itself. Unencumbered capitalism and the juggernaut of imperialism that follows in its wake has the greatest potential to wreak havoc upon the world in terms of further imperialist wars, not to mention ecological destruction of the entire planet.

Sociologist William Robinson has discussed the development of a new transnational model of accumulation in which transnational fractions of capital have become dominant. New mechanisms of accumulation, as Robinson notes, include a cheapening of labor and the growth of flexible, deregulated and de-unionized labor where women always experience super-exploitation in relation to men; the dramatic expansion of capital itself; the creation of a global and regulatory structure to facilitate the emerging global circuits of accumulation; and neo-liberal structural adjustment programs which seek to create the conditions for unfettered operations of emerging transnational capital across borders and between countries.

Oligarchies such as the U.S. power elite benefit from the consolidation of numerous matrices of power, whose generation of surplus value potential is transnational in reach, and whose multifarious and decentralized institutional arrangements are organized around the industrial, bureaucratic and commodity models that have commonly been associated with the military industrial complex. All of these "power complexes" have intersecting social, cultural and political spheres that can be managed ideologically by means of powerful, all-encompassing corporate media apparatuses and the culture industry in general, including both popular and more traditional forms of religious dogma and practice. Taking on a role of increasing importance today is the religious industrial complex that provides the moral alibi for acts of war and military incursions throughout the world, so necessary for imperialist expansion. All of these power complexes tacitly and manifestly teach values, and produce ideational schemata that serve as interpretive templates or systems of intelligibility through which the popular majorities make sense of everyday life via the language of technification, corporatization, bureaucratic administration, and commodification knitted together (in the United States) by ideological imperatives of religious ideology, American exceptionalism, and the coloniality of power. These have been easier to consolidate and integrate organically into the fabric of U.S. corporate life during the rise of neoliberal capitalism with its supranational integration of national classes and productive structures and the frenzied dynamics of marketization and the destruction of completing ideologies such as socialism and thus have succeeded in becoming integrated into the structural unconscious of the American public more securely than ever before. While national capital, global capital, regional capitals, are still prevalent, the hegemonic fraction of capital on a world scale is now transnational capital. We are witnessing the profound dismantling of national economies, the reorganization and reconstitution of national economies as component elements or segments of a larger global production and financial system which is organized in a globally fragmented way and a decentralized way but in a manner in which power is concentrated and centralized. In other words, as Robinson notes, there is a decentralization and fragmentation of the actual national production process all over the globe while the control of these processes—these endless chains of accumulation—is concentrated and centralized at a global level by a transnationalist capitalist class.

While all of these power complexes overlap and interpenetrate each other at the level of capital accumulation and value production, and reinforce the sovereign ideologies of the capitalist state through both new and old media technologies, the production of dominant ideologies is neither lock-step nor harmonious but it does result in an over-determination that enables major "class" conflicts to be avoided.

The academic industrial complex is one of the more pernicious developments that has accompanied neoliberal globalization. Never before in modern history have we been so close to the demise of public education and so far from the promise of educational equality. With President Obama's enthusiastic support, a two million dollar marketing grant by Bill Gates, and a showing at the White House, the film *Waiting for Superman* has been touted as a road map toward saving U.S. schools from bad teachers. In reality, it is an attack on what remains of public schooling, and a shrewd attempt to promote for-profit charter schools and allow private corporations an opportunity to let hedge funds, finance capital and betting on the stock market dictate the future of our schools. According to the film, public schools are not only to blame for the dire results of the U.S. race for academic global dominance, but are also responsible for the economic crisis and the increased poverty and crumbling urban infrastructure that has resulted. It's a tired refrain that conveniently ignores not only the shady real estate deals engaged in by various charter school leaders (some of whom pay themselves salaries of $300,000–$400,000 a year) but also the fact that charter schools in the main do not do as well as public schools. In addition, many of these for-profit charter schools have a strong evangelical Christian religious orientation that challenges the separation between the church and the state and operate in a metaphysical netherworld of premillennial dispensationalism in which dialectical logic is mocked as an intellectual tool of the secular elite.

It is one of the cruel ironies today that capitalism has never been more accessible to conscious and conceptual revision. Yet among the popular majorities, many are not demanding its overthrow. In their eyes, there is nothing credible with which to replace it. The prevailing conviction that there is no alternative than simply to sit out the crisis of capital and wait for better times has somehow passed for verisimilitude. The causes of this misperception are many and sundry.

The Tea Party, the prehensile tail of libertarianism, has made a vertiginous descent into the bowels of the American Armageddon psyche; its comic panorama of self-deception and folly fills the airwaves, only to provoke the radical right to more extreme acts of political mania. Tea Party "patriots," whose words are clothed in the theocratic language of a resurgent fascism, have set in their sights any and all efforts to challenge a world dominated by capital. Seizing this historical moment to their advantage, Tea Party advocates attack big government, undocumented immigrants, health care reform, financial reform, and the separation of church and state, claiming that the United States was founded on a violent revolt against Britain's King George III. Not surprisingly, they fail to mention that this nation was also founded on genocide perpetuated against first nations people and on the slavery of the Middle Passage.

One might think it is an imbecilic habit of the right to play on their general supposition that we are near the end-of-times and must take back civilization from the secular humanists who have destroyed it. But this message has a powerful effect on those who have already conflated democracy with authoritarianism, believing that America must reassert itself as a civilizing force throughout the globe in order to defeat the forces of evil (with Muslims and socialists counting among the most prominent). American exceptionalism has always confronted itself with the half-memory of the blood that was shed for the sake of its imperial grandeur (some critics place the number of those slaughtered by the U.S. military and as a result of U.S. strategic support at 8,000,000 since WWII).

It should come as no surprise that some of Europe's biggest polluters are funneling money to the Chamber of Commerce and to the campaigns of Tea Party candidates. BP and several other big European companies such as BASF, Bayer and Solvay are funding the midterm election campaigns of Tea Party members who deny the existence of global warming or oppose Barack Obama's energy agenda. Approximately 80 percent of campaign donations from a number of major European firms were directed toward senators who blocked action on climate change.

The cataclysmic social and political changes of this present historical moment has unleashed aspirations among the modern Manicheans of the Christian right such that even those who confuse the actor John Wayne with John Wayne Gacy, the serial killer clown, who believe that scientists have created mice with fully functioning human brains, who claim that unemployment insurance is unconstitutional because you can't actually find the term in the original Constitution of the United States, and maintain that evolution, if true, should allow us to see monkeys turn into human beings right before our eyes, have a serious opportunity to inaugurate a new reign of guns and wars for God. As part of a one-sided polemic, generally in the form of bumptious talk show hosts or political commentators, the media for the most part have given their leadership and ideology full reign: A controversial preacher from Florida becomes the center of an international conflagration when he threatens to burn a copy of the Koran. Another anti-abortion Tea Party activist creates a video imploring fellow activists to enter the public square like Samuel Adams, and pull Koran-tearing stunts to garner more media attention. The Governor of Virginia declares Confederacy History Month and fails to mention slavery. Texas Republican congressional candidate Stephen Broden, a South Dallas pastor who called the Obama administration "tyrannical," admitted that he would not rule out violent overthrow of the government if elections did not produce a change in leadership. Broden, who once described the economic crash in the housing, banking and automotive industries as "contrived" and a "set up" by the Obama administration, claimed that the constitutional remedy for the current government is armed "revolution." Had a leftist politician said that, he or she would likely be arrested. Earlier Broden had criticized politically complacent Americans for not being more outraged over government intrusion, comparing them to Jews "walking into the furnaces" under the Nazi regime in Germany. "They are our enemies, and we must resist them," he said of the current administration in Washington.

Of course, the production of social life—even in U.S. political life—is never seamless and there are always cracks and fissures into which critical agents can insert themselves and attempt to pry open spaces of opposition. However, given that even the partially autonomous public sphere has become so fully commodified by the logic of capital, the possibilities for the kinds of public debates and policies that will lead to transformation in the direction of increasing social justice for the popular majorities seem increasingly slim. Some argue that the production of new media technologies will ensure that spaces of resistance will always be available to contest the dominant ideologies of neoliberal capitalism. While this may be the case in some instances, the lack of alternatives to the present capitalist system that seem viable in the eyes of the public has hindered the struggle for a post-capitalist future. The media and religious "complexes" that combine to unleash forms of insecurity and fear serve as an ideological wedge to inflict doubt and distrust among the popular majorities who might come to consider strikes or uprisings in the face of neoliberal capitalism's epidemic of underemployment and unemployment.  This unholy alliance can also be seen in the growing Christianization of the US military and the growth of warriors answerable only to God, and a concomitant rejection of human and constitutional governance in the name of Jesus. All of these complexes converge to shape the decisions of persons who are the subjects and objects of the mechanisms of power but they exist conjuncturally and work synergistically in such a way that their interdependence is not readily visible and is easily mystified by media pundits.

It is our wager in this book that the lives of these individuals can be understood in a much deeper sense when we are able to break through this mystification and situate the production of global humanity in a larger nexus of complexes that either humanize or dehumanize them. Not all of the forces linked to these complexes are dehumanizing, but when taken together, and by understanding their cumulative effect, we can see that they work for the greater interests of the transnational capitalist class. And we can gain an even deeper understanding of how these complexes work symbiotically when we understand how they are linked historically to the global/racial/gender/sexual/ spiritual/class hierarchy that emerged with European colonial expansion in the Americas. In other words, when we examine critically the global matrix of domination within the formation of what Peruvian social theorist, Anibal Quijano, calls the "coloniality of power" and the European colonization of the Americas. This can give us greater critical purchase on understanding the distribution of social and political power by means of social antagonisms such as the racial hierarchical system, sexism and class exploitation or what social theorist Ramon Grosfoguel calls, after Anibal Quijano, the colonial power matrix ("patrón de poder colonial") or the entangled "global racial/gender/ sexual heterarchy" that emerged with the arrival of European/capitalist/ military/christian/patriarchal/white/heterosexual/males as a part of the European colonial expansion and that continues to be reproduced the European colonial expansion and that continues to be reproduced in the modern/ colonial/capitalist world-system, one that needs to be decolonized. The continuous privileging of European culture over non-European culture, of white-associated culture over the culture of indigenous people and people of color, of Christian doctrines over indigenous belief systems, of the historical distribution of social identities and forms of control over labor that favor Anglo-Americans over other ethnic and racial groups, of the myth of

Anglo-European cultural superiority over other national groups, of clichéd stereotypes of cultural duality leading to a Manichean "us" against "them" logic over non-dualistic conceptions of a common humanity, and of the Eurocentric evolutionist perspective of linear and unidirectional movement and changes in human history over multilinear and dialectical conceptions of historical development, still cling to the conceptual integuments of American life. The high rates of exploitation and low wages in the export-oriented peripheral countries that has given rise to a crisis of overproduction, and the resulting surge of immigrants from Latin America attempting to gain entrance into the United States in order to escape this crisis, have been targeted as the sources of the problem, rather than victims of the global economic crisis.

We all live with a certain image that is constantly being embellished: that we live in a meritocracy where we are rewarded fairly for our hard work and perseverance. However, when we look around us at the age in which we live through the conceptual and analytic categories of *The Global Industrial Complex*, we see a ruling class with an unimaginable dense accumulation of wealth resulting from new forms of financial organizations designed to reproduce hegemonic social practices through the various internally related industrial complexes. The key here is the notion of "internal relations."

Marx explains capitalism in terms of internal relations—those types of relations that are central to his dialectical conceptualization of capitalism—because he found this type of relation in the real world of capitalism. Of course this was not the world of capitalism that we experience daily but the reality of capitalism that Marx was able to reveal through his penetrating analysis of the surface phenomenon of capitalism—those surfaces that constitute our immediate and illusory experience. When we examine social relations, we focus on the opposites in the relations as well as the ongoing internal development within those relations. According to Marx's analysis of capitalism, the dialectical contradiction that lies at the heart of capitalism is the relation between labor and capital. This relation together with the internal relation between capitalist production and circulation/exchange constitutes the essence of capitalism. The labor-capital relation produces the historically specific form of capitalist wealth—the value form of wealth. Value is not some hollow formality, neutral precinct, or barren hinterland emptied of power and politics but the very matter and anti-matter of our social universe of capitalism. Value is wealth in monetarized form. For Marx, the commodity is highly unstable, and non-identical. Its concrete particularity (use value) is subsumed by its existence as value-in-motion or by what we have come to know as "capital" (value is always in motion because of the increase in capital's productivity that is required to maintain expansion). The issue here is not simply that workers are exploited for their surplus value but that all forms of human sociability are constituted by the logic of capitalist work. Labor, therefore, cannot be seen as the negation of capital or the antithesis of capital but the human form through and against which capitalist work exists. Capitalist relations of production become hegemonic precisely when the process of the production of abstraction conquers the concrete processes of production, resulting in the expansion of the logic of capitalist work.

Here we need to adopt a form of relational thinking rather than categorical thinking and analysis. When two or more entities might come together and interact, and the change that occurs is external to the entities, then the result can be said to exist independently from the original entities once it has come into existence. An example could be when a male and a female of some species produce an offspring that continues to exist even when the parents do not. This is an example of external relations. Unlike external relations, the results of internal relations do not obtain a separate existence, despite the fact that they often appear to have done so. If the original entities/opposites cease to exist, which can only occur if the relation is abolished, then the result also ceases to exist.

Capital and labor, for instance, are both shaped within their relation to the other. These opposites could not be what they are or what they are to become outside of this relation. When this is an antagonistic relation, the existence of each opposite is variously constrained or hampered by virtue of the fact that it is in an internal relation with its opposite; however, one of the opposites, despite these limitations, actually benefits from the relation. It is in the interest of this opposite, often referred to as the positive, to maintain the relation. In this case the positive relation is capital. The other opposite, the negative, although it can better its circumstances temporarily within the relation, is severely limited by its relation to its opposite and sometimes to the point of devastation; therefore, it is in its interest to abolish the relation. This abolition is referred to as "the negation of the negation." The individuals constituting the negative opposites do not cease to exist, but they do cease to exist as the negative, and inferior, opposite they have been due to their existence within an internal relation/dialectical contradiction. The complexes discussed in *The Global Industrial Complex* are internally related to the capitalist system; they could not exist without value production. To dismantle these complexes we need to abolish the relationship that they have to capital. This means that we have to stop treating the symptoms of the present crisis in order to create a future outside of the social universe of capitalist value production—a socialist future.

President Obama has never considered treating anything more than the symptoms of the present crisis, so he bailed out the banks which are now doing an even better job of carrying out their neoliberal finance capital agenda than ever before, the same agenda that got us into this economic maelstrom in the first place. And he continued Bush's war against the terrorists in the name of universal values of justice. In a traditional annual speech at the opening of the United Nations General Assembly, he said: "We also know from experience that those who defend these [universal] values for their people have been our closest friends and allies, while those who have denied those rights—whether terrorist groups or tyrannical governments—have chosen to be our adversaries." As Bill Blum (2000) notes, this is a bald-faced lie. Blum elaborates:

> It would be difficult to name a single brutal dictatorship of the Western world in the second half of the 20th Century that was not supported by the United States; not only supported, but often put into power and kept in power against the wishes of the population. And in recent years as well, Washington has supported very repressive governments, such as Saudi Arabia, Honduras, Indonesia, Egypt, Kosovo, Colombia, and Israel. As to terrorist groups being adversaries of the United States—another item for the future Barack Obama Presidential Library; as I've discussed in this report on several occasions, including last month, the United States has supported terrorist groups for decades. As they've supported US foreign policy.[1]

Blum goes on to note that in the post-World War Two period, in Latin America alone, the US has had a similar hostile policy toward progressive governments and movements in Guatemala, Salvador, Nicaragua, Honduras, Grenada, Dominican Republic, Chile, Brazil, Argentina, Cuba, and Bolivia. These were leftist governments that offered a viable alternative to the capitalist model. This was the ideology of the Cold War and remains the prevailing ideology that governs U.S. foreign policy.

Since the end of World War Two the United States has, according to Blum:

- Endeavored to overthrow more than 50 foreign governments, most of which were democratically-elected.
- Grossly interfered in democratic elections in at least 30 countries.
- Waged war/military action, either directly or in conjunction with a proxy army, in some 30 countries.
- Attempted to assassinate more than 50 foreign leaders.
- Dropped bombs on the people of some 30 countries.
- Suppressed dozens of populist/nationalist movements in every corner of the world.

What can be done to prevent such global systemic domination and to change the political response to it by the United States leadership? Clearly, as

critics and protagonists of the revolutionary process, we need to work toward
the full development of human beings, and this means creating a social order
in which market relations must be subordinated to a democratic regime based
on direct popular representation. An assembly-style democracy would help
control the content and direction of market exchanges. The focus must be on
the creation and reconstruction of essential links between domestic economic
sectors, and the creation of socio-economic linkages between domestic needs,
latent demands, and the reorganization of the productive system. Crucial in
this process is a pedagogical mobilization and development of the capacities
of the poor and the powerless through a focus on the ideological and cultural
education of working people in the values of co-operation, solidarity, equality
and protagonist democracy. The socialism of which many of us strive to bring
into being reflects the concept of "buen vivir" (living well) and is opposed to
the notion of "buen mejor" (living better). Bolivian President Evo Morales
has noted (see Magdoff and Foster, 2010) that living better stipulates harmo-
nizing oneself to the disharmony of capitalism; it is to exploit humanity; it
is to plunder the earth and to foster the Western hemispheric characteristics
of egoism and individualism marinated by neoliberal capitalism's vampirish
quest for value augmentation. Living better fails to cultivate solidarity and
reciprocity among human beings and it is always achieved at the expense
of others. By contrast, living well underwrites sustainable human development as opposed to sustainable economic development. It animates the fact
that the fate of others is deeply tied to our own actions and that the other is
deeply embedded in ourselves. This is captured by the Mayan concept of
"In'Laketech" which means "tu eres mi otro yo" or "you are my other self."

We cannot underestimate the importance of grasping the interlocking
relationality or entanglement of capitalist relations of power and privilege
on a planetary scale. We can now say to the so-called "green" corporations
(Dell, Hewlett-Packard, Johnston & Johnson, Intel and IBM) who hock with
a forked tongue the snake oil premise that we can expand consumption, grow
the economy, and enhance our purchasing power and profits without feeling
guilty or responsible for the fate of the world's toilers: Ya basta! Que se vayan
todos! (Enough! Out with them all!) Under the cover of their corporate straw
hats, frayed overalls, pitchforks and dust covered Kodiak boots, they saturate
the environment with pollutants, they deny universal access to decent food
and enhance the stratification of wealth and power between nation states
(Magoff and Foster, 2010).

This book seeks the disestablishment of this institutionalized, interlocked
mystification, this motivated amnesia and this culture of silence where
humanity's lifeblood his been sucked dry by capital's black hole, by its solar
anus whose fury vacuums up human life and expels it as dregs and detritus

across the apocalyptic desert of dry bones with the force of a Saharan dust storm.

I want to end this book with a warning—one that has recently been sounded by Gregory Meyerson and Michael Joseph Roberto (2006, 2007). In several important—and I hope not prophetic—publications, Meyerson and Roberto mount evidence for what they call an emerging fascist trajectory in US politics that could lead to a form of fascism in the United States very much unlike its historical predecessors given the changing structure of world capitalism and the world economy as a whole and the undermining of the structure of capitalist rule. They relate this crisis directly to the structural crisis of transnational capital: the historical convergence of a profound and irreversible economic crisis and an endless succession of wars. They also consider multiple crises now in their acute phases (such as resource wars in the Mideast and the crisis of the dollar economy) flowing from an empire in decline and the volatility of *Pax Americana*. They warn that "*if* the general crisis of Pax Americana in its acute phase contains a fascist trajectory, it will result from a crisis of capitalist rule, as history reveals" and "it will look quite different from past fascist trajectories." Opposing the idea that fascism or an intensification of fascist processes constitutes a type of rogue ruling class or autonomous right-wing force that has a contradictory relationship with capital and that draws mass support largely by advocating a revolution against established values and institutions, or both, Meyerson and Roberto argue that if the intensification of *fascist processes* arrive in the United States, they will emerge from the ruling class as a whole. They make an ominous claim that "the intensification of fascist processes would unfold in a bipartisan political context, liberals and conservatives acting in concert—the whole ruling class." It is important here to recognize that contrary to many commentators on the history of fascism, crises of rule are not primarily ideological; they could, in fact, emerge from within the well-entrenched parliamentarism of the United States democratic state. I would certainly claim with Meyerson and Roberto that fascist processes are clearly rooted in properties intrinsic to class rule, "like the contradictions of capitalism or the permanent desire of the masses to resist its ruling classes—a desire that expresses the substantive values. . . . at odds with modern democratic states." Meyerson and Roberto (2006) conclude with a commentary on a recent article by Nafeez Mossadegh Ahmed, author of *Behind the War on Terror and The War on Freedom: How and Why America Was Attacked:*

> Ahmed claims that the "global system has been crumbling under the weight of its own unsustainability . . . and we are fast approaching the convergence of multiple crises that are already interacting fatally. . . ." These crises include

peak oil and climate tipping points, and a dollar denominated economy on the verge, according to no less an authority than Paul Volcker, of a currency crisis (the contradictory character of U.S. plans are indicated by the currency problem, both cause and consequence of a desperate strategy). Ahmed asserts that senior level planners in the policy making establishment have appeared to calculate "that the system is dying" but the last "viable means of sustaining it remains [sic] a fundamentally military solution" designed to "rehabilitate the system . . . to meet the requirements of the interlocking circuits of military-corporate power and profit."

Ahmed ends his very recent article (July 24) with Daniel Ellsberg's warning that another 9–11 event "or a major war in the Middle East involving a U.S. attack on Iran . . . will be an equivalent of a Reichstag fire decree," involving massive detention of both Middle Easterners and critics of the policy, the latter deemed terrorist sympathizers. Ahmed is well aware of how contingencies can postpone such plans. Nevertheless, we must all be aware of these plans and the crises which might bring them into being.

Each and every day, as the structural crisis of capital unfolds, we witness the possibilities grow of more equivalents to the Reichstag fire decree, and we seek to jumpstart those struggles that are necessary to avoid the catastrophe that looms. Meyerson and Roberto (2008) describe the nature of the catastrophe ahead:

The fascism we see may be significantly more dysfunctional than past forms. We do not see it, as does Leggett, as a prelude to the solar capitalist era. If ecosocialists like John Bellamy Foster are right, capitalism will not be reconstituting itself as a new regime of accumulation. If capitalism is becoming unsustainable, if U.S. capitalism in particular—due to its free market worship and auto-based economy among other things—is especially prone to sustainability crises, this decline of capitalism is no cause in and of itself to celebrate. The working class will be hit hardest, perhaps harder than ever, black and Latino workers hardest of all. Competition for resources will almost surely intensify racial and gender inequality, along with anti-immigrant hysteria, even as the United States may be electing its first black president. The ideological climate is likely to be confusing, chaotic and volatile. Thus, the call to organize is urgent; moreover, if we are entering what is in effect a sustainability crisis, the fight must no longer be for a bigger piece of a growing pie, but for massive redistribution immediately—working-class power for distributive and contributive justice.

While I agree that we need a plan for massive redistribution and working-class power for distributive and contributive justice, it is obvious that we also need to create a world outside of value production and the value form of labor itself—a world of socialism. The alternative to capitalism that we seek is not necessarily to be found in the European traditions of socialism (although there is much of value to be had here) but also in new forms of sustainable existence found in indigenous communities worldwide. We would like to think that *Systems of Domination* is taking an important step in providing a template with which to understand the interconnectedness of systems of oppression and how they are currently playing out in a world riven and splayed by the fault lines of capital. And such an understanding we hope will prove valuable in creating a viable plan of what an alternative to the current social universe of capital might look like. We need such an alternative. And we need it now.

We would like to think that *The Global Industrial Complex* is taking an important step in this direction.

REFERENCES

Blum, William. (2010). In Struggle with the American Mind. The Anti-Empire Report. October 1, 2010. As retrieved from: www.killinghope.org.

Grosfoguel, Ramon. (2004). Race and Ethnicity or Racialized Ethnicities? Identities within Global Coloniality. *Ethnicities*, vol. 4, no. 3: 315–336.

Magoff, Fred, and John Bellamy Foster. (2004). What Every Environmentalist Needs to Know about Capitalism. *Monthly Review*, vol. 61, no. 10 (March): 1–30.

Meyerson, Gregory, and Michael Joseph Roberto. (2006). "It Could Happen Here," *Monthly Review,* October 2006, as retrieved from: www.monthlyreview .org/1006meyerson.htm

Meyerson, Gregory, and Michael Joseph Roberto. (2008). "Fascism and the Crisis of Pax Americana." *Socialism and Democracy,* 47, volume 22, no 2, July.

NOTES

1. William Blum, "The Anti-Empire Report" (October 1st, 2010), available at killinghope.org/bblum6/aer86.html.

Index

Contributors

Carl Boggs is the author of numerous books in the fields of contemporary social and political theory, European politics, American politics, U.S. foreign and military policy, and film studies, including *The Impasse of European Communism* (1982), *The Two Revolutions: Gramsci and the Dilemmas of Western Marxism* (1984), *Social Movements and Political Power* (1986), *Intellectuals and the Crisis of Modernity* (1993), *The Socialist Tradition* (1996), and *The End of Politics: Corporate Power and the Decline of the Public Sphere* (Guilford, 2000). With Tom Pollard, he authored a book titled *A World in Chaos: Social Crisis and the Rise of Postmodern Cinema*, published by Rowman and Littlefield in 2003. He edited an anthology, *Masters of War: Militarism and Blowback in an Era of American Empire* (Routledge, 2003). He is the author of *Imperial Delusions: American Militarism and Endless War* (Rowman and Littlefield, 2005). A new book, *The Hollywood War Machine: Militarism and American Popular Culture* (co-authored with Tom Pollard), was released by Paradigm Publishers in 2006. He is currently finishing a book titled *Crimes of Empire: How U.S. Outlawry is Destroying the World*. He is on the editorial board of several journals, including *Theory and Society* (where he is book-review editor) and *New Political Science*. For two years (1999–2000) he was Chair of the Caucus for a New Political Science, a section within the American Political Science Association. In 2007 he was recipient of the Charles McCoy Career Achievement Award from the American Political Science Association. He has written more than two hundred articles along with scores of book and film reviews, has had three radio programs at KPFK in Los Angeles and was a political columnist for the *L.A. Village View* during the 1990s. After receiving his Ph.D. in political science at U.C., Berkeley, he taught at Washington University in St. Louis, UCLA, USC, U.C., Irvine, and

Carleton University in Ottawa. For the past 20 years he has been professor of social sciences at National University in Los Angeles, and more recently has been an adjunct professor at Antioch University in Los Angeles.

Noam Chomsky joined the staff of the Massachusetts Institute of Technology in 1955 and in 1961 was appointed full professor in the Department of Modern Languages and Linguistics (now the Department of Linguistics and Philosophy). In 1976 he was appointed Institute Professor. Professor Chomsky has received more than twenty honorary titles. He is a Fellow of the American Academy of Arts and Sciences and the National Academy of Science. In addition, he is a member of other professional and learned societies in the United States and abroad, and is a recipient of the Distinguished Scientific Contribution Award of the American Psychological Association, the Kyoto Prize in Basic Sciences, the Helmholtz Medal, the Dorothy Eldridge Peacemaker Award, the Ben Franklin Medal in Computer and Cognitive Science, and others. Chomsky has written and lectured widely on linguistics, philosophy, intellectual history, contemporary issues, international affairs and U.S. foreign policy. His works include: *Aspects of the Theory of Syntax*; *Cartesian Linguistics*; *Sound Patterns of English* (with Morris Halle); *Language and Mind*; *American Power and the New Mandarins*; *At War with Asia*; *For Reasons of State*; *Peace in the Middle East?*; *Reflections on Language*; *The Political Economy of Human Rights, Vol. I* and *II* (with E.S. Herman); *Rules and Representations*; *Lectures on Government and Binding*; *Towards a New Cold War*; *Radical Priorities*; *Fateful Triangle*; *Knowledge of Language*; *Turning the Tide*; *Pirates and Emperors*; *On Power and Ideology*; *Language and Problems of Knowledge*; *The Culture of Terrorism*; *Manufacturing Consent* (with E.S. Herman); *Necessary Illusions*; *Deterring Democracy*; *Year 501*; *Rethinking Camelot: JFK, the Vietnam War and US Political Culture*; *Letters from Lexington*; *World Orders, Old and New*; *The Minimalist Program*; *Powers and Prospects*; *The Common Good*; *Profit Over People*; *The New Military Humanism*; *New Horizons in the Study of Language and Mind*; *Rogue States*; *A New Generation Draws the Line*; *9–11*; and *Understanding Power*.

Ward Churchill is a Creek and enrolled Keetoowah Band Cherokee, professor, longtime Native rights activist, acclaimed public speaker, and award-winning writer. A member of the Governing Council of the American Indian Movement of the Colorado chapter of the American Indian Movement, he also serves as Professor of Ethnic Studies and Coordinator of American Indian Studies for the University of Colorado. He is a past national spokesperson for the Leonard Peltier Defense Committee and has served as a delegate to the United Nations Working Group on Indigenous Populations (as a Justice/Raporteur for the 1993 International People's Tribunal on the Rights of Indigenous Hawaiians), and is an advocate/prosecutor of the First Nations International Tribunal for the Chiefs of Ontario.

Michael Dawson holds a Ph.D. in Sociology from the University of Oregon and is Lecturer in Sociology of Portland State University. In 2003, Dawson published *The Consumer Trap: Big Business Marketing in American Life* as part of the University of Illinois Press's "History of Communications" book series, which is edited by Robert W. McChesney. This book garnered praise from renowned scholars Noam Chomsky and Mark Crispin Miller. Its aim was to help readers better understand the institutional roots of the inexorable growth of corporate marketing endeavors and their sociological impact. Contrary to the conventional academic habit of chalking those processes up to ill-defined concepts such as "consumer culture" or "consumer society," Dawson took pains to investigate and explain the historical evolution of on-the-ground, behind-the-scenes practices of actual corporate marketers. Dawson's book, *Automobiles Über Alles: Capitalism and Transportation in the United States*, is forthcoming from Monthly Review Press. This book explains the deep socio-economic importance of the car-centered transportation order of the United States to the viability of domestic and international corporate capitalism. It also elucidates the on-the-ground, behind-the-scenes practices of the corporate marketers, corporate lobbyists, and mainstream politicians who unwaveringly promote this increasingly dangerous and irrational (but exquisitely profitable) transportation order.

Angela J. Hattery is Professor of Sociology at Wake Forest University. She completed her B.A. at Carleton College and her M.S. and Ph.D. at the University of Wisconsin, Madison, before joining the faculty of Wake Forest in 1998. She spent the 2008–09 academic year at Colgate University as the A. Lindsay O'Connor Professor of American Institutions, Department of Sociology. Her research focuses on social stratification, gender, family, and race. She is the author of numerous articles, book chapters, and books, including *Interracial Intimacies: An Examination of Powerful Men and Their Relationships Across the Color Line* (Carolina Academic Press, 2009 with Earl Smith); *Interracial Relationships in the 21st Century* (Carolina Academic Press, 2009 with Earl Smith); *Intimate Partner Violence* (Rowman and Littlefield, 2008); *Globalization and America: Race, Human Rights, and Inequality* (Rowman and Littlefield, 2008 with Earl Smith and David Embrick); *African American Families* (Sage, 2007 with Earl Smith) and *Women, Work, and Family: Balancing and Weaving* (Sage, 2001).

M. Asif Ismail heads "Pushing Prescriptions," a Center for Public Integrity project that tracks the political influence of the pharmaceutical industry and its consequences. (The Center is a Washington-based nonprofit, nonpartisan, non-advocacy, independent journalism organization.) Launched in early 2005, the project has released more than a dozen in-depth, investigative reports that highlight access to medicine, drug pricing, availability, and other issues. Besides covering the pharmaceutical industry, Ismail has reported on a number of issues, including stem cell research, human cloning, the Enron scandal, and Pentagon contracts. He is a co-author of *The Buying of the President 2004* (Charles Lewis and The Center for Public Integrity, Harper-Collins, January 2004), a New York Times bestseller. The book detailed the ties between candidates in the '04 presidential elections and various special interests. As part of the Center's investigative team, he has won several top journalism awards, among them a 2006 Society of Professional Journalists award and a 2004 Investigative Reporters and Editors prize. He is also a winner of the South Asian Journalists Association award in 2004 and 2005. Ismail started his journalism career with *The Times of India* in New Delhi in the mid-1990s. He holds a master of philosophy degree in international relations (Jawaharlal Nehru University, New Delhi), a master's degree in English literature (University of Calicut, India), and a master's in journalism (American University, Washington, D.C.)

Toby Miller is Chair of the Department of Media & Cultural Studies at University of California, Riverside. His research interests include film and TV, radio, new media, class, gender, race, sport, cultural theory, citizenship, social theory, cultural studies, political theory, cultural labor, and cultural policy. Editor of *Television & New Media* and *Social Identities,* and the book series *Popular Culture and Everyday Life* (Lang), he has also been Chair of the International Communication Association Philosophy of Communication Division, editor of *Journal of Sport & Social Issues,* and co-editor of *Social Text,* the *Blackwell Cultural Theory Resource Centre,* and the book series *Sport and Culture* (Minnesota), *Film Guidebooks* (Routledge), and *Cultural Politics* (Minnesota). Miller is the author of numerous books, including: *The Well-Tempered Self: Citizenship, Culture, and the Postmodern Subject; Technologies of Truth: Cultural Citizenship and the Popular Media;, SportSex;,* and his latest, *Cultural Citizenship.* Toby Miller has taught media and cultural studies across the humanities and social sciences at the following schools: University of New South Wales, Griffith University, Murdoch University, and NYU.

Mechthild Nagel, Ph.D., is director of the Center for Gender and Intercultural Studies, professor of philosophy at the State University of New York,

College at Cortland, and Senior Visiting Fellow at the Institute for African Development at Cornell University. She is author of *Masking the Abject: A Genealogy of Play* (Lexington, 2002), co-editor of *Race, Class, and Community Identity* (Humanities, 2000), *The Hydropolitics of Africa: A Contemporary Challenge* (Cambridge Scholars Press, 2007), *Prisons and Punishment: Reconsidering Global Penality* (Africa World Press, 2007), and *Dancing with Iris: The Political Philosophy of Iris Marion Young* (Oxford University Press, 2009). Nagel is editor-in-chief of the online journal *Wagadu: A Journal of Transnational Women's and Gender Studies* (wagadu.org). As a graduate student at Umass Amherst, she was blacklisted for a while from teaching philosophy after leading a strike for union recognition. She can be reached at nagelm@cortland.edu.

Cary Nelson was born in 1946 and grew up in Philadelphia and Bucks County, Pennsylvania. He received a B.A. from Antioch College in Ohio (1967) and a Ph.D. from the University of Rochester in New York (1970). Since the fall of 1970 he has taught modern poetry and literary theory at the University of Illinois at Urbana-Champaign, where he is Jubilee Professor of Liberal Arts and Sciences and Professor of English. His campus work has included a decades-long project of building up the holdings in modern poetry and the Spanish Civil War in the library's Rare Book and Special Collections Department. Nelson is known not only as a blunt and devastatingly witty commentator on higher education but also as an activist working hard to reform it. He was active in the effort to unionize the Champaign-Urbana faculty in the 1970s and in the drive to recognize a graduate employee union twenty years later. As a member of the Modern Language Association's Delegate Assembly he co-authored a number of reform proposals, including a major project to document salaries for contingent faculty in English and foreign languages. As a member of the organization's Executive Council he helped assure that these projects were completed. For the last ten years he has served on the National Council of the American Association of University Professors, the past six as second Vice President. He coauthored the Association's Redbook statements on graduate students and on academic professionals. He has published more than twenty books including *Will Work for Food: Academic Labor in Crisis* (1997), *Academic Keywords: A Devil's Dictionary for Higher Education* (1999), *Revolutionary Memory: Recovering the Poetry of the American Left* (2001), *Office Hours: Activism and Change in the Academy* (2004), and *No University is an Island: Saving Academic Freedom* (2010).

David Nibert is Professor of Sociology at Wittenberg University, where he teaches Animals & Society, Global Change, Social Stratification, and Law and Society. He has worked as a tenant organizer, as a community activist and in the prevention of mistreatment and violence against devalued groups. He is the author of *Animal Rights/Human Rights: Entanglements of Oppression and Liberation* (Rowman and Littlefield) and *Hitting the Lottery Jackpot: State Governments and the Taxing of Dreams* (Monthly Review Press). He has published articles in such journals as *Child Welfare; the Journal of Interpersonal Violence; RESPONSE: To the Victimization of Women and Children; Critical Sociology; Race, Gender, Class; Society and Animals; and the International Journal of Sociology and Social Policy*. He co-organized the section on *Animals and Society* of the American Sociological Association. His research interests include the historical and contemporary entanglement of the oppression of humans and other animals.

Vandana Shiva, born in India in 1952, is a world-renowned environmental leader and thinker. Director of the Research Foundation on Science, Technology, and Ecology, she is the author of many books, including *Water Wars: Pollution, Profits, and Privatization* (South End Press, 2001), *Biopiracy: The Plunder of Nature and Knowledge* (South End Press, 1997), *Monocultures of the Mind* (Zed, 1993), *The Violence of the Green Revolution* (Zed, 1992), and *Staying Alive* (St. Martin's Press, 1989), which dramatically shifted the perception of Third World women. In 1990 she wrote a report for the FAO on Women and Agriculture entitled, "Most Farmers in India are Women." She founded the gender unit at the International Centre for Mountain Development (ICIMOD) in Kathmandu. Before becoming an activist, Shiva was one of India's leading physicists. Dr. Shiva has been a visiting professor and lectured at the Universities of Oslo, Norway, Schumacher College, U.K., Mt. Holyoke college, U.S., York University, Canada, University of Lulea, Sweden, University of Victoria, Canada, and Organisations and Institutions worldwide on ecology, feminism and globalisation. Dr. Shiva has also served as an adviser to governments in India and abroad as well as NGOs such as the International Forum on Globalisation, Women's Environment and Development Organisation and Third World Network. She is also Chair of the International Commission on the Future of Food. The Government of India nominated Dr. Shiva for the SAARC Autonomous Women's Advocacy Group. *Time Magazine* identified Dr. Shiva as an environmental "hero" in 2003 and *Asia Week* has called her one of the five most powerful communicators of Asia. She also has been nominated for the Nobel Peace Prize 2005.

Andrea Smith received her Ph.D. in History of Consciousness at University of California, Santa Cruz in 2002. She currently is an Associate Professor in

Media and Cultural Studies at University of California, Riverside. Previously, she taught in the Program in American Culture at the University of Michigan. Her publications include: *Native Americans and the Christian Right: The Gendered Politics of Unlikely Alliances* and *Conquest: Sexual Violence and American Indian Genocide.* She is also the editor of *The Revolution Will Not Be Funded: Beyond the Nonprofit Industrial Complex,* and co-editor of *The Color of Violence, The Incite! Anthology.* She currently serves as the U.S. Coordinator for the Ecumenical Association of Third World Theologians, and she is a co-founder of Incite! Women of Color Against Violence. She recently completed a report for the United Nations on Indigenous Peoples and Boarding Schools.

Earl Smith, PhD, is Professor of Sociology and the Rubin Distinguished Professor of American Ethnic Studies at Wake Forest University. He is the Director of the American Ethnic Studies Program and the former chairman of the Department of Sociology (1997–2005). Professor Smith has numerous publications, including eight books, research articles and book chapters in the areas of social stratification, criminology, and urban sociology. He has also published extensively about the sociology of sport, including books, peer reviewed articles, and book chapters. His most recent sports publications include, "Race Relations Theories: Implications for Sport Management" in the *Journal of Sport Management* (2010), *Sociology of Sport and Social Theory* (2010), and *Race, Sport and the American Dream* (2009).

Editors

Steven Best is Associate Professor of Humanities and Philosophy at University of Texas, El Paso. Author and editor of 12 books and over 150 articles and reviews, Best works in the areas of philosophy, cultural criticism, mass media, social theory, postmodern theory, animal rights, bioethics, and environmental theory. Two of his books, *The Postmodern Turn* and *The Postmodern Adventure* (both co-authored with Douglas Kellner) won Philosophy Book of the Year awards. With Anthony J. Nocella II he is co-editor of the acclaimed volumes, *Terrorists or Freedom Fighters? Reflections on the Liberation of Animals* (Lantern Books, 2004) and *Igniting a Revolution: Voice in Defense of the Earth* (AK Press, 2006). His forthcoming book is *Animal Liberation and Moral Progress: The Struggle for Human Evolution* (Rowman and Littlefield, 2012). Many of his writings can be found at: www.drstevebest.com and http://drstevebest.wordpress.com/.

Richard Kahn is the author of *Critical Pedagogy, Ecoliteracy, and Planetary Crisis: The Ecopedagogy Movement* (Peter Lang, 2010) and co-author of *Education Out of Bounds: Reimagining Cultural Studies in a Posthuman Age* (Palgrave Macmillan, 2010). He is presently at work on *Ecopedagogy: Educating for Sustainability in Schools and Society* (Routledge, forthcoming). A critical theorist of education, he earned his Ph.D. in Social Science and Comparative Education at UCLA, where he worked closely with Douglas Kellner. His interdisciplinary work has explored issues such as the democratic potential of new media, the alterglobalization movement, and the ways in which a total liberation pedagogy and politics might be effectively organized, and it has been collected in a wide variety of books and journals, including *The Critical Pedagogy Reader* (2nd edition); *The Blackwell Companion to*

313

Globalization; and *Cultural Studies: Keyworks.* Previously an Assistant Professor of Educational Foundations and Research at the University of North Dakota, he is now Core Faculty in Education at Antioch University Los Angeles. For more information, see his website at: http://richardkahn.org.

Peter McLaren, formerly Professor in the Division of Urban Schooling, the Graduate School of Education and Information Studies, University of California, Los Angeles, McLaren is now Professor, School of Critical Studies in Education, Faculty of Education, University of Auckland, New Zealand. He is the author and editor of forty-five books and hundreds of scholarly articles and chapters. Professor McLaren's writings have been translated into 20 languages. Four of his books have won the Critic's Choice Award of the American Educational Studies Association. One of his books, *Life in Schools,* was chosen in 2004 as one of the 12 most significant education books in existence worldwide by an international panel of experts organized by The Moscow School of Social and Economic Sciences and by the Ministry of Education of the Russian Federation. McLaren was the inaugural recipient of the Paulo Freire Social Justice Award presented by Chapman University, California. The charter for La Fundación McLaren de Pedagogia Crítica was signed at the University of Tijuana in July, 2004. La Cátedra Peter McLaren was inaugurated in Venezuela on September 15, 2006 as part of a joint effort between El Centro Internacional Miranda and La Universidad Bolivariana de Venezuela. Professor McLaren's latest books are *A Critical Pedagogy of Consumption, Living and Learning in the Shadow of the "Shopocalypse"* (with Jennifer Sandlin, Routledge) and *Academic Repression: Reflections from the Academic Industrial Complex* (with Steven Best and Anthony Nocella, AK Press).

Anthony J. Nocella II is an activist, academic, and author. While working on his Ph.D. at Syracuse University, Anthony is a visiting professor in the School of Education, Hamline University. He is the Executive Director of the Institute for Critical Animal Studies and the Central New York Peace Studies Consortium. He has been involved in numerous political campaigns, organizations, and international demonstrations fostering direct democracy and is a co-founder of more than fifteen active political organizations including Save the Kids and the Academy for Peace Education. He is co-founder of four scholarly journals and is the founder and editor of the Peace Studies Journal. He is on the board of more than five NGO boards including the American Friends Service Committee. He has written more than twenty-five scholarly articles and is working on his tenth book edited with Richard Kahn and Samuel Fassbinder, *Greening the Academy: Ecopedagogy in the Liberal Arts* (Sense Publishing, forthcoming). His other books include *A Peacemaker's Guide for Building Peace with a Revolutionary Group* (PARC 2004); co-editor with Steven Best, *Terrorists or Freedom Fighters? Reflections on the Liberation of Animals* (Lantern Books 2004); and co-edited with Steven Best and Peter McLaren *Academic Repression: Reflections on the Academic Industrial Complex* (AK Press 2010). His site is: www.anthonynocella.org.

Hey, the deadline to apply for housing is tomorrow. I was just wondering if you were still planning to do it?

CPSIA information can be obtained at www.ICGtesting.com
Printed in the USA
BVOW071958021211

277432BV00001B/1/P